Refugee Repatriation

Voluntary repatriation is now the predominant solution to refugee crises, yet the responsibilities states of origin bear towards their repatriating citizens are under-examined. Through a combination of legal and moral analysis and case studies of the troubled repatriation movements to Guatemala, Bosnia and Mozambique, Megan Bradley develops and refines an original account of the minimum conditions of a 'just return' process. The goal of a just return process must be to recast a new relationship of rights and duties between the state and its returning citizens, and the conditions of just return match the core duties states should provide for all their citizens: equal, effective protection for their security and basic human rights, including accountability for violations of these rights. This volume evaluates the ways in which different forms of redress such as restitution, compensation and truth-telling processes may help enable just returns and traces the emergence and evolution of international norms on redress for refugees. The book concludes by exploring hard cases involving the protracted displacement of stateless refugees, such as the Palestinian refugee situation. While return and redress are invariably imperfect processes, this analysis demonstrates that reparations may play a critical role in promoting a measure of justice for returnees, and accountability for forced migration.

MEGAN BRADLEY is an Assistant Professor in Conflict Studies at Saint Paul University and a Fellow in the Foreign Policy Program at the Brookings Institution. She holds a doctorate in international relations from St Antony's College, University of Oxford, and has worked with a range of organisations concerned with humanitarian, human rights and development issues including the Office of the United Nations High Commissioner for Refugees, the International Development Research Centre and the Canadian Department of Foreign Affairs and International Trade.

Refugee Repatriation

Justice, Responsibility and Redress

Megan Bradley

CAMBRIDGE
UNIVERSITY PRESS

CAMBRIDGE UNIVERSITY PRESS
Cambridge, New York, Melbourne, Madrid, Cape Town,
Singapore, São Paulo, Delhi, Mexico City

Cambridge University Press
The Edinburgh Building, Cambridge CB2 8RU, UK

Published in the United States of America by Cambridge University Press, New York

www.cambridge.org
Information on this title: www.cambridge.org/9781107699557

First published 2013

Printed and bound in the United Kingdom by the MPG Books Group

A catalogue record for this publication is available from the British Library

Library of Congress Cataloguing in Publication data
Bradley, Megan, 1980–
Refugee repatriation : justice, responsibility and redress / Megan Bradley.
pages cm
Includes bibliographical references and index.
ISBN 978-1-107-02631-5 (hardback) – ISBN 978-1-107-69955-7 (paperback)
1. Repatriation. 2. Return migration. 3. Refugees. I. Title.
JV6217.5′B73 2013
325 – dc23 2012043992

ISBN 978-1-107-02631-5 Hardback

Contents

Acknowledgements

My explorations of accountability for displacement and the questions of justice raised by refugee repatriation processes began almost a decade ago, when I first started graduate studies at the University of Oxford. As this project has moved towards fruition, I have been lucky enough to accrue debts of gratitude to more people than I can name.

Matthew Gibney and Richard Caplan were invaluable guides and sounding boards as I examined these issues as a doctoral student. I could not have asked for better supervisors. Matthew and Richard continuously challenged me to rethink my assumptions and sharpen my analyses, and I sincerely appreciate their flexibility, humour, and warm support for my work and professional development. It was only when I began teaching my own students that I fully realised how lucky I was to have two such exceptional scholars and teachers working with me over the years.

I am also grateful to the many friends and colleagues who shared their insights and support as I refined this work. I am especially grateful to Roger Zetter, Anne Hammerstad, Alex Betts, Henry Shue, Adam Roberts, Graeme Rodgers, Katy Long and Stephanie Silverman for their comments on earlier versions of some of these chapters. This project succeeded only with the support of many friends, including Cathy John, Kate Spencer Ellis, Anni Oskala, Stephen Doughty, Leah Gray, Emily Schaming, Anna Sheftel, Kate Desormeau, Chau Le, Shani Winterstein, Rachel Brulé, Meredith Williams, Tania Esposito, Clarice Reis and Catherine Lu. Any errors or shortcomings are of course my own responsibility.

In addition, I would like to thank the organisations who provided the financial and institutional support necessary to make this project possible, including the Wingate Foundation, the Pirie-Reid Scholarship Fund at the University of Oxford, the British government's Overseas Research Student Award Programme, the Sauvé Foundation, and the International Development Research Centre, where I had the wonderful opportunity to work alongside stimulating colleagues, including Tim Dottridge, Roula El-Rifai, Gisèle Morin-Labatut and Luc Mougeot. As a Cadieux-Léger Fellow in the Canadian Department of Foreign Affairs and International

Trade (DFAIT), I benefitted from the chance to enhance my research through discussions with policymakers and the staff of DFAIT's Policy Research Division. I am especially grateful to Mariève Dubois and Jessie Thomson for their help and insights. At Saint Paul University my colleagues, particularly Karlijn Desmasure, Jean-Guy Goulet and Paul Rigby, were a great source of encouragement and advice, while at the Brookings Institution I would like to thank the members of the Brookings-LSE Project on Internal Displacement, especially Bryce Campbell and Beth Ferris. In recent years I have benefitted from the chance to work on an investigation of the interface of displacement and transitional justice with colleagues from Brookings and the International Center for Transitional Justice. Participating in this project deepened my appreciation of the complexities that accompany efforts to redress displacement, and I am especially grateful to Roger Duthie for shaping my thinking on these issues.

The introduction and Chapter 3 include material published in 'Rethinking Refugeehood: Statelessness, Repatriation, and Refugee Agency' *Review of International Studies* (2013, First View), © British International Studies Association, published by Cambridge University Press. Chapter 2 features material previously published in 'Return in Dignity: A Neglected Refugee Protection Challenge' *Canadian Journal of Development Studies* 28(3) (2009), pp. 371–382, published by Taylor & Francis and 'Back to Basics: The Conditions of Just Refugee Returns' *Journal of Refugee Studies* 21(3) (2008), pp. 285–304, published by Oxford University Press. I am grateful to the publishers for their permission to reproduce these articles.

Working with Cambridge University Press has been a great pleasure. I would like to thank John Haslam and Carrie Parkinson, as well as the anonymous reviewers who shared such thoughtful and constructive comments.

This project has helped me understand better both the complexity and preciousness of coming home. My homecomings are always joyful, thanks to the unfailing love and support of my family, particularly my parents Mary Lou and Roger Bradley, and my husband, Tim Wideman. I dedicate this work to them, with much gratitude and all my love.

List of Acronyms

AJR	Association for Justice and Reconciliation
BiH	Bosnia and Herzegovina
CALDH	Centre for Human Rights and Legal Action
CCPP	Permanent Commissions of Guatemalan Refugees
CEAR	Special Commission to Aid Repatriates
CEH	Commission for Historical Clarification
CERD	Committee on the Elimination of Racial Discrimination
CIO	Rhodesian Central Intelligence Organisation
CIREFCA	International Conference on Central American Refugees
COHRE	Centre on Housing Rights and Evictions
CONDEG	National Council of Displaced Guatemalans
CONTIERRA	Presidential Office for Legal Assistance and Resolution of Land Conflicts
CRPC	Commission for Real Property Claims of Displaced Persons and Refugees
ECHR	European Court of Human Rights
FAO	Food and Agriculture Organisation
FONATIERRA	National Land Fund
FONTIERRAS	Land Fund
FORELAP	Work and Production Reintegration Fund
FRELIMO	Front for the Liberation of Mozambique
GPA	General Peace Agreement for Mozambique
GRICAR	International Advisory and Support Group for the Return of the Guatemalan Refugees
HDZ BiH	Croatian Democratic Union of BiH
IACHR	Inter-American Court of Human Rights
ICC	International Criminal Court
ICG	International Crisis Group

ICISS	International Commission on Intervention and State Sovereignty
ICJ	International Court of Justice
ICTR	International Criminal Tribunal for Rwanda
ICTY	International Criminal Tribunal for the former Yugoslavia
IDMC	Internal Displacement Monitoring Centre
IDPs	Internally Displaced Persons
ILA	International Law Association
ILC	International Law Commission
INTA	National Institute for Agrarian Transformation
IOM	International Organisation for Migration
IRO	International Refugee Organisation
JNA	Yugoslav People's Army
MINUGUA	United Nations Verification Mission in Guatemala
NGO	Non-Governmental Organisation
OAU	Organisation of African Unity
OCHA	Office for the Coordination of Humanitarian Affairs
OHR	Office of the High Representative
ONUMOZ	United Nations Operation in Mozambique
PA	Palestinian National Authority
PACs	Civil Defence Patrols
PCIJ	Permanent Court of International Justice
PCPSR	Palestinian Centre for Policy and Survey Research
PIC	Peace Implementation Council
PLIP	Property Law Implementation Plan
PLO	Palestine Liberation Organisation
PNC	Palestinian National Council
REMHI	Recovery of Historical Memory Project
RENAMO	Mozambican National Resistance Movement
RRTF	Reconstruction and Return Task Force
RS	Republika Srpska
RSG	Representative of the United Nations Secretary-General on Internally Displaced Persons
SDA	Party of Democratic Action
SDS	Serbian Democratic Party
UNCC	United Nations Compensation Commission

UNCCP	United Nations Conciliation Commission for Palestine
UNGA	United Nations General Assembly
UNHCR	Office of the United Nations High Commissioner for Refugees
UNHCR EXCOM	Office of the United Nations High Commissioner for Refugees Executive Committee
UNRRA	United Nations Relief and Rehabilitation Agency
UNRWA	United Nations Relief and Works Agency for Palestine Refugees in the Near East
URNG	Guatemalan National Revolutionary Unity
WOLA	Washington Office on Latin America

Introduction

Certain crimes lie beyond the reach of repair. From torture and systematic rape to enslavement and ethnic cleansing, many of the violations that force refugees from their homes count among those injustices for which it is impossible to truly make amends. During the Cold War, many if not most refugees were resettled in western countries, defusing the explosive question of how refugees may be reconciled with their states of origin. Today, however, permanent resettlement is a rare solution to refugee crises. For millions of refugees, repatriation to their countries of origin is no longer an option but an imperative, the only alternative to the limbo of protracted displacement. This raises some critical questions: What can refugees legitimately expect from return? Are they entitled to anything more than a haphazard journey back to ruined or reoccupied homes in communities where their livelihoods are uncertain and their welcome lukewarm at best? If so, what are the conditions of a *just return* process? Who is obliged to ensure these conditions are met? While sometimes fierce public and academic debates probe the obligations states of asylum owe to those harboured within their borders, the issue of what states of origin owe to returning refugees has often been overshadowed. Yet experiences from Guatemala and Cambodia to the Balkans and Afghanistan indicate that identifying the state of origin's responsibilities to returnees and ensuring these duties are met is integral to safe and sustainable repatriation and peacebuilding processes and, in turn, a stable political future.

Historically, questions of justice and the ability of impoverished refugees to straggle back to their homes have rarely found space on political or scholarly agendas. However, over the past 25 years, the repatriation of refugees and the rectification of past injustices have emerged as multifaceted, pressing challenges for state policymakers and humanitarian practitioners alike. As former United Nations Secretary-General Kofi Annan argued in 2005, 'The return of refugees and internally displaced persons is a major part of any post-conflict scenario. And it is far more than just a logistical operation. Indeed, it is often a critical factor in sustaining a peace process and in revitalising economic activity' (Annan 2005). The success of return operations depends on the ability of governments and non-state actors to confront and respond to the questions of justice the repatriation process puts front and centre, from the resolution of land disputes to accountability for the atrocities and inequalities that fuel forced migration.

Drawing on the tools of international law, moral theory, and political and historical analysis, this book focuses attention on the responsibilities states of origin bear towards their repatriating citizens and articulates a minimum account of a just return process. I contend that the goal of a just return must be to put returnees back on equal footing with their non-displaced co-nationals by recasting a new relationship of rights and duties between the state and its returning citizens. The conditions of just return match the core duties a legitimate state must provide for all its citizens: equal, effective protection for their security and basic human rights, including accountability for violations of these rights. Indeed, in the following chapters I will argue that remedies such as property restitution, compensation, apologies and truth commissions play a critical role in creating the conditions for a just return, as it is through such forms of redress that the state of origin may re-establish its legitimacy by acknowledging and attempting to make good on the duties it abrogated by forcing its citizens into exile. However, redress and return are invariably imperfect processes. While this book maintains that reparations are a critical expression of accountability for forced migration, and an essential component of a just return, it also engages in a detailed examination of the legal, moral and pragmatic political problems associated with efforts to uphold at least a degree of state responsibility for displacement and provide redress to returnees.

The rise of return: political origins and practical implications of the focus on repatriation

Although the right to return is acknowledged in numerous United Nations resolutions and Article 13(2) of the Universal Declaration of Human Rights, 'the right of return has not figured prominently in general discussions of refugee rights. The major thrust of these discussions has been on the right *not* to be returned' (Dowty 1994: 26). Indeed, the 1951 Convention Relating to the Status of Refugees refers to repatriation principally in the negative terms of *refoulement*.[1] In contrast, the UNHCR Statute identifies the facilitation of repatriation as one of the organisation's principal functions and calls on the High Commissioner to 'provide

[1] I use repatriation and return as synonyms throughout.

for the protection of refugees . . . [by] . . . assisting governmental and private efforts to promote voluntary repatriation or assimilation within new national communities' (UNGA 1950). However, throughout much of the Cold War, return was often sidelined in favour of other solutions that better served western political interests. It was only in the aftermath of the Cold War that return emerged as the predominant solution to displacement, and with it a wide range of policy challenges, from the provision of protection and development support in return communities to the resolution of returnees' land claims. Although UNHCR (2011: 5, 17) statistics show a consistent decline in refugee repatriation rates since the end of 2004, the refugee agency insists that 'voluntary repatriation remains the preferred solution among most of the world's refugees', not to mention its governments. Even with declining repatriation rates, the overall number of returnees remains considerable: between 1998 and 2007, 11.4 million refugees returned to their countries of origin through more than 25 large-scale repatriation programmes; for every refugee resettled between 1998 and 2008, 14 returned to their home countries (UNHCR 2008: 10).[2]

Return in the early post-WWII years and during the Cold War

Noting that the three durable solutions to displacement, voluntary repatriation, local integration and resettlement, are often listed in order of preference, Goodwin-Gill (1995: 32) suggests that, much like many contemporary governments, the drafters of the UNHCR Statute regarded voluntary repatriation as the ideal resolution to displacement. This early preference for repatriation is reflected in the fact that between 1945 and 1947, the United Nations Relief and Rehabilitation Agency (UNRRA) spent more than $3.6 billion on relief and repatriation for those displaced by World War II (Martin et al. 2005: 82).[3] However, only a few years later, the United States and France attempted to 'torpedo' the inclusion of repatriation in the mandate of the High Commissioner for Refugees (Holborn 1975, Harrell-Bond 1989: 46). For the western powers confronting the rise of the eastern bloc, 'it was virtually inconceivable that refugees from . . . the USSR would be willing to return home, or should be forced to repatriate. Nor was the West able or willing to conceive of refugee problems outside Europe' (Harrell-Bond 1989: 46, Holborn 1975).

2 Interestingly, while refugee repatriation rates have declined in recent years, increasing numbers of internally displaced persons (IDPs) have returned, with some 2.9 million IDPs returns recorded by UNHCR in 2010, the largest amount in some 15 years.

3 This text focuses on repatriation movements post-World War II. For analyses of earlier return processes, see, for example, Long (2009).

By the time the OAU Convention Governing the Specific Aspects of Refugee Problems in Africa was signed in 1969, the proliferation of refugee problems outside Europe was all too clear. The OAU Convention (Article 5.5) emphasises the importance of the voluntary repatriation of refugees, calling for 'every possible assistance by the country of asylum, the country of origin, voluntary agencies and international and intergovernmental organisations, to facilitate their return'. In practice, however, in the first decades of the modern refugee regime, many influential countries and international organisations were hesitant to promote voluntary repatriation as a solution to refugee crises. After World War II, UNHCR's precursor, the International Refugee Organisation (IRO), did not encourage the repatriation of displaced persons to Communist countries where they could be persecuted as traitors. In the early years of UNHCR's work, the use of repatriation as a durable solution was limited as millions of refugees who 'voted with their feet' against repression and conflict in Communist-aligned countries were offered permanent resettlement in the west. In essence, resettlement was used by the west as a sharp political slight against the eastern bloc (Loescher 2001a, Martin et al. 2005: 81–86).

Certainly, the Cold War period saw several significant if troubled repatriations processes. For example, UNHCR facilitated the repatriation of almost 10 per cent of those who fled during the 1956 Hungarian refugee crisis. In spite of the initial opposition of western governments to the operation, UNHCR viewed the facilitation of repatriation to Hungary as an opportunity to overcome its almost total isolation from the eastern bloc (Loescher 2001b: 36). A few years later, the largest repatriation movement on record began with the return of some 10 million displaced persons to the newly independent state of Bangladesh between 1971 and 1972 (UNHCR 2000: 59–60). Despite the complexity and importance of some of these cases, the ethos of the refugee regime nonetheless remained focused on the resolution of displacement through resettlement and local integration. With the decline of Cold War rivalries, however, the political logic underpinning the large-scale resettlement of refugees evaporated, and permanent resettlement opportunities 'largely withered away' (Hathaway 1997: 533).

Increasing returns in the aftermath of the Cold War: rewards, risks and a changed regime

A few years before the end of the Cold War, the refugee regime began to address the question of repatriation in a more explicit manner. In Conclusion No. 40 of 1985, the UNHCR Executive Committee articulated an institutional doctrine to guide voluntary repatriation activities, and by the late 1980s, UNHCR, donors and many host states were broadly united in the effort to transform repatriation from a rhetorical concession into the principal durable solution for refugees. UNHCR declared the 1990s the 'Decade of Repatriation', and during this period return programmes expanded considerably, framed as a contribution to regional stability and international security (Hammerstad 2000: 392–396). At the same time, local integration opportunities waned as the developing countries hosting the vast majority of the world's refugees adopted increasingly restrictive asylum policies, in part as a protest against inadequate progress in establishing 'burden sharing' mechanisms between the global North and South (Kibreab 2003: 26, Loescher et al. 2008: 48–50, Ogata 2005).

This shift towards return in the late 1980s and early 1990s elicited a volley of critiques from scholars and refugee advocates alike. While UNHCR, reluctant host states and governments that scaled down their resettlement quotas were – and are – quick to aver that most refugees prefer return as the durable solution to their displacement, critics rightfully underline that the evidence substantiating such claims is often thin (Harrell-Bond 1998, Takahashi 1997). Many scholars, practitioners and policymakers contend that the upshot of the focus on return is the erosion of asylum rights, the legitimisation of restrictive policies intended to prevent refugees from accessing shelter in wealthy western democracies and the creation of unrealistic expectations among the displaced (Adelman and Barkan 2011, Chimni 1993, Hathaway 2007). Many of the same critics see self-interested motivations behind the promotion of return and question the voluntary nature of many repatriation movements. Indeed, temporary protection and 'mandated return' programmes often make little or no pretence towards voluntariness, in spite of the risks associated with privileging the judgement of states over that of refugees, who may better understand the specific dangers posed by repatriation (Chimni 1993: 454).

Many of these critiques remain highly relevant. But despite the risks associated with return as a durable solution to displacement, a strong conviction has emerged that voluntary repatriation movements should be supported because they have the potential to help to consolidate peace processes. This conviction is reflected in UN Secretary-General Boutros Boutros-Ghali's influential 1992 report *An Agenda for Peace*, which argued that 'Peacemaking and peace-keeping operations, to be truly successful, must come to include comprehensive efforts to identify and support structures which will tend to consolidate peace and advance a sense of confidence and well-being among people. Through agreements ending civil strife, these may include disarming the previously warring parties and the restoration of order . . . [and] repatriating refugees' (UNSG 1992, para. 55). In keeping with the view that peace processes and return movements are closely connected, virtually all of the dozens of peace agreements concluded since 1995 recognise the right of the displaced to return not only to their country of origin, but to their original homes (Phuong 2005).

Undoubtedly, repatriation movements unfolding in the context of volatile peace processes have in some instances been more limited in scope than is often implied by UNHCR, particularly in cases of ethnic conflicts when refugees would be minorities in return communities (Adelman 2002, Adelman and Barkan 2011, Dumper 2006: 13). However, it has nonetheless become clear that the success of repatriation movements and peace operations are indeed often closely intertwined (Black et al. 2006, Dumper 2006b, 2007, Weiss Fagen 2003, 2005, 2006). In some circumstances, return movements can help to stabilise insecure border regions and may serve as an important expression of confidence in fledgling peace processes. As the 2009 *Report of the Secretary-General on peacebuilding in the immediate aftermath of conflict* argues, 'visible peace dividends that are attributable to the national authorities, including early employment generation and supporting returnees, are . . . critical to build the confidence in the government and the peace process' (UNSC 2009, para. 18). In addition, refugees may return with important training and skill sets developed while in exile, which may enable them to make valuable contributions to peacebuilding and development (Milner 2009: 27–28).

Yet in many instances, repatriation has not been a boon for peace processes. Almost inevitably, repatriation movements generate tensions at the local level as returnees attempt to reclaim lost properties and have to confront former neighbours who may have been complicit in the violations that forced them from their homes. Influxes of returnees may further stretch already limited services such as schools and clinics, may be met with hostility on the part of those who were unable to seek shelter abroad and perceive returnees as having been 'spoiled' with international support. In worst-case scenarios – which are all too common – premature and forced return movements can overwhelm and undercut 'fragile institutions' in countries struggling to emerge from conflict, exposing returnees to unnecessary and unacceptable risks, and ultimately setting back peace processes by potentially reigniting conflict and forced migration flows (Milner 2009: 26–27, Rodicio 2001, 2006, Utting 1994). These risks are particularly pronounced in cases of massive return movements. For example, Afghanistan has seen the repatriation of some 5 million refugees since 2002, representing approximately one-quarter of the country's population. Reflecting on the failure to provide returnees with the support essential to make repatriation a sustainable contribution to peace, the head of the UNHCR mission in Afghanistan recently characterised the agency's approach to return as 'a big mistake, the biggest mistake UNHCR ever made' (AFP 2011, IRIN 2012).

High-level initiatives such as the development by the UN Secretary-General's Policy Committee of a 'Preliminary Framework for supporting a more coherent, predictable and effective response to the durable solutions needs of refugee returnees and IDPs' attempt to minimise these risks, and maximise the contributions returns may make to peacebuilding processes.[4] However, this initiative focuses on prompt access to durable solutions for those recently displaced by conflict and does not address the millions of refugees now in conditions of protracted displacement. Perhaps the greatest difficulty associated with the increased focus on return as the 'preferred' solution to displacement is that many refugees now remain in an indefinite limbo, forced to wait for beleaguered peace processes to gain traction, or for stagnant conflicts to move towards resolution, rather than having the opportunity to access local integration or resettlement opportunities.[5] By the end of 2010, approximately 7.2 million refugees were in situations of protracted displacement, as viable conditions for return had not yet taken hold, but other solutions were foreclosed to them (UNHCR 2011: 2). In a 2010 speech to the United Nations General Assembly, UN High Commissioner for Refugees, António Guterres lamented that 2009 was the 'worst [year] in two decades for the voluntary repatriation of refugees', due to the impossibility of return to countries locked in conflict. Nonetheless, his speech underlined the regime's persistent focus on return as the preferred and predominant solution to displacement. 'Despite the lower number of refugees able to return to their countries in conditions of safety and dignity', Guterres (2010) argued, 'voluntary repatriation remains a vital solution. Indeed, with major conflicts failing to resolve, it becomes all the more important to act on the opportunities which do exist for voluntary repatriation.'

In short, since the end of the Cold War, the refugee regime has changed dramatically and perhaps irrevocably. The problems associated with

[4] Framed as a follow-up to the Secretary-General's 2009 Report on Peacebuilding, the framework emphasises a rights-based approach premised on the state of origin's responsibility for its displaced citizens. It will be piloted in three countries in 2012 and 2013. See Secretary-General's Policy Committee Decision 2011/20 (UNSG 2011a).

[5] Adelman and Barkan (2011) suggest that this problem is particularly acute for refugees who would be ethnic minorities if they were to return to their countries of origin and suggest that the insistence that refugees have the right to return is in large part to blame for this conundrum.

return are troubling for anyone concerned with the rights and wellbeing of refugees, but this does not alter the political realities now underlying the international refugee regime: affluent countries lack the incentive and domestic support necessary to resuscitate large-scale resettlement programmes. The lauded tradition of hospitality towards refugees in the developing world, and particularly in Africa, is flagging and unlikely to be revived without a substantial breakthrough in donor support and burden sharing. The prospects of such a breakthrough are bleak, as evidenced by the confounding of UNHCR's recent attempts to enable the permanent local integration of Burundian refugees who have been living in Tanzania for decades. While efforts to improve the protection of refugees and ensure their access to a sufficiently wide range of durable solutions remain of the utmost importance, increased focus on repatriation is not a passing trend but a definitive change in the structure of the international refugee system. Scholars and advocates should be concerned that, despite this change, repatriation has attracted only modest attention from researchers to date, and the theoretical framework underpinning return remains comparatively undeveloped (Takahashi 1997: 593, Zetter 2004: 299). For example, in spite of UNHCR's mantra that repatriation must take place 'in conditions of safety and dignity', the UNHCR *Handbook on Voluntary Repatriation* offers little discussion of the meaning of dignified return beyond setting out a dictionary definition of dignity (UNHCR 1996: 11). As the onus has shifted from states of asylum and resettlement countries to states of origin to provide a durable solution to displacement in the form of repatriation, there is a pressing need for more rigorous examination of the conditions of just return and how states may realise these conditions.

Theoretical implications of the focus on repatriation

The rise of return as the dominant durable solution to displacement also has significant implications for the prevailing theoretical conceptions of the refugee predicament. Historically, few political theorists and philosophers have systematically engaged with the problem of refugees, with the notable exception of Hannah Arendt. As a refugee from Nazi Germany, Arendt discusses refugees and statelessness in *The Origins of Totalitarianism*, a text that has become a touchstone for scholars grappling with the nature and consequences of forced migration. Theorists such as Giorgio Agamben (1994) have drawn on Arendt to position the refugee as the 'central figure of our political history', and her contribution continues to illuminate certain aspects of the refugee problem. However, structural changes in the international system, including the increased focus on repatriation, mean that Arendt's depiction of refugees as stateless, rightless 'scum of the earth' no longer so clearly reflects or suggests avenues for resolving the challenges faced by the majority of the world's refugees (Arendt 2004: 343).

Arendt was principally concerned with European Jewish refugees who fled the Holocaust. Many of these refugees were indeed literally stateless as the denaturalisation laws of the Third Reich stripped millions of unwanted minorities of their citizenship. This practice has since been explicitly forbidden under international law, with the development of treaties such as the 1961 Convention of the Reduction of Statelessness.[6] At the time, however, the minorities' legal predicament was more ambiguous, as international law did not yet fully conceive of individuals as the subjects of international rights and obligations (Benhabib 2004: 54, 68).[7] Certainly, Arendt's concerns with statelessness ran much deeper than questions of legal status. For Arendt, the displacement of refugees across Europe exposed the poverty of human rights rhetoric and the 'fiction' of justifying the state system in terms of the protection and promotion of human rights (Agamben 1994). Although Arendt (2004: 344) writes that 'the very phrase "human rights" became for all concerned – victims, persecutors, onlookers alike – the evidence of hopeless idealism or fumbling feeble-minded hypocrisy', she is nonetheless adamant about the political and ethical value of this very discourse (Isaac 2002: 507). Her principal observation and concern was that refugees were powerless to stop their state from robbing them of their rights as citizens. Left without the protection of a state, refugees were unable to find 'a community willing and able to guarantee any rights whatsoever' (Gibney 2004: 2). The 'right to have rights', Arendt concluded, depended on membership of a political community; as membership was distributed according to the

[6] Article 9 of the 1961 Convention on the Reduction of Statelessness provides that 'a contracting state may not deprive any person or group of persons of their nationality on racial, ethnic, religious or political grounds', while Article 7 indicates that 'if the law of a contracting State permits renunciation of nationality, such renunciation shall not result in loss of nationality unless the person concerned possesses or acquires another nationality'. The 1961 Convention entered into force in 1975, and was preceded by the 1954 Convention Relating to the Status of Stateless Persons. It is important to note that international support for both treaties has been lacklustre: the 1954 Convention has 59 signatories, while the 1961 Convention has only 31. However, instruments such as the 1948 Universal Declaration of Human Rights also provide some general protection against statelessness. For instance, Article 15(2) of the Universal Declaration of Human Rights underlines that 'No one shall be arbitrarily deprived of his nationality.'

[7] The minorities treaties overseen by the League of Nations purported to provide some protection to minorities against acts such as forced denationalisation. However, the protection provided by these treaties was meagre and not universal, and members of the affected minority groups had no standing in the legal bodies responsible for the implementation of the treaties (Roucek 1929).

prerogative of states, citizens risked being rendered 'stateless' refugees or, as Arendt put it even more bluntly, 'superfluous' (Benhabib 2004: 50). In other words, 'the loss of citizenship rights . . . contrary to all human rights declarations, was politically tantamount to the loss of human rights altogether' (Benhabib 2004: 50).

While aspects of Arendt's argument continue to resonate, this book suggests that Arendt's focus on refugees as powerless and fundamentally stateless is now rather anachronistic (Bradley in press). This is attributable to factors such as changes in the geographic scope and political impetus of refugee flows; the codification of human rights in international law; and, perhaps above all, the increasing importance of repatriation and the reconstitution of the relationship between refugees and their states of origin, a possibility largely unforeseen by Arendt. As Gibney (2004: 4) observes, 'the circumstances that confronted Europe with refugees between 1930 and 1950 had their source in what have turned out to be relatively transient forces . . . that emanated from *within* Europe'; most refugee crises now originate *outside* Europe, due to civil wars, ethnic strife, and the persistent difficulties associated with building solid state structures in conditions of impoverishment. Unlike in Arendt's time, most contemporary refugees are not technically stateless but remain citizens of their states of origin.[8] Refugees certainly lack effective state protection, but this is unfortunately true for almost every citizen of deeply dysfunctional states such as Afghanistan and Haiti, displaced or not. If it is to maintain its analytic incisiveness, 'statelessness' cannot simply mean a lack of robust state protection. Very different courses of action are required to resolve the predicament of people who are literally stateless, and to ensure that the citizens of abusive or failing states, including refugees, can avail themselves of stronger state protection systems. While a stateless person must carve out a fresh space for herself as a recognised member of a state's political community, a refugee can already lay claim to a place in a state's political community, albeit one in marked need of improvement.

[8] In this connection, it is helpful to note the distinction between *de jure* and *de facto* statelessness. According to Batchelor (1998: 170–174), a *de jure* stateless person is one who 'is not considered as a national by any State under the operation of its law'. This reflects the formal definition of statelessness set out in the 1954 Convention relating to the Status of Stateless Persons. While the drafters of the 1954 Convention and the 1951 Convention relating to the Status of Refugees assumed an overlap between refugees and *de facto* stateless persons, in light of refugees' inability to benefit from effective national protections, 'neither *de jure* nor *de facto* statelessness necessarily signifies the existence of a well-founded fear of persecution under the terms of the 1951 Convention . . . if stateless persons are really to benefit from the provisions of international or regional instruments developed to resolve cases of statelessness, they must be able to show *de jure* statelessness' (Batchelor 1998: 172). Statelessness and refugeehood are, therefore, not legally synonymous.

In the aftermath of the Holocaust, it was inconceivable to Arendt and her contemporaries that Jewish refugees should be expected to return to and reconcile with their states and former neighbours. Arendt (2004: 372) wrote that the first loss refugees suffered was 'the loss of their homes, and this meant the loss of the entire social texture into which they were born and in which they established for themselves a distinct place in the world'. Arendt saw this loss as permanent and irreparable, and, indeed, Holocaust survivors who returned to their homes were often cast out of what remained of the Jewish community as traitors (Borneman 2004: 129). I do not wish to debate whether the Holocaust was the pinnacle of human atrocity; however, it must be acknowledged that many other sweeping genocides have followed on from the *Shoah*. In recent decades, millions of refugees who survived these crimes have had to return to their countries and face the task of rebuilding their lives and their place in the political community of the state. This has never been an easy process, but the practical experience of returnees demonstrates that while Arendt's diagnosis of the refugee's dilemma may be prescient, her despair at finding a remedy to their predicament is premature.

Even while displaced, many refugees are engaged in the process of pursuing political membership in their state of asylum or, more importantly for the purposes of this book, regaining space in the political community of their country of origin. Arendt argues that the life of a refugee separated from her community is 'mere existence in all matters of public concern. This mere existence . . . can be adequately dealt with only by the unpredictable hazards of friendship and sympathy, or the great and incalculable grace of love' (Arendt 2004: 382). However, many refugees have proven themselves to be astute political actors in multiple arenas, using diaspora networks to affect political change in their country of asylum and in their home communities (Van Hear 1998). In particular, some refugees manage to leverage the rights accorded to them under international law to negotiate the conditions of their return with their states of origin. The significance of the inclusion of individuals as subjects under international law and the codification of human rights was unanticipated by Arendt, but has arguably been one of the defining features of international politics since the end of World War II. Without doubt, many of the international legal provisions designed to protect individuals' human rights remain notoriously weak, particularly due to the absence of effective domestic and international enforcement mechanisms. However, international human rights laws have at least limited the ability of states to violate the rights of their citizens without consequences, and increased the ability of refugees and their advocates to voice compelling claims for assistance and recompense.

Turton (2005: 278) argues that 'to emphasise the horror and pain of the loss of home . . . and to say nothing – or little – about the work of producing a new home or neighbourhood, whether in a refugee camp, resettlement site, detention centre, city slum or middle class suburb, is to treat the displaced as fundamentally flawed human beings, as lacking what it takes to be social agents and historical subjects. It is to see them . . . as a category of "passive victims" who exist to be assisted, managed, regimented and controlled'. While Arendt (2004: 382) saw the refugee as robbed of 'his political status in the struggle of his time', the actions of refugees from Guatemala to Mozambique have shown this theoretical picture to be incongruous with the reality of refugees as political actors. 'Displacement', Turton (2005: 258) writes, 'is not just about the loss of place, but also about the struggle to *make* a place in the world, where meaningful action and shared understanding is possible'. Equally, it may be about the struggle to *regain* one's place in the world – a process that merits greater attention as geo-political changes and alterations in the structure of the international refugee regime have pushed repatriation to the forefront of efforts to find durable solutions to displacement.

Although not principally concerned with Arendtian theory, this book will serve as a rejoinder to the prevailing Arendtian conception of refugees as fundamentally stateless. It will in effect argue for the need to shift the discourse on the nature of refugeehood from a focus on the refugee as stateless to the refugee as an actor who bears legitimate claims for the reconstitution of her relationship with her state of origin. Further, this book will emphasise the importance of reorienting theorising on refugees so that it is relevant to the experience of the majority of contemporary refugees who remain in the developing world, without the opportunity to secure membership in a new political community. Theorists such as Benhabib (2004) are helpfully building on Arendt's articulation of the dilemmas posed by lack of protection and disenfranchisement from the political community by arguing for the right of refugees to gain new citizenships. However, the significance of this type of project is limited by the current political reality in which only a tiny minority of refugees have the opportunity to seek asylum or acquire citizenship in the affluent, multicultural democracies of primary concern to Benhabib. Rather than assuming that the answer to the refugee's dilemma lies in the acquisition of a new political community, this book will investigate how refugees may regain membership in their original political communities, but on new, more equitable terms. These terms must involve the acknowledgement and rectification of past injustices and a concomitant redistribution of power, so that returning refugees are not at the mercy of their state but have the ability as citizens to hold the state accountable for the protection of their rights.

Reparations: a new threshold for morality in international politics?

Although unforeseen by Arendt and largely overlooked by the refugee scholars who have followed in her tradition, reparation is emerging as a key tool to promote accountability for human rights violations and help reconstitute the relationship between abusive states and the victims of injustice, particularly refugees. The individual's right to redress under international law evolved out of the post-World War II human rights regime, and is reflected in agreements such as the International Covenant on Civil and Political Rights. Prior to the emergence of the modern human rights regime, the 1928 Permanent Court of International Justice *Chorzów Factory* ruling laid down the basic remedial norms for violations of international law. The court ruled that 'reparation must, so far as possible, wipe out all the consequences of the illegal act and re-establish the situation that would, in all probability, have existed if that act had not been committed' (PCIJ 1928, Shelton 2002: 835).

According to the United Nations Basic Principles and Guidelines on the Right to a Remedy and Reparation for Victims of Gross Violations of International Human Rights Law and Serious Violations of International Humanitarian Law (hereafter UN Reparation Principles), the term 'reparations' encompasses five main types of remedy: restitution, compensation, satisfaction, rehabilitation and guarantees of non-repetition (UNGA 2005a). Restitution aims to restore the conditions that existed prior to a violation, and often involves the return of homes, artefacts or land (Du Plessis 2003: 630). Traditionally seen as the legally preferable form of remedy, restitution is 'required of the responsible state unless it is materially impossible' or 'involves a burden out of all proportion to the benefit deriving from restitution instead of compensation' (Arzt 1999, Shelton 2002: 849). It is often impossible to restore the conditions that existed prior to the human rights violations that cause citizens to seek asylum, such as torture. In these cases, remedy is often achieved through compensation, which principally involves monetary payment for material or moral injuries, or satisfaction, which addresses non-material injuries through mechanisms such as official apologies; judicial proceedings; and truth commissions (Gillard 2003: 531–532). Rehabilitation involves the provision of assistance such as medical, psychological and social services as a form of redress, while guarantees of non-repetition of the violation from the offending state may require legal and institutional reform, with a view to both remedying past crimes and deterring future abuses (UNGA 2005a).

While these legal definitions are informative, redress is not simply a legal principle, but is also rooted in political, ethical and religious discourse. Barkan (2001: xviii) contends that the legal tools of remedy, such as restitution, compensation and satisfaction, 'are all different levels of acknowledgement that together create a mosaic of recognition by perpetrators for the need to amend past injustices'. Drawing on Barkan's work, I shall base this discussion on a comprehensive political conception of reparations or redress as the 'entire spectrum of attempts to rectify historical injustices' (Barkan 2001: xix). Although broad, this definition is salient because it encompasses the diverse yet interrelated approaches that may be taken to remedy injustice, including legal initiatives such as trials, administrative processes such as property restitution commissions, and political efforts such as apologies and truth commissions. I use reparations and redress as synonyms, and conceptualise the struggle to 'redress the legacies of massive human rights abuses that occur during armed conflict and under authoritarian regimes' as the central concern of transitional justice (Duthie 2011: 243). While I draw more on the terminology of reparations politics than transitional justice, I understand these to be intimately connected if not overlapping enterprises.

The provision of redress by West Germany to the state of Israel and individual Holocaust survivors was the first major example of a modern reparations process, which played a decisive role in the political rehabilitation of Germany and establishment of the Israeli state (Lustick 2005). However, the fledgling reparations movement largely stagnated until the early 1990s when class action suits were filed in US courts against three prominent Swiss banks for their complicity in the Holocaust. This sparked renewed interest in the question of addressing historical injustices and launched several complex reparation cases onto domestic and international political agendas, including compensation for Korean 'comfort women' and Japanese North Americans interned during World War II, and apologies for the abuse of indigenous peoples in Canada and New Zealand (Bazyler 2002: 15). Longstanding debates on reparations for slavery were reinvigorated in the United States, at the same time as South Africa struggled to recognise and redress the history of apartheid. Although numerous pressing reparation cases remain sidelined the world over, Barkan (2001: xvii) argues that the growing push to redress past injustices 'provides a new threshold for morality in international politics'.

This trend has engaged national governments, donors, NGOs, survivors' groups, various UN agencies and other inter-governmental organisations. Although different reparations mechanisms have been woven into many recent peace agreements and reconstruction plans, it nonetheless appears that in some instances this 'new threshold for morality' has struggled to exert influence in post-conflict scenarios where the stakes are often highest. This book will consider redress for returning refugees as a testing ground for the traction of international norms on redress, and how they can be translated into politically volatile domestic contexts. Clearly not only refugees but all victims of serious human rights violations have a right to redress, and a stake in the transitional justice processes through which remedies may be conveyed (Roht-Arriaza 2004). However, I will argue that redress for refugees is particularly crucial because remedies such as real property restitution, compensation and truth-telling processes may help to create just conditions of return and have important implications for fostering security and development in post-conflict states. In essence, providing redress and creating conditions of just return is often in states' long-term interests. Given that the provision of redress is morally and legally well grounded, and is often a prudential policy for states in the process of political transition, this book will question why so many refugees have been denied access to redress, and why reparations programmes involving refugees have been at best only partially successful. Various reasons for states' resistance to initiate reparations programmes will be explored, including their reluctance to engage in time-consuming, politically contentious and costly negotiations. In many cases, efforts to redress refugees' land losses and other grievances are simply sidelined in favour of traditional, aid-based approaches to facilitating return and establishing security (Foley 2008).

Reparations have often been examined as a legal process and an abstract philosophical conundrum, but it is only in recent years that studies have begun to emerge on the links between transitional justice and displacement, and the possibility that the provision of different forms of redress may be a critical component of efforts to address displaced persons' concerns and strengthen societies in the process of reconstruction.[9] While the body of research on the interface of displacement, transitional

[9] See, for example, Leckie (2003b, 2008), Williams (2007), Duthie (2011, 2012a), and Bradley (2012a). Organisations that have taken a leading role in examining the connections between transitional justice and displacement include the Refugee Law Project, the Brookings Institution and the International Center for Transitional Justice (see http://ictj.org/our-work/research/transitional-justice-and-displacement).

justice, reconciliation and redress is growing rapidly, many of the studies that have been conducted to date have focused on isolated cases of real property restitution programmes evaluated from legal or socio-legal perspectives and have not explored the practical and conceptual links between property restitution commissions and other transitional justice initiatives such as trials, truth commissions and grassroots reconciliation projects. This has made it difficult to appreciate the significance for refugees of the reparations movement in its totality, both theoretically and in terms of its concrete impact in post-conflict communities. By adopting an approach that brings together legal, moral and political analysis to inform the study of redress and return, this book aims to advance understanding of the connections between these processes.

Structure and scope of analysis

This book has three main parts. Part I (Chapters 1, 2 and 3) addresses the moral and legal foundations of the responsibility of states for displacement and sets out a minimum account of what must be involved in a just return process. In Chapter 1, my discussion of the legal dimensions of the responsibilities states of origin bear for forced migration concentrates on human rights law and the international law of state responsibility, while my examination of the moral foundations of state responsibility draws on the work of David Miller, as well as the distinctive insights Andrew Shacknove offers into issues of responsibility, refugeehood and return. Briefly, Shacknove (1985) suggests that states and citizens are bound by a minimal relation of rights and duties, the breakdown of which engenders refugees. When the state fails to respect citizens' rights, the bond between the citizen and the state is fractured. Chapter 2 argues that the state has a moral and legal duty to attempt to remedy this rift by creating just conditions for return, and applies the tenets of human rights law, rights-based theories and philosophical discussions of human dignity to develop a picture of the minimum conditions a state is obliged to guarantee for its repatriating citizens. At a minimum, I argue, a just return must establish or re-establish returnees as equal citizens entitled to benefit from a legitimate relationship of rights and duties with the state and effective, equitable protection for their basic human rights and security. This must include accountability for past violations of these rights, expressed through the provision of appropriate forms of redress, such as property restitution, compensation and apologies. These reflections on the conditions of just return and the role of reparations in establishing these conditions is informed by an analysis of the international refugee regime's repatriation framework, which stresses that return must be voluntary, and must take place in 'safety and dignity'. Chapter 3 begins the work of connecting this normative argument to the practice of states and other key actors in the refugee regime by tracing the emergence and evolution of international norms on redress for refugees, which have at times been intimately tied to the desire of host and donor states to promote repatriation as the primary durable solution to displacement.

The arguments developed in Part I are based on the premise that it is important to consider states' legal and moral obligations, and the pragmatic political conditions for action in concert with one another. Large-scale repatriations processes are one of the many cases in which the 'neat separation of politics and law', and indeed also morality, 'seems increasingly anachronistic' (Reus-Smit 2004: 1). It is clear that legal principles, moral argument and political practice influence one another to varying degrees and that both legal and moral principles, if they are to have any practical import, must grapple with the competing interests and constraints faced by states domestically and in the international arena. A three-pronged approach that considers the interplay between politics, law and moral argument is essential, as no one element can provide a comprehensive response to the puzzle presented by state responsibility for displacement and just return.

Since abstract explanations of state responsibility for forced migration and just return naturally cannot capture all the complexities inherent in actual reparation and return processes, Part II examines efforts to redress refugees repatriating to Guatemala (Chapter 4), Bosnia and Herzegovina (Chapter 5) and Mozambique (Chapter 6), drawing out the insights these cases hold for the account of just return and state responsibility for displacement developed in Part I.[10] These cases raise important theoretical questions about the nature, allocation and exercise of responsibility for displacement, and serve as valuable sources of insight into the characteristics of effective reparations programmes for returnees. In this connection, a secondary goal of the case studies is to use them to identify some of the key qualities of redress initiatives that are conducive to supporting the safe, durable and ultimately just resolution of displacement. Rather than attempting to generate a checklist or blueprint for planning just return and redress processes, the aim is to stimulate productive reflection on the challenges of shifting from theory to practice. With this in mind, the cases of Guatemala, Bosnia and Mozambique were selected

[10] This is of course not to suggest that the actors involved in repatriation and redress processes in Guatemala, Bosnia and Mozambique were committed to enabling the just return of refugees in the vein suggested in Part I. Indeed, the repatriations to Guatemala, Bosnia and Mozambique fell far short of the conditions of just return set out in Part I.

because they share several critical characteristics that enable meaningful comparison, but also raise distinct challenges. These cases all involved the repatriation of refugees under peace agreements, signed in the early to mid-1990s, were facilitated with the support of the international community and followed on from wildly destructive armed conflicts in which state agents were complicit in human rights violations. Yet these cases also vary in terms of the size of the movements; the role of international actors; the involvement of refugees in negotiating the conditions for their return; the types of reparations mechanisms used; and the intensity of calls for redress from local, national and international actors. The cases are, therefore, sufficiently similar to make structured, focused comparison possible, while also demonstrating variations that challenge different aspects of my normative argument. Examining the Mozambican case is particularly important in this respect, because the return to Mozambique is widely considered in the international community to have been a success, despite the fact that the justice issues associated with the war and the massive uprooting of the civilian population were not tackled head on by formal national or international institutions. In this case, redress was typically mediated by 'traditional authorities' who subvert simple categorisation as state or non-state actors, bringing into relief the complexity and diversity of approaches to redress in historically weak states.

Each case explores four critical issues: the historical and socio-economic context; the framework for repatriation and redress established in peace treaties, national laws, UN resolutions and key political statements; the mechanisms used to redress grievances including but not limited to land claims; and the roles played by key actors including the state of origin, international agencies and refugees themselves. In each case, I consider the implications of redress for the durable, equitable reintegration of returnees into the political community of their countries of origin. In the conclusion of each case study I examine the particular challenges and insights raised by the case, such as the implications of state collapse for the attribution of state responsibility for displacement in Bosnia, and the significance of the direct involvement of Guatemalan refugees in negotiating the conditions of their own return.

Through these cases, I probe the stark practical and theoretical limits of redress as an expression of state responsibility and a vehicle for reconciling returnees and their states of origin. Two of the threads that run throughout these cases are the observation that enabling just return and ensuring accountability for the crimes at the root of displacement require a long-term approach, and that although remedies for refugees (where available) have typically focused on the return of real property, the state is also obliged to redress non-material human rights violations inflicted on refugees through mechanisms such as apologies, truth commissions and criminal tribunals. Chapter 7 elaborates on these and other key points raised by the cases and discusses the characteristics of reparations programmes that may make good on the state of origin's obligation to redress its returning citizens.

In light of this analysis, Part III goes on to examine the challenges presented by 'hard cases' involving the protracted displacement of (*de jure*) stateless refugees. By extending my analysis to tackle the case of the Palestinian refugees, I interrogate how questions of state responsibility, redress and just return are affected when the displaced cannot make their claims for redress as citizens. While the Palestinian case is indisputably difficult, this discussion seeks to demonstrate that it is not entirely *sui generis* (Dumper 2006a, 2006b, 2007). Indeed, some of the earliest political debates on redress for returnees took place at the United Nations in response to the Palestinians' displacement, and set the stage for the development of international norms on reparations for refugees which have helped inform the resolution of various subsequent cases of forced migration. Rather than bolstering a trend of overly introspective scholarship on the Palestinian refugees, Chapter 8 identifies the implications of the concept of just return for hard cases, such as that of the Palestinian refugees, and explores how the insights on the negotiation and implementation of reparation and return in Bosnia, Mozambique and Guatemala may be applied to advance the resolution of the Palestinians' longstanding exile. At the same time, I use the Palestinian case as an entry point for a discussion of some of the most complex questions surrounding redress and just return, including the resolution of inter-generational claims, and link between reparations and the acceptance of moral responsibility for the historical injustices surrounding displacement.

States of asylum, internally displaced persons (IDPs) and those ousted to make way for development projects may also have legitimate claims to redress. Indeed, it is widely accepted that those uprooted through processes such as slum clearances and the construction of infrastructure such as dams have a right to compensation for their losses, and a significant body of literature has developed on the aims and strategies of effective reparations programmes for 'oustees'.[11] However, this discussion focuses more narrowly on redress for returning refugees. While there are numerous competing and compelling definitions of the term 'refugee', this discussion concentrates on people who have fled their countries because of persecution and lack of effective state protection.

11 See, for example, Cernea and Mathur (2008), Cernea and McDowell (2000) and Penz (2003).

Cases where the state is in principle willing but in practice unable to offer protection raise challenging questions for any theory of state responsibility for forced migration, which are addressed in part through the case study of Mozambique in Chapter 6.

Contested terms and concepts

Some of the terms and concepts that run throughout this book demand a word of clarification. As stated above, I conceive of redress, or reparations, as the 'entire spectrum of attempts to rectify historical injustices' (Barkan 2001: xix). Although I primarily use the language of reparations politics rather than transitional justice, I understand these to be closely intertwined endeavours. My discussion of state responsibility for displacement and just return focuses principally on refugees as citizens who have been compelled to flee their states of origin due to persecution or lack of state protection from violence (Part III considers the predicament of refugees who are *de jure* stateless). Chapter 1 engages in a detailed examination of the notion of state responsibility for displacement from a range of moral perspectives and in light of international legal norms. Following Krasner (1983: 2), I view norms as 'standards of behaviour defined in terms of rights and obligations'.

Just return intersects with various conceptions of justice, including cosmopolitan, retributive, restorative and distributive justice. While the development of a complete theory of justice is well beyond the scope of this book, Chapter 2 argues that a theory of just return can be constructed on the basis of a minimum conception of justice that puts a premium on liberty, equality and accountability. Conceptions of justice vary widely across cultures and between individuals, particularly in the aftermath of the atrocities that often accompany refugee flows. It must therefore be stressed that I have not taken on the presumably impossible goal of developing an account of just return that could meet each and every returnee's expectations or perceptions of justice. Rather, my much more modest aim is to identify the minimum obligations that states of origin may reasonably be expected to shoulder in the context of a return movement, leaving room for returnees and their states of origin to negotiate additional actions that may need to be undertaken in order to render return viable and just from the particular perspective of different groups. At the outset, it must also be clarified that I do not wish to overstate the role that attending to justice issues may play in shaping the 'success' of a return operation. Other, related factors such as: the availability of effective reintegration and reconstruction programmes and development assistance; land scarcity; popular attitudes towards return;

the conditions in host states and access to information on conditions in return communities will also decisively affect the security and durability of repatriation as a solution to displacement (Koser 1997, Zetter 2005). Ultimately, the relationship between the justice and perceived success of a reparation movement will depend largely on how success is defined. If success is understood simply as relieving host countries of their 'burdens', then the justice of a return movement may well be unrelated to its success. My contention is that from a legal and moral angle, the justice issues raised by return cannot be legitimately scuttled, and should be factored into calculations of success in return operations. Given the propensity of historic grievances to fester and undermine community cohesion, attending to these concerns in a forthright manner also appears to be a prudent course of action for states and other actors concerned with promoting stability and reconciliation in countries emerging from conflict and widespread displacement. Thus, if success is understood more comprehensively as the safe, dignified and durable resolution of displacement in a way that advances broader processes of transitional justice and peacebuilding, returnees' justice claims must figure centrally.

In addition to responsibility and justice, citizenship is another foundational concept in this book that eludes simple definition. This work rests on the basic conviction that in general 'everyone living under the authority of a state should have a say – an equal say – in how that authority is exercised' (Gibney 2006: 11). In this respect, my work reflects a perhaps predominately western conception of citizenship as closely tied to claims for equal standing among the individual members of the polity. This vision of citizenship has been critiqued by theorists concerned with citizenship in post-colonial states, who underline the discord between the borders drawn by colonial powers and the boundaries of pre-existing political communities, and suggest that membership in sub-state groups may be more important, practically and analytically, than the notion of the citizenry as a collective of equal individuals.[12] Yet contestations over which individuals should be counted as citizens in non-western countries make it clear that notions of citizenship as an individual claim to equal membership rights exert significant influence even in states where individualistic traditions are not necessarily deeply rooted. This notion of citizenship therefore represents a reasonable point of departure for a discussion of the obligations states of origin bear towards their returning citizens (Gibney 2006: 11–12).

[12] See, for example, Kabeer (2002) and Adejumobi (2001).

Last, what does the notion of repatriation itself entail? Hammond (1999: 230) argues that

> Amongst the most problematic terms in the repatriation canon are the words *return* and *returnee*, which imply that by re-entering one's native country a person is necessarily returning to something familiar. These terms are riddled with value judgments that reflect a segmentary, sedentary idea of how people ought to live, what their relation to their homeland should be, and ultimately how they should go about constructing their lives once the period of exile ends. The implication of these terms is that returnees should seek to move backward in time, to recapture a quality of life that they are assumed to have enjoyed before becoming refugees or that those who remained behind might currently enjoy... because post-repatriation life, or 'home' in the discourse of repatriation, is rooted in the country of origin it is considered by outsiders to be necessarily better than the life in exile.

In a related vein, Ranger (1994: 289) reflects that:

> The concept of 'repatriation' derives from the idea of a 'patria' and this in turn implies that an individual's primary identity, rights and obligations derive from the membership in a 'nation'. The nation encapsulates 'home' in terms of language, culture, rights to citizenship and land. Yet this is precisely what is at stake in many countries which generate refugees and returnees... Even where the idea of return to one's 'country' is a national as well as a local sentiment, that idea co-exists and sometimes conflicts with many other senses of identity and entitlement.

Similar concerns have also been expressed by scholars who question both the assumption that refugeehood is necessarily inferior to life in the country of origin, and that the 'natural' solution to displacement is for refugees to return not only to their state but to their 'original' homes (Allen and Turton 1996, Malkki 1992, 1995). This discussion of just return does *not* presuppose that return is the inherently preferable solution to displacement, that refugees identify strongly with their state of origin or that a primordial connection links exiles to their 'homelands'. While repatriation itself may in some cases represent a valuable form of redress for refugees who have long dreamed of going back to their countries and birth places, return should not be narrowly defined as refugees' resumption of residency in their former homes or on their ancestral lands.[13] Conceptualising repatriation merely in terms of returnees' geographic location obscures the broader political challenges at stake in the process. Rather than idealising return as the preferred solution to displacement, I simply contend that the responsible exercise of sovereignty requires states to recognise and redress the thwarted claims to equal

[13] For contrasting perspectives, see, for example, Warner (1996: 162).

membership in the political community borne by citizens who have been forced to seek shelter abroad. In this account, repatriation is not so much about crossing a border, returning to a particular physical location or reviving lost ways of life, as it is a critical opportunity to restructure political relationships between states and citizens, with a view to ensuring a more equitable, peaceful future.

Part I

Foundations of state responsibility and just return

1 Forced migration and the responsibilities of states

Moral and legal perspectives

'Rights talk' pervades the refugee regime. In order to make sense of the right to redress and the conditions of a just return, it is necessary to clarify the responsibilities that link states and citizens, and to understand what becomes of these responsibilities when a citizen is made a refugee. There are numerous actors who influence the creation and resolution of refugee crises, including states of origin, states of asylum, resettlement countries, donors, inter-governmental organisations, humanitarian agencies, local communities, and individuals, from state leaders and officials to refugees themselves. Typically, states of asylum, donors and international organisations such as UNHCR receive the lion's share of attention in debates on responsibility for refugees. Why is it important, both theoretically and practically, to focus on the responsibility of the state of origin for forced displacement? What is meant by responsibility in this context? What is the link between a state's legitimacy and its exercise of responsibility towards refugees?

This chapter will examine these questions, with the objective of laying the groundwork for the ensuing discussion on the state's responsibility to deliver on the refugee's right to just return and redress for displacement. My aim is to clarify the aspects of responsibility that are at stake during repatriation and redress processes, and the particular significance of efforts to ensure that states of origin exercise responsibility for forced migration. While it is critical to ensure that the individual engineers of atrocities and mass exoduses are held to account for their actions, I argue that effective remedies and the attainment of post-conflict security also require accountability at the state level. In support of this view, the first section of this chapter focuses on the notion of responsibility in political theory. The subsequent section examines the concept of responsibility under international law, and the insights human rights law offers into the obligations legitimate states bear towards their citizens. The final section explores the implications of a state subverting its responsibilities towards its citizens by forcing them into exile. This section argues that rectifying the relationship of rights and duties linking the citizen and the state is essential to the state's legal and moral legitimacy, and points to the need for reparations to advance this process. Holding states of origin accountable for displacement is not simply a question of backward-looking liability, but is also a question of forward-looking responsibility for the future wellbeing of displaced persons whose rights have been violated and for the broader citizenry.

My legal and moral analyses share the common conclusion that states have the duty to protect their citizens and that states bear at least some degree of remedial responsibility when they actively harm their citizens, or otherwise fail to provide effective protection to their citizenry. Why is it important to pursue both legal and moral examinations of the question of the responsibility states of origin bear for forced migration? First, in terms of motivating political action, it is significant that the demands of both morality and contemporary international law intersect regarding the state's obligation to strive to remedy the wrongs associated with forced migration. This lends added weight to calls to uphold refugees' right to redress. Second, although international legal provisions on accountability for human rights violations are rapidly evolving, it cannot be assumed that these developments will always accord with moral demands regarding responsible state behaviour. For example, while the creation of the International Criminal Court may be considered a significant step towards greater accountability for human rights violations, this advance is tempered by various states' increasingly restrictive interpretations of the obligations imposed on them by the Geneva Conventions. These restrictive interpretations may be legally tenable, but persuasive moral arguments may be mounted to suggest that the actions states seek to justify through these restrictive interpretations (such as the indefinite detention of suspected terrorists) are inconsistent with the moral requirements faced by responsible, rights-respecting states. In essence, I suggest that legal and moral analyses of responsibility for forced migration are mutually reinforcing, but neither perspective is sufficient on its own. On one hand, it is essential to consider the international law perspective, as international law can wield significant influence over state behaviour, particularly in comparison to the more modest influence of abstract moral arguments. On the other, legal provisions do not exist in a vacuum and must be closely interrogated to ascertain whether they are consistent with moral demands.

Responsibility in political theory

As David Miller (2001: 455) suggests, responsibility is a notoriously 'slippery' concept, and 'potentially one of the most confusing terms in the lexicon of moral and political philosophy', not to mention international law (Miller 2004: 244). It is, therefore, imperative to clarify the different theoretical notions of responsibility that are at issue in this discussion, including causal, moral and, in particular, remedial responsibility. These different senses of responsibility repeatedly intersect with one another in cases of forced migration, but it is important to distinguish their meanings, and to explore the ways in which responsibility for displacement may be both backward-looking, in the sense of being concerned with who is to blame for refugee crises, and forward-looking, in the sense of being concerned with who is responsible for protecting the rights and wellbeing of formerly displaced persons in the future. In this section I contend that states of origin often but do not always bear backward-looking responsibility for uprooting refugees, but even when they are not primarily to blame for displacement they still have forward-looking responsibilities to redress displacement and enable return.[1]

Causal responsibility refers to an agent's role in generating a particular state of affairs, based on a 'common sense understanding of causation' (Hart and Honoré 1985: 26–83). Causal responsibility may or may not be linked with moral responsibility, which involves the evaluation of an agent's conduct in terms of moral blame or praise. Moral responsibility may be incurred for acting wrongly or, for not acting as duty requires. For example, if I walk down the street, accidentally trip and knock down another pedestrian, I am causally responsible for the accident, but not morally responsible. However, if I collided with the pedestrian purposefully, or due to negligence, I would be both causally and morally responsible for the results (Miller 2001: 455–458).

As it is defined in the 1951 Convention Relating to the Status of Refugees (Refugee Convention), refugeehood typically involves both causal and moral responsibility on the part of the state of origin. The 1951 Refugee Convention defines a refugee as 'any person who is outside the country of his nationality . . . because he has or had well-founded fear of persecution by reason of his race, religion, nationality, membership of a particular social group or political opinion and is unable or, because of such fear, unwilling to avail himself of the protection of the government of the country of his nationality'. Although the Convention focuses on the duties of host states and the rights of refugees while in exile, the assumption undergirding this definition is that the

[1] As Richardson (1999: 247) underlines, the 'traditional philosophical issue of moral responsibility . . . tends to pose the question in binary terms: Was the agent responsible for what he or she did, or not?' While it is important to consider which agents are to blame for refugee crises, it may be equally important to ask the forward-looking question: 'For what is the agent responsible?'

state of origin or its agents are responsible for causing the refugee's 'well-founded fear of persecution'. This places causal and moral responsibility for the creation of refugees squarely on the shoulders of the state of origin.

Of course, displacement occurs due to a much wider range of factors than those articulated in the 1951 Refugee Convention. For example, the Convention's assumption that the state of origin is responsible for refugee outflows does not reflect the complexities of cases such as the Palestinian refugee situation. Arguably, the state of Israel bears the bulk of causal and moral responsibility for the creation and perpetuation of the Palestinians' displacement, yet Israel is not the refugees' state of origin in a straightforward sense.[2] The state may not be causally or morally responsible for displacement owing to emergencies such as tsunamis, particularly if the state did everything it could to prepare for and mitigate the effects of natural disasters. Assessing the extent of the state's causal and moral responsibility for the creation of refugees is also particularly difficult in cases where citizens are displaced owing to external invasions or the actions of non-state actors outside the government's control. Furthermore, attributing causal and moral responsibility for displacement is complicated by the interconnected structural injustices that contribute to the creation of refugee flows and constrain states' capacity to respond to them, such as economic disparity and cripplingly inequitable trade rules. As Castles (2003: 18) argues, in many cases 'the North does more to cause forced migration than to stop it, through enforcing an international economic and political order that causes under-development and conflict.'

Undoubtedly, in some cases, such as the displacement of refugees from Darfur by *janjaweed* under the control of the government of Sudan, the state of origin's primary causal and moral responsibility for displacement is clear enough. However, given that causal and moral responsibility for refugee crises is much murkier in many other cases, in what other senses may states of origin be responsible for redressing and resolving forced migration situations? Beyond causal and moral responsibility, the essential principle to consider here is remedial responsibility. 'To be remedially

[2] The Palestinian Authority positions itself as responsible for or at least accountable to the refugees as members of the Palestinian nation, and it may be assumed that the government of a future Palestinian state would adopt a similar position. However, this should not be confused with acceptance of causal or moral responsibility for the refugees' longstanding displacement. In this case, the Palestinian Authority's acceptance of 'responsibility' for the refugees may be better understood in terms of solidarity rooted in a common national identity or as part of efforts to build up the legitimacy of the Palestinian Authority and calls for an independent Palestinian state.

responsible for a bad situation means to have a special obligation to put the bad situation right, in other words to be picked out, either individually or along with others, as having a responsibility towards the deprived or suffering party that is not shared equally among all agents' (Honoré 1999, Miller 2001: 454). When determining remedial responsibility for a wrong, the main question that must be answered is: 'What connects a particular agent A to a particular patient P in such a way that A is singled out as having a remedial responsibility towards P that others, in general, do not have?' (Miller 2001: 454). Miller's connection theory suggests that remedial responsibility for a bad situation may be distributed by examining and balancing factors, including not only causal and moral responsibility but also whether particular actors reaped benefits from the harm; the diverse capacities of the actors involved; the usefulness of the aid they could offer; the relative cost each actor would have to bear for remedying the situation; and whether the actors who could assist and those in need of a remedy have 'special responsibilities' towards each other, owing, for instance, to family links or nationality (Miller 2001: 460–462, Miller 2007: 99–104). In this way, Miller's connection theory is both backward looking and forward looking. By attributing remedial responsibility on the basis of a pluralistic balancing of moral, causal and outcome responsibility, capacity to assist, whether an actor benefitted from the harm, and community connections, his theory respects the view that for the most part actors 'should be held responsible for the harm that they do' (Miller 2001: 466). At the same time, however, the connection theory acknowledges that the effective distribution of remedial responsibility must be sensitive to whether the actor recognised as bearing remedial responsibility is actually able to redress the harm (Miller 2007: 103–104). According to Miller, there is 'nothing paradoxical . . . in assigning remedial responsibility on the basis of causation, say, in one case and on the basis of communitarian relations in the next case . . . Where two or more of the principles apply, the theory tells us to look at the strength of the various connections . . . In some cases it may recommend dividing responsibility between two or more agents, where this makes practical sense, and the ties are of comparable strength' (Miller 2001: 471, Bradley 2012b: 154–155).

Under this account, then, remedial responsibility for displacement may be borne by or shared between different actors, such as states of origin, states of asylum, donor states and international organisations. Why should states of origin be held remedially responsible – among others, perhaps – for resolving refugee situations, and what does remedial responsibility for displacement involve? First, remedial responsibility for refugees must entail the provision of a durable solution to their displacement, be it repatriation, resettlement or local integration. As discussed in the Introduction, historically, many states of origin have not been held remedially responsible for creating refugees. Indeed, the architects of the international refugee regime sought to remove refugees as a potential source of conflict between states by emphasising the responsibilities of host countries over states of origin, and underscoring the purportedly non-political nature of the work of UNHCR and the act of extending asylum to refugees. While the definitively political foundations of the refugee regime have since been underscored by scholars such as Forsythe (2001) and Loescher (2001a), international law still lacks the robust enforcement mechanisms necessary to hold states responsible for creating refugees, and, particularly during the Cold War, politically powerful countries generally did not pressure states of origin to exercise accountability towards their displaced citizens. Instead, international actors shouldered remedial responsibility for refugees by facilitating resettlement or providing the opportunity for refugees to integrate into their countries of asylum. Beyond the pragmatic recognition that host and resettlement states are now adopting increasingly restrictive policies towards refugees – in effect refusing to accept remedial responsibility for the displaced – are there compelling reasons to require states of origin to accept responsibility for contributing to the resolution of refugee crises by establishing just conditions for return? When considering this question, it is important to note that while return is a right recognised under international law, there is no legal right to resettlement or local integration. Many political theorists have also argued strongly for the state's prerogative to control entry and membership in the political community (Walzer 1983). While others have called for more open borders, few would suggest that refugees' claims on resettlement or local integration opportunities are as strongly supported, legally and morally, as their right to return. In light of this situation, it is reasonable to focus a greater amount of attention on ensuring that the state of origin shoulders its remedial responsibility for its displaced citizens by enabling them to return in just and secure conditions. As Miller's connection theory suggests, integrating the state of origin into the distribution of remedial responsibility for forced migration does not preclude other actors such as states of asylum from providing a remedy to displaced persons, for example, through local integration.[3]

[3] Depending on factors such as the causes of displacement and conditions in the host community, in some cases the provision of asylum and permanent local integration opportunities may be an important form of redress for displacement (see Souter (in press) for a defence of this view). Importantly, even if there is an obligation in some instances

The view that states of origin should figure centrally in the distribution of remedial responsibility for displacement is bolstered by the widespread and deep-seated belief that if B is causally and, in particular, morally responsible for harming C, then B is obliged to remedy the situation. As discussed above, the creation of refugees is often a crime of the state – that is, it is carried out through the purposeful mobilisation of state resources against the citizen, or at the hands of non-state actors who are able to violate citizens' rights because the state is negligent or incompetent. For example, during the Guatemalan civil war, the widespread displacement of Maya civilians was carried out by the national army in conjunction with state-supported paramilitaries. As the state of origin is so often intrinsic to the creation of refugees, it is difficult to see how remedial responsibility could be entirely devolved to another level, such as to individuals or to external organisations.

To be sure, as Miller (2001: 471) recognises, there is 'no algorithm' for dividing up responsibility for alleviating deprivation and suffering. Assigning responsibility for forced migration is particularly complicated in light of the wide range of actors involved, including individual leaders. The judges at Nuremberg famously concluded that 'international wrongs are committed by individuals and not by abstract entities' (Echeverria 2002). While the importance of individual accountability cannot be underestimated, it is equally crucial that *states* be held liable for abuses in order to deter human rights violations at all levels and ensure effective remedies are available to the victims of injustice. The pursuit of individual accountability to the exclusion of state responsibility is particularly problematic as an individual, no matter how far beyond the moral pale, cannot shoulder sole responsibility for the systematic human rights violations that so often spark massive refugee flows. Individual leaders may mastermind atrocities, but both the individual and the institution must be held accountable for state-sanctioned crimes, if only because the duty to make amends for these crimes cannot be discharged by an individual.[4] Even if a war criminal had extensive financial resources that could be appropriated to fund the reconstruction and reparations programmes necessary to remedy his crimes, it would be profoundly inappropriate for him to be responsible for the delivery of these programmes,

for other states to provide asylum and permanent local integration opportunities as a form of redress, the state of origin may still be remedially responsible for enabling a safe, dignified and ultimately just return. As a right protected under international human rights law, refugees should have the option to return and may exercise this option in concert with other durable solutions to displacement.

[4] Equally, national groups often lack the institutional structures necessary to make collective decisions and take responsibility for them.

as this would likely be offensive to the survivors and unlikely to meet their needs. This duty rightfully falls upon the more abstract political entity of the state.

Given these concerns, it is both reasonable and expedient to focus more attention on the state of origin's remedial responsibility for refugee crises. However, Miller is right to emphasise the complexities associated with the delegation of remedial responsibility. What should we make of cases where, for example, the state of origin bears little or no causal or moral responsibility for displacement, or may lack the capacity to discharge this responsibility without external support? Briefly, Miller's connection theory suggests that even if the state of origin is not to blame for the outflow of refugees, it may still bear forward-looking remedial responsibility towards its displaced citizens because, for example, it is specially situated as the primary actor with the capacity to enable exercise of the right of return.[5] Furthermore, the state of origin has 'special obligations' towards its displaced citizens as members of the admittedly fractured political community of the state; under Miller's account these ties represent a strong reason to consider the state of origin remedially responsible (Miller 2007: 104). When the state of origin lacks the capacity to discharge its remedial responsibilities towards its exiled citizens without external support, this responsibility may be shared with international actors. In Parts II and III, I will return to Miller's work to elucidate the responsibilities international actors bear in terms of supporting just return and holding states of origin accountable for causing refugee flows. For the moment, however, it is worth noting that alongside Miller's connection theory of remedial responsibility, a modified version of Iris Marion Young's social connection model of responsibility for global injustices may provide a compelling conceptual foundation for explaining why other actors – particularly wealthy western states – may have a responsibility to support the state of origin so that it can redress the wrongs that forced its citizens from their homes and enable a just return process.[6] Although it cannot be discussed at length here, Young's social connection model of responsibility is prescient because

[5] States of origin often help their citizens exercise their right to return to their country of origin, even when the state is not to blame for the circumstances that have resulted in their citizens being outside the country and needing assistance to return. For example, after the 2004 Indian Ocean tsunami, the Canadian government, like many others, facilitated the return of its citizens who were stranded in the affected areas.

[6] Young's theory focuses on individuals' responsibilities in contexts of global structural injustice, whereas I am primarily concerned with institutional responsibilities, and particularly states' responsibilities. However, many of the arguments Young develops regarding individual responsibility may apply to states.

it focuses on instances in which particular wrongs are linked to conditions of structural injustice, and suggests that 'obligations of justice arise between persons' and potentially also between states 'by virtue of the social processes that connect them' (Young 2006: 102). More precisely, the social connection model of responsibility indicates that 'all agents who contribute by their actions to the social processes that produce injustice have responsibilities to work to remedy these injustices' (Young 2006: 102–103). While refugee flows are not the exclusive result of structural injustice, inequitable global distributions of resources and power undeniably render some regions and groups more vulnerable to displacement. The countries that are in a position to help impoverished and conflict-stricken states of origin exercise remedial responsibility for their displaced citizens are often those wealthy states that are directly connected to and have benefitted from structural injustices linked to displacement. Under Young's account, they may therefore share responsibility for rectifying the harms associated with these structural injustices. Like Miller's account of remedial responsibility, Young's view is based on the conviction that in some circumstances, 'finding an agent responsible does not [necessarily] imply finding the agent at fault or liable for a past wrong, but rather refers to the agents' carrying out activities in a morally appropriate way and aiming for certain outcomes . . . Where there is structural injustice, finding some people' or institutions 'guilty of perpetrating specific wrongful actions does not absolve others whose actions contribute to the outcomes from bearing responsibility' (Richardson 1999: 218–249, Young 2006: 119–120). These theories are therefore both particularly well suited to exploring problems such as the resolution of forced migration situations, in which different kinds of responsibility may be shared among many different actors. In such situations, those actors with backward-looking responsibilities for uprooting refugees may not necessarily be the sole or primary actors with forward-looking responsibilities for resolving displacement crisis.

This preliminary discussion of states' remedial responsibilities for forced migration and the more detailed arguments that follow rest on several assumptions about responsibility that are important to acknowledge, although an in-depth examination of them is not possible here. First, I assume that we can meaningfully assign responsibilities, including moral and remedial responsibilities, to collective or institutional agents including states. Following Erskine (2001: 72), I assume that a collectivity such as a state qualifies for moral agency if it has 'an identity that is more than the sum of the identities of its constituent parts . . . a decision-making structure; an identity over time; and a conception of itself as a unit'. Discussions on the nature and scope of state responsibility must take into account the diverse empirical and normative conditions and capacities that characterise contemporary states. Many states have a limited capacity to make and implement independent moral decisions, and 'a state, like an individual, cannot be said to bear a duty that circumstances render it incapable of discharging' (Erskine 2001: 83). Yet, I assume that the capacity to exercise moral agency and shoulder responsibility can exist in degrees, and that a state's present inability to make amends for past wrongs does not render it immune to arguments that it *should* develop this capacity (Erskine 2001: 72–82).[7] I also assume that a state's responsibility for past injustice may persist despite the passing of generations. This is a particularly important consideration for the displaced as major refugee exoduses now last an average of 17 years. More than 7.2 million people are considered to be in 'protracted' refugee situations, and thousands of children are born into displacement every year (UNHCR 2006a, 2011: 2). The complexities associated with longstanding or inter-generational wrongs may in fact provide another reason to focus attention on the level of state responsibility for displacement: according to the legal principle of state continuity, the state retains its legal identity and responsibilities for past violations despite changes in government or the passage of time. Demonstrating the identity of states over time may be a complex task from a political or theoretical point of view, given the radical changes many states experience in terms of their demographic composition and political character. However, this is likely to be far less problematic than the argument that responsibility for remedying grave historic injustices can be inherited and dispensed by nations or individual descendants of wrongdoers.[8] The challenges associated with resolving inter-generational wrongs will be addressed in greater detail in Chapter 8, building on the insights international law offers into the responsibility states of origin bear for forced migration.

The responsibilities of states: legal views

The international law of state responsibility and international human rights law are the two bodies of international law with greatest relevance to the question of the state of origin's obligation to redress forced migration and the crimes associated with it. Although legal perspectives on responsibility tend to focus on backward-looking liability for violations of obligations under the law, legal conceptions of states' responsibilities

[7] For further theoretical perspectives on state and institutional responsibility, see Erskine (2003), Green (2002) and Luban, Strudler and Wasserman (1992).

[8] For an alternative perspective, see Miller (2005).

may also be forward looking insofar as the ultimate goal of these legal systems is to protect the security, dignity and rights of all individuals.

The doctrine of state responsibility is one of the core tenets of international law. As a legal term of art, state responsibility is 'simply the principle which establishes an obligation to make good any violation of international law producing injury', and arises from the legal maxim stated by Grotius in 1646 that 'every fault creates the obligation to make good the loss' (Lee 1986: 536–537). As states are the conventional subjects of international law, technically speaking, the law of state responsibility applies only between states. Duties a state owes to its citizens are left out or on the margins of the law.

The International Law Commission (ILC) Articles on State Responsibility affirm this traditional, state-centric definition of state responsibility; crystallise customary international law on state responsibility; and set out restitution, compensation, satisfaction and guarantees of non-repetition as the basic legal tools states have to remedy injuries (Crawford 2002). Although the ILC Articles on State Responsibility took 40 years to negotiate, 'the greatest relevance of the . . . articles may ultimately lie outside the scope of the project' as many states have now taken on new legal obligations that are 'unilateral or vertical, in the sense that they concern duties owed by states to individuals . . . Breach of these duties is unlikely to injure another state directly or give rise to a classic claim for reparations' (Shelton 2002: 834). Nonetheless, many jurists argue that the law of state responsibility also pertains to the internationally recognised obligations states bear towards individuals, and the Articles have been referenced in the judgements of influential human rights bodies such as the Inter-American Court of Human Rights (Shelton 2000: 93).

These developments reflect the relatively recent but fundamental shift in international law towards recognition of the rights and duties of individuals (Ellis and Hutton 2002: 352).[9] Agreements including the International Covenant on Civil and Political Rights, the International Covenant on Economic, Social and Cultural Rights and various pieces of international humanitarian law clearly delineate individual rights the state is bound to respect, if not for moral reasons then because, by signing these conventions, states have created binding legal responsibilities for themselves. Several provisions contained in international human rights and humanitarian law clearly proscribe arbitrary displacement, and require (at least in principle) that states be held responsible for this crime (Williams 2007: 6–7). For example, Article 49 of the Fourth Geneva Convention relative to the Protection of Civilian Persons in Time of

[9] See also Shelton (2000).

War prohibits individual and mass forcible transfers and deportations. Building on the prohibitions in the Geneva Convention, the Statute of the International Criminal Tribunal for the Former Yugoslavia and Article 7(1)(d) of the Rome Statute of the International Criminal Court recognise the transfer or deportation of civilian populations as crimes against humanity.

The progress made in codifying the state's responsibilities to individuals has prompted some progressive scholars and governments to argue that a state's claim to sovereignty is dependent upon the state effectively shouldering its primary responsibilities, including safeguarding human rights. Francis Deng (1995) captures this idea in his discussion of 'sovereignty as responsibility'. According to Deng, when a state grievously fails to behave responsibly towards its citizens, the state temporarily forfeits its claim to sovereignty and the international community may be permitted to intervene.[10] Morally compelling and legally innovative, the notion of sovereignty as responsibility gained traction through its incorporation into the work of the International Commission on Intervention and State Sovereignty and the inclusion of the concept of the 'responsibility to protect' in the outcomes of the 2005 United Nations September Summit (ICISS 2001, UNGA 2005b). However, these developments have not translated into strong enforcement mechanisms to curtail the sovereignty of irresponsible states and remedy severe violations of human rights. As Shelton (2000: 1–2) argues,

> For all its revolutionary advances, human rights law has yet to develop a coherent theory or consistent practice of remedies for victims of human rights violations . . . The international law of state responsibility is an inadequate model because it derives from inter-state cases between juridically equal parties, where diplomatic concerns and broader issues of cooperation or conflict affect the results. International human rights law is the first area of international law where individuals may bring actions against states in international tribunals, but the imbalance in respective power and juridical status between states and individuals affects the procedures and the perceived role of the human rights institutions in affording remedies.

Indeed, while bodies such as the European Court of Human Rights and the Inter-American Court of Human Rights allow individuals to bring forward claims against states, these organs are simply out of reach

[10] Sovereignty as responsibility is fundamentally a forward-looking conception of responsibility, as it is concerned not so much with whether the state is *liable* for past abuses, as it is with whether the state can and will protect citizens' current and future wellbeing. Regardless of whether it is to blame for past rights violations, a state that wishes to legitimately claim the prerogatives of sovereignty must shoulder responsibility for the protection of its citizens' rights, including their remedial rights.

for the vast majority of refugees, who lack the resources and political clout necessary to navigate the international legal system and use it to hold their states to account. Although progress has been made through the International Criminal Court (ICC) and the International Criminal Tribunals for Rwanda and the Former Yugoslavia (ICTR, ICTY) to help ensure individuals are held responsible for egregious human rights violations, states can often evade this duty despite its strong normative and legal underpinnings. Legal history was made in February 2006, when the first trial of a *state* charged with genocide opened at the International Court of Justice (ICJ). The case was initially filed by Bosnia-Herzegovina against Serbia (then Yugoslavia) in March 1993 in an attempt to pressure Belgrade to cease the killing and expulsion of Bosnian Muslims. Although the ICJ issued a prompt ruling ordering Yugoslavia to do everything within its power to prevent genocide in Bosnia, the verdict was disregarded, and it took 13 years of legal wrangling for the case to come before the court for a full hearing. In February 2007, the ICJ affirmed that Belgrade failed to comply with its obligation under international law to prevent genocide and punish the perpetrators of this crime. However, the court found that 'the acts of genocide at Srebrenica cannot be attributed to the Respondent [Serbia] as having been committed by its organs,' and dismissed Bosnia's compensation claim, ruling that '[f]inancial compensation is not the appropriate form of reparation' (ICJ 2007: paragraphs 395 and 462).

While the ICJ's verdict was disappointing to many Bosnian Muslims, *Bosnia and Herzegovina* v. *Serbia and Montenegro* was undisputedly a historic effort to ensure state-level responsibility for genocidal acts in which mass displacement figured centrally. However, the ICJ, like the ICTY, ICTR and ICC, is not a venue that can be approached by individuals seeking to hold their own state responsible for human rights violations. A ruling in favour of Bosnia would not have altered the international legal system's lack of accessible venues through which *citizens* can lodge claims against their own governments. It must, therefore, be concluded that while international law clearly prohibits arbitrary displacement and calls for states to be held responsible for forced migration, more accessible and robust enforcement mechanisms are required to ensure that international law can be brought to bear to hold states accountable for driving out their own citizens (Andreu-Guzmán 2012).[11]

[11] This discussion has focused on cases in which the state of origin is principally to blame for the displacement of its citizens and has stressed the difficulty of using current legal tools and processes to hold states responsible for this violation. However, in instances

Breaking the bond and the imperative of repair: theorising responsibility for forced migration

Feeble as legal instruments for ensuring state responsibility for forced migration may be, moral arguments often hold even less sway over states. Nonetheless, Shacknove's discussion of the refugee definition illuminates the relationship of mutual rights and duties that links the citizen and the state, and provides a starting point for examining the obligations that arise when this relationship is undermined by citizens being forced into exile.[12] Along with many scholars from a broad range of theoretical schools, Shacknove embraces the widely held view that a fundamental duty of a legitimate state is to protect its citizens.[13] Shacknove (1985: 275) argues that the refugee definition offered in the 1951 Refugee Convention is predicated on the assumption that 'a bond of trust, loyalty, protection, and assistance between the citizen and the state constitutes the normal basis of society' and that 'in the case of the refugee, this bond has been severed'. Persecution, conflict and alienage are the physical manifestations of this severed bond. 'It is the absence of state protection', Shacknove (1985: 277) argues, 'which constitutes the full and complete negation of society and thus the basis of refugeehood'. Shacknove (1985: 281) insightfully notes that 'in exchange for their allegiance, citizens can minimally expect that their government will guarantee physical security, vital subsistence, and liberty of political participation and physical movement. No reasonable person would be satisfied with less. Beneath this threshold the social compact has no meaning'. The upshot of Shacknove's argument is that if every state subverted its responsibilities by creating refugees, the justification for the state system itself would crumble.

Although this outcome seems extreme, owing to scarce resettlement and local integration opportunities, millions of refugees are denied the chance to forge new bonds of citizenship with another state and so are left outside the logic of the state system. These refugees are compelled either to continue in limbo with only limited rights in their country of

where actors other than the state of origin are largely to blame for the generation of refugee crises, international legal systems are equally, if not more, ill-equipped to ensure accountability for such violations.

12 As recognized above, the actions of the state of origin are not always the primary cause of displacement. However, following Shacknove, I am focusing on those paradigmatic cases in which the state of origin is causally and morally responsible for displacement.

13 Various theoretical justifications may be offered in support of this view. For example, social contract theory and much of Christian and Islamic political thought supports the conclusion that a legitimate state is fundamentally obliged to protect the security and wellbeing of its citizens. However, a detailed discussion of the theoretical underpinnings of this widely accepted position is not within the scope of this work.

asylum or to return to their state of origin. This reality forces the question of rectifying the relationship between states and their exiled citizens onto the political and moral agenda. The implications of this question are ethically and politically significant, because in the repatriation process the rights and obligations that bind the citizen and the state can be made explicit and enforceable in the context of reformed state institutions. The restructured 'terms' of the state-citizen relationship may be reflected in instruments such as peace agreements and new national constitutions. Certainly, refugees do not often have the opportunity to participate directly in peace talks and constitutional negotiations. In cases such as Burundi and Guatemala, however, displaced populations have played an active role in negotiating peace agreements or, in more theoretical terms, new social contracts with their states (Accord 1997, de Rivero 2001, Jonas 2000, Mooney 2006, UNIFEM 2000).

In comparison to refugees who resettle in affluent, multicultural democracies, returnees often face much more serious obstacles in re-establishing themselves as equal, rights-bearing citizens. Refugees are often members of social groups that the dominant powers prefer to remain estranged from the state. However, this ostracism is ill-conceived, both practically and theoretically. On the theoretical level, scholars such as Kant offer compelling defences of the natural equality of moral status between individuals. In light of this natural equality, individuals should deal with one another even-handedly, and should receive similar treatment from institutions such as the state. Grounding his theoretical arguments in practical recognition of the nature of power dynamics, Hobbes contends that it is in the state's interest to treat its citizens equally. Hobbes stresses the physical equality that exists between individuals, underlining that although individuals have markedly different degrees of physical power, virtually every person has the capacity to harm another, especially as the weak may use technology to augment their power (Buchanan 1975, Kymlicka 1991: 188). In light of individual citizens' physical and moral equality, as expounded by Hobbes and Kant, the state of origin has good reason to adopt an equitable approach to the assessment of its obligations towards returnees and the restoration of its relationship with them.

Beyond the state's responsibilities towards its repatriating citizens, restoring a functional state-citizen relationship also raises the perplexing question of the duties returnees bear towards the state. In 'Obligation, Loyalty, Exile', Judith Shklar blends legal and theoretical analyses of the predicament facing the displaced to illuminate the nature of obligation and loyalty as political virtues. Shklar (1993: 190) opines that 'legality is the core of the legitimacy of the modern state' and, similarly to Shacknove, argues that 'when legally created expectations, based on a public and published system of rights and duties, are cast aside... [this] violates trust in a way that renders the very basis of public life unreliable, and vitiates the chief reasons for our obligation to obey the law'. Shklar reviews the experiences of prominent historical exiles such as the Jewish French Army Captain Alfred Dreyfus, who maintained his sense of loyalty and obligation to France despite his expulsion to Devil's Island on the basis of entirely erroneous and unsubstantiated allegations that he passed military secrets to Germany. Despite his experience of overt persecution and anti-Semitism from the French state, Dreyfus returned to France as soon as he had the opportunity and even re-enlisted in the army, going on to defend France with distinction in World War I. While many admire Dreyfus' unwavering obligation and loyalty to the French state throughout his exile and afterwards, Shklar (1993: 191) admits that she 'think[s] he was crazy'.

Although exiles like Dreyfus may successfully preserve a sense of respect and obligation towards their state of origin, Shklar (1993: 193) argues that refugees such as the Holocaust survivors 'have been expelled beyond all hope of return and have no political obligations at all to their former state. After such an expulsion, there is no point in trying to reclaim one's rights.' Shklar (1993: 193) explains the expellees' condition in 'Lockean terms': 'both contracts had been broken, the first between members of society as well as the second between citizens and the state. They were betrayed at both levels, excluded from civil no less than from political society'. While her analysis effectively illuminates refugees' disenfranchisement from the state as well as from their fellow citizens, Shklar, like Arendt, does not completely capture the current political problem confronting refugees. Shklar presciently suggests that psychologically many refugees may be past the point where they could ever hope for return, or reconciliation, with their state of origin. Yet in the contemporary international refugee regime, fewer and fewer refugees, neither victims of the Taliban nor orphaned Tutsis, are 'expelled beyond all hope of return'. Too often, finding secure and permanent asylum is an even bleaker prospect than repatriation, and the 'hope of return' must be faced, regardless of whether it is a welcome homecoming.

Shklar may be correct when she suggests that refugees have few or no obligations to their state of origin while in exile. At this point, the state–citizen relationship is in tatters. However, through the repatriation and reintegration processes, the formerly displaced must surely take on both the rights and the obligations of regular citizens. This is essential to the establishment of both social equity and long-term stability. While many refugees welcome the restoration of 'normal' relations with their neighbours and their state as the long-desired conclusion to their exile, for others this may seem like an unreasonable expectation. Returnees might ask why they should be required to support, contribute to and submit to the laws of a state that egregiously wronged them (or at least failed to protect them), particularly if that harm is not fully acknowledged. Reparations, reconciliation and reintegration programmes can play an essential, albeit complex, role in enabling returnees to accept the authority of the reformed state, and are examined in detail through case studies in Part II. Equally, these programmes may promote the political rehabilitation of the state so that it becomes an institution more worthy of trust and capable of wielding authority responsibly.[14]

In short, both legally and theoretically, the state is 'constituted by a set of duties owed to its citizens that are integral to its authority to act' (Gibney 1999: 175). When these duties have been violated through the creation of refugees, the state must repair the broken bond between itself and its exiled citizens if it is to regain legal and moral legitimacy. Indeed, Principle 1 of the Cairo Declaration of Principles of International Law on Compensation to Refugees affirms that the 'responsibility for caring for the world's refugees rests ultimately upon the countries that directly or indirectly force their own citizens to flee' (ILA 1992). Establishing just conditions for return is one of the principal ways in which the state of origin makes good on its obligations towards its exiled citizens, thereby opening the way for an eventual reconciliation process.

[14] See, for example, Barkan's discussion of the role of reparations in the rehabilitation of the German state (Barkan 2001).

2 The conditions of just return

A minimum account

In his 2005 Tanner Lectures on Human Values, Israeli philosopher Avishai Margalit (2005: 214) points out that 'we tend to talk of peace and justice as we do of fish and chips – as two complementary things'. Linking peace and justice is *de rigeur* in the international political arena, and to argue against a just peace is, as Margalit suggests, like standing up against motherhood or friendship (Palmer 2005). Given the demonstrated link between peace and repatriation processes in countries such as Bosnia, Cambodia, Tajikistan, El Salvador and Namibia and Mozambique (Druke 2000, Petrin 2002, Utting 1994, Weiss Fagen 2003, 2005: 513–519), scholars and policymakers have good reason to be concerned with just return as an essential element of a just and sustainable peace. Yet the notion of justice for returnees has attracted little attention in international politics. Indeed, in hastily planned, under-resourced repatriation operations where 'the lucky ones' get a bag of seeds and a plastic tarpaulin, talk of justice may seem overly ambitious or utterly irrelevant.

In this chapter, I argue that the question of just return merits greater scholarly and political attention, and sketch a minimum account of the conditions of just return. I develop this account by drawing on international legal principles, as well as moral arguments on rights, dignity and state responsibility. There is no standard mould for a just return. However, building on the arguments set out in Chapter 1 on the importance of ensuring that states – particularly states of origin – are held responsible for this injustice, I contend that broadly speaking, the goal of a just return process must be to put returnees back on equal footing with their non-displaced co-nationals by restoring or creating a new relationship of rights and duties between the state and its returning citizens.[1] The conditions of just return match the essential duties a legitimate state

[1] Admittedly, in some countries a respectful relationship of rights and duties between citizens and the state is the exception rather than the norm. This analysis does not extend to cases where the state of origin purposefully eschews protection responsibilities for the majority of its citizens, displaced or otherwise. In these cases, it is highly unlikely if not impossible for any of the conditions of just return to be met.

must ensure for its citizens: equal, effective protection for their security and basic human rights, including accountability for any abuses of these rights.[2] Establishing these conditions is a critical expression of the state of origin's remedial responsibility for forced migration, as discussed in Chapter 1. These conditions are also implicit in the international refugee regime's norms on repatriation.[3]

The norms developed by UNHCR and UN Member States on voluntary repatriation and return in 'safety and dignity' provide the framework within which a just return may be pursued. However, the notions of voluntary, safe and dignified return have typically been discussed in legal and operational terms; their moral dimensions have been neglected or interpreted inconsistently. As a response to this analytical gap, this chapter examines the moral and political origins and implications of these interconnected norms, focusing in particular on the under-examined notion of *dignified* return. This discussion underlines the importance of upholding the principle of refugee choice, and points to the role of redress as the crux of the just return process. My analysis begins with an examination of why just return merits greater practical and scholarly consideration, focusing on the status of return as a morally and legally defensible right.

Before embarking on this analysis, however, it must be stressed that the model of just return developed in this chapter is an ideal (albeit minimum) account that naturally cannot apply neatly to practice in every circumstance. I suggest that creating just conditions for return is an essential demonstration of the state of origin's remedial responsibility for forced migration, and that just return is best understood as the restoration (or creation) of a legitimate relationship of rights and duties between returnees and the state, such that returnees and their non-displaced co-nationals are rendered equal as citizens. What relevance does this model have for situations such as the conflict in the Balkans, where refugees returned to states that did not exist prior to their displacement? What insight does this account hold for cases such as the Palestinian refugees, in which the vast majority of the displaced are not citizens of the state that bears perhaps the greatest share of responsibility for their continued displacement? In Chapter 5, I will address the challenges disruptions in state continuity pose for this model. While the account of just return offered in this chapter focuses on the paradigmatic case of refugees who are citizens of the state responsible for their displacement, in Part III I

[2] For detailed discussions of basic rights and state legitimacy, see, for example, Shue (1996) and Buchanan (2004).

[3] Portions of this chapter appear in Bradley (2008) and Bradley (2009b).

will discuss how this model can be used as a starting point to elucidate the responsibilities states may hold towards non-citizens and *de jure* stateless persons whom they have displaced.

Why worry about just return?

Internationally supported repatriation movements are complex logistical feats, and the justice issues at stake in these processes can get lost amidst the provisions of operational handbooks and heavy bureaucratic structures. In this chaotic environment, why is it important to focus attention on the seemingly ambiguous, ambitious idea of *just* return, rather than the more modest goal of a simply sustainable return? Why argue for a minimum account of just return, rather than an expansive list of ideal conditions for a just repatriation process?

Historically, the durable solutions system has not functioned with justice considerations first in mind. In his 1954 Nobel Peace Prize lecture, the first UN High Commissioner for Refugees, G. J. van Heuven Goedhart, commented that resettlement took place according to 'reversed Darwinistic principles' that privileged the 'exodus of the fittest'. In the same speech the High Commissioner opined that 'voluntary repatriation is no longer of great importance' (van Heuven Goedhart 1955). Time has disproved this assessment, but the international refugee regime has retained many of the Darwinian qualities Goedhart identified. For example, it is widely recognised that well-resourced, educated refugees are more likely than their illiterate, impoverished counterparts to find permanent asylum or resettlement opportunities in affluent democratic countries. The upshot of this trend is presumably that the majority of returnees are likely to come from economically disadvantaged or socially marginalised backgrounds, which may hamper their ability to organise themselves politically to demand that the conditions of their return are just.[4] This renders it all the more important for refugee advocates and scholars to give the issue of just return due consideration, in order to ensure that they are able to effectively amplify returnees' claims and concerns.

[4] Certainly, some displaced persons who secure permanent asylum or resettlement in the North return to their countries of origin and often play key leadership roles in new governments. For example, returnees have held influential positions in the post-Taliban and post-Baathist governments in Afghanistan and Iraq, respectively. These high-ranking, politically connected former refugees are certainly not 'typical' returnees, although they may have suffered many of the same injustices as those who repatriate in more humble circumstances, and may help raise the profile of the justice concerns facing the broader returnee population.

Contemporary international political rhetoric posits strong, mutually reinforcing links between peace and justice on the one hand, and between peace and repatriation on the other.[5] If these links are as firm as the rhetoric suggests, then there are compelling pragmatic reasons to take the question of just return seriously, in order to avoid future conflict. Yet history suggests that the connection between peace and justice cannot be taken for granted. For example, sustainable peace was achieved in post-apartheid South Africa without a comprehensive legal justice process. Indeed, many commentators suggest that South Africa's apartheid leaders would have prolonged their hold on power if trials rather than amnesties had been on the political horizon. In recent years, western powers adamantly underlined the link between peace and justice in the former Yugoslavia, where they had invested heavily in justice apparatuses such as the International Criminal Tribunal for the Former Yugoslavia (ICTY). However, it is far from certain that the ICTY and related justice processes have translated into a sustainable peace in the Balkans. Many remain deeply distrustful of the ICTY, and sceptics and supporters of the court alike acknowledge that the Tribunal was above all a face-saving mechanism launched, in the view of one UN official, 'more as a substitute for an effective political or military intervention by the Security Council than as a [display of] genuine belief in the virtues of international justice' (Beigbeder 2002: 50).

Margalit's theoretical work also challenges the purported indivisibility of peace and justice. In an exposition on the morality of political compromise, Margalit (2005: 194) argues that 'peace is justified if it is not based on a rotten compromise [which establishes or maintains a political order based on systematic cruelty and humiliation] . . . Peace can trump the pursuit of justice if the pursuit of justice endangers peace.' Margalit does not dispute that conflicts *should* be resolved in a just manner. Indeed, this 'is so clear and so boringly right that there is nothing useful to add to it' (Margalit 2005: 222). However, Margalit recognises that the winning party in a war is rarely swayed by claims about what is right, and argues that in certain circumstances it is morally permissible, and even morally required, for negotiators from the weaker side to seize the opportunity to make a decent peace, even if it means compromising on principles of justice. Margalit's proposal challenges assumptions about the inseparability of peace and justice, while advancing an alternative approach to thinking about peace in terms of decency and honour. What are the implications of this argument for the pursuit of just return? To what extent are the conditions of return (and return itself) subject to

[5] See, for example, Annan (2005) and Jorda (2001).

compromise? Can return be understood as an issue of decency, rather than as a question of justice?

Return must be discussed as an issue of justice because first and foremost, return is a human right; respecting rights is not simply a question of decency, but a matter of justice. The right of return is set out in numerous UN resolutions and international agreements. Perhaps most famously, Article 13(2) of the Universal Declaration of Human Rights provides that 'Everyone has the right to leave any country, including his own, and to return to his country.' The right to return also is implicit in the argument that the state's legitimacy derives from its role as the protector of its citizens (Deng 1995, ICISS 2001). If the state is to maintain its legitimacy, it cannot dole out protection on a selective basis; its exiled citizens must have the right to return to the state and benefit from its protection.

Admittedly, many refugees are loath to repatriate but have little choice other than to exercise their right of return as access to other durable solutions is often scarce. At the same time, many refugees thirst for the chance to return to their homelands and experience their continued exile as a humiliation or act of systematic cruelty. For example, for many indigenous Guatemalan refugees with strong connections to their lands, their displacement was not only physically and economically damaging, but was also a grievous spiritual and psychological injury (Commission for Historical Clarification 1999). This suggests that attempts to limit or compromise on refugees' right to return should be treated with caution because, in Maraglit's terms, this is often the kind of trade-off that smacks of rotten compromise (Margalit 1995, 2005, 2010). This is not to say that the process of return is exempt from negotiation simply because it is a right. Indeed, each return operation presents unique challenges and conflicts of interest that must be negotiated if the right of return is to be realised. However, these discussions must be based on the recognition that return is an issue of justice, given its status as a right.

Beyond legal and moral arguments surrounding the right of return, there are compelling pragmatic reasons why just return merits greater political and scholarly attention. First, many refugee populations are highly politicised, with clear views on their rights; how their situation compares to other cases of displacement; and how their dilemma should be resolved. For example, as Karen Koning AbuZayd, former Commissioner-General of the United Nations Relief and Works Agency (UNRWA), has noted,

> Palestinians – refugees and non-refugees alike – are astute, seasoned observers of the international scene. They are aware that in the standard refugee paradigm,

refugee status is not meant to be permanent. They know that in other contexts, refugee situations are resolved when international pressure is applied through international political channels to resolve the root causes of a conflict. And they know that such resolution enables refugees to return voluntarily in safety and dignity to their countries of origin. (Koning AbuZayd 2006)

Palestinian refugees are increasingly informed about international standards on justice and repatriation, and are prepared to argue that their situation should not be immune from the application of these standards. Identifying a clear account of the conditions of just return and applying these conditions in an even-handed manner in different displacement situations may help gain refugees' support for repatriation plans, and is essential in ensuring that expectations are realistic and return sustainable.

The experiences of South Africa and the former Yugoslavia notwithstanding, it behoves policymakers to be concerned about the justice of return because if the conditions of repatriation are widely seen to be unfair, this may spark future conflict. In his influential 1795 pamphlet 'Toward Perpetual Peace', Kant (1991: 93) argued that 'no treaty of peace shall be held valid in which there is tacitly reserved matter for future war.' Margalit (2005: 208–223) shares Kant's concern with irredentism, arguing that a political compromise reached in the name of peace cannot be considered decent or honourable if it is likely to serve as an impetus for future conflict. Most modern peace treaties include articles on the return of refugees and IDPs, with many mirroring the extensive provisions on return laid out in the 1995 General Framework Agreement for Peace in Bosnia and Herzegovina. In some recent peace agreements, however, certain key principles are conspicuously absent. For example, neither the 1992 General Peace Agreement for Mozambique nor the Interim Agreement for Kosovo affirm the voluntary nature of return (Phuong 2005: 5–6). Other agreements are silent on issues such as property restitution and amnesties for returnees who did not complete military service. If peace agreements do not set the stage for a just return process, returnees' grievances will likely go unanswered and may be exacerbated. In turn, this heightens the prospects of future conflict, on local or larger scales.[6] In cases such as Bosnia, nationalistic actors tried to impede the return processes, often with the express intention of stirring up conflict. Generally speaking, however, prolonged conflict is decidedly against the interests of the state of origin, its citizens

[6] See Part II for more detailed analyses of the relationship between treaty provisions on return, the creation of just conditions of return, and the successful conclusion of peace processes.

and neighbours, and the international community. Just return is therefore not only a legal and moral enterprise but is also a question of stark self-interest.

Given that return merits serious moral, political and legal concern, what is the rationale for attempting to articulate a *minimum* account of the conditions of just return? Why not set out an expansive, ideal account of returnees' entitlements? First and foremost, the conditions of just return cannot be a wish-list if the concept is to be analytically incisive or practically useful. Large-scale repatriation operations take place in remarkably diverse cultural contexts, typically in countries that are emerging from war and struggling to achieve even basic development standards. A theory of just return must respond to this reality. It must resonate in different cultural contexts, and take into account that the chief actor responsible for just return, the state of origin, most likely lacks the capacity to establish even minimum conditions of just return without support from donors and international agencies.[7] While in exile, many refugees benefit from superior conditions than those endured by IDPs and their non-displaced former neighbours. It is neither realistic nor fair to suggest that conditions in return communities must meet the standards enjoyed in affluent countries of asylum before refugees can reasonably be expected to return, or before return can be said to be minimally just. Rather, basic conditions of security and respect for human rights must be in place, with reasonable prospects for the economic development that is necessary to sustain these conditions.

Walzer's concept of 'thick' and 'thin' morality is particularly instructive when considering the salience of a minimum account of the conditions of just return. In contrast to scholars who argue in support of an expansive set of purportedly universal human rights, Walzer (1994: 2) emphasises that '[m]oral terms have minimal and maximal meanings; we can standardly give thin and thick accounts of them, and the two accounts are appropriate to different contexts, serve different purposes.' While elements of thin or universal morality exist within thick, particular moral systems, thick morality is robust because it is embedded in a political community's history and culture (Walzer 1994: xi). When moral debates occur *within* a particular community, the discussion takes place in terms of the thick morality that arises from shared experience and nuanced understanding of cultural and political values. Owing to the

[7] As discussed in Chapter 1, actors such as donors and international agencies may share remedial responsibility for displacement; supporting the establishment of conditions amenable to a just return is one of the ways in which this remedial responsibility may be executed.

depth of thick moral values, Walzer (1994: 6) argues, these commitments go hand in hand with more 'qualification, compromise, complexity and disagreement'. Thin morality only comes into play when moral arguments are being made that reach across different cultures or local contexts. An argument about the general conditions of just return that seeks to be relevant in dramatically different repatriation scenarios must therefore be based on principles of thin morality. Although only a minimal set of moral values resonate across cultures, this does not mean that thin morality is 'substantively minor or emotionally shallow' (Walzer 1994: 6). As Walzer (1994: 6) freely admits, 'There isn't much that is more important than "truth" and "justice" minimally understood.'

While various objections can be raised to Walzer's concept of thick and thin morality, his account compellingly underlines the importance of not overstretching claims about universal principles or values. A sounder approach is to reason from the basis of a limited set of moral values or obligations that can realistically be expected to hold in diverse cultural and political circumstances. The moral systems of political communities that have undergone mass migrations are likely to experience serious shockwaves. Yet even in such turbulent circumstances, cultural mores persist that affect how individuals perceive justice and engage in political processes, including those associated with repatriation and reintegration. A minimum account of just return should identify core principles and obligations to guide policymakers, while leaving ample room to expand on the concept of a just return and the activities that may be undertaken in pursuit of it, in accordance with particular values and beliefs.

The foundations of just return: legal provisions on repatriation and their moral and political implications

Article 13(2) of the Universal Declaration of Human Rights sets out the right of return, but places no conditions on the quality or characteristics of this homecoming. Yet just as there are conditions such as access to legal counsel and an impartial judiciary that must be met before a defendant can be said to enjoy her right to a fair trial, there are conditions that govern the just implementation of the refugee's right to return. As Zieck (2004: 33) points out, the 'handful of legal norms that govern the solution [of return] are fairly simple, yet in their straightforwardness prone to concealing its complexity'. International law states that repatriation processes must be voluntary and must take place in 'conditions of safety and dignity'. These terse legal norms have garnered widespread support from states, international organisations, scholars and advocates, and represent the pillars of legal justice for returnees. They must therefore be accounted for in any politically and legally tenable theory of just return. Thinking about the conditions of just return is an opportunity to contextualise these legal provisions, and explore their political and moral nuances. The analysis offered in this chapter suggests that international legal norms on voluntariness, safety and dignity are bound up with the compelling moral principles of equality, liberty and accountability, which must underpin any defensible account of just return.

In this section, I discuss the evolution and implications for just return of international norms on voluntary repatriation and return in conditions of safety and dignity. This discussion must be prefaced with the recognition that a vital precondition for just return is the cessation of the conditions that forced refugees to flee their homes in the first place. Internationally-supported repatriation processes typically take place before the official cessation of refugee status for all the members of a particular refugee group. The cessation of refugee status is intended to take place only when the actors involved are soundly convinced that the causes of flight have been permanently resolved, and it is tacitly understood that the conditions under which return takes place may fall short of the standards for cessation (Zieck 2004: 37). International agencies such as UNHCR *facilitate* or actively *promote* return, depending on the extent to which conditions have improved in the country of origin. The facilitation of return involves services such as coordinating transportation and documentation for those refugees who request assistance to repatriate. In contrast, when UNHCR promotes return, it directly encourages refugees to consider return as a viable solution to their displacement, and often negotiates tripartite agreements with the states of origin and asylum, to govern the return process. When UNHCR promotes rather than facilitates return, it also offers a wider range of assistance programmes, such as 'go and see' visits and local reintegration initiatives.

International organisations like UNHCR play a pivotal role in working with states of asylum and states of origin to ensure that conditions of return are viable. However, any discussion of just return must be informed by the recognition that humanitarian actors such as UNHCR often face dilemmas in which they are pushed by countries of asylum or other actors to actively promote repatriation, even when conditions in the country of origin are far short of ideal (Zieck 2004: 37–40). In these cases, UNHCR's policy has been to support return operations 'when the life or physical integrity of refugees in the country of asylum is threatened to the point that return is the safer option' (UNHCR 2002: paragraph 29). Although this type of balancing act is an unfortunately necessary reaction to the political realities of the contemporary refugee regime, it unavoidably has negative consequences for the preservation of the voluntary nature of repatriation processes.

The voluntary character of return

The conventional insistence that return may only take place at the refugee's voluntarily expressed wish is often seen as the upshot of the refugee regime's cardinal rule against *refoulement.* While provisions on return in 'conditions of safety and dignity' did not begin to appear in major international agreements until the late 1980s, the 1950 Statute of the Office of the United Nations High Commissioner for Refugees gives the Commissioner a mandate to facilitate *voluntary* repatriation. The 1969 OAU Convention Governing the Specific Aspects of Refugee Problems in Africa was the first major international refugee agreement to elaborate on the principles of voluntary return, stressing the 'essentially voluntary character of repatriation' (Article 5.1). Similarly, the 1984 Cartagena Declaration on Refugees affirms the 'voluntary and individual character of [the] repatriation of refugees' (Article 12). UNHCR Executive Committee Conclusion No. 40 (XXXVI) of 1985 set out the terms for the agency's rapidly expanding involvement in repatriation operations, emphasising that 'the repatriation of refugees should only take place at their freely expressed wish and the voluntary and individual character of [the] repatriation of refugees . . . should always be respected'.

UNHCR's courage of conviction on this point has wavered over the past decades: over the course of the 1990s, involuntary returns became increasingly commonplace. Prompted by the popularisation of temporary protection measures, UNHCR, UN Member States and refugee advocates became enmeshed in a fierce and still unresolved debate on whether return can be involuntary, and yet legally and morally just. In other words, is 'mandated repatriation' simply a euphemism for *refoulement*? (Hathaway 1997: 554). Hathaway and Chimni have served as two of the foremost protagonists in this debate. Arguing from a legal perspective, Hathaway (1997: 551) maintains that refugees are entitled to 'dignified and rights-regarding protection *until and unless* conditions in the State of origin permit repatriation without the risk of persecution'.[8] Chimni (1993: 454) counters that 'to substitute the judgement of States and institutions for that of refugees, is to create space for repatriation under duress, and may be tantamount to *refoulement*'.

[8] Hathaway revised this position in some of his later work.

Given the dearth of firm legal guidance on the permissibility of mandated return, a normative analysis may help guide practice. Clearly part of what makes the creation of refugees so heinous is that it strips citizens of much of their capacity to make free decisions about their lives. A just return process should counteract this coercive experience by empowering returnees to choose between as wide a range of options as possible regarding their repatriation. This does not mean that refugees must always have the right to stay in their country of asylum indefinitely. Repatriation may run against the refugee's preference, but this does not necessarily entail that it is unjust. Generally speaking, a sovereign state is entitled to restrict the entrance of non-members but is obliged to forgo this prerogative when a refugee is seeking asylum.[9] However, when conditions in the refugee's country of asylum are stable and the reasons for the refugee's flight have been resolved, a country of asylum may legitimately require the refugee to repatriate, as it reasserts its right to limit non-members' access to its political community. Certainly, many host states have abused this right by prematurely terminating protection for refugees. Albeit repugnant, this abuse of power does not vitiate the argument that, in certain instances, asylum may legitimately be extended on a temporary basis and revoked at the discretion of the host state.

Although the crucial choice of whether or not repatriation occurs may ultimately be made by the host state, the country of asylum is only one of the many actors who determine the range of choices open to the returnee. The state of origin can, and should, put other important choices into the refugee's hands, such as whether to return to original homes or relocate to a new community and what shape reintegration programmes should take. The legally and morally problematic nature of involuntary return underlines the importance of international cooperation to create the best possible conditions of return. If just conditions of return are in place, refugees are more likely to make the choice to return voluntarily, thereby sidestepping the difficult question of forced repatriation.[10]

[9] See Walzer (1983) for a defence of this widely accepted view. This perspective is challenged by various protagonists in the 'open borders' debate. See, for example, Mark Gibney (1988).

[10] If conditions of just return are in place and the refugee still does not wish to repatriate, then it may in some cases be morally acceptable to initiate cessation procedures. The acceptability of cessation will depend on factors such as whether major socio-economic constraints hinder the permanent local integration of refugees, and whether the state of asylum bears particular remedial responsibilities towards the displaced that may best be upheld by allowing the refugee to remain. As Walzer (1983) and Souter (in press) suggest, in some cases host states may have a responsibility to permanently accept refugees due to their complicity in their initial displacement.

Return in 'conditions of safety and dignity'

Safety and dignity are an ancient pairing. Chapter 30 of the Book of Job finds the longsuffering Job driven from his home, impoverished and enfeebled, so that he cries out,

> Terrors overwhelm me;
> my dignity is driven away as by the wind,
> my safety vanishes like a cloud.
> (Zondervan 1998: 749)

The voluntary nature of repatriation and refugees' ability to exercise choice are closely intertwined with the notion of a safe and dignified return. The concepts of safety and dignity also bear heavily on the pursuit of justice in return.

Provisions on return in conditions of safety and dignity emerged relatively recently in the international refugee regime, yet this norm is evolving into a critical principle for the protection of returnees. Without doubt, the notion of dignity has deep roots in both 'hard' and 'soft' international law. For example, Article 1 of the Universal Declaration of Human Rights proclaims that 'All human beings are born free and equal in dignity and in rights.' However, there is no commonly accepted definition of dignity (or, indeed, of safety) in international instruments or national laws.

The 1969 OAU Convention and the 1984 Cartagena Declaration were the first major international instruments to emphasise the importance of return in conditions of safety, with Article 12 of the Cartagena Declaration stating that repatriation must 'be carried out under conditions of absolute safety, preferably to the place of residence of the refugee in his country of origin.' Neither agreement mentions dignity. The 1989 Declaration and Concerted Plan of Action in favour of Central American Refugees, Returnees and Displaced Persons, adopted by the International Conference on Central American Refugees (CIREFCA) appears to be the first major agreement to include provisions on the safety and dignity of returnees. The signatories affirmed their commitment to the return of refugees 'under conditions of personal security and dignity that would allow them to resume a normal life' (Article 3).

Following the 1989 CIREFCA Declaration, references to return in conditions of safety and dignity increased sharply in international agreements, declarations and UN resolutions. The United Nations Security Council has underscored the need for the return of refugees in conditions of safety and dignity in numerous resolutions on conflicts in locations including the former Yugoslavia, Georgia, the Caucasus and

Darfur.[11] A wide range of UN General Assembly resolutions also address return in conditions of safety and dignity, including the Millennium Declaration. The inclusion of the duty to enable internally displaced persons (IDPs) to return to their homes 'in safety and with dignity' in the Guiding Principles on Internal Displacement (Principle 28.1) is a particularly strong sign of the traction of return in conditions of safety and dignity as an international legal norm, as the Guiding Principles are based on international humanitarian and human rights law and analogous refugee law, although they are not themselves legally binding. Language on return in safety and dignity has also been included in multiple peace agreements, such as the treaties for Georgia, Guatemala and Cambodia, as well as in national laws such as the Decree on the Dignified Return of Refugees, issued by Hamid Karzai in 2001 as President of the Interim Afghani Administration.

While there are abundant and increasing references to safe and dignified return in international agreements and UN resolutions, these documents offer only limited insight into the origins and meaning of the idea of safe and dignified return. An analysis of the speeches delivered by the UN High Commissioners for Refugees between the late 1970s and 2006 demonstrates that UNHCR rhetoric on safe and dignified returns predated and potentially prompted the inclusion of principles on repatriation in safety and dignity in major international agreements. In total, 92 per cent of the High Commissioners' speeches from this period addressed the repatriation of refugees. The rhetoric of return in 'conditions of safety and dignity' was included in 25 per cent of the speeches, with High Commissioner Hocké largely responsible for popularising the language of return in safety and dignity. From 1986 to 1989, Hocké discussed repatriation in 100 per cent of his public addresses and connected return with the notion of dignity in more than two-thirds of his speeches.[12] Safe and dignified return has remained a significant part of UNHCR's rhetoric on return ever since.

[11] See, for example, UN Security Council Resolutions 874 (1993b), 1036 (1996), 1258 (1999b) and 1564 (2004b).

[12] I arrived at these figures through a content analysis of 455 speeches delivered by the six High Commissioners who served between 1978 and 2006. This analysis included only those speeches posted in UNHCR's online archive at the time. It is possible that various speeches were missing from this collection. However, the online archive provided a large sample of 455 speeches, including the High Commissioners' key policy statements to the UNHCR Executive Committee. The sample included 55 speeches from High Commissioner Hartling (1978–1985), 30 speeches from High Commissioner Hocké (1986–1989), 15 speeches from High Commissioner Stoltenberg (1990), 270 speeches from High Commissioner Ogata (1990–2000), 73 speeches from High Commissioner Lubbers (2001–2005) and 15 speeches from High Commissioner Guterres (2005–October 2006).

Although the concept of return in safety and dignity has evolved into an important protection norm that is foundational to the concept of just return, the idea has troubling antecedents. Barnett and Finnemore (2004: 101) suggest that when UNHCR became actively concerned with human rights conditions in refugees' countries of origin in the 1980s, the agency 'tried to avoid offending sovereignty-sensitive governments by asking for "safety and dignity" and not a marked improvement in human rights'. In a 1992 speech on displacement in the former Yugoslavia, High Commissioner Ogata infamously stretched the rhetoric of safety and dignity far beyond its breaking point, arguing that protection 'means not only the right to seek asylum from persecution, it also means the right of return for all those who so desire, and above all, it means the right to be allowed to remain in one's home in safety and dignity' (Ogata 1992). Doubtlessly, strong theoretical arguments can be mounted in support of the right to remain. However, the situation in much of the former Yugoslavia had deteriorated so dramatically that conditions of safety and dignity could not possibly be upheld. At the time, advocating for the right to remain was incompatible with due regard for civilians' wellbeing. As Hathaway (1994) has argued, and the massacres in Srebrenica and Foča proved, the right to remain during the war in the former Yugoslavia was the 'right to be toast'. Using the language of safety and dignity in this way undermines both its credibility and its relevance to the concept of a just return.

Beyond the troubling origins of this norm, the concept of return in safety and dignity has at times proven difficult to use as a practical guideline for the governance of return processes. This is in part because the concepts of return in safety and dignity are, as Zieck (2004: 37) acknowledges, 'rather indeterminate'. Undoubtedly, UNHCR has made considerable progress in articulating benchmarks on safety for returnees. For example, the 1996 UNHCR *Handbook on Voluntary Repatriation: International Protection* discusses the question of safety in commendable detail, focusing on the physical, legal and material safety of returnees. This tripartite approach to safety for returnees is further developed in documents such as UNHCR's background paper on voluntary repatriation for the Global Consultations on International Protection (UNHCR 2002). According to UNHCR, physical safety entails a: secure return environment in which there is protection from attacks and harassment; guaranteed freedom of movement; and access to de-mined or at least demarcated land. Legal safety involves the equal recognition of returnees as citizens before the law, and 'non-discriminatory access [to] and exercise of civil, economic, social, political and cultural rights' (Englbrecht 2004: 101).[13]

[13] See also UNHCR (2002) *Global Consultations on International Protection – Background Paper on Voluntary Repatriation*.

Material safety implies access to humanitarian assistance and essential services in the early phases of the return process and, in the longer term, sustainable reintegration and economic development opportunities (Englbrecht 2004: 101–102). Levels of physical, legal and material safety are interdependent, and have repercussions not only for returnees but also on the wellbeing of other members of return communities. Resolution 1998/26 of the UN Sub-Commission on the Prevention of Discrimination and the Protection of Minorities is tantamount to a checklist of many of the aspects of just return that fall under the rubric of physical, legal and material safety. The resolution acknowledges:

> the right of all returnees to the free exercise of their right to freedom of movement and to choose one's residence, including . . . their right to privacy and respect for the home, their right to reside peacefully in the security of their own home and their right to enjoy all necessary social and economic services, in an environment free of any form of discrimination.

By emphasising the need to abolish all forms of discrimination, Resolution 1998/26 affirms that re-establishing the returnee as an equal citizen in her country of origin is an integral part of the pursuit of physical, legal and material security for repatriating refugees. Taken in total, resolutions such as 1998/26 and the UNHCR repatriation handbooks provide reasonably detailed insight into the content of safety as a core condition of just return. These details are consistent with the expectations a repatriating citizen can justifiably bear towards a reformed, responsible, legitimate state of origin. To draw again on Shacknove's words: 'No reasonable person would be satisfied with less' (1985: 281).

In contrast to the progress made in identifying criteria to judge the safety of return operations, in its 1996 *Handbook on Voluntary Repatriation*, UNHCR (1996: 11) admits that 'the concept of dignity is less self-evident than that of safety', and makes only a perfunctory attempt to clarify it by offering a dictionary definition of dignity as 'serious, composed, worthy of honour and respect'. UNHCR's reliance on a dictionary definition of dignity certainly implies that room remains for the organisation to devote greater consideration to the meaning and consequences of this pivotal concept. Fortunately, the 1996 *Handbook* provides some additional commentary on the application of the concept of 'return with dignity', explaining that,

> In practice, elements must include that refugees are not manhandled; that they can return unconditionally and that if they are returning spontaneously they can do so at their own pace; that they are not arbitrarily separated from family members; and that they are treated with respect and full acceptance by their

national authorities, including the *full restoration of their rights*. (UNHCR 1996: 11, italics added)

These provisions support the notion that a just return must involve protection for human rights, including accountability for past violations. Notably, the *Handbook on Voluntary Repatriation* links respect for returnees' dignity with the durability of repatriation, a connection which is bolstered by many NGOs involved in return operations (Ferris 2002, UNHCR 1996: 14).[14] Notably, the 2004 *UNHCR Handbook for Repatriation and Reintegration Activities* makes a strong connection between dignity and the ability of refugees to return to their original homes, encouraging authorities to create conditions conducive to realising refugees' right to return with safety and dignity to their places of origin or former habitual residences (UNHCR 2004: 144).

In general, the UNHCR Handbooks are overly prone to treating 'conditions of safety and dignity' as an item on a checklist for repatriation planning, rather than as an overarching, multifaceted concept to guide a just return. Indeed, ensuring that return occurs in conditions of safety and dignity is the first item on the Checklist of Main Protection Activities in the *Handbook on Voluntary Repatriation*. Yet upholding dignity is not easily condensed into a checklist item, not least because it crosscuts every aspect of a just return process. The theoretical perspectives on dignity developed by philosophers and political theorists can shed greater light onto the meaning of dignity and its implications for the conditions of just return.

Philosophical expositions of dignity are remarkably muddled, even before any attempt to apply the concept to the repatriation process. Dignity is depicted by some scholars as an inherent, inalienable characteristic of human beings and the source of human rights, but by others as a good to which everyone has a right, or which is obtained through respect for human rights. Many theorists concerned with dignity stress its relation to equality among human beings, but recognise that dignity can be expressed differently depending on the cultural context.[15] The notion of dignity was perhaps most famously articulated by Kant, who argued that everyone is possessed of dignity by virtue of being autonomous, and that

[14] The *Handbook* states that return can be actively promoted 'when a careful assessment of the situation shows that the conditions of safety and dignity can be met: in other words, when it appears that objectively, it is safe for most refugees to return and that such returns have good prospect of being durable' (UNHCR 1996: 14).

[15] For example, Meyer (1989: 524) argues that 'one's human dignity, if it is a mark of anything, is a mark of one's equality on some fundamental level with other human beings.'

respecting this dignity means never treating one another merely as means but as ends in themselves.

In contrast to the Kantian tradition, Feinberg stands out for his vigorous criticism of the view that rights are inherent to human beings by virtue of their dignity. Instead, Feinberg argues that human dignity is better understood as the 'recognisable capacity to assert claims. To respect a person, then, or to think of him as possessed of human dignity, simply is to think of him as a potential maker of claims' (Feinberg 1970: 252). Meyer embraces Feinberg's view that the capacity to make claims is a central aspect of human dignity, but compellingly argues that an additional component of dignity must be the capacity for self-control. 'A person who has human dignity', Meyer (1989: 533) writes, 'is fundamentally a person who is self-possessed; he at least has the capacity to give direction to his own life. The fact that he is self-possessed implies that he is not possessed by either of two potential enemies to his dignity: other people or random, uncontrolled desires from within', such as alcoholism or phobias. Although Meyer's argument is based on Feinberg's decidedly un-Kantian precepts, his emphasis on the importance of autonomy and the ability to exercise choice strongly echoes key components of Kant's moral framework. In Meyer's view, an abusive or overbearing state represents a serious threat to the individual's dignity, as such a state undermines the citizen's ability to direct her own life and may turn a deaf ear to her legitimate claims. Pritchard and Spiegelberg advance a popular conceptualisation of dignity as self-respect. However, both share Meyer's view that dignity must involve the ability to exercise choice, suggesting that 'respecting something requires standing back from it with an attitude of non-interference' (Pritchard 1972: 305, Spiegelberg 1971).

It is important to note that the majority of the relevant literature portrays dignity as something that can be lost or stolen, and restored. Goodwin-Gill (1989: 9), for instance, argues that the 'purpose of international protection must be to support refugees, and to try to restore their dignity so as to enable them to exercise their essential rights'. This approach distorts the highly subjective nature of dignity, implying that there are clear routes to losing and regaining one's dignity. The subjectivity of dignity is evident when we consider the different experiences of people exposed to discrimination and political violence. For example, South Africa's apartheid policy was a clear affront to human dignity, whether conceived in Kantian terms or otherwise. Yet, it would be a mistake to conclude that all those at the brunt of this policy were stripped of their dignity. Despite the degrading treatment he endured, Nelson Mandela (1995: 391) unequivocally declared that 'Any man or institution that tries to rob me of my dignity will lose, because I will not part with it at any price or under any pressure.' Equally, many survivors of apartheid say they lost their dignity under white rule, but regained it through the proceedings of the South African Truth and Reconciliation Commission. For others, the idea that the Commission could revive their trampled dignity was a farce (Minow 1998: 52–90).

Given dignity's inherent subjectivity and the multiple theoretical interpretations of the concept, how should policymakers act to uphold the oft-reiterated commitment to enabling return in conditions of safety and dignity? How do the notions of safety and dignity relate to a just return? Although they approach the question from different angles, the theorists discussed above successfully establish the connection between dignity and the ability to exercise choice. There is also general agreement about the need to demonstrate equal respect for the dignity and rights of others. Equality and choice are not only central to the notion of dignity. As Maraglit (2005: 214–215) suggests, the notion of justice itself is constituted by two values, liberty and equality. By ensuring refugees' security and protecting their human rights, a just return process enables returnees to enjoy their liberty on equal terms with their fellow citizens.

States' commitment to upholding returnees' safety and dignity, and by extension their liberty and equality, demands that serious inequalities and injustices are recognised, and steps taken to rectify them. Just as there is a subjective element to dignity, there are innumerable competing conceptions of justice. Integrating reparations into return operations therefore cannot guarantee that returnees will perceive the process as wholly dignified or just. However, the responsibility of the state of origin and other key actors such as UNHCR must be to ensure that the conditions of return are commensurate with respect for dignity in terms of liberty and equality. The provision of redress is a critical demonstration of this respect.

At the heart of the matter: return and redress, return as redress

> The same moviemaker of the subconscious who, by day, was sending her bits of the home landscape as images of happiness, by night would set up terrifying returns to that same land. The day was lit with the beauty of the land forsaken, the night by the horror of returning to it. The day would show her the paradise she had lost; the night, the hell she had fled. (Kundera 2002: 16–17)

There is no panacea for all the risks of return. As exiled Czech author Milan Kundera captures in his novel *Ignorance*, the prospect of repatriation melds together great optimism and almost overwhelming trepidation for returnees. A dignified, safe and ultimately just return requires that a complex array of factors be brought into alignment, from the presence of peacekeepers and de-mining teams, to the creation of functioning legal systems and opportunities for economic development. Given the wide range of challenges that must be surmounted in the course of a successful repatriation process, why focus on redress as the crux of the just return issue? In this section I will argue that the duty to provide redress is implicit in the commitment to respect returnees' dignity and human rights.[16] Redress advances respect for returnees' dignity and human rights because it recognises the unacceptability of the abuses at the root of displacement, repositions the refugee as a citizen empowered to make claims against the state and ideally deters future violations of returnees' rights. Furthermore, reparations initiatives such as compensation and real property restitution make valuable contributions towards increasing returnees' security, while expanding the range of choices the refugee can make in the context of the return process (Williams 2006b: 39). This increases the likelihood that refugees may voluntarily decide to return, thereby ideally circumventing the controversy surrounding 'mandated' repatriation. Redress is therefore instrumentally valuable, as it supports the political goal of enabling sustainable return and contributes to efforts to realise principles such as the right to security and due process under the law. Yet redress also has intrinsic value as a requirement of justice and a reflection of respect for refugees' dignity.

In stressing the centrality of reparations to just return, my intent is not to downplay the importance of other facets of the return process, such as reconstruction efforts and local integration initiatives. While these types of activities are essential to the success of repatriation operations and may have significant implications for the creation of conditions conducive to just return, my view is that redress is the aspect of the return process most closely connected to questions of *justice*. Although my focus is on reparations for returnees, I do not wish to imply that non-returning refugees and non-displaced citizens may not also have legitimate claims for redress. However, because refugees have been physically, politically and morally estranged from the state, reparations processes have particularly significant and unique implications for returnees. For returnees, reparations can help overcome the material and socio-economic challenges associated with repatriation, as well as address the moral and political problem of putting returnees on equal ground with their fellow citizens and re-establishing them as full members of the political community.

In the 1996 *Handbook on Voluntary Repatriation*, UNHCR (1996: 11) confirms that it sees the full restoration of refugees' rights as a core

[16] A more detailed discussion of redress as a right is provided in Chapter 3.

element of a dignified return. The full restoration of refugees' rights is a forward-looking process, but it must also involve efforts on the part of the state of origin to recognise and redress past violations of refugees' rights. Kant (1991: 98–99) captured the theoretical connection between redress and dignity, arguing that 'the dignity of humanity in us' creates a duty that we do not 'suffer [our] rights to be trampled underfoot by others with impunity.' In Feinberg's terms, redress is inextricable from dignified, just repatriation processes because reparations programmes restore the refugee's ability to make claims, in particular against the state of origin. Reparations achieve this outcome in a variety of ways. In particular, redress mechanisms such as trials and claims commissions reposition the refugee as a citizen with clear legal and moral entitlements, such as the right to lodge a grievance with national or quasi-international authorities, and to receive an even-handed response to this concern.[17] Internationally mandated reparations processes underline that there are consequences for the state when citizens are stripped of their ability to make reasonable claims for security, protection and respect.

By exposing refugees to physical and economic insecurity, return can erode their sense of dignity and restrict the choices available to them for the future. Reparations such as property restitution and compensation help to counteract this process. For instance, restoring lost housing and land provides returnees with shelter and a valuable resource. Indeed, regaining lost property is often a core component of just return because many returnees' economic security hinges on access to their land, which they use for activities such as agriculture or commerce. Furthermore, 'few things are as sacred to people as their homes, properties and lands' (van Boven 1993: x). Enabling return to original homes may go further to creating a sense of psychological security and justice for repatriating refugees than any other initiative (Kibreab 2003: 27). The musings of an elderly refugee woman from Banja Luka who regained her home through the Bosnian property restitution effort illustrate this point:

> You must be persistent. If I hadn't been persistent, I would never have returned to my home. I still have lots of problems. My house needs repairs and the secondary occupants stole all my possessions. But I am home. I have my freedom. (Badil 2002)

Albeit contestable, many UN resolutions and peace agreements espouse the increasingly predominant view that the right to return

[17] See the case study on Bosnia (Chapter 5) for a discussion of how reparations processes for displaced persons can affirm returnees' right to equal treatment before the law and bolster broader efforts to uphold equity and respect for human rights in return communities.

involves not only the right to repatriate, but also to reclaim and reoccupy one's original home (Leckie 2003c: 4). Reparations, particularly housing and property restitution processes, are clearly essential to making good on this interpretation of the right to return. Yet just as reparations are essential to enabling the right to return, return itself can be seen as a form of redress. Indeed, this is explicitly recognised in the UN Basic Principles and Guidelines on the Right to a Remedy and Reparation for Victims of Gross Violations of International Human Rights Law and Serious Violations of International Humanitarian Law (Article IX, para. 19). Recrossing a border is merely one of a long series of steps that comprise the return process, and which together contribute to rectifying the injustice of forced migration by restoring the conditions that existed prior to displacement, where appropriate, and establishing a viable, respectful relationship of rights and duties between the state and its returning citizens.[18] While Takahashi (1997: 593) points out that 'the theoretical framework for voluntary repatriation remains relatively underdeveloped, compared to other aspects of the refugee issue', this chapter suggests that redress may serve as an overarching theoretical concept through which to understand the return process. In reflecting on processes of restoration and responsibility, we may find the origins of a broader theory of return.

[18] If the conditions that existed prior to displacement were systematically unfair, they clearly should not be restored in the name of a 'just' return process. This issue is discussed in greater depth in Chapter 7.

3 The tools of repair

Redress for returning refugees

I and the public know
What all schoolchildren learn,
Those to whom evil is done
Do evil in return.

–W.H. Auden (1940), 'September 1, 1939'

The prospect of repatriation is often met with trepidation, not only by refugees, but also among national authorities and displaced persons' former neighbours, who fear that returnees may seek to avenge the crimes that drove them from their homes.[1] In Chapter 2, I argued that as an expression of its remedial responsibility for forced migration, the state of origin is obliged to establish conditions of just return, principally by using reparations to restore (or create) a respectful relationship of rights and duties between the state and its returning citizens. This may also be a prudential course of action: by redressing the violations endured by the displaced, states of origin may help defuse grievances and, in turn, facilitate smoother repatriations processes. This argument accords with the view, espoused by an increasing number of scholars and practitioners, that different forms of redress, including but not limited to housing and property restitution, can make valuable – albeit complex – contributions to return and reintegration processes.[2]

This chapter examines the emergence and evolution of international norms on redress for past injustices, particularly as they pertain to refugees and returnees. The discussion is informed by Stephen Krasner's widely accepted conception of norms as 'standards of behaviour defined in terms of rights and obligations' (Krasner 1983: 2). International norms exist in varying degrees of strength, and this analysis demonstrates that while there is widespread and growing support among national and international actors for displaced persons' right to redress, international law on this issue is still at a relatively early stage of

1 See, for example, Hansen (1999), and Chayes and Minow (2003).

2 See, for example, Duthie (2011, 2012a), Leckie (2003b, 2008) and Williams (2007, 2012).

development. The chapter underscores the close connection that has often been made between redress for displacement and enabling return as the 'preferred' solution to displacement, and stresses that although efforts to redress forced migrants from regions such as the Balkans have garnered extensive attention and praise, international norms on redress for displaced persons are still not evenly implemented. In short, the tools of redress have been honed remarkably since the end of World War II, with the past 20 years witness to particularly commendable progress. Yet, redress is still a clumsy tool in the hands of states and international actors, and must be further sharpened in order to enable just return.[3]

This discussion is prefaced by a brief exploration of different legal and political conceptions of redress, and a short introduction to the modern reparations movement. This examination of the history and cogency of contemporary norms on reparations for the displaced is intended to serve as a springboard for Part II, in which I will examine how international norms on redress for returnees were applied in three key cases, and draw upon the insights from these experiences to identify the key characteristics of reparations programmes that may make good on the state of origin's responsibility to create conditions amendable to a just return.

Competing conceptions of redress

Redress is a terminological minefield. Efforts to advance and understand claims for justice are continually hampered by confusion and disagreement over the meaning of even the basic terms of debate. Like the notion of state responsibility, the right to a remedy is affirmed by both international law and moral arguments rooted in the human rights tradition. Legally and theoretically, the right to a remedy may be considered a secondary right that follows from the breach of primary rights, such as the right not to be tortured, or to be arbitrarily displaced (Andreu-Guzmán 2012, Zegveld 2003: 503).[4] Beyond the legal and theoretical senses of the term, redress is also a deeply rooted and hotly contested religious, cultural and political concept. Misalignment between legal and theoretical definitions of reparations is widespread in contemporary scholarship on transitional justice. While recognising the critical role of legal frameworks in the pursuit of justice for victims of human rights violations, I do not believe that legal and political conceptions of redress can be neatly

[3] For detailed discussion of the challenges and opportunities associated with using different forms of redress – including restitution, compensation, truth-telling and trials – to respond to the problem of displacement, see Duthie (2012a).

[4] See also Arzt (1999).

dissociated: remedies and the struggle to achieve them are inherently political, and must be understood as such.

Legal perspectives

It is a 'basic maxim of law' that harms should be redressed, and every legal system requires that this obligation be met in some form (Roht-Arriaza 2004: 12). While the modern right to a remedy was expressed in Article 8 of the 1948 Universal Declaration of Human Rights, the basic remedial norms for violations of international law were set out some 20 years earlier in the Permanent Court of International Justice's landmark ruling on the *Chorzów Factory* case (Williams 2007: 3).[5] The *Chorzów Factory* decision indicates that 'reparation must, so far as possible, wipe out all the consequences of the illegal act and re-establish the situation that would, in all probability, have existed if that act had not been committed' (PCIJ 1928).

Legal definitions of reparations are set out in documents including the International Law Commission (ILC) Articles on State Responsibility and the Basic Principles and Guidelines on the Right to a Remedy and Reparation for Victims of Gross Violations of International Human Rights Law and Serious Violations of International Humanitarian Law (UN Reparation Principles; UNGA 2005a). The UN Reparation Principles were prepared over the course of 15 years under the auspices of two independent experts, Theo van Boven and Cherif Bassiouni, and were adopted unanimously by the General Assembly in 2005.[6] A significant contribution to the codification of norms on the right to redress, the Principles clarify current and emerging international legal principles on reparation, with a view to providing effective and enforceable remedies to victims of human rights abuses, and upholding the public interest by deterring future violations of international law (Echeverria 2002: 2). While the *Chorzów Factory* ruling and the ILC Articles on State Responsibility pertain primarily to obligations between states, the UN Reparation Principles concern the obligations states owe to individual victims of human rights violations, as subjects of international law. The Principles use 'reparation' as an umbrella term for five main types of remedy: restitution, compensation, rehabilitation, satisfaction and guarantees of non-repetition.

[5] Article 8 states that every person has 'the right to an effective remedy by the competent national tribunals for acts violating the fundamental rights granted him by the constitution or by law.'

[6] See UN General Assembly Resolution 60/147 (2005a).

Traditionally seen as the 'first form of reparations', restitution aims to remedy violations by restoring the *status quo ante*, often through the return of assets including homes, land and cultural artefacts (Shelton 2002: 849). The Principles address the restoration of lost property as an important form of redress, and recognise that return to one's home may in itself represent a form of restitution. However, they do not explicitly affirm restitution's conventional place at the top of the remedial hierarchy, but list restitution as one of several approaches to redress that may be employed depending on the relevant circumstances (UNGA 2005a: Section IX, paragraph 18).[7] Compensation involves monetary payment for material and moral injury, and may be better placed than restitution to remedy the irreversible crimes that often push citizens into exile, such as torture and rape. According to the UN Reparations Principles (UNGA 2005a: Section IX, paragraph 20), 'compensation should be provided for any economically assessable damage, as appropriate and proportional to the gravity of the violation and the circumstances of the case.' This may entail cash payments for physical and mental harm; loss of professional and educational opportunities; loss of earnings and earning potential; medical expenses; and psychological and social services. Responsible states may also provide rehabilitation assistance, including medical, psychological and social services, as a form of reparation (Section IX, paragraphs 20–21). Satisfaction addresses non-material injuries and may involve official apologies, judicial proceedings, and truth-telling processes (Gillard 2003: 531–532). In addition, satisfaction may necessitate 'effective measures aimed at the cessation of continuing violations'; the search for 'disappeared' persons; assistance in locating, identifying and reburying the bodies of people who were killed; commemorations and tributes in the victims' honour; and the revision of educational materials to reflect victims' experiences of abuse. Guarantees of non-repetition strive both to remedy past crimes and contribute to prevention and deterrence efforts, and may involve the reform of laws and national institutions (UNGA 2005a, Section IX, paragraphs 22–23).

Scholars differ over the present ability of the international legal system to provide meaningful redress to the victims of violations, and the strength of the right to a remedy for displacement in and of itself. Undoubtedly, the piecemeal development of international law over the past 50 years has resulted in an uneven proliferation of domestic and international

[7] See also Williams (2007: 4, 2012). See Chapter 7 and Part III for a more detailed discussion of debates surrounding the restoration of the *status quo ante* as the preferred form of redress.

standards, and mechanisms to remedy rights violations (Echeverria 2002: 2–3). Regarding criminal responsibility for displacement, 'there is certainly sufficient international jurisprudence to prosecute the crime of forced displacement, but it is not as strong as it is for other serious crimes . . . Often, [the] focus [of criminal prosecutions] is on the crimes connected to displacement rather than the crime of forced displacement in itself. Displacement is frequently seen as a "natural" consequence of other crimes or as an inherent effect of armed conflict, and so the criminal responsibility of the numerous actors involved in these crimes is not investigated' (Andreu-Guzmán 2012). While Lee (1993: 157–159) is optimistic about the ability of international law to deliver compensation as a form of redress for both refugees and their countries of asylum, Garry (1998) questions whether current enforcement mechanisms are strong enough to secure reparations for refugees and deter future crimes. Concerning property restitution as a remedy for forced migration, Williams (2012, Williams and Gurel 2011) underscores the importance of recent decisions from regional human rights courts that temper displaced persons' right to reclaim lost properties in light of factors such as long-standing occupancy by other parties.[8] Reflecting on the broader status of international legal norms on reparations for human rights violations, Falk (2006: 484) maintains that the right to redress has won widespread acceptance, but presciently points out that the implementation of this right has been largely limited to states that are generally respectful of human rights in the first place. In a more conservative assessment of the situation, de Greiff (2006: 6–7) argues that '[w]hatever consensus there is in international law about reparations, it is only just emerging, and the boundaries of the obligation remain porous.' Although there is growing legal consensus regarding the obligation to redress specific crimes such as unlawful deaths and disappearances, de Greiff (2006: 7) contends that 'there is much weaker or no consensus on whether the obligation extends to territorial displacement.' As de Greiff (2006: 7) recognises, 'decisions concerning the catalogue of rights whose violation triggers reparations benefits have been made in a way that excludes . . . those who have been

[8] See, for example, the European Court of Human Rights (ECHR) decisions in *Demopoulos v. Turkey*, as discussed in Williams (2010a), and the ECHR's decisions on property claims in Cyprus. Williams and Gurel (2011: 1) argue that the ECHR's decisions do not hold up or strike down a straight-forward right to property restitution, but 'define the outer parameters within which the parties have a degree of political space to arrive at a mutually acceptable compromise . . . the Court's recent judgments do no more – and no less – than to exclude the more extreme aspects of the proposals that have been put forward by both sides'. Importantly, the decision of the African Commission on Human and People's Rights in the *Endorois* case suggests that for some 'vulnerable categories of victims', such as indigenous groups, restitution may still be the preferred remedy. See Williams (2012).

traditionally marginalised, including women and some minority groups'. Refugee and IDP populations are also often politically and socially sidelined, and it is not surprising, therefore, that their justice claims have so often been overlooked.

Political and theoretical perspectives

Although international law on reparations is evolving rapidly, some of these principles are not yet uniformly accepted as hard law. This does not mean, however, that these principles do not represent obligations the state is bound to respect (Mendez 1997: 4). Indeed, the reparations movement illustrates the close connection between legal developments, political advocacy and contemporary normative debates on states' duties towards their citizens. Despite these close links, some researchers argue that reparations should be understood first and foremost as a legal remedy, and discourage the 'politicisation' of reparations processes (Williams 2007: ii). This 'juridification of politics' risks obscuring the inherently political nature of the narration of suffering, calls for redress, and the struggle to advance progressive legal interpretations of states' obligations towards their citizens (Torpey 2006: 159). Furthermore, focusing exclusively on remedial rights under international law may inadvertently preclude consideration of stronger claims returnees and other survivors of human rights violations may be able to make against their state under domestic laws, and in the national political arena.[9] It is therefore essential to discuss not only legal definitions, but also moral and political conceptions of redress.

Perhaps the most comprehensive normative discussion of reparations is presented by Elazar Barkan (2001: xii–xvii, xviii), who writes that redress 'represents the historical bridging of animosity between enemies', and contends that the legal tools of remedy 'are all different levels of acknowledgement that together create a mosaic of recognition by perpetrators for the need to amend past injustices'. For the purposes of this discussion, I will adopt Barkan's comprehensive notion of reparations as the 'entire spectrum of attempts to rectify historical injustices' (Barkan 2001: xix).[10]

9 For example, Colombia has detailed laws on remedies for displacement, and highly active domestic advocacy organisations working to secure redress for forced migrants. See Cantor (2011).

10 In *The Guilt of Nations*, Barkan (2001) principally uses the term 'restitution' to denote the broad range of efforts undertaken to remedy historical injustice. This is not a standard usage of the word, as restitution is most commonly associated with remedies that aim to restore the *status quo ante*. In his later work, Barkan (2005, 2007) uses 'reparations' as a general term, in the place of 'restitution'.

The broadness of this definition runs counter to de Greiff's call for scholarship that clarifies the boundaries of the notion of reparations, and the relationship between reparations and other transitional justice measures. Although de Greiff (2006: 2, 13) correctly stresses the need for a clearer vision of justice that resonates in cases of large-scale, gross violations of human rights, his primary focus on reparations-as-compensation is discordant with legal definitions of reparation and risks creating arbitrary divides between compensation and other forms of redress such as property restitution. In contrast, Barkan's definition helpfully encompasses the diverse yet interrelated approaches available to remedy past injustice.[11]

From the long shadow of Versailles: the modern reparations movement

The crushing extraction of reparations from Germany under the auspices of the Treaty of Versailles was perceived by the Allied powers as intrinsic to a 'peace of justice', but by Germany as the unabashedly 'victorious violence of our enemies' (Lu 2002: 10).[12] Scathing in his criticism of Versailles, Kennan condemned the Allies' 'foolish attempts to draw the blood of reparations and war debts from the veins of the exhausted peoples of the continent', and advanced the now-familiar argument that the vindictive, economically crippling nature of the World War I reparations regime set Europe on the path to a second catastrophic war (Kennan 1996: 16). While this popular revisionist interpretation of the Treaty is now questioned, Germany's experience under Versailles undoubtedly gave reparations a bad name, associated primarily with the merciless seizure of money from the vanquished (Boemeke, Feldman and Glaser 1998, Lu 2002: 4–6).

The Treaty of Versailles reflected the prevailing pre-World War II conception of reparations, and particularly restitution, as the preferred approach to remedying wrongs between states. The post-World War II era saw a seismic shift in which reparations were reconceived as an obligation states may owe to individual victims of human rights

11 De Greiff (2006: 13) suggests that unlike in the 'massive cases', there is 'solid consensus about the criterion of reparatory justice for the relatively isolated case, namely *restitutio in integrum* – the effort to re-establish the situation prior to the wrongful act (or omission), or to compensate the victim in proportion to the harm suffered'.

12 See 'German Observations on the Draft Treaty of Peace' and 'Reply of the Allied and Associated Powers to the Observations of the German Delegation on the Conditions of Peace, and Ultimatum' in *The Treaty of Versailles and After: Annotations of the Text of the Treaty* (1944: 39).

violations (Torpey 2006: 159, Williams 2007: i). This shift took place parallel to and as a consequence of the proliferation of human rights law, which repositioned individuals as subjects of international law. Barkan (2001: 3–29) points to Germany's efforts to compensate Holocaust survivors as the first example of a large-scale, modern redress process, but this case in fact straddled emerging notions of reparation as an individual right, and older approaches that focused on remedies negotiated and administered between states. Germany's redress for the survivors of the Holocaust was negotiated with international Jewish organisations and the newly founded Israeli government, and, since 1952, has involved the transfer of over 60 billion dollars from Germany to both individual survivors and the state of Israel (Bazyler 2002: 38).

The incipient reparations movement largely stalled until the early 1990s when class action suits were filed in the United States against three prominent Swiss banks for their complicity in the Holocaust. This reinvigorated interest in redressing historical injustices, and catapulted several complex reparations cases onto political agendas worldwide, including compensation for Japanese North Americans interned during World War II, and Korean women forced to serve as sex slaves ('comfort women' or *ianfu*) for the Japanese Imperial Army (Bazyler 2002: 15). Debates on reparations for slavery were revived in the United States, while United Nations delegates deliberated van Boven and Bassiouni's Reparations Principles, as well as issues such as remedies for colonialism. The 1990s also saw the emergence of new types of institutions designed to confront and respond to historical injustices. For example, the South African Truth and Reconciliation Commission was a major institutional innovation that has become a 'paradigmatic international model' for countries transitioning to democracy (Hamber and Wilson 2002: 35). At the same time, the United Nations Compensation Commission pioneered new approaches to resolving mass claims lodged by individual victims of war. In addition to individualised, court-mandated reparations, this period saw the development of community-oriented, flexible, collective approaches to redress. These include linking community development programmes to reparations goals; having perpetrators carry out community service as a form of atonement; and giving the survivors of human rights violations preferential access to social services (de Greiff and Duthie 2009, Roht-Arriaza 2004: 122, 129–136). The high political profile of reparations issues, and the key role redress was perceived to play in democratic transitions were illustrated by the fact that the first law passed by Nelson Mandela's ANC government in South Africa addressed the restitution of land rights lost under apartheid (Gibson 2009, ICG 2004a: 142).[13]

In short, by the year 2000 reparations politics had reached a heightened pitch – in Nigerian Nobel Laureate Wole Soyinka's words, a '*fin de millénaire* fever of atonement' (Soyinka 1999: 90). Reparations have now been 'routini[sed] . . . as a political pursuit'; the 'ideal of reparations has . . . been disseminated throughout the world and constitutes a crucial resource in the arsenal of contemporary politics' (Torpey 2006: 5, 159). Torpey (2006: 3–4) suggests that reparations politics remains 'vibrant', but has calmed somewhat since the terrorist attacks of 11 September 2001 and the subsequent 'war on terror', which have drawn away the attention of human rights advocates. The vibrancy of the reparations movement notwithstanding, refugees remain in the eddies of mainstream political discussions on reparations and transitional justice, and their problems are often overlooked by scholars concerned with the efficacy and significance of redress programmes. Yet, closer examination demonstrates that refugees have had a significant if overshadowed role in the modern reparations movement, with specific norms on redress for the displaced developing alongside the broader international norms that inform contemporary reparations politics.

Refugees in the reparations movement: recent history of an emerging norm

Refugees have long been intertwined with the law and politics of redress. As early as 1939, Jennings argued for refugees' legal right to redress, and in 1952, a reluctant Israel engaged in reparations negotiations with West Germany because it was financially crippled and in urgent need of $1.5 billion to resettle Jewish refugees from Europe. Germany paid two-thirds of the resettlement costs (Bazyler 2002: 38, Garry 1998: 98). Yet efforts to redress displacement have, to date, garnered much less political and scholarly attention than efforts to remedy other crimes such as disappearances and murder.[14]

13 See the Restitution of Land Rights Act of 1994, available at http://land.info.gov.za/acts/1944/a22-94.pdf.

14 Many of the authors who have examined the development of specific international norms on reparations for displacement are practitioners who have served on the staffs of claims commissions, or humanitarian agencies and inter-governmental organisations involved in real property restitution. See, for example, Cox and Garlick (2003), Garlick (2000), Philpott (2005), Worby (2001), Madsen (2001), Leckie (2003b, 2008) and Williams (2007).

In this section, I contend that the strengthening of international norms on remedies for refugees is evident in developments such as: the proliferation of provisions on redress for the displaced in peace treaties, UN resolutions and documents; the creation of new positions and institutions committed to advancing refugees' right to redress; the integration of forced migration into the mandates of transitional justice mechanisms such as truth commissions and trials; and the provision of significant levels of financial support for reparations initiatives involving displaced persons (particularly restitution processes). Although international norms on remedies for refugees are not consistently applied, the implementation of these norms in increasingly diverse circumstances is a further sign of their growing traction.

How can this pattern of norm development be explained? To respond to this question, a number of factors must be taken into account. First, the rise of the broader reparations movement over the course of the 1990s provided a propitious legal and political framework within which to pursue refugees' specific claims. Arguably, the fact that displacement was a major (albeit largely unacknowledged) factor in almost all of the major reparations cases of the 1990s provided especially fertile ground for advancing claims focused more specifically on displacement and the violations associated with it. Most importantly, however, reparations programmes for refugees garnered strong support because they were seen as instrumental to the goal of ending displacement by enabling durable solutions, especially return. As Stefansson (2006: 115) argues, the international community views return as critical to post-conflict peace processes. In particular, many actors view housing and property restitution as essential to the success of repatriation movements. This perspective accords with Williams' trajectory of international norms on restitution for the displaced: prior to World War II, reparations were primarily applied to remedy harms between states. After World War II, the view emerged that the states responsible for human rights violations owed reparations to the individual victims of abuse. In the post-Cold War era, restitution has come to the fore as the primary remedy for forced displacement (Williams 2007: 1). In recent years the post-Cold War tendency to 'subordinate restitution to physical return of displaced persons' has given way in some cases to the 'promotion of restitution as a right in itself', which may be seen as 'equivalent to other forms of reparation' (Williams 2012). However, many states and other stakeholders remain fixated on return as the 'preferred' solution to displacement, and restitution as the remedy most conducive to realising this goal. Notwithstanding the current status of restitution as the predominant approach to redress for forced migrants, in the upcoming sections I argue that legally, morally and pragmatically, international norms on redress for refugees must extend beyond restitution to encompass other forms of reparation, if redress is to facilitate just return.

Beyond donor and host states' desire to promote the return of refugees, several additional factors have contributed to the evolution of international norms on remedies for the displaced. These include the efforts of refugee leaders and human rights advocates; governments' desire to create conditions amenable to foreign investment and economic growth, particularly by resolving land claims and upholding private tenure rights; and the determination of donors and international organisations who have staked their reputations on the success of reparation and repatriation operations.[15] On the other hand, the evolution and implementation of strong norms on reparations for refugees has been diminished by factors such as disparate levels of interest among donors and international agencies in different displacement situations; conflicting priorities in post-conflict and transitional environments; the difficulty of implementing reparations programmes in chaotic, impoverished circumstances; the shortage of accessible legal venues through which refugees can advance claims against their states; and the lack of sincere interest and commitment from many recalcitrant countries of origin.

Reparations for the refugees of Nazism

Both property restitution and the facilitation of sustainable returns 'arguably represent emerging human rights requirements on post-conflict states', with the right to return 'now increasingly understood to obligate states to permit individuals and groups displaced in conflicts to return not only to their country, but their actual home of origin' (Williams 2006b: 51). Yet most efforts to provide redress to the refugees created by the policies of the Third Reich and the destructiveness of World War II were not intended to facilitate return, but the resettlement of Holocaust survivors. Debate took place at a remarkably high level, and the reparations issue was integrated into the mandates of key refugee-serving agencies. For example, UNHCR's precursor, the International Refugee Organisation (IRO) employed a Reparations Director, who worked in concert with counterparts from the German, Allied and Israeli governments, as well as key non-governmental agencies, such as the Jewish Restitution Successor Organisation. It would be almost 50 years until UNHCR exhibited a strong interest in reparations, and the issue is still

15 Interview with Scott Leckie, former Executive Director of the Centre on Housing Rights and Evictions, 27 November 2007.

not institutionalised in the High Commissioner's office to the extent that it was in the IRO.

In addition to the reparations Germany paid to individual Holocaust survivors and the $1 billion it transferred to Israel to help fund the resettlement of the Jewish refugees, a proportion of Germany's external assets (i.e. Germany's holdings outside its borders) was also harnessed as reparations to support the resettlement of refugees. The Final Act of the December 1945 Paris Reparation Agreement allocated $25 million for those who 'suffered heavily at the hands of the Nazis and now stand in dire need of aid to promote their rehabilitation' (Rubin and Schwartz 1951: 379). Although $25 million was 'pitifully small in relation to any conceivable measure of compensation', representatives of the Inter-Allied Reparations Agency and the Inter-Governmental Committee on Refugees agreed that the reparations money would be best applied to support the rehabilitation and resettlement of refugees (Rubin and Schwartz 1951: 379). Interestingly, the Agreement on a Plan of Allocation of a Reparation Share to Non-Repatriable Victims of German Action stipulated that the money could not be used for individual compensation, but must be directed towards rehabilitation and resettlement services for the broader group (Rubin and Schwartz 1951: 379).

Writing in the 1950s, the proponents of reparations for the Jewish refugees lamented that 'despite the moral force that lies behind it, the principle [that Germany should redress the victims of Nazism] has been implemented to a pitifully small extent' (Rubin and Schwartz 1951: 377–378). Yet in retrospect, efforts to redress World War II-era refugees stand out as some of the most well-financed and extensive on record. Reflecting on the reparations programme for refugees of the Holocaust underlines the extent to which norms on reparations for refugees have evolved (or, indeed, regressed) since the 1940s and 1950s. First and foremost, 'non-repatriable victims' is no longer part of the lexicon of the contemporary durable solutions regime. Rather, the focus is more often on survivors' 'resiliency' and their right to return, a rhetorical shift that reflects the new orientation of the refugee regime towards repatriation, and may in part be intended to excuse the foreclosure of refugees' access to other durable solutions. Second, while the reparations programme for the European Jewish refugees involved both individualised and collective remedies, since the end of the Cold War most reparations initiatives for refugees have focused predominantly on individualised remedies. This pattern is slowly changing as community-level redress processes are also gaining traction. Third, it is striking that unlike the reparations programme for the refugees of the Holocaust, most contemporary reparations efforts that are focused on material losses do not address assets other than land

and housing. This reflects a profound change in the socio-economic background of the 'average' refugee, and the priorities of donors and international agencies. Whereas refugees from conflict and persecution in Europe tended to have considerable personal assets, the vast majority of contemporary refugees are from poorer Southern countries, and have far fewer material resources to lose. The recovery of their assets may nonetheless be extremely important to Southern refugees, but donors and international agencies have shown much less willingness to help refugees regain possessions other than land. This may most plausibly be attributed to the fact that the restitution of land or homes is seen as the remedy most directly connected to enabling repatriation. This change may also denote a decline in the amount of money and energy western countries are willing to invest in reparations processes for displaced persons and other victims of human rights violations from strikingly different cultural backgrounds.

Redress for refugees in post-World War II treaties and resolutions: consolidation of the focus on return

In a cruel moment of political irony, just as the Holocaust survivors were negotiating the compensation agreement that enabled them to resettle in Israel, another group of refugees in need of redress was created. Some of the most important, precedent-setting political statements on reparations for refugees arose after some 750,000 Palestinians were displaced in 1948, alongside the establishment of the Israeli state (Fischbach 2003: xxi, Shiblak 2009: 2). Unlike the reparations programmes for European Jewish refugees, these statements clearly linked reparations and return. In 1948, the UN Mediator on Palestine, Count Bernadotte, identified the 'twin rights of repatriation and compensation' as essential to the settlement of the Palestinian question (Lee 1986: 534). Bernadotte wrote,

> The right of the Arab refugees to return to their homes in Jewish-controlled territory at the earliest possible date should be affirmed by the UN, and their repatriation, resettlement and economic and social rehabilitation, and payment of adequate compensation for the property of those choosing not to return, should be supervised and assisted by the UN. (UN Mediator on Palestine 1948)

UN Member States echoed a revised version of Bernadotte's recommendations in General Assembly Resolution 194 (III) of 1948, which resolves that

> refugees wishing to return to their homes and live at peace with their neighbours should be permitted to do so at the earliest practicable date, and that compensation should be paid for the property of those choosing not to return and for

loss of or damage to property which, under principles of international law or in equity, should be made good by the Governments or authorities responsible. (UNGA 1948)

Although never implemented, these provisions have been repeated yearly in General Assembly resolutions, and are oft-cited pieces of political rhetoric that have helped to consolidate the political connection between refugees' right to return and their claims for redress. Indeed, some advocates have argued that because Resolution 194 (III) has been so regularly reaffirmed by the General Assembly, it now has the status of international law (Boling 2001). While this interpretation may be tenuous, the regular reaffirmation of Resolution 194 (III) ensured that the question of reparations for refugees retained a foothold on the international political agenda, and prompted further debate on the issue. In 1981 the General Assembly deliberated the notion of 'adequate compensation', which was developed with a view to resolving the Palestinians' displacement, but also has significant implications for other redress, return and resettlement processes. This approach was subsequently elaborated upon by Benvenisti and the UN Group of Governmental Experts on International Cooperation to Avert New Flows of Refugees (1986) in their report to the General Assembly.[16] Drawing on Resolution 194 (III), the non-governmental International Law Association also discussed refugees' right to reparations at conferences in 1988 and 1990, and in 1992 adopted the Cairo Declaration of Principles of International Law on Compensation to Refugees (Lee 1993). Although efforts to redress the Palestinian refugees and resolve their displacement have not moved beyond the level of political rhetoric, these discussions helped refine individual, governmental and institutional views on reparations for refugees, at a time when efforts on the issue were otherwise largely stagnant.

Following on the heels of the end of the Cold War, the United Nations Compensation Commission (UNCC) reinvigorated international activity on the issue of reparations for the victims of large-scale violence, and set crucial precedents regarding displaced persons' right to redress. Established in 1991, the UNCC addressed harms suffered by individuals, corporations and states as a result of Iraq's invasion of Kuwait. The UNCC was not a court but a political organ that aimed to process claims promptly, transparently and fairly, and blended classic reparatory principles with streamlined decision-making procedures to offer remedy to large numbers of claimants, focusing on the needs of individuals. The Commission specifically strived to compensate the millions forced

[16] See also Benvenisti (1999). See Chapter 8 for a more detailed discussion of this approach.

to flee Iraq and Kuwait, and thus represented the first large-scale, institutionalised attempt to provide reparations to refugees in the post-Cold War era. The UNCC distributed its final payments to individuals in 2007. It was generously funded through Iraqi oil sales, and it is doubtful whether future initiatives based on the UNCC model could succeed without access to comparable resources. Nonetheless, the UNCC serves as a source of important lessons on providing timely remedies to refugees, which have influenced the creation and operation of subsequent claims commissions (Crook 1993, Wooldridge and Elias 2003).

Four years after the establishment of the UNCC, a watershed moment occurred in the struggle to achieve redress for the displaced: the signing of the 1995 General Framework Agreement for Peace in Bosnia and Herzegovina (Dayton Agreement). Provisions on refugees' right to return and reclaim their property had been incorporated into several earlier peace treaties, such as the 1992 General Peace Agreement for Mozambique and the 1994 Agreement on the Resettlement of the Population Groups Uprooted by the Armed Conflict in Guatemala. However, these provisions tended to be perfunctory and difficult to enforce. The Dayton Agreement was the first peace treaty to explicitly recognise refugees' right to return to their prewar homes, and far surpassed previous agreements in terms of its specificity, and the determination of the international community to ensure that the rights to return and restitution were realised. Annex 7 of the Dayton Agreement is devoted to refugees and displaced persons, and famously states:

> All refugees and displaced persons have the right freely to return to their homes of origin. They shall have the right to have restored to them property of which they were deprived . . . and to be compensated for any property that cannot be restored to them. The early return of refugees and displaced persons is an important objective of the settlement of the conflict in Bosnia and Herzegovina. (General Framework Agreement for Peace 1995)[17]

Through this ambitious provision, refugee return and property restitution were placed at the heart of efforts to build peace in Bosnia. The Dayton Agreement's provisions on reparations and return have been echoed in several subsequent agreements, with virtually every peace treaty signed since 1995 recognising refugees' right to return and redress in some form (Phuong 2005: 12, Williams 2012). The *Peace Agreement Drafters' Handbook* prepared by the Public International Law and Policy Group (2005) includes model articles on reparations and refugee returns, implying that

[17] See Chapter 5 for a more detailed discussion of repatriation and reparation processes in Bosnia and Herzegovina.

such provisions are now accepted as staples in any agreement that aspires to end a conflict involving extensive displacement. The proliferation of articles on reparations and repatriation in peace agreements signed since the end of the Cold War was complemented by an array of national laws on property restitution and other forms of redress, which further bolstered these budding international norms.[18]

Yet Annex 7 of the Dayton Agreement (and the many treaties, laws and resolutions that followed it) had its genesis not simply in the altruistic desire to assist the displaced and spur on the growing reparations movement, but also in states' self-interest. The history of the Dayton peace negotiations underlines the close connection between western support for refugees' right to redress, and their determination to reduce the number of refugees living within their borders. As chief American negotiator Richard Holbrooke (1999: 275) recalled,

> With over three hundred thousand Bosnian refugees in their country, Germany wanted to reduce the burden that the refugees had put on its social services and budget . . . Bonn had given [its representative at Dayton] one firm instruction: any agreement must encourage the refugees to return home.[19]

At the same time as refugees' rights to return and reparations were being enshrined in peace agreements and national laws, various international bodies and agencies became more actively involved in shaping norms

[18] See Leckie (2007) *Housing, Land and Property Restitution Rights of Refugees and Displaced Persons: Laws, Cases, and Materials* for a compilation of more than 240 international laws, peace agreements, tripartite agreements, UNHCR Executive Committee Conclusions, UN resolutions, and national laws on displaced persons' right to restitution. See also COHRE (2001). Domestic laws on redress for displaced persons typically focus on property restitution and/or compensation. While international law, including the Rome Statute of the International Criminal Court, enables the prosecution of forced displacement ('acts of deportation or forcible transfer') as a crime against humanity or a war crime, most domestic criminal law systems do not presently include laws prohibiting forced displacement (Andreu-Guzmán 2012; UN Commission on Human Rights Resolution 2003/52).

[19] Williams (2007: 39) writes that post-Dayton there was a 'fundamental shift in the international community's perception of the justification for restitution, from promoting return *per se* to supporting durable solutions.' This could be taken to undermine the connection between the development of norms on reparations for the displaced, and the North's desire to promote return as the preferred durable solution. However, this is largely a matter of how return is defined. The fact that many displaced Bosnians did not, in the end, return to their original homes does not undermine the political efficacy of restitution from the perspective of begrudging host countries. Restitution and the resale of properties made it possible for the displaced to achieve a durable solution *within* their (newly reconstituted) country of origin. While European host and donor states certainly preferred that the displaced return to their original homes, the critical point was that refugees should leave their host countries. Entrenching the right to return and restitution in the treaty effectively promoted the achievement of this goal.

on reparations, often with the goal of promoting return as the preferred solution to displacement.[20] For example, the UN Security Council passed more than 30 resolutions between 1992 and 2005 supporting the refugees' right to return to and reclaim their original homes.[21] The United Nations human rights architecture played a particularly active role in stimulating the development of norms in this field. While the Commission on Human Rights spearheaded debate on the UN Reparations Principles, the drafters of the 1998 Guiding Principles on Internal Displacement (Principle 29.2) confirmed that

> Competent authorities have the duty and responsibility to assist returned and/or resettled internally displaced persons to recover, to the extent possible, their property and possessions which they left behind or were dispossessed of upon their displacement. When recovery of such property and possessions is not possible, competent authorities shall provide or assist these persons in obtaining appropriate compensation or another form of just reparation.

This provision is a strong indication that displaced persons' right to reparations has reached the status of a norm in international law, as the Guiding Principles do not aim to create new obligations for states, but to clarify already existing responsibilities under international law.[22] However, the Guiding Principles attach several broad provisos to this right: the responsible state is only obliged to facilitate restitution 'to the extent possible', and is not obliged to guarantee that the displaced person secures compensation or another appropriate remedy. Rather, only the state's 'assistance' is required.[23] This modest reading of the law stands in sharp contrast to the more wide ranging interpretation of the state's obligations embraced by the UN Sub-Commission on the Promotion and Protection of Human Rights.

In 1997, the Committee on the Elimination of Racial Discrimination (CERD) set in motion the first focused attempt by the United Nations to grapple with the scope and implications of this issue when it asked the

[20] See Thiele (2001) for a discussion of UN engagement in the development of norms on restitution for returnees in the 1990s.

[21] See, for example, UN Security Council Resolution 787 on Bosnia and Herzegovina (1992); Resolution 999 on Tajikistan (1995); Resolution 1244 on Kosovo (1999a); and Resolution 1545 on Burundi (2004a).

[22] The 2009 Convention for the Protection and Assistance of Internally Displaced Persons in Africa (Kampala Convention) also recognises arbitrary displacement as an offence, and elaborates on displaced persons' right to reparations.

[23] The 2010 IASC Framework on Durable Solutions for Internally Displaced Persons elaborates on the implications of Principle 29.2, devoting considerable attention to the issue of IDPs' access to restitution and other reparations mechanisms (Inter-Agency Standing Committee 2010, paras. 76–83, 94–105).

Sub-Commission on the Promotion and Protection of Human Rights to examine the return of displaced persons' property. A year later, the Sub-Commission adopted Resolution 1998/26 on Housing and Property Restitution in the Context of the Return of Refugees and Internally Displaced Persons. The Commission on Human Rights encouraged the Sub-Commission to continue its work on this topic, and in 2001 the Sub-Commission accordingly requested Brazilian expert Paulo Sérgio Pinheiro to author a working paper on the issue. The Sub-Commission made Pinheiro Special Rapporteur on Housing and Property Restitution for Refugees and Internally Displaced Persons in 2002, and considered his report the following year. At the Sub-Commission's request, the Special Rapporteur used the conclusions of his preliminary study to prepare draft principles on restitution, which were initially presented to the Sub-Commission in 2004. After extensive feedback from members of the Sub-Commission and consultations with lawyers, non-governmental organisations, UN agencies and governments, the final text of the UN Principles on Housing and Property Restitution for Refugees and Displaced Persons (Pinheiro Principles) was presented to the Sub-Commission in August 2005, at which time the Principles received the formal endorsement of the Sub-Commission (Leckie 2005: 4).

The first 'consolidated and universal approach' to displaced persons' housing and property restitution claims, the Pinheiro Principles represent a landmark in the development and consolidation of international norms on reparations for the displaced (Leckie 2005: 4). Following the adoption of the Principles by the Sub-Commission, a programme of activities was launched to popularise the standards and promote their implementation.[24] Some of these activities have attracted significant high-level support. For example, in 2007 a handbook on implementing the Pinheiro Principles was cooperatively developed by UNHCR, UN-Habitat, the Food and Agriculture Organisation (FAO), the Office for the Coordination of Humanitarian Affairs (OCHA), the Office of the High Commissioner for Human Rights, and the Norwegian Refugee Council. The foreword to the handbook, signed by leaders including the UN High Commissioner for Refugees, the High Commissioner for Human Rights and the Under-Secretary General for Humanitarian Affairs welcomes the Pinheiro Principles, and emphasises the connection between restitution and return (FAO, NRC, OCHA et al. 2007: 3). The Principles have been referenced in the 2006 Great Lakes Protocol on the Property

[24] For more information on the Centre on Housing Rights and Evictions, one of the key organisations that spearheaded efforts to popularise the Pinheiro Principles, see www.cohre.org.

Rights of Returning Persons; a 2007 ruling by Colombia's Constitutional Court; the 2008 Iraqi IDP strategy; and in decisions of the European Court of Human Rights and the African Commission on Human and People's Rights (Williams 2010b, 2012). The UN Secretary-General's 2011 report on the rule of law and transitional justice in conflict and post-conflict societies recognise the Pinheiro Principles as 'an important step in the emergence of internationally agreed best practice on housing, land and property rights issues in post-conflict settings' (UNSG 2011b: para. 53).

Despite this high-level recognition, the Principles have not garnered unanimous support. Indeed, a number of forceful critiques of the Pinheiro Principles have been mounted by scholars and practitioners. For example, some critics charge that the Pinheiro Principles' rigid interpretation of remedial rights and concerted focus on return risks undermining fledgling peace processes and may run counter to the interests of displaced persons who do not wish to return (Ballard 2010, Pantuliano 2009, Pantuliano and Elhawary 2009, Smit 2012). While advocates of the Principles maintain that they are 'grounded firmly within existing international human rights and humanitarian law', it may be argued that in fact the Principles take an activist approach, stretching beyond accepted interpretations of the requirements of current international law (Leckie 2005: 4). Critics have also suggested that the Pinheiro Principles focus too strongly on restitution, with insufficient attention devoted to other remedies such as compensation. Furthermore, the Principles fail to adequately delineate the circumstances in which restitution is the most appropriate remedy for displacement.[25] By simply calling on states to 'demonstrably prioritise the right to restitution as the preferred remedy for displacement and as a key element of restorative justice', the Principles shirk the difficult but critical task of determining how longstanding displacements and secondary occupations affect refugees' claims for redress (UN Sub-Commission on the Protection and Promotion of Human Rights 2005: Principle 2.2). Certainly, international law offers no clear guidance on this issue. The drafters may have been hesitant to recognise this reality, out of concern that it would undermine the Principles' authority. Their hesitation to confront or even acknowledge these 'hard questions' may also be connected to their desire to support refugees' struggle to return and receive reparations, even in controversial cases such as that of the Palestinian refugees. Principle 2.2 proclaims that 'the right to restitution exists as a distinct right, and is

[25] Views expressed by a prominent international legal expert on displacement. Electronic communication, 18 September 2007.

prejudiced neither by the actual return nor non-return of refugees and displaced persons entitled to housing, land and property restitution', but Special Rapporteur Pinheiro and the Principles that bear his name undoubtedly conceive of restitution and return as mutually reinforcing rights. While Principle 10.1 concedes that '[r]efugees and displaced persons should be able to effectively pursue durable solutions to displacement other than return, if they so wish, without prejudicing their right to the restitution of their housing, land and property', the Principles contain an entire section on 'The Right to Voluntary Return in Safety and Dignity', and are virtually silent on how the right to restitution pertains to the other durable solutions. This is perhaps unsurprising, as Pinheiro is unequivocal in his support for return, attesting that the

> best solution to the plight of millions of refugees and displaced persons around the world is to ensure they attain the right to return freely to their countries and to have restored to them housing and property of which they were deprived during the course of displacement, or to be compensated for any property that cannot be restored to them. It is the most desired, sustainable, and dignified solution to displacement. (Centre on Housing Rights and Evictions 2005)

To the relatively limited extent that other remedies such as trials, truth commissions, commemorations, and justice-sensitive security sector reform have been used to address the injustices associated with displacement, these efforts have not concentrated so explicitly on enabling return. However, it is increasingly common for organisations that work with displaced populations, including UNHCR, to cooperate with transitional justice bodies such as truth commissions, and this cooperation is often undertaken in the hopes that these mechanisms may help open up durable solutions to displacement. In comparison to international norms on restitution for displaced persons, norms on integrating displacement into other transitional justice mechanisms are even more nascent, with the engagement of refugee populations and the incorporation of displacement as a substantive concern typically approached in an ad hoc manner. However, there is a notable trend towards counting displacement itself as one of the violations to be addressed through transitional justice initiatives, and including displaced persons as beneficiaries of these measures. Indeed, many diaspora organisations have taken a leading role in the push for accountability for past abuses, whether or not their members intend to return permanently (Bradley 2012a, 2012c, Caparini 2012, Duthie 2012b, Van der Auweraert 2012, Young and Park 2009).

The contribution and creation of national and international institutions

The shortcomings of the Pinheiro Principles are reflective of the gaps that exist in the broader body of laws, resolutions and treaties that address remedies for the displaced, and confirm that despite the adoption of hundreds of provisions on this issue since the end of the Cold War, international norms on redress for refugees are still in the early stages of development. However, a remarkably wide range of national and international actors are devoting unprecedented attention to the question of restitution and other forms of redress for refugees (Leckie 2005: 3). This includes UNHCR and the International Organisation for Migration (IOM), as well as local and national governments, donors, tribunals, peacekeepers, and even military forces operating in areas experiencing conflict between returnees and local residents.[26] The involvement of such a broad array of organisations attests to the growing resonance of international norms on this issue, and it may be hoped that their contributions will eventually result in appropriately nuanced interpretations of these norms, which may more effectively inform state behaviour. This section will review the contributions organisations such as UNHCR and IOM have made to the development of norms and practice on redress for refugees, and will examine how the creation of new institutions specifically focused on the provision of redress have also shaped the evolution of these norms.

UNHCR expressed clear support for refugees' right to restitution during the Global Consultations on International Protection (Voluntary Repatriation), and endeavours to ensure that the state of origin's obligations regarding redress for the displaced are delineated in the tripartite agreements that govern return operations.[27] Over the past 15 years, the agency has taken modest steps to institutionalise its commitment to supporting remedies for the displaced, nominating a 'contact person' for real property restitution issues, developing a Checklist on the Restitution of Housing and Property, and cooperating closely with various trials and truth-telling processes (Bradley 2012c, Feller 2009: 93, UNHCR 2001).

26 For example, Human Rights Watch (2004) documented the involvement of the United States military in land restitution issues involving displaced communities in Northern Iraq. While it is not uncommon for military, peacekeeping and police forces to be involved in implementing the decisions made by claims commissions, in this case the US forces were also involved in convening local negotiations on restitution and attempting to mediate disputes between returnees and secondary occupants.

27 See UNHCR *Handbook on Voluntary Repatriation: International Protection* (UNHCR 1996: 82, 88) and UNHCR *Handbook for Repatriation and Reintegration Activities* (UNHCR 2004: 142). See also the background paper *Global Consultation on International Protection: Voluntary Repatriation* (UNHCR 2002: 4–5).

Under High Commissioner Ogata, the agency was also actively involved in a range of reconciliation or 'coexistence' activities, such as the 'Imagine Coexistence' programme, which moved beyond property restitution to address issues such as the peaceful use of public space and resources by returnees and their former neighbours. UNHCR's 'Imagine Coexistence' programme was partially a pragmatic response to UNHCR's involvement in repatriation to deeply divided communities in Bosnia and Rwanda, but was also fuelled by Ogata's personal conviction, inspired by the work of Martha Minow, that if returns were to be sustainable and peace consolidated, 'the fabric of society would have to be stitched back together. This meant looking at individuals and their communities in the most holistic way and designing integrative projects that amalgamated social, economic, cultural and spiritual aspects into a cohesive whole' (Haider 2009, Ogata 2003: xi–xvi).

Although the evaluators of the Imagine Coexistence programme concluded that UNHCR should continue to provide long-term support to coexistence activities, the agency's commitment to this type of reparative work seems to have waned under subsequent High Commissioners (Babbitt 2002). This lack of sustained engagement has arguably undermined efforts to strengthen norms on redress for refugees, and expand the types of remedies available to the displaced. However, UNHCR's involvement in promoting redress and reconciliation in communities affected by large-scale displacement may be poised to expand. The agency's 2008 'Policy Framework and Implementation Strategy: UNHCR's Role in Support of the Return and Reintegration of Displaced Populations' includes sections on 'Rights, justice and reconciliation' and 'Protection, reconciliation and the rule of law', and articulates a fairly comprehensive approach to supporting reconciliation, building on local initiatives and UNHCR's engagement with formerly displaced populations. The 2008 Policy Framework is based on the assumption of a close link between transitional justice and reconciliation processes, which UNHCR is to support through peace education and co-existence initiatives (UNHCR 2008: 13, para. 60). Similarly, the 2011 Decision of the Secretary-General's Policy Committee on Durable Solutions and the accompanying 'Preliminary Framework for supporting a more coherent, predictable and effective response to the durable solutions needs of refugee returnees and internally displaced persons' has a strong focus on reconciliation, and envisions a leading role for UNHCR in promoting transitional justice and reconciliation, with a view to enabling durable solutions, particularly return (UNSG 2011a: paras. 9, 12). The pilot implementation of the Preliminary Framework in 2012–2013 should provide an opportunity for UNHCR to deepen its contribution to issues of redress and reconciliation (Bradley 2012a).

While UNHCR's engagement with reparations issues has been somewhat scattergun, the International Organisation for Migration (IOM) has demonstrated a deep and sustained interest in the provision of reparations to the displaced, and developed considerable technical expertise on this front. For example, the IOM managed the delivery of redress to Holocaust survivors in the Swiss banks case, and has overseen the complex technical processes associated with delivering restitution and compensation in unstable conflict and post-conflict circumstances, such as Iraq and Colombia. By providing its technical services, the IOM Claims Programme has been instrumental in helping states of origin make good on their obligation to redress their displaced and returning citizens. The IOM has also played a leading role in identifying effective approaches to implementing norms on restitution and compensation for returnees, with the goal of ensuring that refugees in different parts of the world can access redress on a more equitable basis. For instance, the IOM Claims Programme has completed extensive research synthesising the technical and legal lessons the organisation has learned through these processes, in order to determine how this might inform the development of effective claims commissions for protracted displacement situations such as the case of the Palestinian refugees (IOM 2009).[28]

While norms on reparations for refugees have influenced and been influenced by the behaviour of well-established organisations such as UNHCR and the IOM, dozens of national, international and quasi-international organisations have been created specifically to give expression to emerging remedial norms. These institutions may be divided into two main groups. The first group encompasses institutions such as ad hoc courts, truth and reconciliation commissions and compensation commissions, which respond to a wide array of human rights violations, but may be tailored to ensure that they address the crime of displacement, and are accessible to the displaced.[29] Although international institutions like the UNCC, the European Court of Human Rights (ECHR) and the International Criminal Tribunal for the Former Yugoslavia (ICTY) have taken modest but significant steps to uphold state and individual responsibility for the crime of displacement, other international bodies and national-level institutions have been much less open to engaging

[28] See van der Auweraert (2012) for discussion of a range of cases in which the IOM has facilitated the provision of various forms of redress in societies affected by large-scale displacement.

[29] On innovations in including displaced and diaspora populations in the work of national truth commissions, see, for example, Young and Park (2009).

refugees and confronting the issue of forced migration.[30] For example, displaced and exiled claimants were purposefully excluded from the reparations processes initiated in Brazil, Chile and the Czech Republic (de Greiff 2006, Williams 2007). In other countries, the displaced were not consciously barred from the institutions intended to redress grievous wrongs against citizens, but because efforts to accommodate their particular needs were insufficient or non-existent, they were unable to lodge grievances or participate in the justice process. For example, in some cases information about the mandate and services offered by the national institutions responsible for reparations is not widely available outside the country of origin. As a result, refugees may fail to file their claims.

The second group is comprised of institutions specifically designed to adjudicate cases raised by the displaced. More than a dozen such institutions have been mandated under peace treaties, national laws and international agreements signed since the end of the Cold War. A smaller number have in fact become operable, such as the Commission for Real Property Claims in Bosnia and the South African Land Claims Court.[31] Typically, these institutions focus on housing and property restitution for the displaced, although some also have a mandate to provide compensation in lieu of restitution. Where such fora have been available, refugees and displaced persons have typically been very enthusiastic about using them to advance their claims. While a more detailed discussion of the emergence and evolution of some of these institutions is presented in Part II, at present it is worth noting that the creation and operationalisation of administrative institutions with immediate responsibility for resolving property claims has often proven instrumental to the realisation, at least in part, of refugees' right to return and reparations. In the absence of specially tailored, internationally supported and financed institutions with the mandate to resolve claims *en masse* (rather than through a case-by-case adversarial legal process), restitution rights have generally gone unimplemented. This is not to say that the creation of such

[30] See Andreu-Guzmán (2012) for a detailed discussion of the development of norms on international criminal justice and forced displacement.

[31] Other institutions created with a view to resolving claims raised by displaced persons include: the Albanian State Committee for Restitution and Compensation of Property; the Southern Sudan Land Commission; the Sudanese National Land Commission; the Georgian Commission on Restitution and Compensation; the Iraqi Commission for the Resolution of Real Property Disputes; the Iraqi Property Reconciliation Facility; and the Technical Committee established under the 1994 Accord on the Resettlement of the Populations Uprooted by the Armed Conflict in Guatemala. While the 2000 Arusha Peace and Reconciliation Agreement for Burundi called for the establishment of a National Commission for the Rehabilitation of *Sinistrés*, with a Sub-Commission on Land, the Commission and Sub-Commission do not appear to have ever become operable.

institutions is sufficient to uphold refugees' right to redress and return.[32] Although refugee-serving institutions such as the Kosovo Housing and Property Directorate have been relatively successful, bodies such as the Iraqi Property Claims Commission and Afghanistan's Special Property Dispute Resolution Court have struggled to fulfil their mandates in conditions of ongoing instability. Indeed, the Special Court in Afghanistan imploded due to corruption and lack of capacity, and was shut down despite the fact that the country is inundated with returnees bearing unresolved restitution claims.[33] Despite the shortcomings of these bodies, bilateral donors have shown remarkable readiness to finance institutions intended to implement norms on reparations for the displaced, particularly in cases such as Bosnia and Kosovo, in which the donor countries were also major host countries and had a keen desire to realise the repatriation of refugees.

Innovations in the application of norms on redress for refugees

An additional indicator of the increasing potency of international norms on redress for refugees is the extent to which these norms have been applied in cases that deviate from the 'standard' model of resolving refugees' reparations claims with a view to enabling an imminent and ideally permanent return. This demonstrates that states and other international actors are increasingly willing to move beyond predominantly self-interested interpretations of the obligations these norms place upon them, and creatively apply reparations to advance the protection of displaced persons. For example, the World Bank has financed a project in Colombia that takes a proactive approach to implementing norms on reparations for returnees. Although return is not yet a viable option for most displaced Colombians, the project worked with displaced communities who lack formal deeds to their land, to map out and register their territories, in preparation for their eventual return and the launch of restitution claims.[34] In Lebanon, the government has expressed its intention to apply international principles on redress to facilitate the return of the Palestinian refugees forced from Nahr El Bared camp in 2007 as a result of the government's 105-day siege against Fatah al-Islam militants occupying the camp.[35] Through posters identifying the Republic of Lebanon,

[32] For detailed discussion of the shortcomings of some of these efforts, see Smit (2012).
[33] Interview with Conor Foley, former Coordinator of Norwegian Refugee Council Legal Aid Program for Afghanistan/Expert on Property Restitution, 14 June 2008.
[34] See 'Colombia: Protection of Patrimonial Assets of Internally Displaced Populations' (World Bank 2004).
[35] Leaders from Nahr El Bared have voiced clear calls for the refugees to be able to return to the camp, rather than be integrated elsewhere in Lebanon. As camp resident Abdel

the Presidency of the Council of Ministers and the Lebanese-Palestinian Dialogue Committee as 'partners in responsibility', the government publicised the following commitment (superimposed over an image of intertwined Lebanese and Palestinian flags):

> Our Palestinian brothers and sisters. Your departure from Nahr El Bared is a safety precaution . . . The Lebanese Government is adamant on the return of all those who were forced to flee the fighting and will strive to ensure their homecoming as soon as the current conflict comes to an end. The Government is also determined and committed to assist in redressing all the damage suffered by Palestinian civilians and their possessions.

Although progress in implementing these commitments has been decidedly lacklustre, Lebanon's rhetoric demonstrates the credibility adherence to these norms can lend a government in the eyes of the international community. The stance signals that despite its history of inflicting policies of crippling discrimination against the Palestinian refugees it hosts, the beleaguered Lebanese government remains a legitimate authority that can be trusted to play its part in the reconstruction of the camp. The Lebanese government's readiness to facilitate the refugees' return and redress their losses also serves to highlight the inadequacy of Israel's response towards the Palestinian refugees' claims to return and redress.

The reparation programmes discussed above assume that the returnees who participate in them are innocent civilians. However, in some cases returnees have themselves committed offences, ranging from grievous violations to petty crimes, which must be redressed if they are to reintegrate into their communities of origin. It is a sign of the gradual maturation of norms on reparations and return that they have in some cases been successfully adapted to account for such situations. For example, the Commission for Reception, Truth and Reconciliation in Timor-Leste established innovative procedures to deal with displaced perpetrators of minor crimes who wanted to return to their home communities.[36] These prospective returnees could request the Commission to convene meetings with their victims and other community members, during which the parties would discuss the past crimes and propose an agreement under which the perpetrator would pledge to carry out reparative acts, such as apologies, repayment of damages, or community service. Once an agreement was reached, the District Court ordered that the redressed

Hakim Sheref observed, 'People only want to return to Nahr Al-Bared. It is a step on our way to Palestine.' See Groult (2007).

36 'Less serious' crimes included theft, minor assault, burning houses, stealing, and destroying crops and livestock. Grievous crimes such as murder and rape were to be formally prosecuted.

acts would be immune from further prosecution, and the community promised that the offender could return in safety. Abrogation of the agreement is treated was a criminal offence (Harris-Rimmer 2010, Roht-Arriaza 2004: 133–134, Vieira 2012). Timor-Leste's facilitation of this unique process bridges the gap between individual accountability and the state's remedial responsibility, and enables the state to support the creation of return conditions that are just for both the returnee and the community.

While many contemporary reparations programmes that have actively involved refugees have done so with a view to ensuring their return, the legitimacy of displaced persons' claims for redress certainly does not hinge on their intention to repatriate. As the Special Rapporteur on Housing and Property Restitution acknowledges, redress is a 'free-standing, autonomous right' owed to displaced persons irrespective of their intentions regarding return (Special Rapporteur on Housing and Property Restitution 2002: 6). Beyond their claims against their state of origin, refugees often experience abuse at different stages in the displacement cycle, which may give rise to legitimate reparations claims against other agents. For those concerned with the entrenchment of refugees' right to redress, it is heartening that some of these claims are gaining attention, nationally and internationally. For example, the Swiss banks' Holocaust settlement, which was negotiated and financed by the banks as well as the Swiss state, identified five classes of eligible claimants, including a 'Refugee Class'. This class consisted of individuals who attempted to gain asylum in Switzerland and were either denied entry or, after gaining entry, were refouled or mistreated (Bazyler 2002: 15). This little-known case is one of the only examples of a state of asylum acting on its responsibility to redress refouled refugees.

Debate on restitution and compensation for resettled refugees and immigrants has also been ignited through a US-based campaign entitled 'Justice for Jews from Arab Countries', which aims to ensure that Mizrahi Jews who left their countries after the creation of the state of Israel are recognised as refugees, and to secure restitution and compensation for them. The campaign calls for a 'tit-for-tat' arrangement in which all references made to the Palestinian refugees and their reparations claims must be matched with parallel references to the predicament of the Mizrahi Jews. Although this is arguably not so much an attempt to secure meaningful redress for the Mizrahi as a tactic to stymie any productive discussion of the Palestinians' claims, the campaign has been well-received in the United States, with resolutions on the issue introduced in the Senate and House of Representatives in February 2007

(Shenhav 2003).[37] However, it was initially given a cold shoulder by the Israeli government and has been opposed by many Israeli Mizrahi Jews who see the effort as a derisive reinterpretation of their history, in which they are cast as hapless refugees who came to Israel under duress, rather than as active supporters of Zionism.[38] for its part the Israeli government was for many years loath to encourage claims against Arab governments for fear of Palestinian counter-claims, the establishment of ministerial and steering committees on the issue reflects the growing traction that the campaign has gained in Israel, particularly under the government of Prime Minister Netanyahu. While the campaign's outcome remains to be seen, this case exemplifies the complex, strategised nature of contemporary reparations politics involving refugees, in which non-governmental organisations, diaspora groups and national governments utilise norms on reparations, not only to achieve, but also to undermine return.

A norm in progress

Although refugees' claims for redress remain on the fringes of mainstream reparations politics, there has been a flurry of interest in reparations for the displaced since the end of the Cold War, with many host countries, donor states, international organisations and refugees themselves particularly keen to promote housing and property restitution as a stepping-stone to return. The emergence and evolution of norms on reparations for the displaced is evidenced by the profusion of provisions on redress and return in peace treaties and UN documents; the behaviour of national and international institutions, including those specifically created to administer returnees' right to restitution; and the implementation of norms on reparations for the displaced in increasingly diverse and often difficult circumstances. There is a growing consensus that reparations should be

[37] The Resolutions indicate that 'it would be inappropriate and unjust for the US to recognize rights for Palestinian refugees without recognizing equal rights for former Jewish, Christian, and other refugees from Arab countries', and instruct the US President to ensure that when the question of refugees in the Middle East is discussed in international fora, US representatives insist that 'any explicit reference to Palestinian refugees is matched by a similar explicit reference to Jewish and other refugees, as a matter of law and equity.' See S. Res. 85 (110th Congress, 1st Session) and H. Res. 185 (110th Congress, 1st Session). The introduction of these Resolutions was followed by Congressional hearings on the issue on 8 May 2007.

[38] For example, former Knesset speaker Yisrael Yeshayahu insisted, 'We are not refugees. [Some of us] came to this country before the state was born. We had messianic aspirations' (Shenhav 2003). At a Knesset meeting on the issue, Israeli Mizrahi Ran Cohen declared, 'I have this to say: I am not a refugee . . . I came at the behest of Zionism, due to the pull that this land exerts, and due to the idea of redemption. Nobody is going to define me as a refugee' (Shenhav 2003). In addition see Shenhav (1999, 2002).

provided on an equitable, timely, transparent basis, but norms on redress for refugees nonetheless remain in the early phases of their development, and must be further refined, both theoretically and operationally, if they are to establish just conditions of return. This is illustrated by persistent disagreement over the interpretation of the relevant international laws; the narrow focus on restitution and return, often to the exclusion of other forms of redress and other durable solutions; and by the lack of systematic, effective efforts to implement rhetorical commitments to redress in any form in the vast majority of displacement situations.

While the 'norm entrepreneurs' involved in the development and dissemination of the Pinheiro Principles have attempted to present return and redress as ironclad, inter-connected rights, uncertainty remains regarding the legal and moral obligations these norms entail for states subject to a range of competing responsibilities (Finnemore and Sikkink 1998: 893). Can a refugee's right to a remedy such as restitution trump the claims of secondary occupants who have resided in the refugee's homes for decades? Can community development programmes substitute for individualised reparations? Must redress programmes attempt to restore the *status quo ante* if they are to enable just return? In Part II, I will examine three case studies that provide insight into these unresolved normative debates, as well as the challenges associated with attempting to uphold state responsibility for forced migration through the provision of redress to returnees, and the characteristics of reparations programmes that may make good on refugee-creating states' obligation enable just return. Presently, however, Rubin and Schwartz's reflections from 1951 on the state of international norms on redress for refugees remain remarkably prescient: 'In the context of a world but lately at war, and with the clouds of a threatened general war hovering overhead, the problems of refugees and resettlement', and no less return, 'are generally overshadowed. What can be done is pitifully small in terms of what damage remains to be repaired, and what losses are irreparable. But in a picture whose pervading colour is dark, there is some light' (Rubin and Schwartz 1951: 393).

Part II

Historical experiences of return and redress

Introduction to Part II

Scholars concerned with issues of peacebuilding, human rights and humanitarianism must 'occupy the difficult terrain between empirical and normative inquiry. In whichever context it arises, the question of "how we should act" requires both an appreciation of the political conditions of action *and* an understanding of the good(s) we wish to achieve' (Reus-Smit and Snidal 2008: 261). Recognising that scholars and practitioners concerned with accountability for displacement must appreciate the origins and evolution of normative commitments towards returning refugees and other forced migrants, Chapter 3 traced the emergence and development of international norms on redress for the displaced, which I argue play a critical role in confronting the injustices at the root of displacement and recasting the fractured relationship between refugees and their states of origin in the context of a just return process. This section will strengthen the bridge this work endeavours to build between empirical and normative aspects of repatriation by exploring efforts to redress refugees returning to Guatemala, Bosnia and Mozambique, drawing out the insights these cases hold for the account of just return and state responsibility for displacement set out in Part I.

As discussed in the Introduction, the purpose of these case studies is to illuminate the obstacles and opportunities that accompany efforts to uphold state responsibility for displacement and employ reparations with a view to enabling the just return of refugees. I also use these cases to identify some of the key characteristics of reparations programmes that may help to make good on the state of origin's responsibility to create conditions amenable to just return. The goal here is not to generate a simple checklist, but to use the cases as a springboard for empirically informed discussion of the theoretical and strategic challenges associated with redressing returnees. The troubled experiences of Guatemala,

Bosnia and Mozambique raise compelling questions about the arguments on state responsibility for displacement and just return that I developed in Chapters 1 and 2. For example, these cases prompt important questions about responsibility for displacement in the context of state collapse and extremely limited state capacity; the importance of moving beyond an exclusive focus on property restitution to integrate different types of redress for returnees; the role of refugees themselves in creating conditions of just return; the culpability of actors beyond the state of origin; and the roles and responsibilities of external actors such as donor states and UN agencies. Engaging with these empirical cases thus highlights the practical implications of my theoretical contentions, and provides an opportunity to clarify and add nuance to my arguments in light of the challenges of practice.

Having set out the aims of these case studies, it is also important to clarify the purposes they are *not* intended to serve. First, while the cases generally support the contention that responding effectively to returnees' justice claims is a significant factor shaping repatriation operations, and thus a prudent course of action for those seeking to facilitate safe, durable and dignified returns, their primary function is not to make inferences for empirical theory. Rather, I employ them mainly to elucidate the challenges practice poses for my normative account. In Chapter 7, I do discuss the insights these cases offer into the characteristics of effective reparations programmes for returnees; however, I do not assume that the Bosnian, Guatemalan and Mozambican cases are representative of repatriations processes around the world, or that the insights they have to offer can serve as a simple blueprint for reparations programmes elsewhere. Instead, my aim is to reflect on the hurdles encountered in these cases and draw out a modest number of contingent generalisations that may apply to similar situations.

Second, although significant efforts were made in each case by actors at different levels to confront the accountability and justice issues associated with repatriation, I do not wish to imply that the actors involved were necessarily trying to enable the just return of refugees along the lines I set out in previous chapters. Nor am I arguing that these processes met the conditions of just return that I articulated in Chapter 2, although the Mozambican case in particular has often been hailed as a success, at least in terms of its durability and the lack of large-scale violence surrounding return. However, if success is also evaluated in normative terms, incorporating issues such as fairness and the development of a solid relationship of rights and duties between the state and its returning citizens, all three cases are clearly problematic. Indeed, many of the actors involved in these cases, including state agents, actively tried to undermine the return process, particularly efforts to resolve returnees' justice claims. These cases are therefore instructive as much for their failures as for their modest successes. My conclusion that, despite extensive international support, these cases failed to meet the minimum conditions of a just return begs the question of whether these minimum conditions are in fact unrealistically high. I explore this possible criticism in Chapter 7.

Part II begins with an examination of return and redress in Guatemala. This case is the most straightforward of the three in terms of the attribution of responsibility for displacement, as the exodus from Guatemala was caused principally by the Guatemalan state, which continues to exist today. In Chapters 5 and 6 I examine the cases of Bosnia and Mozambique, where the attribution of responsibility for displacement is complicated by factors such as state disintegration, the extensive involvement of non-state actors and extremely limited state capacity. Each case examines four key issues: the historical and socio-economic context; the relevant framework for return and redress, as reflected in peace treaties, tripartite agreements, national laws and political statements; the specific mechanisms used to redress both land claims and other grievances; and the roles of key actors including governments, international organisations and refugee groups. I then proceed to analyse the implications of reparations for the durability of repatriation and the equitable reintegration of returnees into the political community of their state of origin. The experiences of each country raise some unique questions and challenges, which I engage in the conclusion of each case study.

In Chapter 7, I analyse the cases as a group, drawing out their insights in terms of the characteristics of reparations programmes that may help make good on the state of origin's remedial responsibility to enable just return, and the interlinked practical and theoretical difficulties associated with using reparations to help create conditions of just return and uphold state responsibility for displacement. This analysis points to the need to conceptualise the just return process as a long-term endeavour that extends well beyond the initial border crossing. Indeed, although most refugees who returned to Guatemala, Bosnia and Mozambique did so well over a decade ago, reintegration, reconciliation and the reconstitution of the political community represent ongoing if often overlooked challenges in each of these countries.

4 Return and redress in Guatemala

The civil war that prompted a refugee exodus in the 1980s was not an aberration from the historical trajectory of the Guatemalan state, but a direct consequence of the racism and class discrimination that have characterised the country since the Spanish *conquistadores* and their descendents evicted indigenous Maya from their traditional territories and claimed ownership over the vast majority of the country's arable land. Although most Guatemalans are indigenous or Ladino *campesinos* (peasants) who rely on farming to survive, a direct and inverse relationship emerged in the country between the amount of land a proprietor owns, and the amount cultivated (Painter 1996: 149–150).[1] The Guatemalan civil war was triggered by President Jacobo Arbenz's efforts to rectify this inequality by expropriating and redistributing certain categories of uncultivated private lands. Arbenz's reforms threatened the interests of Guatemalan elites and foreign companies including the US-based United Fruit Company. At the urging of United Fruit, in 1954 the CIA orchestrated a coup against Arbenz, replacing him with Carlos Castillo Armas who repealed Arbenz's land reform laws and restored 99.6 per cent of the redistributed lands to private interests or the state. Under Castillo and his successors, Guatemala implemented further counter-reforms that resulted in large-scale evictions of peasants, and the reallocation of land to politicians, military leaders and other elites, consolidating one of the most unequal land distribution patterns in the world (Costello 1995, Naqvi 2004: 76).[2]

Persistent social inequality and heavy-handed military rule prompted the development of several leftist insurgent groups based in the

[1] 60 per cent of Guatemala's population of 12 million are indigenous, while 30–40 per cent are Ladino. Ladinos have mixed indigenous and European backgrounds, but do not identify themselves as indigenous. See Carey (2004: 92) and IDMC (2006). Guatemala is home to a diverse range of indigenous groups, which are collectively known as Maya peoples. However, many indigenous Guatemalans identify more strongly with their particular group than with being Maya.

[2] For a detailed history, see Schlesinger and Kinzer (2005).

country's remote highlands. In 1982, four groups united to form the *Unidad Revolucionaria Nacional Guatemalteca* (URNG), a political and military movement that boasted 6,000–8,000 fighters and 500,000 supporters at the height of its power in the early 1980s (Costello 1995). In response, the military initiated a scorched-earth policy that aimed to 'remove the water from the fish' – in other words, to undercut the rebels' support base by depopulating the highlands (Stepputat 1994: 179). Anyone considered sympathetic, or even potentially sympathetic, to the rebels' cause was a legitimate target; the indigenous *campesinos* presumed to form the backbone of the insurgents' support network bore the brunt of the violence (Worby 2001: 17). Through their conscription into paramilitary civil defence patrols (PACs) 900,000 Guatemalan men and boys participated in the assault on their own communities. Willingly or unwillingly, PAC members committed an estimated 18 per cent of the atrocities during the civil war, which included the killing or disappearance of 200,000 citizens and the destruction of 440 Maya villages (CEH 1999, de Rivero 2001: 8). However, the PACs were subservient to the state, which the country's UN-sponsored truth commission found responsible for 93 per cent of the violence and violations committed during the civil war. The majority of these crimes took place in the early 1980s, during the scorched-earth campaign. Of the victims, 80 per cent were Maya prompting Guatemala's truth commission to declare the state guilty of genocide (CEH 1999: Conclusions, Section I, paras. 2, 15, 25, Section II, paras. 111, 122).

Displacement figured centrally in the genocide, with at least 20 per cent of the population forced from their homes, often under gruelling conditions specifically intended to cause death (Seils 2002: 43, Worby 2001: 17). While 1.5 million were internally displaced, scores of Guatemalans sought asylum throughout North and Central America, including some 800,000 to 1.5 million people who travelled through Mexico to find shelter in the US. Although many of these Guatemalans presumably could have mounted compelling refugee claims, relatively few applied for asylum. Consequently, this population remained largely 'under the radar' of the humanitarian community. Political, humanitarian and scholarly attention focused instead on the 200,000 Guatemalans who took refuge in Mexico. UNHCR recognised more than 45,000 of these Guatemalans as refugees and helped to establish them in camps in the border state of Chiapas (Bradley 2011: 88–89, Cheng and Chudoba 2003: 9–12, Jamal 2000: 5).[3] Conditions in the camps were highly

[3] Relatively little is known about the 155,000 Guatemalan refugees in Mexico who were not registered by UNHCR. They are presumed to have integrated into local communities or moved north to the United States.

insecure: the Mexican government documented more than 60 incursions by the Guatemalan army onto Mexican territory, some of which resulted in the murder of refugees. The refugees were suspected of inciting unrest among the indigenous host population, and in 1984 Mexico forcibly relocated 18,500 refugees to camps in Campeche and Quintana Roo on the Yucatán Peninsula. Some refugees refused to move so far from their homelands, and spontaneously repatriated in spite of extreme risk (Riess 2000: 9, Worby 1999).

The scorched-earth campaign saw the militarisation of both displacement and durable solutions. The army 'recovered' and resettled displaced persons in 'model villages' and 'development poles' where they maintained tight control over social life and development processes. If the displaced were not 'recovered' and resettled in the short term, their lands were redistributed by the army and the National Institute for Agrarian Transformation (INTA) under Decree 1551, which provided that property 'voluntarily' abandoned for more than a year would fall under the ownership of the state (Painter 1996: 150–151, Stepputat 1994: 179, Worby 2001: 17). The resettlement programme aimed to consolidate military control; prevent the return of 'subversives'; improve the army's image; and cover up evidence of massacres and ecological destruction (Costello 1995, Williams 2007: 42). As a carefully crafted policy to divide communities and sever ethnic ties, the resettlement scheme was, in short, genocidal.

Although the military attempted to play an equally domineering role in the repatriation process, the return operation did not simply take place on the army's terms. Rather, major portions of the refugee community mobilised to negotiate a collective, organised return that involved significant reparations and contributed directly to the national peace process. Consequently, many observers have hailed the Guatemalan operation as a 'best-case scenario' (Worby 2001: 17). At first glance, the Guatemalan repatriation also appears to coincide neatly with the theoretical accounts of state responsibility and just return set out in Chapters 1 and 2. The Guatemalan state clearly bore primary responsibility for the refugee crisis; publicly recognised its culpability; and demonstrated accountability by establishing state institutions to facilitate return, negotiating with the refugees, and extending diverse types of redress including apologies, a truth commission, property restitution and compensation. The refugees voluntarily chose to return, and secured internationally backed guarantees for their safety. The refugees' slogan 'Return is struggle, not resignation' reflected their awareness of the risks inherent in repatriation, but also their conviction that engaging in the struggle and attempting to renegotiate their relationship with the state was a powerful expression of their dignity as individuals, indigenous peoples and Guatemalans (Riess 2000).

Upon closer examination, however, the Guatemalan case is at best a qualified success that falls short of the conditions of a just return.[4] Although more than 20,000 refugees chose integration in Mexico over repatriation, the displaced did not have equal access to different durable solutions. While refugees in Campeche and Quintana Roo were offered local integration and land acquisition opportunities, those in Chiapas were pushed to return, despite threats and attacks from the army and secondary occupants opposed to return (Riess 2000: 2, Worby 2001: 23). The relatively progressive conditions for return negotiated by the refugees in Mexico were realised at extraordinarily high financial cost, and directly benefited less than 5 per cent of the total number of those displaced (Cheng and Chudoba 2003: 10, Worby 1999). This discrimination in access to assistance and redress engendered new injustices and exacerbated inequalities between the refugees and those who were not able to seek asylum outside the country. Yet even access to comparatively plentiful aid and reparations did not necessarily translate into a sustainable, just return: within 2 years of the end of the official repatriation process, more than 500 former refugee families returned to Mexico, claiming that they were the victims of 'economic violence'. As a representative of the displaced testified, 'We are not being killed by bullets, we are being starved to death' (Bailliet 2003: 167).

In this chapter I suggest that while the Guatemalan case is clearly not an unblemished success, it offers critical insights into the interplay between repatriation and peace processes, and the role of citizens (displaced and non-displaced alike) in creating just conditions of return and upholding state responsibility for displacement. It also raises a range of compelling questions: how are remedial rights affected when returnees belong to disadvantaged indigenous groups? Can a return be just if the state extends reparations only to certain groups? While the Guatemalan case stands out from other repatriation operations of the time, insofar as it involved a relatively small population with extensive international support and at least partial access to a range of durable solutions, it illuminates common challenges regarding capacity building, popular participation and the difficult compromises of principle required to achieve even a modicum of justice for returnees in practice.

Negotiating return, negotiating peace

In the Guatemalan case, return 'did not wait for peace, it helped forge it' (Jamal 2000: 2). Indeed, 80 per cent of returns took place before the

[4] See Bradley (2011) for a reconsideration of the successfulness of the broader humanitarian operation in Central American in the 1980s and 1990s.

1996 Accord on a Firm and Lasting Peace was signed, ending 36 years of war (Williams 2007: 46). To understand the interlacing of peace and return in Guatemala, these processes must be examined at the local, national, regional and international levels. By 1986, the army recognised the need to revive Guatemala's abysmal international reputation by restoring civilian rule in word if not in deed, and three decades of military rule gave way to a civilian, elected president. Although some hardliners favoured continued efforts to definitively defeat the enervated URNG, factors including donor pressure and the acceleration of regional peace and democratisation processes led the government to agree to pursue a negotiated resolution of the conflict. The 1987 Esquipulas II agreement laid the groundwork for subsequent negotiations between the Guatemalan government and the URNG. Esquipulas II called for parallel peace processes across Central America, and recognised displacement as a critical factor in the region's conflicts. The agreement was augmented by the 1989 Declaration of the International Conference on Central American Refugees (CIREFCA), which recognised, in a limited manner, the need for states to redress returnees by ensuring equitable access to land.[5] Taken in combination, these agreements provided a foothold for negotiations on return and redress in Guatemala.

The collective return movement

While regional negotiations were under way, the new Guatemalan government dispatched delegations to Mexico to 'woo the refugees home', in a bid to restore the state's credibility and attract aid (Costello 1995, Worby 2001: 18). Known as *repatriados*, the refugees who accepted the government's invitation to return were promised property restitution and an amnesty covering their purported support for the insurgents. The repatriation process was facilitated by UNHCR and the Special Commission to Aid Repatriates (CEAR). Established in 1986, the CEAR embodied the Guatemalan state's conflicted attitudes towards the returnees. CEAR representatives provided returnees with medical assistance, basic supplies and identity documents described by officials as a 'moral promise from the army and the government to safeguard the life and goods of these people like any other citizen' (WOLA 1989: 16). The promise was of dubious worth, as the refugees were being returned to an active war zone where, as a CEAR worker commented, 'every day it gets worse, worse, worse. It's part of military tactics, and we don't

[5] Signatories pledged to 'respect . . . access to the means of subsistence and land [for returnees] under the same conditions as other national of their countries'. See the CIREFCA Declaration and Concerted Plan of Action (1989), para. 2(21)(f).

control that' (WOLA 1989: 21). Although some observers applauded CEAR's 'impressive' commitment to the returnees, others argued that the Commission retained close ties to the military and characterised CEAR reception efforts as 'rehabilitation camps' where returnees were 're-educated' before being sent to development poles (Stepputat 1994: 179, WOLA 1989: 17).

Deep scepticism regarding the government's promises prompted the exiles to establish a network of Permanent Commissions of Guatemalan Refugees (CCPP) dedicated to achieving a collective and organised return. Beginning in 1987, elected CCPP representatives worked alongside refugee organisations (*sectores*), including the prominent women's group Mamá Maquín. Although many of the refugee leaders were poorly educated *campesinos* with little political experience, they built on efforts among indigenous communities to fight poverty and racism, inspired in part by the tenets of liberation theology (Konefal 2003, Krznaric 1997: 64–65, Leffert 2001). Participants in the collective return movement were known as *retornados*, and distinguished themselves morally, politically and socially from the *repatriados*. In the movement's terms, a *retornado* was a 'real refugee' who 'perceives exile as transient and therefore does not attach himself too much to life in Mexico' (Stepputat 1994: 181).[6]

Inspired by the Salvadoran repatriation movement, the *retornados* envisaged creating a number of segregated return communities, in which some families would remain, while others eventually moved on to their original lands. Participation in the collective return movement stoked the creation of new political identities among the refugees, as many began to reflect on themselves as Guatemalans, while a concept of their collective identity as indigenous peoples emerged that spanned linguistic and cultural sub-divisions within the population. These new identities were buttressed by the appropriation of a 'new language of rights', which pervaded the agreement on return signed by the CCPP and CEAR on 8 October 1992 (Krznaric 1997: 71). Known as the October Accord, it was the first repatriation agreement negotiated between a government and its exiled citizens, and a critical public recognition by the state (in spite of protests from army hardliners) of the peaceful, civilian character of the refugee population. Although the government considered the agreement to be political rather than legally binding, the accord mandated

[6] A group of 32,000 Guatemalan IDPs known as the *Comunidades de Población en Resistancia* (CPRs) also organised themselves while in hiding and negotiated a collective resettlement involving access to land, education and economic development programmes, and assistance with documentation. See Inter-American Commission on Human Rights (1994).

several measures to backstop the implementation process, including the creation of a Mediation Group and an International Advisory and Support Group for the Return of the Guatemalan Refugees (GRICAR).[7] The October Accord stipulated that the 'return of refugees must be a voluntary decision, individually expressed, undertaken in a collective and organised fashion, under secure conditions and with dignity'. More specifically, it recognised returnees' right to personal and community security; free association and organisation; and freedom of movement. While the CCPP was unable to negotiate limits on the army's presence in return communities, they did secure a guarantee that returnees would be permanently exempt from serving in the PACs (Stepputat 1994: 181).

The most detailed provisions in the October Accord focused on remedial rights and access to land. Most of the refugees were from longstanding highland communities, or from remote lowland regions, settled in the 1960s and 1970s under state and church-run colonisation schemes. While some were landless, many had lived in cooperatives with collective title over private tracts. The refugees' aim of reclaiming their lands was hampered by the fact that in many cases their lands had been resettled for more than a decade. In these cases, the government pledged to negotiate with the *nuevos* (secondary occupants) to vacate the land. In the event of unsuccessful negotiations, the refugees could pursue their claim in court or waive their restitution rights, and the government would provide alternative land (Painter 1996: 154).[8] The agreement also guaranteed that all landless adult returnees could become landowners through a 'revolving credit' scheme under which land purchase loans would be repaid to a community development fund rather than to the state. The refugees celebrated this solution as both a just response to their displacement during the civil war and reparation for the systematic dispossession of the Maya since the colonial era (Leffert 2001, Worby 2001: 20). However, even CCPP supporters 'wondered at the government's apparent demagoguery in promising generous terms that at best would not be replicable to any group in Guatemala other than the refugees and at worst would simply be unworkable because of the resources they would require' (Worby 2001: 19–20).

[7] The Mediation Group was charged with helping to solve problems associated with the collective returns, such as land conflicts, while the GRICAR acted as a witness to mediation efforts, and pressured the Guatemalan government to respond to refugees' concerns (Worby 2001: 19). On the role of international accompaniment in the Guatemalan return, see Levitt (1999).

[8] Problematically, the accord failed to specify secondary occupants' rights, and did not quantify the amount of time and resources the government would devote to securing restitution for returnees.

When the first group of 2,500 returnees re-entered Guatemala in January 1993, they were welcomed by hundreds of activists, diplomats, officials, reporters and fellow *campesinos*. Before returning to the land set aside for them, the returnees undertook a three-week, cross-country caravan designed to raise awareness of their experiences and goals. The 'grand tour' was both a 'symbolic reappropriation of citizenship' and an astute strategy based on the returnees' recognition that their security depended on 'popular support and visibility in (the very limited) public opinion' (Stepputat 1994: 178, Thoresen 1995). In the return community, christened Victoria 20 de Enero (Victory 20 January), the state's ambivalence towards the return was reflected in the army's attempts to intimidate the community, and delays in negotiating restitution and securing alternative land. Coupled with a coup in May 1993, these problems thwarted refugee advocates' prediction that the October Accord would jump-start large-scale returns. When civilian rule was restored and collective returns resumed at the end of 1993, they took place with much less fanfare but in equally insecure circumstances. Attacks against the *retornados* and their supporters included the 'sniper-like' assassination of a returnee girl; the hostage-taking of UN and NGO staff by *nuevos* opposed to collective returns; and the October 1995 massacre by Guatemalan soldiers of 11 returnees in Xaman who were peacefully protesting army presence in their community. Following the Xaman massacre, return rates slowed considerably, with the last collective returnees arriving in April 1999 (Krznaric 1997: 64–65, Roberts 1996: 12, Worby 1999: 13–14).

Although return rates were modest, many officials, scholars and refugees contend that the return made a direct and substantial contribution to peace in Guatemala.[9] Returnees advanced the peace process by bringing issues of violence and repression into the public arena for discussion, while their efforts set the stage for extensive popular participation in the national peace process. Furthermore, the October Accord served as a 'partial blueprint' for the June 1994 Accord on the Resettlement of Populations Uprooted by the Armed Conflict (Resettlement Accord), one of the 13 agreements reached by the government and the URNG to officially end the civil war (Jamal 2000: 5).

[9] See, for example, various contributors in North and Simmons (1999). Much of the literature that portrays the Guatemalan return as a grassroots triumph challenging the nature of the Guatemalan state was written in the mid-to-late 1990s, when optimism about the Guatemalan peace process was running high. More recent analyses are generally more circumspect in their assessment of the case, in light of the failure of the national peace process to substantively transform the Guatemalan state. See, for example, Long (2008) and Bradley (2011).

The Guatemalan peace negotiations aimed to transform the rebels into a legitimate political party, but were also an opportunity for the military to revise and reconsolidate its grip on power.[10] Culminating with the signing of the Accord on a Firm and Lasting Peace on 29 December 1996, the accords resulting from this negotiation process 'extend beyond the realm of traditional ceasefire arrangements', setting out over 300 socio-economic and human rights reforms necessary to resolve the root causes of the war, including racism, landlessness and displacement (Bailliet 2003: 171). Under the Resettlement Accord (1994: Section I, Principles, 1), the government 'undertakes to ensure that conditions exist which permit and guarantee the voluntary return of uprooted persons . . . in conditions of dignity and security'.[11] According to the 1994 agreement (Section I, Principles, 6), the process 'shall not be discriminatory, and shall promote the reconciliation of interests of the resettled population groups and the population groups already living in the resettlement areas.' The agreement specifically connects durable solutions with the need for state reform, underlining that one of the main objectives of return is to 'develop and strengthen the democratisation of State structures, ensuring that the constitutional rights and duties of the uprooted population groups are respected at the community, municipal, departmental, regional and national levels' (Resettlement Accord 1994, Section I, Objectives, 4). In terms of land access and restitution, the Resettlement Accord's provisions benefit the entire uprooted population but are far weaker than the assurances in the October Accord, obliging the government only to 'promote' land access for the displaced (Resettlement Accord 1994, Section II, 9). Returnees' remedial rights were further weakened by the fact that the agreement explicitly makes redress contingent upon international assistance and authorises the prioritisation of resources to support 'macro-economic stabilisation and modernisation of the economy' (Resettlement Accord 1994, Section IV.3, IV.2, Painter 1996: 157). The Resettlement Accord's weakness is attributable in part to the signatories' pragmatic awareness of the difficulty of redressing such a large population, but more so to the state's continued distrust of the displaced and its commitment to privileging the interests of national elites. While the URNG courted displaced communities' support during the conflict, at the peace talks the debilitated force made concessions on

10 The transformation of the URNG into a political party was effected through the 1996 Accord on the Incorporation of the URNG into Society.

11 The Resettlement Accord (1994: Section I, Definitions, 1) defines resettlement as 'the legal process of return of uprooted population groups and individuals to their place of origin or another place of their choice in Guatemalan territory, and their relocation and reintegration therein.'

uprooted persons' rights in order to strengthen its hand on other issues more important to the rebel leadership (Painter 1996: 160).

Realising return and redress

From the outset, return, redress and reintegration were complicated by the polarisation of the collective returnees and those who weathered the war in Guatemala. While many of the 43,600 refugees who returned between 1984 and 1999 had learned to challenge authorities and actively claim their rights, those who stayed in Guatemala endured a process of militarisation intended to decimate their ability to organise politically (de Rivero 2001: 10). The groups also embraced different interpretations of the source of their strife, with returnees typically blaming the military and their former neighbours often pointing the finger at the URNG for abandoning them to the scorched-earth campaign. Return and reparation efforts were also plagued by doubts surrounding the capacity and integrity of the government, while coordination problems were rife among the many international actors eager to support the novel situation of a refugee-negotiated return (de Rivero 2001: 10, Naqvi 2004: 93, Mahony 1999: 34, Taylor 1998: 148).

Donors provided comparatively abundant, if short-lived, financial support for the operation, at the rate of more than $2,000 per returnee (Stepputat 2006: 128). UNHCR invested extensively in the return, providing personal documentation, cash grants, in-kind assistance, mediation services and quick impact projects designed to promote reconciliation in return areas (Worby 1999). Nonetheless, some of these programmes accentuated disparities between returnees and the non-displaced and 'shoehorned' returnees into inflexible assistance packages focused on land acquisition (Jamal 2000: 2). Beyond UNHCR's activities, the return movement was supported by more than 700 NGOs and by the UN Verification Mission in Guatemala (MINUGUA) (Bailliet 2003: 175). In 2001, MINUGUA declared that after the rapid cessation of open hostilities, the peace process had stagnated in its socio-economic aspects, and questioned the utility of its own mandate, admitting that 'it is difficult to verify something which is not happening' (Bailliet 2003: 174).

A partial remedy: Redressing land claims

The resolution of land claims was among the thorniest problems confounding return and the consolidation of peace. Several major obstacles emerged to resolving returnees' restitution and land access claims. Arguably the foremost obstacle to peaceful reintegration in Guatemala, conflicts between returnees and secondary occupants thwarted restitution efforts and resulted in some of the most confrontational episodes of the entire return operation (Painter 1996: 151, 161–166). The cooperative-cum-confrontational dynamics between the *retornados* and *nuevos* are captured in the statement issued by the CCPP leader in Santa María Tzejá to the community's secondary occupants:

> We represent all of the refugees of Santa María, and we are coming back. You who are occupying our lands will have to leave, and you should leave soon. We know that you, like us, are poor *campesinos*, and like us have a right to land in our country. But we have a prior claim to this land . . . We will work with you, if you like, to acquire other lands to which you can move – but you must leave here . . . We left here against our will, running like animals, but we return with pride and determination. (Taylor 1998: 73)

A second major problem was the limited supply of land available to accommodate the landless and those who agreed to make way for other claimants. Third, pervasive government corruption undercut restitution efforts, as funds earmarked for land access programmes were diverted, and INTA 'lost' refugees' land titles (Bailliet 2003: 173, Painter 1996: 164). Fourth, the military mounted formidable opposition to return and redress. For example, when returns began in 1986, the military base in Huehuetenango sent no less than 56 memos to the President declaring its 'total rejection' of repatriation, and suggesting that returnees should be forced onto reservations where the army could 'subject them to psychological operations' (WOLA 1989: 24). Although the army publicly expressed high-level support for return in 1987, in the field it continued to undermine returnees' security and restitution claims. Fifth, local authorities often posed a significant obstacle, as the state's commitments had to be implemented by individuals who had vested interests in preventing return, in order to maintain their favoured positions in local property and political relations (Williams 2007: 43). The effects of local-level obstructionism were compounded by disunity within the national government and the consequent lack of coherent country-wide claims policies and processes. For instance, while the CEAR vocally opposed INTA's application of 'voluntary abandonment' laws, INTA stoked fears of renewed conflict, charging that 'One cannot return the land to the repatriates for it would mean a new human displacement, and the worst, a new war between the repatriates and the newcomers, the latter of which are not going to easily return their parcels of land' (Painter 1996: 162).

These problems were accentuated by a shortage of viable options for resolving land disputes. Recourse to the courts was unrealistic for most returnees, due to lack of education, money and trust in a system known as overburdened, non-responsive and politically biased. The Presidential Office for Legal Assistance and Resolution of Land Conflicts (CONTIERRA) was created in 1997 to offer 'conciliation services' as a low-cost, non-adversarial dispute resolution option. However, many displaced persons were dissatisfied with CONTIERRA due to its lack of independence and enforcement capacity, and its inability to investigate corruption (Bailliet 2000a: 199–200, 2000b: 16–19, 2003: 198). In addition to the courts and CONTIERRA, various traditional dispute resolution mechanisms were applied to adjudicate arguments between indigenous communities. However, their efficacy was limited by their lack of legal standing and resources to investigate land disputes (Bailliet 2000a: 198, 207, Williams 2007: 44). Given the paucity of accessible avenues for resolving claims, UNHCR became heavily involved in mediating disputes. Some UNHCR representatives questioned the wisdom of this engagement, arguing that 'assuming responsibility for a whole spectrum of abuses, including land issues . . . is ineffective and risks bypassing national institutions that should be concerned with them' (Jamal 2000: 2). Despite this scepticism, UNHCR's efforts were undertaken in response to a clear demand from the returnees, and were one of the agency's first forays into active involvement in promoting reparations for the displaced.

Even when dispute resolution mechanisms functioned reasonably well, the fairness of the process was compromised, as displaced persons with similar claims had markedly different rights depending on whether they returned under the October Accord. Yet, neither the strength of returnees' legal claims nor their rights under the different repatriation accords fully explains their success in regaining their lands. *Retornados* who achieved restitution were not necessarily those with the strongest legal claims. Rather, they won their claims by convincing powerful actors such as GRICAR to intervene on their behalf and bringing their cases to national and international attention through tactics such as sit-ins and marches. Some 30 per cent of collective returnees regained their lands in this way, while the rest obtained new lands under government-supported purchase programmes (Worby 2001: 17–20). Non-collective returnees and IDPs rarely mobilised promptly in this manner and, consequently, did not enjoy equal levels of access to restitution and compensation.

To the extent that they were accessible, Guatemala's land purchase programmes enabled displaced persons who were denied restitution to 'finance their own reparation' in accordance with the interests of Guatemala's land-holding elites (Bailliet 2000a: 205). Under these programmes, the government bought land at market rates and allowed returnees to repay the purchase gradually. In one of the most costly land purchase initiatives on record, the government and donors spent $29.7 million on land for collective returnees through the FORELAP and FONATIERRA programmes (Worby 2001: 20). Based on the 'revolving credit' scheme negotiated by the Permanent Commissions, FORELAP was available only to returning refugees. In contrast, FONATIERRA was open to IDPs and poor families, but on much less favourable terms. Both programmes were phased out in 1999 upon the establishment of the peace treaty-mandated land fund FONTIERRAS. Far from a coherent attempt at land reform, the land acquisition programmes avoided the sensitive question of large-scale land redistribution. Whether this represented a strength or weakness is a matter of debate, but the land purchase programmes were undoubtedly compromised by a range of other glaring problems. First, the system allowed landowners to offload unproductive properties at highly inflated prices thus creating financial incentives for the government to crowd returnees onto cheap, isolated land. Repayment schedules were unfeasible given the poor quality of the purchased land, prompting some returnees to abandon the land, thus burdening their remaining neighbours with heavier debts. The programmes struggled to attract support from donors justifiably concerned that they simply lined the pockets of wealthy landowners and even perpetrators of major human rights violations. Indeed, General Fernando Romeo Lucas García, one of the architects of the counter-insurgency, sold three estates to returnees in 1994. As the land purchase programmes proved so expensive, the government was unwilling to provide further assistance, resulting in impoverishment in the villages set up on newly acquired land (de Rivero 2001: 10, Egan 1999: 95, 105, Painter 1996: 154, Refugees International 2007, Worby 2001: 20–23).

Taken in total, these problems virtually paralysed the land purchase programmes: by 2006, it was estimated it would take over 800 years to ensure access to land for all of Guatemala's landless and land-seeking citizens (IDMC 2006). Consequently, many returnees simply became IDPs. Yet as early as 1993, the government began to downplay the number of IDPs in the country in order to evade responsibility for redressing and resolving their displacement. Today, the government and most international agencies no longer consider there to be IDPs in Guatemala.[12] IDPs are categorised as 'poor', rather than displaced persons with specific remedial rights. Despite this manoeuvre, active land disputes in

12 In 2012, the Internal Displacement Monitoring Centre (IDMC) indicated that some Guatemalans remain internally displaced as a result of the civil war but was unable to provide an estimate for the size of the population (IDMC 2012: 16, 59).

Guatemala are on the rise, while tens of thousands of disputes remain latent, destabilising the political landscape and discouraging both foreign and domestic investment (Bailliet 2003: 170, IDMC 2006, Williams 2007: 47).

While land-based approaches to redress are 'critical to the ultimate goal of national reconciliation', they have addressed 'neither the immediate effects of the conflict nor the long-term effects of historical injustice' (Painter 1996: 182, Williams 2007: 41). This is perhaps unsurprising: the deep cleavages between the returnees and their government, and among the returnees themselves, could not be bridged through a myopic focus on the question of land. At the same time, conflict among the *retornados* detracted from their ability to secure their remedial rights, as many returnee settlements became mired in disputes over the control of land and development plans (Krznaric 1997: 62, 75). Female returnees' claims for equal remedial and tenure rights were often stymied as men who had supported refugee women's organisations in Mexico pressured the women to revert to traditional roles once the immediate goal of return had been achieved. While many returnee women were eager to speak out about the denial of equal land rights, many of their groups were muzzled or compelled to disband in the face of pressure from male community members, and the need to focus on the daily struggle for survival (de Rivero 2001: 10, Jamal 2000: 12, Krznaric 1997: 72, Worby 2001: 21–22).

The failure of the 1999 referendum was a clear testament to the persistence of deep social divisions in the country, in spite of costly if not wholehearted efforts to redress the theft of land during the war. The referendum focused on legal reforms that would have given the peace accords precedence over other national laws, including the 1985 Constitution, thus promoting social equality and greater respect for customary indigenous law. Although the proposed reforms and the reasons for their failure were complicated, Ladinos in Guatemala City are credited with successfully rallying the 'no' vote by arguing that giving increased rights to the indigenous population would renew the civil war (Carey 2004: 70).[13] 'Ironically,' as Carey (2004: 84) observes, 'after the military had killed 200,000 Maya . . . Ladinos were still fearful of ethnic violence initiated

[13] National debate on more than 50 proposals for constitutional reform contained in the referendum was dominated by a 'campaign of misinformation' while the government stood at the sidelines (Williams 2007: 44, Carey 2004). While many international observers interpreted the failure of the referendum as the death knell of the peace process, Carey (2004: 90–91) argues that Maya citizens did not necessarily perceive it as a profound setback. Indeed, many Maya voted against the referendum because they opposed the process, or felt that the reforms were not sufficiently ambitious.

by the victims' survivors.' Reconciliation and accountability initiatives undertaken in the aftermath of the referendum have made at best meagre headway in building trust among Guatemala's divided peoples, and between the citizenry and the state.

Pursuing reconciliation and accountability: returnees' roles

Return and reconciliation are explicitly linked in the Guatemalan peace accords, which state that return should 'promote genuine reconciliation, fostering a culture of peace in the resettlement areas and at the national level based on participation, mutual tolerance, reciprocal respect and commonality of interests' (Resettlement Accord 1994, Section I.5, Objectives). Return was taken as a sign of progress in the peace process, while returnees are credited with having advanced reconciliation and accountability by frankly recounting their experiences of militarisation and violence. Indeed, many urban Guatemalans and government officials only learned about the devastating impact of the scorched-earth campaign when the refugees returned and told their stories to the media (Naqvi 2004: 94, Worby 1999: 5). While scholars such as Stepputat justifiably question the tendency to romanticise or overstate returnees' part in reconciliation and reconstruction, the refugees undoubtedly played a considerable role in many of the country's redress processes as both leaders and claimants.[14] Beyond their involvement in land restitution and compensation programmes, returnees contributed to the national truth commission, as well as efforts to raise monuments, locate clandestine cemeteries, and facilitate mass exhumations. In addition, they have helped spearhead the push to prosecute the architects of the scorched-earth campaign and secure financial compensation for grave human rights violations.

Although the government and URNG signed the Accord mandating the Commission for Historical Clarification (*Comisión para el Esclarecimiento Histórico*) (CEH) in June 1994, the Commission was not formally established until 1997. It was given only 1 year to investigate more than three decades of civil war, and was precluded from convening public hearings, issuing subpoenas or naming perpetrators. The Commission built on the work of initiatives such as the Recovery of Historical Memory Project (REMHI), gathering 7,338 testimonies from over 2,000 communities, including 500 collective testimonies (Quinn and Freeman 2003:

[14] For example, Stepputat (2001: 90–91) challenges Egan's assertion that the return communities represent 'positive symbols for other rural Guatemalans' (Egan 1999: 108).

1122).[15] Returnees served as witnesses for the Commission and helped the CEH to gather testimony from other survivors. Although many victims found testifying to be a powerful experience, rural survivors' participation was typically perfunctory and superficial, hindered by their remote location and fear of reprisals. The army's participation was also limited: the army refused to release documents and testify before the Commission in a deliberate strategy to undermine the process (Jamal 2000: 5, Seils 2002: 36, 39–40).

The CEH's final report was released in a packed public ceremony in Guatemala City in February 1999. The report's hard-hitting economic and social analysis and unequivocal condemnation of the violence as a genocide against the Maya people far surpassed the expectations of Guatemalan civil society (Quinn and Freeman 2003: 1122–1123, Seils 2002: 42). Significantly for returnees, the report specifically recognises the suffering and stigma endured by the displaced, as well as the detrimental impact of state discrimination on return and reintegration. The report also documents more than a dozen cases of occupation of refugee lands (CEH 1999, Worby 2001: 19). Although the report contains 84 paragraphs of recommendations, many focusing on the need to provide different forms of redress to the victims, the report has had a negligible impact on Guatemalan public life: 'while activists in the city greeted the report with euphoria, it passed largely unnoticed in the rest of the country', where returnees make their homes (Seils 2002: 36–37).

The official reaction to the report was perhaps the greatest blow to the CEH's efforts to promote national reconciliation: Guatemalan President Arzu refused to accept the report at the release ceremony, but sent a low-ranking cabinet official to represent the state in his place. The 'simple churlishness of his behaviour derailed serious comment on [the report's] findings and set the tone for future discussions. Instead of the [CEH] report being embraced as a building block for the future . . . it was downgraded to the status of a political football' (Seils 2002: 42–43). Four months later, the government declared that the Commission was wrong to conclude that genocide had been committed in Guatemala. Although Arzu's successor accepted the report in full and committed himself to carrying out its recommendations 'as a matter of state responsibility', progress has been notoriously slow, particularly with respect to reparations (Quinn and Freeman 2003: 1123–1124, Seils 2002: 43). Indeed,

[15] REMHI was led by the Archbishop of Guatemala's human rights office and involved over 7,000 interviews with victims of human rights violations, including displaced persons. The REMHI report attributed responsibility to the Guatemalan army for over 90 per cent of the atrocities committed during the war, including 400 massacres. See Martín Beristain (1998: 23–26).

the implementation process had yet to begin when the last refugees returned from Mexico in April 1999. This has made it difficult to assess the effect of inclusion of displacement issues in the CEH on efforts to ensure that repatriation was safe, dignified and just. The government was fairly prompt in addressing CEH recommendations such as issuing a presidential apology and declaring a National Day of Dignity for the Victims of the Violence. However, just as many returnees had to finance their own land-based reparations, they had to fight for critical expressions of state responsibility such as trials and financial compensation.

The CEH report set a clear remedial standard, stating that the government must undertake '[m]easures for the restoration of material possessions so that, as far as possible, the situation existing before the violation be re-established, particularly in the case of land ownership' (CEH 1999: Recommendations, Section III, para. 9a). The report also called for financial compensation for the most serious injuries, as well as psychological rehabilitation; medical, legal and social services; and moral and symbolic reparations (CEH 1999: 6). However, progress on financial compensation was only achieved after President Portillo agreed in 2003 to distribute over $220 million in compensation to former PAC members who were not paid during the war. The decision to indemnify PAC members before redressing the survivors 'violated the victims anew', and generated fresh pressure for action (IDMC 2006, Martín Beristain 2007: 41). After prolonged negotiations, a Reparations Commission and National Reparations Program were created by decree in 2003. However, the reparations fund was seriously underfinanced, and only a modest number of cases have been redressed, typically with very modest awards. In 2006, the National Council of Displaced Guatemalans (CONDEG) indicated that no IDPs have been redressed through the commission, although displacement is recognised as a crime eligible for compensation (IDMC 2006, Martín Beristain 2007: 41).

Beyond individual reparations, the CEH report recommends collective redress initiatives that strive to advance reconciliation and development in communities afflicted by the war. This raises the important question of whether development initiatives may serve as a form of redress. Although development support is clearly critical to the impoverished survivors of the war, the CEH's vision of this process diverges from the basic purpose of reparation. The CEH report states that collective reparations should 'promote reconciliation, so that in addition to addressing reparations [they] . . . favour the entire population, without distinction between victims and perpetrators' (CEH 1999: 6, para. 10). While reincorporating offenders into society may be a critical element of peacebuilding, redress processes must make a legal and moral distinction between abusers and the abused. Reparations should attempt to remedy violations suffered by victims, not reap benefits for the perpetrators. Beyond these legal and moral problems, efforts to provide assistance and redress without 'taking into account the particular experiences, claims, and concerns of the potential beneficiaries resulted in "neglect of the special needs of displaced persons, and an overall lack of justice and restitution for the displacement that they suffered"' (Bradley 2012c, Fitigu 2005: 3).

While restitution and compensation have not been easily won in Guatemala, trials are perhaps the most elusive form of justice for the victims of the war. Amnesty laws including the 1996 Law of National Reconciliation underpin a deep-rooted culture of impunity in Guatemala. In light of this culture, survivors have appealed to courts outside the country to hold individual leaders and the state responsible for egregious violations. For example, Nobel Laureate Rigoberta Menchú and several co-claimants have charged General Ríos Montt with genocide and crimes against humanity in the Spanish courts under universal jurisdiction laws.[16] Several groups have successfully held their state responsible for extreme abuses in front of the Inter-American Court of Human Rights. For instance, in a settlement with 'undeniable collective impact', the court ruled in 2004 that the Guatemalan state was responsible for the Plan de Sánchez massacre and ordered the government to pay generous reparations to the victims (IACHR 2004, Martín Beristain 2007: 40). Trials in Guatemalan courts against individual state agents are also progressing, albeit slowly. The Association for Justice and Reconciliation (AJR), a group of indigenous Guatemalans from 20 communities, has been instrumental in bringing forward cases against Montt and his predecessor, General Fernando Romeo Lucas García, for massacres resulting in 2,300 deaths and the displacement of 50,000 people, many of whom fled to Mexico. The cases have been delayed due to constant changes to the prosecutorial team, and ongoing threats against the forensic anthropologists, witnesses and lawyers involved in the cases, many of whom have themselves been forced into exile (Carey 2004: 75, Martín Beristain 2007: 40, Seils 2002: 51).[17] Furthermore, the cases have struggled because the Guatemalan Public Ministry, which is responsible for the prosecution, is only theoretically autonomous from the Guatemalan state. In practice, the different arms of the state protect each other and the

[16] See Centre for Justice and Accountability, www.cja.org. The Spanish Supreme Court confirmed that the case can be prosecuted under the country's universal jurisdiction laws, but the Guatemalan government refused to extradite Montt.

[17] Personal communication, Jesus Tecu Osorio, survivor of the 1982 Rio Negro massacre, and key witness in court cases against the Guatemalan government and military leaders, Guatemala City, 27 April 2008.

national elite, as reflected by the failure of the Public Ministry lawyers to challenge the arguments mounted by the defence. Groups such as the AJR must therefore rely on the intervention of independent human rights lawyers acting on their behalf rather than the state institutions charged with ensuring accountability for their suffering.[18] In early 2012, a Guatemalan court ruled that the trial against Montt for genocide and crimes against humanity will move forward, generating optimism that after years of exploiting his parliamentary immunity, the General will finally be held responsible for masterminding the atrocities of the civil war.

A model return?

The Guatemalan repatriation clearly falls short of the conditions of a just return set out in Chapter 2, insofar as the process failed to create a legitimate relationship of rights and duties between the state and its returning citizens. Rather than upholding accountability for the crimes at the root of displacement, the state buttressed the privileged position of elite landowners at the expense of returning refugees seeking equal treatment as citizens. As Long (2008: 26) argues, 'the state's interest in repatriation was not the initiation of any programme of political inclusion, but to ensure physical jurisdiction and authority over its returned population.' Yet the collective return was nonetheless a powerful expression of justice for those who were exiled to Mexico. The returnees' mantra 'Struggle to return! Return to struggle!' underlined both their lack of faith in the Guatemalan state, and their conviction that return was nevertheless a right and an opportunity to advance their claims for democracy, equality and accountability (Stepputat 1999: 210, Taylor 1998: 10). Returnees' involvement in ongoing efforts to commemorate and repair unresolved grievances attests to their determination to change the character of their state and the quality of political life in Guatemala.

In spite of its shortcomings, the Guatemalan case holds numerous insights for scholars and practitioners concerned with just return. For example, it demonstrates that despite the risks involved in using return to reinforce faith in a nascent peace process, returnees can serve not only as a symbol of progress but as active leaders in accountability and reconciliation movements. In addition, the Guatemalan experience illuminates the close connection between just return and choice among

[18] Personal communication, J. Soto, Coordinator, Justice and Reconciliation Program, Centre for Human Rights and Legal Action (CALDH) and lawyer for the Association for Justice and Reconciliation (AJR), Guatemala City, 27 April 2008.

durable solutions. Albeit limited, refugees' access to durable solutions other than return enabled them to engage in negotiations with the state from a relatively strong position (Jamal 2000: 2).

Beyond these insights, the case raises various unresolved questions that bear on the account of just return developed in Part I. Perhaps the most pressing relate to the selective nature of access to justice for displaced Guatemalans. The fairness of the return and redress processes was clearly compromised by the fact that the vast majority of displaced persons were purposefully excluded from the relatively generous terms negotiated by the Permanent Commissions. However, even if the government had been willing and able to confront ideological opposition to redressing such a large number of returnees, it would not have had the resources to do so. Given this situation, should the state not have granted such generous terms to the *retornados*? Would it have been better, morally and politically, to privilege equity among victims over the chance to do justice to a few? I would advance the somewhat paradoxical view that given the inevitably unsatisfactory nature of justice in the aftermath of atrocity, the government was right to agree to the *retornados*' demands. Although this decision exacerbated inequalities among the victims, it created a precedent for more generous settlements and demonstrated to other groups how lobbying tactics may be successfully applied to defend rights and obtain redress. (Undoubtedly, 'doing right' was hardly the government's guiding concern; rather, it was concerned to suture the damage the refugees were causing to the state's reputation and ability to maintain aid flows.)

Another set of questions raised by this case pertains to the indigenous identity of many of the Guatemalan refugees. How are claims for return and redress affected when the displaced are indigenous peoples with strong cultural and spiritual ties to their lands? Does indigeneity imply special obligations for the state of origin, such as a stronger duty to privilege returnees' claims for restitution over compensation? How longstanding must indigenous refugees' ties to the land be in order for their claims to be given any added weight? This is an important question in the Guatemalan case, as many Maya were forced from land they had only settled 10 to 20 years previously. Nolin (1997: 1) argues that the Maya had an 'intimate connection' to both their ancestral lands and land on which they laboured, and that this link motivated their efforts to return. In contrast, Stepputat (2006: 123) contends that rather than being an innate response to exile, 'the will to return' was a politically constructed aspiration that 'had as much, or even more, to do with the question of how to provide the political conditions for their livelihood'. In any case, it is entirely possible that indigenous secondary occupants could have developed strong spiritual, cultural and socio-economic ties to the land they toiled in the refugees' absence, thus complicating the role of indigeneity in resolving restitution claims. While the Guatemalan case offers no clear-cut answers to these issues, it illustrates the power of claims to indigeneity in the context of the struggle for return and redress. Indeed, groups such as the Palestinian refugees who have not historically identified themselves as indigenous peoples have attempted to bolster their claims for return and redress by publicly labelling themselves as indigenous peoples, and participating in the relevant international forums (Kymlicka 2007). Although a more detailed examination of how indigenous identity politics shaped the Guatemalan experience is not possible here, such an investigation could help illuminate cases where claims to indigeneity are much murkier, and advance understanding of what the creation of an equitable relationship of rights and duties between the state and its displaced citizens, as called for under the conception of just return developed in Part I, might look like from the perspective of different indigenous communities.

Last, the Guatemalan experience proffers both insights and questions regarding the participation of diverse citizens and state actors in accepting responsibility for displacement, and creating just conditions for return. Refugees' direct participation in negotiating their return has been lauded as the most innovative and successful aspect of this repatriation movement, setting the stage for the inclusion of provisions in documents such as the Pinheiro Principles on the importance of consultation and participation in decision-making on restitution for displaced populations. Yet was there a downside to this approach? Stepputat argues that while the collective return movement's hands-on, participatory strategy was successful in terms of increasing security and challenging the national historical record, it was less practical as an approach to achieving development in the return communities. Similarly, in MINUGUA's assessment, 'the imperative on participation and consensus-building has at times slowed the implementation process, enabling the government and other state institutions to evade their responsibilities and substitute dialogue for action' (MINUGUA 2004).

International actors such as UNHCR and MINUGUA were instrumental in amplifying the refugees' ability to demand action, and enabling the state, however grudgingly, to shoulder some responsibility for its displaced citizens.[19] Yet the Guatemalan state's acceptance of responsibility

[19] The Guatemalan case also raises the question of whether international actors such as the US government and the United Fruit Company may be liable for reparations for their role in instigating the civil war and perpetuating the refugees' displacement (Cheng and

for displacement is by no means straight forward. Clearly the state is not a monolithic rational agent but an institution comprised of multiple actors with conflicting interests. The incoherence of Guatemala's expressions of responsibility for displacement is attributable in part to the fact that the peace process achieved only a partial transition. Although the peace process required the military, landowners and other elites to make some significant concessions, they nonetheless retained their hold on power and thus avoided binding commitments to reparations (Williams 2007: 43). Unlike in other Latin American countries, there is no basic consensus among Guatemalan state actors on the illegitimacy of the war and the need for accountability for the losses that resulted from it.[20] Consequently, reparations initiatives are typically supported only by governmental decrees, rather than by state laws, which means that administrations can easily change the state's policy, undoing the meagre progress made in redressing the displaced. Under these conditions, reparations may in fact hinder progress towards more equitable, rights-respecting national politics: the REMHI report warns against accepting reparations that 'might lead to new forms of social control or to legitimising the state', stressing that 'the value of the support needs to be weighed up both in terms of its practical benefits and in terms of maintaining people's sense of dignity' (Martín Beristain 1998).

How do *citizens* figure in *state* responsibility for displacement? While displaced citizens were key drivers in the push for accountability and state reform, other groups of Guatemalan citizens such as the landowning elite were clearly complicit in the policies that led to the refugees' displacement, and frustrated their efforts to return and reintegrate. For example, the members of the Guatemalan Association of Agriculturalists refused to sell any land to returnees in the south of the country. At the same time, Guatemalan elites refused to pay the taxes required to finance the implementation of the peace accords (Bailliet 2003: 168, Nolin 1997: 6). As the 1994 Resettlement Accord recognises, 'responsibility for solving the problems of resettling the uprooted population falls on the entire Guatemalan society, and not on the Government alone. Broad sectors of Guatemalan society must unite their efforts to ensure its success.'

Chudoba 2003: 8, Taylor 1998: 23). However, this issue is largely outside the scope of this work.

20 Schirmer's work on the Guatemalan military elucidates this state actor's refusal to fully recognise and accept responsibility for the crimes that were committed during the war. Schirmer (1991, 1999) argues that the Guatemalan military sees itself as the protector of democracy and stability in Guatemala: while elected governments change, the military brings continuity to the state apparatus, and co-governs with whatever party is in power. From this standpoint, the army viewed the scorched-earth campaign as a legitimate reaction to a serious threat to the stability of the state.

How can diverse state agents and citizens, from demobilised guerrillas to wealthy agriculturalists, be engaged in the process of acknowledging and attempting to remedy the grievances of the war and the deep cleavages in Guatemalan society? In the absence of a shared interpretation of the wrongs of the past and a unifying vision for the future of the state, popular participation in the ongoing processes of reintegration, reconciliation and redress is likely to be limited to those who felt the brunt of the war. As Seils (2002: 43) laments,

> Far from being at peace, Guatemala lives in a twilight zone between denial and triumphalism. Those who won the war, in general, do not want to acknowledge either its causes, their responsibility for those causes, or the role they played in the atrocities committed during it. Victory is not only victory. It is vindication over those who dared to challenge the order or presented, even momentarily, a real or potential threat.

In short, if just return requires the (re)construction of an equitable, rights-based relationship between the state and its returning citizens, the Guatemalan case must serve less as a beacon of hope and more as a word of warning.

5 Return and redress in Bosnia and Herzegovina

The enormity of the Bosnian conflict is reflected by many Guatemalans' belief that, even after 36 years of war, their situation could be much worse: Guatemala could be another Yugoslavia (Carey 2004: 84). Yugoslavia's implosion was caused by the confluence of complex factors, including an economic downturn and the manipulation of unresolved historical grievances by opportunistic nationalist leaders after the death of Communist leader Josip Tito in 1980.[1] On 25 June 1991, Croatia and Slovenia unilaterally declared independence from Yugoslavia, prompting Belgrade to dispatch the Serb-dominated Yugoslav People's Army (JNA) to restrain the breakaway republics. Bosnia and Herzegovina (hereinafter Bosnia or BiH) followed suit on 3 March 1992 and was internationally recognised as a state on 6 April 1992.[2] While the wars in Slovenia and Croatia were relatively short lived, ethnically mixed Bosnia became the battleground upon which Serbian, Croatian and Bosniak nationalist aspirations were played out most viciously.[3] Although all sides were complicit in atrocities, Serbian and to a lesser extent Croatian forces were responsible for the most egregious violations as they attempted to create ethnically 'pure', contiguous territories that could secede from Bosnia to join Croatia and the Federal Republic of Yugoslavia (Serbia).

Before the signing of the General Framework Agreement for Peace in Bosnia and Herzegovina (Dayton Accord/Agreement) in December 1995, an estimated 100,000 people were killed in the violence. The war also engendered the worst refugee crisis in Europe since World War II;

[1] For a more detailed analysis of the genesis of the wars in the former Yugoslavia, see Malcolm (2002) and Toal and Dahlman (2011).

[2] See Caplan (2005a) for a detailed discussion of the recognition of the new states that emerged from the collapse of the former Yugoslavia.

[3] Reference to ethnicity in Bosnia is both widespread and misleading. The Bosniaks, Croats and Serbs are all Slavic, but practice different religions (Islam, Catholicism and Serbian Orthodox Christianity, respectively). Although the word 'Bosniak' arguably arose as a nationalist term, I use it in its now commonly accepted sense to refer to Bosnian Muslims in general.

over half the population was displaced, as armed attacks, torture and systematic rape were used in the service of ethnic cleansing (Human Rights Watch 2006: 3). While 1 million Bosnians were internally displaced, 1.3 million sought refuge abroad. These expulsions altered the demographic landscape of the entire country: at the end of the conflict, there were no municipalities in which the prewar demographic composition remained unchanged (Heimerl 2005: 377). Nationalistic powers ensured this new demographic pattern could not be easily unravelled: prewar property ownership records were destroyed; laws were passed to legitimise the usurpation of abandoned homes; and one-third of houses were ruined (Williams 2006a: 441, 478).

From this bleak starting point, Bosnia became a landmark case in the development of international norms on repatriation and redress for returnees, prompting former High Representative Paddy Ashdown to declare, 'We've invented a new human right here, the right to return after a war' (ICG 2002: ii). While the right of return long predates the Bosnian repatriation operation, the innovation in this case was the Dayton architects' attempt to use tools such as large-scale property restitution to enable refugees to return not only to the Bosnian state, but to their prewar homes. This proved no easy task, as the Dayton Agreement split the country into two 'entities', the Bosniak-Croat governed Federation of Bosnia and Herzegovina (the Federation) and the Bosnian Serb-controlled Republika Srpska (RS). Of the Bosnian refugees in Europe 70 per cent were from ethnically cleansed areas that were to be governed largely by members of an 'opposing' group, and where they would now find themselves in the minority (Van Metre and Akan 1997: 2). In order to make return a more viable solution, the Dayton Agreement included detailed provisions on refugees' right to reclaim their original homes, counting that robust remedial rights would translate into high rates of 'minority return'.[4] Beyond property restitution, displaced Bosnians' right to redress was also to be upheld through the work of institutions such as the International Criminal Tribunal for the Former Yugoslavia (ICTY). As Toal and Dahlman point out, despite talk of 'turning back

[4] I use the term 'minority return' to refer to displaced persons returning to communities that are governed by a different ethnic group (Harvey 2006: 108). In the Bosnian context, the terms 'return' and 'minority return' have often been conflated, implying that 'return' has only occurred if a displaced person reoccupies her original or reconstructed prewar home. However, many different forms of return have been practiced in Bosnia, including majority return, seasonal return, and temporary return for purposes such as selling assets or burying loved ones (Stefansson 2006, Pollack 2003). I consider all refugees who repatriated from other countries to have 'returned', and use the terms 'domicile return' or 'minority return', as appropriate, to distinguish those who returned specifically to their pre-war homes (Heimerl 2005: 378).

the tide' of ethnic cleansing, 'None of the major powers supporting the international effort in Bosnia ever seriously thought that the demographic legacy of ethnic cleansing could be [fully] reversed.' Rather, the 'debate was whether to accept it as an unassailable reality and fund local integration of the displaced or to set up and fund a return process that would require people to leave their place of displacement and repossess their property to obtain reconstruction aid' (Toal and Dahlman 2011: 7, Phuong 2000a: 5).

Despite extensive and expensive international efforts to ensure restitution, criminal accountability and minority returns, the Bosnian case failed to meet the conditions of a just return discussed in Chapter 2. In 2011, 16 years after the signing of the Dayton Accords, 176,000 Bosnians remained displaced owing to problems including persistent insecurity and impoverishment in return communities (IDMC 2012: 63, UNHCR 2012a). Many minority returnees faced institutionalised discrimination that relegated them to second-class citizenship (IDMC 2007: 5, UNHCR 2007, RSG 2005: 2, ICG 2002: ii). Rather than subject themselves to such conditions, countless would-be minority returnees simply sold their repossessed properties and resettled elsewhere. Indeed, the conclusion reached by most researchers and practitioners concerned with this difficult case is that while the property restitution effort was an unprecedented success, restitution alone is insufficient to enable dignified, durable returns (Black 2002, Englbrecht 2004, Williams 2006a, 2006b). This chapter will examine the factors that led to this conclusion, and left the Bosnian repatriation process so far short of a just return. These factors range from pervasive insecurity, economic stagnation and the intransigence of ultra-nationalist authorities to the disjointed nature of reparation efforts, which were inordinately focused on property restitution and high-level prosecutions, and did not translate into improved relations at the community level. The concluding section will explore the difficulties associated with promoting return as a statebuilding instrument, as well as the complex questions the case raises about assigning and upholding responsibility for forced migration and just return in the context of state disintegration.

Enabling and undermining return: the Dayton peace process

After 'proximity negotiations' shepherded by the US, the EU and Russia, the Dayton Agreement was signed by the presidents of Croatia, Yugoslavia and Bosnia, the three states most intimately involved in fighting the war. While the Dayton Agreement exceeded the scope of most modern treaties in both its complexity and detail, 'none of the warring parties was satisfied with the outcome of the negotiations, much of which had been conducted over their heads and behind their backs' (Caplan 2000: 213). A 'compromise between *Realpolitik* and idealism', the Dayton Accords embodied numerous internal contradictions (Caplan 2000: 214). First and foremost, although the treaty purported to backstop a united, democratic Bosnian state, it also entrenched the partition achieved through ethnic cleansing. The Dayton Agreement retained Bosnia's international boundaries but divided the country into the Republika Srpska with 49 per cent of the territory, and the Federation of Bosnia and Herzegovina with the remaining 51 per cent. The Federation was further subdivided into cantons, effectively separating Bosniaks and Croats. Each entity had its own citizenship, army and responsibility for key political portfolios, leaving the central government with a comparatively superficial mandate.

While the Dayton Agreement formalised Bosnia's nationalistic rifts, it also reflected the international community's desire – arguably little more than 'pure idealism' – to 'undo' ethnic cleansing through minority returns (Toal and Dahlman 2011: 164). Minority returns were seen by proponents as not only a moral imperative, but also an opportunity to moderate ethno-national extremism and resolve tensions within the treaty between principles such as group and individual rights. Beyond these goals, return was critical for reluctant European host states attempting to fend off a perceived 'asylum crisis' (Harvey 2006: 103–4, ICG 2000: 1). Accordingly, Annex 7 of the Dayton Agreement was devoted entirely to the question of refugees and displaced persons.[5] At its heart was the guarantee in Article 1.1 that

> All refugees and displaced persons shall have the right freely to return to their homes of origin. They shall have the right to have restored to them property of which they were deprived . . . and to be compensated for any property which cannot be restored to them. The early return of refugees and displaced persons is an important objective of the settlement of the conflict in Bosnia and Herzegovina. (General Framework Agreement for Peace 1995)

However, the agreement also contained many 'loopholes' and recognised the 'right not to return' to original homes or communities (Toal and Dahlman 2011: 164).

[5] Other annexes address issues such as security and peacekeeping, the new constitution, human rights, and the implementation and monitoring of the agreement. The Dayton Agreement itself was signed by the Republics of Bosnia and Herzegovina, Croatia and Yugoslavia; however, the Republic of Bosnia and Herzegovina, the Federation and the RS are parties to the annexes, stressing the entire state's responsibility to support the Dayton implementation process (Cox 1998: 603).

The Dayton Agreement was not the first time Bosnians had been displaced *en masse*, and called to return to their original homes. Following World War II, Tito ordered an 'eighth offensive' (*osma ofensiva*), under which 'Everyone was to go home. Everyone was to face his or her neighbours... Anyone who dared to utter an unkind word to someone of another nationality would sit for ten days in jail; if the unkind word was about someone's mother, the sentence would be three months' (Sudetic 1998: 36). UN Security Council Resolution 820 of 1993 is one of numerous UN resolutions on the Bosnian conflict that insist that 'all displaced persons be enabled to return in peace to their former homes.' Article 2 of Annex 7 underscored Bosnian authorities' responsibility to ensure this return could take place 'in safety, without risk of harassment, intimidation, persecution, or discrimination, particularly on account of their ethnic origin, religious belief, or political opinion'. Tellingly, the Agreement did not insist that the refugees must be able to return in dignity; this would have been an audacious promise given the looming prospect of 'mandated repatriations' from Europe, despite the persistence of virulent nationalism across Bosnia.

Annex 7 underlined that international actors also had a critical role to play in enabling return and redress. UNHCR was given 'extraordinary power' under Dayton, as it was charged with developing a repatriation plan the Bosnian authorities would be obliged to implement (Cox 1998: 608). In 'one of the most innovative elements of the peace settlement', the Dayton Agreement established the Commission for Displaced Persons and Refugees, later renamed the Commission for Real Property Claims of Displaced Persons and Refugees (CRPC), a temporary, quasi-international body with responsibility for adjudicating restitution and compensation claims, which will be discussed at greater length (Cox and Garlick 2003: 72).

In short, Dayton put return and redress for the displaced at the centre of efforts to build peace in Bosnia and legitimise the compromises the treaty entailed. Yet return and restitution were not discussed in depth at Dayton. Certainly, the parties' positions were clear enough: Izetbegović demanded that the peace process protect the rights of minority returnees, while Tudjman and Milošević actively opposed minority returns of any kind (Harvey 2006: 105, Van Metre and Akan 1997: 3). Refugees' right to compensation was one of the few Annex 7 issues explicitly negotiated at Dayton, as the Serbs insisted that their co-nationals from the Federation had no interest in return and, thus, required compensation. As Cox (1998: 609, 611) argues, Dayton's 'far-reaching provisions on human rights and refugee returns can only be attributed to the creativity and thoroughness of US State Department lawyers, and the substantial indifference of the delegations themselves to much of the text which they signed'.

Implementing Annex 7: an overview

Annex 7 was predicated on the assumption that while the Bosnian authorities were ultimately responsible for implementing the Dayton Agreement, the international community could 'help' by using a 'mix of bribes, threats and other available leverage' to ensure that local officials took these responsibilities seriously (ICG 1999: i). As it soon became abundantly clear that officials on all sides were not going to be forthcoming in implementing the treaty, particularly Annex 7, the international community spearheaded the push for minority returns as well as related activities including peacekeeping, de-mining, police training, judicial reform, and reconstruction and reconciliation projects. From 1995 to 2001, peacebuilding expenditures in Bosnia totalled an estimated $9 billion annually, with the reconstruction expenditure of $1,200 per person representing more than four times the amount spent on the Marshall Plan (Belloni 2001: 165). That only modest achievements were made with such extensive support is attributable in part to waste and corruption, as well as to the fact that many donor states were also host states with 'mandated repatriation' policies that compromised the sustainability of minority returns (Bagshaw 1997, ICG 2000: 17). Indeed, in analysing the implementation of Annex 7, it is essential to bear in mind that while a sense of unity is often attributed to the 'international community' in Bosnia, in practice international actors were (and are) motivated by disparate, and often conflicting interests (Harvey 2006: 98).

The return process unfolded in two distinct phases, the first of which stretched from 1996 to 1997 and saw little direct international intervention in support of minority returns. The highest rates of return were in 1996 with some 240,000 refugees and IDPs returning to areas where they were part of the demographic majority (Heimerl 2005: 379). However, returns in this period did more to 'consolidate the ethnic carve-up of BiH than reverse it', as minority refugees compelled to repatriate typically relocated to majority areas, or simply became IDPs (Bagshaw 1997: 584, Phuong 2000a: 7). The nascent restitution process stalled and initiatives based on positive conditionality, such as UNHCR's Open Cities programme, failed to stimulate high rates of minority returns (ICG 1998).

These failures convinced international actors that more determined support was required, and 1997–2000 consequently saw a major policy shift that brought the power of the High Representative to bear on the question of the return process. The Office of the High Representative (OHR) was established under Dayton to facilitate the parties' efforts to implement the treaty. In light of intransigence on key peacebuilding issues, the 1997 Peace Implementation Council (PIC) authorised the High Representative to use the 'final authority clause' provided for under Annex 10 to fire obstructionist officials and strike down or rewrite legislation that undermined minority return (Caplan 2005b: 465, Heimerl 2005: 381). The PIC also granted the Reconstruction and Return Task Force (RRTF) increased resources and nominated a Deputy High Representative to implement the Comprehensive Strategy for a Just and Efficient Return Process in Bosnia-Herzegovina (OHR 1999).[6] This action plan focused on three factors critical to minority return: space, security and sustainability. While sustainability entailed equitable access to employment and social services, creating space for return necessitated a much stronger focus on restitution (Prettitore 2006: 189). Accordingly, in 2000 the OHR unveiled the Property Law Implementation Plan (PLIP) and replaced positive conditionality with the principle that 'the same pressures, demands and expectations must be applied to all officials and municipalities' (Belloni 2005: 442). Owing to these strategic changes; the growing impatience of displaced populations to access a durable solution; and regime changes in neighbouring states, a breakthrough of sorts was achieved in minority returns from 2000 to 2003. In service of this breakthrough, UNHCR channelled virtually all its operational budget towards minority returns. However, the entities and cantons devoted only a tiny proportion of their budgets to this issue, and significant funding gaps emerged related to return (ICG 2000: 17, 2002: 2, Heimerl 2005: 378–382, 388).[7]

The long-term results of this change in tack are unclear. In September 2004, UNHCR announced that over 1 million refugees and IDPs, or almost 50 per cent of all those displaced, had returned to their prewar homes; just under half this number were reported to be minority returns (Heimerl 2005: 383–384).[8] Heimerl (2005: 384) calls this a 'relatively high proportion', while Williams (2006a: 456) says these rates

[6] From 1997 to 2003, the RRTF served as a forum for managing and coordinating the return process. The Task Force was made up of representatives from human rights, humanitarian and development agencies.

[7] Donors' prioritisation of repatriating refugees' needs also generated resentment among IDPs and the non-displaced (Hovey 2000: 10–11, Black 2002: 133–136, Philpott 2005: 11).

[8] Minority return rates were difficult to track, in part because many minority returnees did not register with local authorities out of fear, or in order to retain access to benefits elsewhere (ICG 2002: 4).

'exceeded all early expectations'.[9] However, minority return rates plummeted after 2003, and no reliable longitudinal data are available on how many minority returnees actually stayed, with anecdotal evidence suggesting that many returnees sold up and moved on after reclaiming their original homes.[10] Particularly in the RS, most minority returnees were elderly people who established isolated enclaves in decimated, abandoned villages (Cousens and Harland 2006: 109, Heimerl 2005: 384–386, ICG 2000: 3). Many who returned to larger centres were effectively 'incarcerated at home', and avoided interaction with the state structure and the dominant ethnic group by forming parallel returnee institutions and separate economic networks (Harvey 2006: 97, ICG 2002: 16, Stefansson 2006: 123).[11]

The low quality of this purportedly durable solution is due in large part to concerted and persistent opposition from nationalist authorities. The presence of war criminals, often in positions of authority, also discouraged return – especially minority return – and undermined its sustainability. Many returnees suffered shootings, beatings, police intimidation, rape, the destruction of homes and the desecration of holy sites. Particularly in the eastern RS, many officials refused to treat violence against returnees

9 Strictly speaking, this is inaccurate. UNHCR optimistically planned for 870,000 returns in 1996 alone, but drastically revised its expectations (Van Metre and Akan 1997: 2).

10 In their important 2011 study *Bosnia Remade*, Toal and Dahlman (2011: 296–299) point out that minority returns have touched almost all regions of the country, and while concurring that statistics on property restitution cannot serve as a proxy for sustained minority returns, they critique the data presented by NGOs such as the Helsinki Committee for Human Rights in Bosnia and Herzegovina that suggest that the implementation of Annex 7 has been an almost unmitigated failure. Pointing to the results of a nationally representative survey conducted on the tenth anniversary of the Dayton Accords, Toal and Dahlman (2011: 300–301) argue that the 'majority of displaced persons, when they reclaimed their property, returned to live in the property (or, at least at the time of the survey this is what they indicated)'. Returning to live in one's original place of residence was the option exercised by almost 75 per cent of displaced respondents in the Federation and just under 50 per cent of displaced survey participants in the RS. Importantly however, this survey did not disaggregate between minority and majority returnees, or provide insight into long-term durable solutions strategies. Reflecting on the success of efforts to implement Annex 7, Toal and Dahlman (2011: 9, 304) contend that 'While the demographic legacy of ethnic cleansing has not been reversed, the "unmixing" of Bosnians into hard-bordered ethnoterritories has not been realised either (though some claim it has) . . . Given the thousands of Bosnians who have been able . . . to repossess their property and return to sell, rent or reinhabit, it is much too glib to describe the annex as a failure . . . Where international officials claim success, with some justification, is in establishing a transparent legal process that created the right of Bosnian citizens to repossess their prewar property and the right to return to live in it if they so chose.' For a more detailed discussion of statistics on minority return, see Tuathail and O'Loughlin (2009).

11 See Jansen (2007) for a discussion of the political economy of return and the feasibility of different forms of return.

as a crime. Although the security situation has improved significantly since the 1990s, violence against returnees was long sanctioned (tacitly or explicitly) by officials such as the RS interior minister who responded to aggression against Bosniak returnees by saying that the perpetrators were just 'having fun' (Amnesty International 2007, Englbrecht 2004: 104–106, Heimerl 2005: 385, ICG 2002: 18–19).

Yet resistance to return was not only physically violent but also bureaucratic and socio-economic. Initially, the Bosnian constitution itself served as a major impediment to return by granting Serbs 'pre-eminent' status in the RS, while Bosniaks and Croats comprised the 'peoples of the state' in the Federation (ICG 2002: 33). Political representation in bodies such as the House of Peoples was reserved for the dominant post-Dayton group, irrespective of pre-war demographics or the presence of minority returnees. In 2000, the Bosnian Constitutional Court struck down these provisions as contrary to the state's obligation to create the 'economic, social and political conditions conducive to return', as per Annex 7. Constitutional amendments imposed in 2002 affirm that Bosnians must enjoy equal status throughout the state, and mandate hiring and political representation quotas for each group. The Court's stipulation that these quotas must stand until Annex 7 is 'fully implemented' sparked a firestorm over how this would be defined (Belloni 2001: 164, ICG 2002: 33, OHR 2002, Williams 2006a: 466). In the absence of a definitive conclusion to this debate, systematic opposition to return continues to be manifested in judicial bias; educational segregation; and discriminatory access to assistance, social services and employment. The latter poses an acute threat to return: while Bosnia's official unemployment rate is 40 per cent, in recent years permanent employment rates among minority returnees have been as low as 3 per cent (Amnesty International 2008, Philpott 2005: 17, RSG 2005: 2, Toal and Dahlman 2011: 303, Williams 2007: 39).

Despite many state officials' complicity in perpetuating these obstacles, on 1 January 2004, the RRTF closed its doors, and Bosnian authorities assumed full responsibility for implementing Annex 7 (OHR 2003, 2004). In late 2004, several international organisations and the governments of Bosnia, Croatia and Serbia launched an initiative to end displacement in the Balkans by 2006. This timeline had to be extended, however, since 2007 saw 180,000 IDPs remaining within Bosnia, while almost 200,000 Bosnian refugees were still in exile (IDMC 2007: 5, 54, UNHCR 2007). A renewed strategy for resolving the vestiges of the displacement crisis was mapped out in 2007–2008, was finally adopted by Bosnian authorities at different levels in 2010, but remained unimplemented in 2011. By this time, the numbers of those still displaced stood at 113,000 IDPs and 63,000 refugees (IDMC 2012: 9, 66, Toal and Dahlman 2011: 298, UNHCR 2012b). In the following sections, I will discuss the remedial initiatives that helped achieve this mixed record of success and the role redress may yet play in resolving Bosnian refugees' now protracted displacement.

Redressing ethnic cleansing: diverse attempts, limited success

Justice is a moving target in post-war Bosnia. Reparations efforts in Bosnia rested on the assumption that trials and property restitution were critical preconditions for peace and sustainable returns. However, transitional justice advocates were compelled to scale back their lofty expectations of institutions such as the ICTY and CRPC when confronted with the formidable obstacles to reconciliation, accountability and return in Bosnia. For their part, Bosnian survivors embraced diverse interpretations of the meaning of justice, but almost unanimously low expectations of any redress that could be meted out by the international actors and divided state that failed so abysmally to protect them in the first place (Weinstein and Stover 2004: 4).

Returning property, resettling people

Under the Dayton Agreement, the CRPC was charged with collecting and adjudicating displaced persons' applications for restitution under a mass claims system but got off to a slow start owing to problems from lack of electricity to entrenched ideological opposition (Phuong 2000a: 5). According to Garlick (2000: 66), the Commission faced three major obstacles: First, the massive scale of displacement slowed the process enormously. Second, the socialist system left behind arcane property laws that were extremely difficult to navigate and had to be overhauled in tandem with the restitution process.[12] Third, the property issue was highly charged on several key levels. On the personal level, the loss of home was a traumatic experience that generated psychological and physical insecurity. On the economic level, land was one of the most valuable assets available in the tumultuous post-conflict context and was thus

[12] For example, Williams (2006a: 478–483) discusses the complex legal issues surrounding the restitution and subsequent privatisation of socially owned apartments. Some observers have suggested that laying the groundwork for Bosnia's neo-liberal economic transformation was a critical if often unacknowledged goal of the restitution process (Garlick 2000: 67). For a detailed discussion of the post-conflict restitution process in Bosnia, see Buyse (2009).

hotly contested. On the political level, property restitution was initially extremely contentious, as it undermined the ethno-nationalistic rationale for the war. The CRPC's ability to contend with these challenges was limited by its own structural weaknesses. For example, the CRPC had no appeals mechanism, which put Bosnia in contravention of the European Human Rights Convention and limited the Commission's ability to respond effectively to particularly complicated cases (Davies 2004: 12). While international involvement in the CRPC may have helped legitimise its decisions in the eyes of local people, the Commission alienated domestic institutions, which was untenable as the CRPC lacked the ability to enforce its own decisions (Cox and Garlick 2003: 74, Smit 2004).

Taken in total, Philpott (2005: 5) argues, these problems reduced the CRPC to little more than a 'useful repository of claims'. Indeed, when the OHR's revamped Property Law Implementation Plan (PLIP) commenced in October 2000, only 15 per cent of restitution claims had been resolved, let alone enforced (Prettitore 2006: 195).[13] PLIP was based on new property laws approved under pressure from the OHR and emphasised technical adherence to the law and cooperation between international and local officials, thereby increasing Bosnia's responsibility for a key remedial process. Under PLIP, the entities adjudicated and implemented claims independently of the CRPC resulting in extensive duplication of efforts but greater 'local ownership' over the process. International representatives monitored domestic adjudications; supported efforts to resolve backlogged cases; and coordinated restitution-related activities, while the International Police Task Force supervised evictions by Bosnian police. Other than in cases involving individuals occupying multiple homes, claims were processed in strict chronological order of submission, with a view to ensuring transparency, impartiality and efficiency (Philpott 2005: 6, Prettitore 2006: 193, Von Carlowitz 2005: 550). Restitution under PLIP was indeed remarkably efficient: while the process would have taken 40 years at pre-PLIP rates, 92 per cent of the 215,000 claims received were decided and enforced in favour of the claimant by December 2003 (Prettitore 2006: 190, Williams 2006a: 443). Although progress was initially stronger in the Federation, parity between the entities was achieved by the end of 2003.

[13] See Hastings (2001) and Van Houtte (1999) for a more detailed discussion of early restitution efforts. Philpott (2005: 9) points out that as many 'PLIP strategies' were already under way before the scheme was announced, the programme's main value was as a public relations exercise that revived donor interest by regularising ad hoc strategies and collecting and publicising useful statistics under a 'catchy new acronym'.

For many returnees, decisions on their property claims 'carried important symbolic and psychological as well as legal value', as other domestic remedies were denied to them (Garlick 2000: 75). Seeing their complaints taken seriously also boosted confidence among returnees in national institutions (Bagshaw 2000: 222). Yet why did formerly obstructive authorities cooperate with the restitution process? For its part, the ruling Bosniak Party of Democratic Action (SDA) was a long-time advocate of Bosniak minority returns as a means to preserve the unity of the state. Although not as keen a supporter of Serb returns to predominantly Bosniak cantons, the SDA recognised the need for reciprocity, and thus ensured cooperation with restitution efforts (Harvey 2006: 97–98, Ito 2001). The Serbian Democratic Party (SDS) and Croatian Democratic Union of BiH (HDZ BiH) were opposed to minority returns, but agreed under pressure from their own constituents to support restitution because selling repossessed property proved essential to financing resettlement in majority areas (Cox and Garlick 2003: 77). Furthermore, local governments facilitated restitution because they were also 'left free to pursue other policies that discourage real return' (ICG 2002: 10–11). Many of these policies took the form of resettlement incentives for majority-group members, such as the distribution of building plots, business premises and construction materials (Heimerl 2005: 379, ICG 2002: 11–13). The SDS also took the more strident steps of declaring Serb returns to the Federation a form of treason; intimidating pro-return organisations; and encouraging the establishment of pro-resettlement groups such as *Ostanak* ('Remain' or 'Stay Put'). 'Anti-return' policies directed at minorities included the obstacles discussed in the previous section, as well as pre-emptively privatising and reallocating contested socially owned land, and concertedly focusing on restoring homes in urban areas rather than in the countryside, where return could be more easily sustained through subsistence agriculture (Harvey 2006: 96, ICG 2002: 3, 6–12, Toal and Dahlman 2011: 247–249).[14]

Given the strength of these barriers, nationalist authorities could be confident that while displaced Bosnians saw restitution as 'important for reasons of morality, justice and economic rehabilitation', they were unlikely to opt in favour of minority return, particularly as many had put down roots elsewhere during the time it took for the restitution process to start moving (Stefansson 2006: 117, 120). The growing rift between the restitution and minority return processes was evident as early as 2000,

[14] Nonetheless, rural returns were undesirable for many urbanised refugees, one of whom asked, 'Why do I want to return to a place where in order to get milk I have to milk a cow that I no longer have?' (Hovey 2000: 10).

when the PLIP Framework Document defined restitution as a means of realising minority returns, but went on to provide a 'comprehensive and explicit assertion of property restitution as', first and foremost, 'a rule of law exercise' (OHR 2000a, Williams 2006a: 526). According to Williams (2007: 39), this reflected a 'fundamental shift in the international community's perception of the justification for restitution, from promoting [minority] return *per se* to supporting durable solutions' and entrenching the rule of law, especially property rights. (Importantly, for Bosnian refugees, these solutions often still involved repatriation, as local integration and resettlement opportunities in third countries were limited.) However, the international community was not unanimous in its support for this shift. For example, UNHCR objected to disconnecting restitution from efforts to realise minority return, which was itself a legal right in Bosnia, and expressed concern that the reformed restitution process did not adequately protect repatriating refugees from internal displacement (Philpott 2005: 15).

Although the restitution process is typically hailed as a remarkable success in an otherwise beleaguered peace process, it struggled with several serious shortcomings beyond the concerns raised by UNHCR. First, both the minority return and restitution processes became a 'numbers game' that paid little regard to the actual consequences for the 'beneficiaries' (Ito 2000: 121, Von Carlowitz 2005: 554). Second, neither the international community nor Bosnian officials made adequate provisions for secondary occupants evicted to uphold restitution rights (Philpott 2005: 20). Third, the restitution process arguably missed valuable opportunities to promote dialogue and reconciliation among the parties. While the restitution process dissuaded victims from violently repossessing their properties or carrying grievances about stolen property forward to future generations, neither the PLIP nor the CRPC created a foundation for direct, peaceful negotiations between returnees and other members of the community. Rather, claims were adjudicated behind closed doors, without individual testimony. Secondary occupants did not have to acknowledge the legitimacy of the original owners' claims, but were simply forced to make way. While more conciliatory options may have been impracticable given the scale of displacement and the depth of antagonism in Bosnia, the restitution process should not be misconstrued as a major victory for reconciliation (Smit 2004). A fourth, formidable shortcoming is that restitution often 'meshed poorly with the economic and social needs of Bosnian society' (Heimerl 2005: 377).[15] The restitution process

[15] Researchers disagree about the relative significance of different barriers to return in Bosnia. In 2002, for example, the ICG (2002: 15) reported that 'economic stagnation

focused on domestic residences and did not allow refugees to repossess businesses and agricultural lands. CRPC data indicates that only 450 of 2,489 claims for the restitution of business premises were resolved. Over 80,000 claims were submitted to the Commission for the repossession of non-residential land. However, the international community did not require municipalities to submit statistics on the resolution of these claims. In the absence of concerted international pressure to restore this land to its owners, it can be assumed that progress on this front was extremely weak, with the upshot that while returnees were guaranteed a place to live, many lacked the means to survive (ICG 2002: 2–3).

Perhaps the most significant shortcoming of the restitution process was its failure to maximise the choices available to refugees regarding the resolution of their displacement. In particular, the unavailability of compensation contributed to the foreclosure of choices for the displaced. Contrary to the promises made at Dayton, compensation mechanisms failed to materialise because they were costly, prone to corruption, and could arguably be seen as legitimising ethnic cleansing (Garlick 2000: 79).[16] Some observers have dismissed the problematic nature of this restriction on refugees' remedial rights, suggesting that the sale of repossessed properties functioned as a form of compensation (Philpott 2005: 21, Prettitore 2006: 197). However, displaced Bosnians' ability to obtain 'compensation' by selling their homes was limited by the OHR's imposition of a 2-year moratorium on the privatisation and sale of repossessed socially owned apartments in the Federation.[17] Furthermore, although Philpott (2005: 21) approvingly asserts that in Bosnia 'the market is the mechanism for delivering compensation', it is unclear that leaving 'compensation' up to the vagaries of the market was in fact effective or fair. Many refugees may have been unable to travel back to sell their properties, while those with destroyed homes are unlikely to have received a fair price. Indeed, it is misleading to suggest that the proceeds from property sales were sufficient to make even majority return a dignified and sustainable choice. Many returnees who resettled alongside their majority group lacked basic support, as their preferences diverged from those of

was *the* single greatest obstacle to return'. In contrast, Black's (2002: 133) research from the same period indicates that concerns about security and harassment predominated and that extensive spending on reconstruction and employment generation programmes was perhaps misled. See also Simpson (1997: 478).

16 Interview with Scott Leckie, former Executive Director of the Centre on Housing Rights and Evictions, 27 November 2007.

17 The moratorium was intended to encourage (or compel) higher rates of minority return. In practice, however, the ban pressured those unwilling to return to forgo their property rights. When the ban was rescinded in July 2001, restitution applications skyrocketed (Heimerl 2005: 386, Williams 2004: 15).

the international community, and nationalist leaders abandoned them once their aim of ethnic homogenisation was secured (Stefansson 2006: 130).

Reflecting on the successes and shortcomings of the Bosnian property restitution process, scholars and practitioners almost unanimously conclude that 'property rights, particularly related to return, should be addressed early, systematically, and from a rule of law perspective' (Black, Eastmond and Gent 2006: 12). This observation is often accompanied by the assertion that while attempts to use restitution to enable minority return were 'hopelessly politicised', the rule of law approach was successful because it 'depoliticised' the issue (ICG 2000: 6, Philpott 2005: 2, 17, Williams 2006b: 41). Indeed, according to the Federation's Ministry for Refugees and Displaced Persons, return is 'no longer considered a political issue but rather a technical matter' (RSG 2005: 9). Such assertions distort the inherently political nature of reparations, and gloss over nationalists' deeply political reasons for acquiescing to the restitution process. While the Bosnian experience certainly confirmed that the 'rule of law' approach is an effective framework within which to promote refugees' remedial rights, facilitating return and redress in this manner is still politicised. The critical point is that the law is marshalled as a tool to manage politics. The OHR's (2000b) 'Non-negotiable Principles in the Context of the Property Law Implementation', which served as the touchstone for restitution under the rule of law approach, illustrates the impossibility of depoliticising return and redress. Rather than employing the cool-headed legal rhetoric one might associate with a rule-of-law approach, the 'Non-Negotiable Principles' are expressed in a bizarre style that reveals restitution advocates' desperation for a political victory on this file. The document ominously states that the 'time for implementation of the property laws has nearly passed . . . Unless great achievements are made from April to October 2000 we will all have to reconsider our presence in this country', and exhorts that 'All decisions, in general, need to be issued in chronological order. NOW' (OHR 2000b, capitals in original).

As Philpott (2005: 20) recognises, the restitution process 'had been all things to all agencies. It was "return" to the Annex 7 agencies and "rights" and "the rule of law" to those of Annex VI'.[18] However, the restitution process was far from being all things to all those it was intended to benefit. Restitution was not enough to make minority returns a plausible choice for many refugees, nor did the sale of repossessed property necessarily provide adequate support for repatriating refugees who

[18] Annex 6 agencies were charged with supporting human rights and the rule of law.

wanted to build a new life elsewhere in Bosnia. In the following section, I will discuss how broader reparations efforts figured in the effort to make return a safe and sustainable, if not entirely just option for Bosnian refugees.

On trials: implications of tribunals and other reparations for return

Beyond a place to live, dignified, durable and ultimately just repatriation processes depend on respectful relations between returnees, their neighbours and the state, from the central government to the municipal level. This in turn depends on how history is interpreted, and grievances resolved. Various initiatives have attempted to acknowledge and redress Bosnia's troubled historical record, including international trials, domestic prosecutions, truth-telling processes, official apologies and community coexistence projects. However, many of these remedial efforts have been undertaken in isolation from one another, and have failed to engage ordinary Bosnians. While some constituent parts of the Bosnian state are increasingly active in advancing reparations, most remedial initiatives have focused on individualising responsibility for atrocities, sidestepping complex questions of shared and institutional responsibility for the injustices of the war.

Redress is pursued within the broader context of efforts to ensure respect for human rights in Bosnia. On paper, the provisions to support this endeavour are strong: in terms of human rights, Bosnia's constitution is one of the most progressive in the world. Human rights are mentioned no less than 70 times in the Dayton Accords, which created several human rights protection mechanisms, including the Commission on Human Rights and the Office of the Ombudsman and Human Rights Chamber (Bagshaw 1997: 576–578, Cox 1998: 605, Englbrecht 2003). Nonetheless, in 1997 Bagshaw (1997: 577) lamented that efforts to establish just conditions of return in terms of human rights had failed, 'unless one equates effective respect for and protection of human rights with the absence of gross and systematic violations'. Conditions have improved significantly since 1997, but efforts to ensure accountability for the crimes that forced Bosnians from their homes have floundered. Trials remain the predominant approach to redress in Bosnia, although many scholars contend that judicial remedies 'contribute far less to the social reconstruction of post-conflict societies than was previously assumed' (Stover and Weinstein 2004: 20).

Established by the Security Council in the heat of the Bosnian war, the ICTY has attracted the lion's share of attention from international actors concerned with justice and accountability in Bosnia. Grounded in the view that 'peace and justice are, if not indivisible, at least close associates', the court was ostensibly intended to deter flagrant violations of international law during the war, although it is commonly recognised that the tribunal was above all a face-saving mechanism established to compensate for UN Member States' lack of effective military and political intervention (Shawcross 2000: 187). The Dayton Agreement obliges Bosnian institutions to cooperate with the ICTY, which attempts to uphold individual responsibility under international law for war crimes, genocide and crimes against humanity. The Hague-based tribunal's focus on individual responsibility comes at a high cost in the aftermath of war crimes systematically committed by thousands of perpetrators: the prosecution of cases is inevitably selective, and the court's impact has been sharply curtailed by the death of its most prominent defendant, Slobodan Milošević, and the long delays in bringing Bosnian Serb leaders Radovan Karadžić and Ratko Mladić to trial. Some contend that overall the trial has made a significant if underappreciated contribution to peacebuilding and democracy in Bosnia (Nettelfield 2010). Arguably, the court not only individualised responsibility for the atrocities but has also stigmatised the nationalists' regime by revealing the 'political and organised character of the crimes committed' (Humphrey 2003: 496–500). However, others question whether, by individualising guilt, the court may 'contribute to a myth of collective innocence' (Fletcher and Weinstein 2002: 580). This concern is apt: the ICTY's inability to instil a strong sense of shared responsibility and atonement has been evident in nationalist authorities' refusal to cooperate in apprehending perpetrators and providing evidence until the 'carrot' of EU membership is dangled before them; even then, cooperation has not been assured (Ellis and Hutton 2002: 352–352).

The ICTY's 'mission of reconciliation' in Bosnia has been hindered by lack of trust; poor public relations; the inaccessibility of the court; and its lacklustre prosecution record: by 2005, the ICTY had rendered judgements on only 51 war criminals, while literally thousands remained at large (Biro et al. 2004: 193, Fletcher and Weinstein 2004: 30–33, Jorda 2001, Meernik 2005: 272–274).[19] Although many defendants erode the tribunal's reconciliatory potential by using the courtroom as a soapbox for nationalistic grandstanding, some such as former RS President Biljana Plavšić have arguably contributed to reconciliation by pleading guilty and

[19] Public opinion research indicates that although the ICTY was the most trusted international institution working in Bosnia as of 2005, within the RS only 4 per cent of the population trusts the court. Croats and Serbs commonly believe the ICTY is biased against their group (Meernik 2005: 271–274, Biro et al. 2004: 193).

expressing remorse for their crimes.[20] However, such confessions seem to have had little impact on Bosnians' daily lives, and the court lacks the mandate to provide compensation, a form of redress that might foster a stronger sense of reconciliation and justice by directly improving victims' socio-economic circumstances (Ellis and Hutton 2002: 351).[21]

Nevertheless, the ICTY has served as a valuable form of redress for many displaced persons and has made significant contributions to enabling refugees to exercise their right to return. Displacement is a clear part of many ICTY indictments, and several ICTY cases have clarified and strengthened international legal norms on forced displacement as a crime against humanity (Andreu-Guzmán 2012). Many former refugees have derived personal satisfaction from carrying out their perceived 'moral duty' to testify before the court (Stover 2004: 106–108). However, establishing a detailed historical record about the events that forced refugees and IDPs from their homes and removing several odious war criminals whose presence deterred repatriation are arguably the foremost contributions the ICTY has made to enabling return in Bosnia (Nalepa 2012).[22] Indeed, a 2004 survey of Bosnian civil society leaders indicated strong support (74 per cent) for the view that ICTY prosecutions 'facilitated the return of refugees' (Nettelfield 2010: 168). The Tribunal's positive effect on return was particularly evident in cities such as Prijedor, where returns increased after a comparatively large number of offenders were arrested promptly under high-profile ICTY indictments. Similarly, four ICTY trials involving over a dozen Croats who spearheaded the 1993 assault on Ahmici played an important role in enabling Bosniaks to return. However, in the short term at least there is 'no indication that these trials have in any way transformed the way in which Croats in the village interpret what happened' (Stover 2004: 116–117). Indeed, when the refugees returned, they found a massive neon cross memorialising the Croats, but not the Muslims, who died there.

20 Plavšić voluntarily surrendered to ICTY in 2001 and arranged a plea bargain under which she acknowledged and apologised for her role in crimes including forced displacement. In exchange, Plavšić was convicted of only one count of crimes against humanity; seven other charges were dropped, including two counts of genocide. However, she retracted her confession in a 2005 interview (BBC News 2003b, B92 2005).

21 See Drumbl (2007) for a detailed critique of the approach to punishment adopted by international courts including the ICTY.

22 Nalepa (2012), for example, maintains that removing prominent perpetrators had a significant effect in enabling return to communities such as Prijedor and Srebrenica. However, on the basis of a micro-level, time-series cross-sectional analysis of all municipalities in BiH, she contends that the ICTY's practice of plea-bargaining, which compelled perpetrators to admit the truth of their role in the atrocities of ethnic cleansing, actually had a more significant effect on minority return rates.

According to ICTY officials, 15,000 to 25,000 individuals were indictable for war crimes in the former Yugoslavia (ICG 2002: 19). With the ICTY slated to complete all trials by mid-2011 and appeals by 2013 (with the exception of Radovan Karadžić, Ratko Mladić and Goran Hadžić), offenders must be prosecuted in domestic courts if trials are to continue supporting the ongoing return and reintegration process. Currently, Bosnian courts prosecute dockets transferred from the ICTY, as well as all cases initiated after October 2004. Established in March 2005, the Special War Crimes Chamber of BiH tries the most serious cases not handled by the ICTY, while others are referred for prosecution in the entities. The first decade post-Dayton saw 'effective impunity' for war crimes in the RS: only two war crimes trials were completed in the RS by 2005, while more than 50 were completed in the Federation, 12 of which involved majority-group perpetrators. However, significant progress has been made in the RS since late 2005, despite limited resources, inadequate police assistance, witness intimidation and the 'non-availability' of suspects (Human Rights Watch 2006: 1–2, 2007: 2). Indeed, the increasingly concerted effort to prosecute war crimes within BiH is arguably the clearest example of the Bosnian state taking responsibility (at both the central government and entity levels) for redressing the violations committed during the war. In contrast to the far-removed ICTY, domestic trials may be better placed to enable further return and reintegration by removing a significant number of perpetrators and promoting recognition of the parties' complicity in atrocities.

A third major effort to use courts to redress the injustices of the war played out at the International Court of Justice (ICJ) which, unlike the ICTY and domestic courts, hears charges against states. In a bid to pressure Belgrade to halt the killing and expulsion of Bosnian Muslims, Bosnia filed a case at the ICJ against Serbia (then Yugoslavia) in March 1993. Although the ICJ promptly ordered Belgrade to do everything within its power to halt the genocide, the verdict was ignored. After the war, Bosnia continued to press its case in an attempt to 'set the record straight' on Belgrade's role, and secure reparations such as apologies and compensation. Bosnia did not specify how much it would seek in compensation; however, in a similar ICJ case against Serbia, Croatia claimed $29 billion in damages (Partos 2006). After 13 years of legal wrangling, the world's first trial of a state charged with genocide opened in February 2006. The ICJ's 2007 verdict recognised that genocide took place in Srebrenica and ruled that Serbia violated the Geneva Conventions insofar as it failed to stop the killings. However, applying a particularly high evidentiary standard, the court opined that Serbia was not directly responsible for the genocide and that 'financial compensation is not the appropriate form of reparation' in this case (ICJ 2007). This decision sparked outrage in the Federation, as well as among Serbian human rights activists who decried the verdict as doing 'nothing to help the country come to terms with its past' (Brkic 2007: 22). However, some observers have suggested that in the long run the verdict could be a victory for reconciliation in the region, as having to pay a cripplingly large settlement would have exacerbated Serbs' acute sense of persecution (Vogel 2007). Yet by requiring nothing of Serbia, the verdict unquestionably prolongs the accountability stalemate in the region.

Inside and outside these courtrooms, reconciliation is stymied not only by citizens' lack of knowledge about the atrocities experienced by other groups but also their readiness to downplay or even gloat over the suffering 'the other side' endured. For example, the Serb-run concentration camp of Trnopolji has reverted to being a primary school. However, local Serbs rescheduled the school's annual celebrations to commemorate the day Trnopolji was transformed into a camp and invited former Bosniak prisoners to attend the party (ICG 2002: 25). The audacity of such actions at once underlines the need for broader reparations activities, such as truth commissions, and why such initiatives have so often failed. In 1995, Izetbegović agreed to support an 'international commission of inquiry' into the war, and over the past decade a handful of Bosnian civil society leaders have spearheaded a campaign to establish a truth commission for Bosnia (Kritz and Finci 2001). The necessary legislation was drafted and in 2001 former ICTY President Claude Jorda (2001) argued that the ICTY and a truth commission could be mutually complementary, particularly if the truth commission examined the role of sectors such as the media, the academy, religious institutions, the judiciary and the education system in stoking the war. By recognising their troubled history and contributing to the reform of institutions, which continue to hinder reintegration, a truth commission could arguably promote acceptance of minority returnees and in turn improve access to durable solutions for those who remain displaced. However, efforts to establish a truth commission for Bosnia have stagnated owing to government opposition, insufficient consultations and lack of popular support among Bosnian citizens who question the wisdom of trying to speak so publicly about the past (Hodzic 2012).

While discussions regarding a regional truth commission (REKOM) are underway, thus far the only major truth-telling initiative in Bosnia has been the RS's Commission for Investigation of the Events in and around Srebrenica between 10 and 19 July 1995, which released a report in 2004 acknowledging Serbian forces' responsibility for the massacre of 8,000 Muslim men and boys.[23] Upon issuing the report, Bosnian Serb authorities offered their first public apology to the survivors of the genocide.[24] The significance of this step was diminished, however, as the commission was convened only at the OHR's insistence, after an earlier RS report minimised the severity of the massacre (Wood 2004). Two days after the ICJ issued its 2007 ruling, the RS offered a broader official apology for the crimes committed against non-Serbs in Bosnia during the war. Several apologies have also been offered at the regional level among the states that emerged from the disintegration of the former Yugoslavia (BBC News 2003a, Biro et al. 2004: 196, RFE 2007). More research is necessary to determine the impact of such gestures on inter-communal relations and return and reintegration processes.

Beyond these higher-level efforts, the international community also supported numerous grassroots reconciliation activities involving Bosnian returnees. For example, UNHCR's 'Imagine Coexistence' programme attempted to temper extreme divisions in public space that undermined the sustainability of return. Englbrecht (2001: 19–20) identifies three phases of the reconciliation process as it relates to return, including the re-establishment of contacts between refugees and their former neighbours; the facilitation of 'peaceful coexistence', focusing on tolerance and anti-discrimination; and the promotion of 'social reconciliation', which entails examining and acknowledging past injustices. Focusing on the first and second phases of this process, the Imagine Coexistence programme encouraged members of conflicting groups to undertake joint peacebuilding activities and share public space such as schools and playgrounds (Babbitt et al. 2002, Chayes and Minow 2003, Haider 2009). Bosnian and international organisations also undertook a wide range of symbolic and commemorative activities, including the reconstruction of the iconic Stari Most bridge, and the erection of an array of memorials such as the 'Monument to the International Community', a larger-than-life can of expired processed meat dedicated by the 'Grateful Citizens of Sarajevo' in recollection of the aid they were provided during the siege (Corkalo et al. 2004: 150–152, Reuters 2007). As reparations efforts continue, one of the challenges will be to tailor

23 While another truth commission was subsequently established to study the siege of Sarajevo, this is regarded as a highly controversial, biased endeavour (ICTJ 2008). In Serbia, former President Kostunica established a Yugoslav Truth and Reconciliation Commission in 2001, but this dissolved in 2003 without producing a report. The Commission was compromised by inadequate consultations and popular participation, as well as a lack of impartiality and credibility.

24 It is interesting to note that the RS's decision to offer an apology on behalf of the Serbian nation may serve as a perverse affirmation of the uniqueness of the Republic's identity, and the need for its continued existence as a political institution.

these initiatives to address not only the continued struggle for reintegration and reconciliation in return communities but also the resolution of the vestiges of the displacement crisis in the Balkans. This will necessitate looking not only at the recent history of the region but also back to World War II and the early history of Yugoslavia. 'Clearly', as Ellis and Hutton (2002: 350) point out, 'from a Serb perspective, restitution and reparations for World War II victims have been insufficient to the degree that victim narratives continue to legitimise military aggression and violations of human rights'. While the tensions between and within Bosnia's interlinked national narratives belie tidy resolution through verdicts, commission reports or apologies, sustained attention to this question is essential to ensure that these narratives cannot be mobilised afresh as a pretext for further human rights violations and displacement.

Disconnects between return, redress and responsibility

The Bosnian repatriation operation embodies the notion that return itself can serve as a powerful form of redress, emphatically rejecting the perverse logic of ethnic cleansing. Yet this repatriation was far from a just return. The safe and dignified character of the operation was undermined early on by the premature repatriation of refugees from host states such as Germany.[25] As the process unfolded, it became clear that unprecedented international support for return and restitution was not a panacea for effective efforts at all levels of the Bosnian state to accept responsibility for the displaced on an equitable basis.[26] At the same time, reparation efforts driven by certain Bosnian state agents and the international community could not substitute for accountability on the part of recalcitrant Bosnian institutions, Serbia and Croatia for their roles in the ethnic cleansing of Bosnia. At the most basic level, the possibility of a just return for displaced Bosnians was thwarted by the preponderance of ethno-nationalistic hatred in post-conflict Bosnia, which undercut refugees' safety, dignity, and their ability to negotiate effective forms of redress. More specifically, efforts to uphold state responsibility and enable just return were hindered by the problematic relationship

25 A relatively low number of refugees were forcibly apprehended and returned from Germany and other European host states. A larger number conceded to return under serious pressure from their host states, including the threat of deportation. See Bagshaw (1997).

26 In some cases the international community in fact inadvertently undermined efforts to enable minority return. For example, international sanctions against the RS foreclosed employment opportunities in return communities, adding to would-be minority returnees' incentives to resettle in the Federation.

between return and statebuilding under Dayton; disconnection between different elements of the reparations process and the needs of survivors; and the difficulties associated with attributing and upholding responsibility for displacement in the context of the collapse and creation of divided states.

By many domestic and international actors, return was perceived to play a critical role in strengthening the fledgling Bosnian state. In the best cases, large-scale minority returns improved relations between the communities and contributed to the marginalisation of extremists, yet these 'best cases' were few and far between (Belloni 2005: 434). More typically, using returnees as a 'vanguard force in the fight for reintegration' resulted in the creation of isolated enclaves that made scant contributions to reintegration and political moderation, at significant risk to the refugees (Heimerl 2005: 388). By doggedly promoting only minority return in the early years of the peace process, the international community and the SDA narrowed the choices available to individual refugees regarding their futures (Chandler 2000: 107). At the same time, the SDS and HDZ used return as a tool of ethno-nationalistic statecraft, curtailing refugees' choices by refusing to support durable solutions other than majority return. Unsurprisingly, the result was inadequate support for both minority and majority return. It is striking that while Bosnian leaders and the international community viewed return as a large-scale statebuilding enterprise, those refugees who were reportedly most satisfied with the repatriation process were not those who benefited from the most generous assistance programmes but those who felt they were treated as individuals, for example, by being provided assistance to transport their important belongings back to Bosnia and receiving follow-up calls from NGOs tasked with facilitating their return (Black 2002: 133). Integrating greater respect for refugees' individual needs and autonomous choices could have improved not only the repatriation process, but also efforts to redress the displaced.

As I have discussed, reparation efforts in Bosnia have focused predominantly on property restitution and high-level criminal trials. While both remedies can make critical contributions to enabling just return, in the Bosnian context these processes have been viewed as almost entirely separate projects, undertaken at the insistence of the international community rather than as an expression of shared responsibility for redressing displacement and enabling return. Neither process has directly engaged significant numbers of survivors, nor have they sufficiently grappled with the fundamental causes of conflict and displacement in Bosnia. This remains a highly relevant goal, but addressing it will require a much broader and more cohesive approach to redress that is more closely attuned to the needs of returnees and other survivors, and better integrates alternative approaches to redress, such as compensation and truth commissions.

While Arendt (2006) maintains that 'Every government assumes political responsibility for the deeds and misdeeds of its predecessor, and every nation for the deeds and misdeeds of the past', responsibility for displacement and creating conditions of just return belies easy attribution in the Bosnian case. Efforts to allocate responsibility for the Bosnian displacement crisis must grapple with acts committed in the midst of state collapse, as well as the complicity of neighbouring states and non-state actors, and the creation at Dayton of a complex state structure involving two robustly autonomous entities under the umbrella of a weak central state. Technically, there are no successor states to the former Yugoslavia, as this was the world's first case of total state disintegration.[27] It is therefore difficult under international law to allocate responsibility to contemporary states for the former Yugoslavia's past wrongs, including abetting and underwriting Bosnian Serb extremists. However, if state responsibility is conceived in political or moral terms, rather than strictly as a legal concept, it may be argued that Serbia bears the lion's share of responsibility at the state level for stoking the ethnic cleansing of Bosnia. Yet multiple new states emerged from the collapse of the former Yugoslavia, bearing common but differentiated responsibility for the complex web of conflicts that wracked the Balkans. Although a regional approach may ultimately be necessary to redress the past and enable just return in Bosnia and in the Balkans more broadly, it has proven extremely difficult for Balkan countries to convince or compel their neighbours to shoulder even a small share of responsibility for displacement in the region, as reflected by the failure of Bosnia's ICJ case against Serbia. Even if stronger legal and political levers were available for Bosnia to secure greater accountability from Belgrade, for example, there is no state-citizen relationship between Serbia and the people of Bosnia. In light of the widely accepted conception of sovereignty as responsibility and the notion of remedial responsibility discussed in Chapter 1, it is reasonable to conclude that while it was not the main architect of its citizens' displacement, the Bosnian state is nonetheless obliged to take a leading role in resolving the ongoing displacement of more than 176,000 of its citizens (113,000 IDPs and 63,000 refugees) and establishing conditions of basic justice for those returnees still struggling in the long process of reintegration. This conclusion dovetails with the Dayton Agreement, which clearly identifies the

27 Serbia initially claimed that it was the successor state to the former Yugoslavia but has given up this contention. See Caplan (2005a).

Bosnian state and its newly created entities as bearing immediate responsibility for resolving and redressing the country's displacement crisis.

However, even after major constitutional reforms, Bosnia's ethnically charged system of entities and cantons does not lend itself to the creation of a legitimate relationship of rights and duties between the state and its citizens, which I have argued is the crux of a just return. The functions of Bosnia's central government are 'so minimal as to mean very little to its citizens, which is only likely to strengthen citizens' sense of identity with their respective entity and further weaken the larger state fabric' (Caplan 2000: 223). In the longer term, justice and equity for minority returnees may necessitate significantly strengthening the central government, making the system imposed by Dayton a 'means to a much more inclusive end, rather than . . . an end in itself' (Ni Aolain 2001: 88). In the present context, however, Bosnian state responsibility for redressing displacement and enabling return must involve not only the central government but also the entities, cantons and municipalities (*opstina*).

Over the past decade, the Bosnian state has made considerable progress in shouldering this duty by becoming a major player in the restitution and criminal justice processes, establishing a centralised Return Fund, adopting an internationally endorsed strategy for the implementation of Annex 7 and ultimately assuming sole responsibility for this process.[28] While these are promising signs, ample grounds remain for scepticism, as this progress was only achieved through the High Representative's exercise of his 'extraordinary powers' over 100 times to prevent infringements on the right to return (Williams 2006b: 49). Although entity laws on return have now been harmonised, various discrepancies continue to limit returnees' choices and equal standing as citizens. For example, many of those who remained displaced as of 2007 were the victims of rape; disparities between the benefits available for rape survivors in each entity have limited options regarding return (IDMC 2007: 69, RSG 2005: 10). In addition, complex obstacles remain regarding the state's willingness and ability to use remedies such as compensation to further support return, reintegration and ultimately reconciliation. As discussed in Chapter 1, remedies such as apologies and compensation typically need to come from the party with acknowledged causal and moral responsibility for past violations, if they are to be personally and politically meaningful. If politically meaningful compensation were to be offered to Bosnian citizens through the state, it may need to be provided

[28] The 2003 Strategy of Bosnia and Herzegovina for the Implementation of Annex 7 was the first joint framework agreed to at the state level since the Dayton Agreement.

through a series of reciprocal (if not equal) efforts made by the governments of each entity to survivors from the appropriate ethnic group. While such compensation remains a very remote possibility, initiatives that engage Bosnia's national groups as actors in the reparations and reconciliation process arguably merit further consideration.[29]

Beyond Bosnia's role in ensuring accountability for displacement and return, this case also broaches the international community's obligation to remedy its own failures in the region. Several international actors have engaged in reparations processes intended to account for their culpability in Bosnia's ethnic cleansing. For example, the Dutch cabinet resigned *en masse* in April 2002, following the publication of an official report on the Netherlands' failure to stop the Srebrenica massacre (BBC News 2002a, NIWD 2002). Prime Minister Wim Kok's explanation of this decision captured the difficulties inherent in attempting to hold the amorphous 'international community' accountable for past wrongs: 'The international community is anonymous and cannot take responsibility. I can and I do' (BBC News 2002b). The succour this step provided was evidently limited, as 6,000 survivors from Srebrenica subsequently launched a suit against the Netherlands and the UN in the Hague District Court (BBC 2008b, International Herald Tribune 2007). Although not always on target, the international community's broad efforts to support return and redress in Bosnia were motivated at least in part by a shared sense of responsibility for the victims, and the need to demonstrate, however disingenuously, that rampant violence and widespread displacement 'would not be tolerated in the emerging international system' (Harvey 2006: 106). Paradoxically, the international community itself has suffered from an 'accountability deficit' in Bosnia, as it usurped many normal state roles and responsibilities, including in terms of reparations and return, but is not answerable to the local population (Caplan 2005b: 463).

While the international community's extensive involvement in Bosnia is gradually winding down, the creation of conditions of just return is an ongoing process in which international actors will continue to have a keen interest and even a direct stake, as Bosnia's efforts to resolve the remnants of its displacement crisis and redress its troubled history are sure to figure in continuing talks on EU expansion.[30] At the same time

29 Discussion of how transboundary nations can exercise responsibility for historical injustice is an important element of this problem, but is unfortunately beyond the scope of the present discussion.

30 Regrettably, the EU's willingness to overlook Croatia's intransigence regarding restitution for displaced Croatian Serbs does not send a strong signal to Bosnia on the importance of confronting historical injustices and redressing those who remain displaced.

as national and international reparations advocates cast a critical eye on Bosnia's contentious past, those who remain displaced also look towards the future. As refugee Branko Tišma reflected, 'The future is my hope. I will live where I can support [my] family and where I can have normal conditions for life. That can be anywhere – we bring our roots with us, the only thing is to find good soil' (Harvey 2006: 108). While Bosnia is making faltering steps towards being that good soil, complacency is a luxury the country can ill afford.

6 Return and redress in Mozambique

Contemporary Mozambicans are the heirs of a long and complex history of displacement. As the colonial power in Mozambique, Portugal forced innumerable communities from their fertile ancestral lands in order to make way for white settlers. In 1962, a cluster of Mozambican exile organisations founded the *Frente de Libertaçao de Moçambique* (Frelimo) and launched a war of independence in 1964. This resulted in additional uprootings, as part of Portugal's counter-insurgency strategy was to force Mozambican peasants into *aldeamentos* (protected villages) where they would be 'safe' from Frelimo's revolutionary influence. After more than a decade of war, Mozambique achieved its independence on 25 June 1975, with Frelimo at the helm of the country's first post-colonial government. Yet independence brought little respite from war and displacement for Mozambican citizens.[1]

In 1977, Frelimo declared itself a Marxist-Leninist vanguard party committed to supporting anti-colonial struggles across the region. The government suppressed internal opposition, and attempted to undermine the role of traditional leaders in rural Mozambique, labelling customary authorities 'backward and superstitious' (Waterhouse 1998).[2] Frelimo leaders nationalised all land, and collectivised agricultural production through 'villagisation schemes', which involved the often forcible transfer of approximately 1.8 million citizens, or 20 per cent of the

[1] For analysis of forced displacement and oppression during the colonial period and the war of independence, see Isaacman and Isaacman (1983), Cann (1997) and Newitt (1995).

[2] The role of 'traditional' or 'customary' authorities in Mozambican politics has often been over-simplified. Although it is not possible to discuss the issue at length here, it must be recognised that the term covers a diverse cast of actors who enjoy varying degrees of support at the grassroots level, including the descendants of precolonial chiefs ousted by the Portuguese, Portuguese-appointed chiefs (*regulos*), traditional spiritual healers, Christian healers, former Frelimo strong-men and democratically elected village secretaries who may cross-identify with one or more of the above categories. On the persistent yet evolving political and cultural importance of traditional authorities and spiritual practices in Mozambique, see West and Kloeck-Jenson (1999), Alexander (1997), Buur and Kyed (2005), Dinerman (2006) and West (1998a, 1998b , 2005).

population, into some 1,200 communal villages, none of which were economically viable (Hanchinamani 2003, Unruh 2005: 151). Although many Mozambicans initially welcomed the promise of new clinics and schools in the communal villages, the largely disastrous implementation of the villagisation plan generated dissatisfaction and resentment among Mozambique's largely rural, agrarian population.[3] In 1977 the government became embroiled in armed conflict with the *Resistência Nacional Moçambicana* (Renamo), a rebel group established by the Rhodesian Central Intelligence Organisation (CIO) to destabilise the country and thereby undermine Mozambican support for Zimbabwean independence forces.[4] Initially bereft of a coherent set of political convictions, Renamo gradually developed a patchwork of ideological commitments, including support for 'traditional authorities' and opposition to Frelimo's Marxist policies.

Shortly before the independence of Zimbabwe in 1980, the Rhodesian CIO transferred control of Renamo to South Africa, which stoked the rebel movement with the goal of further destabilising Mozambique and consolidating Pretoria's economic and political dominance in southern Africa. Under South Africa's tutelage, Renamo earned a reputation for overwhelming brutality, regularly applying tactics such as public torture, mutilation of victims both living and dead, and forcing family members to kill each other. The seeming randomness of Renamo's attacks disguised its nature as a generally well-disciplined insurgency force guided by a strategy of attacking 'soft' civilian targets such as schools, roads and health clinics, in order to underline the government's inability to protect or provide for its citizens (Hall 1990, Vines 1991).

'The cruelty of Renamo mesmerised everyone in Mozambique, from the peasant whose own head sank before its scythe to the members of the many foreign delegations that came to survey the wreckage', yet in some rural areas support for Renamo grew, largely owing to peasants' dissatisfaction with Frelimo's policies of collectivisation and forced relocation, and its disdain for traditional values and governance structures (Finnegan 1992: 23). Although Renamo's reputation for uninhibited violence was due in part to unruly government troops and effective propaganda from Maputo, it is widely agreed that Renamo perpetrated

[3] Approaches to villagisation varied in different parts of the country, however, taken in total, the policy is typically regarded as having been seriously misguided, and a significant if often misunderstood cause of the civil war. See, for example, Roesch (1992), Geffray (1990), Manning (2002: 59–62) and Coelho (1998).

[4] For more detailed discussions of the origins and unfolding of the Mozambican civil war, see Vines (1991), Andersson (1992), Bowen (2000), Chingono (1996), Fauvet (1984), Minter (1994), Cabrita (2000), Geffray (1990), and McGregor (1998).

the majority of atrocities and prompted a massive refugee exodus from Mozambique (Chan and Venancio 1998). However, attributing responsibility for the war and the violations associated with it is a delicate and controversial business. As Dinerman (2004: 123) points out, there is 'no consensus, either within or beyond Mozambique, on the extent to which Frelimo's version of state socialism and its often heavy-handed tactics bear responsibility for fuelling a brutal . . . conflict'. Undoubtedly, Frelimo exacerbated the Mozambican displacement crisis through its policy of 'recuperation', which mandated the forcible relocation of peasants into garrison towns in order to limit Renamo's ability to extract resources from them. The government justified the recuperation policy as critical to 'liberating' citizens from Renamo control, but many local groups vehemently opposed the policy, which often compounded the dissatisfaction with the state generated by Frelimo's villagisation schemes and rejection of traditional authorities (Chingono 1996: 139, Lubkemann 2008: 201–215).

Whether at the hands of their government or Renamo rebels, Mozambicans' exposure to longstanding and repeated displacement devastated the social fabric of the country. By the advent of peace in 1992, Mozambique was home to 3.5 to 4.5 million IDPs from an estimated population of 16 million, and between 1.7 and 2 million citizens had sought refuge in six neighbouring states (RSG 1997). Approximately 1 million people were killed during the war, earning the country the moniker of the 'killing fields of Africa' (Nordstrom 1997: 40). The civil war left Mozambique 'the world's hungriest, most indebted, most aid-dependent country': with an annual gross domestic product (GDP) of $80 per capita, Mozambique's economy was dwarfed even by war-ravaged Somalia, where the GDP per capita was a comparatively robust $120 (Hanlon 1991: 1, Hume 1994). The catastrophic effects of the war were compounded by the worst drought in southern Africa in 70 years, which placed 3 million Mozambicans at risk of starvation, and reached its peak as the peace process accelerated in the early 1990s.

Given these conditions, the success of the Mozambican peace process and return operation was a surprise to many, coming to be dubbed the 'miracle of Mozambique' in humanitarian circles (Wilkinson 1998). Millions of Mozambicans spontaneously returned to their homes before the ink was even dry on the 1992 General Peace Agreement, repatriating under circumstances that in many ways fell short of the conditions of just return set out in Chapter 2 – the country was littered with up to 1 million landmines; infrastructure was decimated; and starvation was an ever-present risk. The government had no ability to enforce law and order in much of the country; neither Frelimo nor Renamo accepted responsibility for the egregious crimes committed during the war; and no formal processes were in place to ensure that returnees could regain access to their former homes and lands, and peacefully reintegrate into their communities. Yet in spite of the risks and injustices inherent in the process, many Mozambican refugees were eager to repatriate, and the process was largely durable, in that few returnees were forced back into exile. The Mozambican case therefore raises several critical questions. What is the relevance of thinking about minimum standards of justice in cases where refugees are evidently willing to return despite endemic poverty and inequality, and expect very little by way of justice (or even basic services) from their state (Lundin 2004: 27)? How should scholars and practitioners think about responsibility for forced migration in cases where the state is in principle willing but in practice is unable to protect its citizens from displacement at the hands of non-state actors? How should accountability for displacement and the injustices associated with it be pursued in the context of abject poverty and bureaucratic incapacity? What does accountability mean in a country where customary governance mechanisms are often seen as having more legitimacy than the state, but where, at the same time, legislation officially recognising the role of traditional authorities in local governance renders the line between the state and these 'informal' actors relatively porous (Alexander 1997: 1, 15–20, Buur and Kyed 2005, Unruh 2001)?[5]

The Mozambican case is often listed by advocates of redress for refugees as one of the many diverse countries in which reparations have been made available to returnees in the form of real property restitution. In this section, I recognise that while no formal reparations programmes have been enacted by the Mozambican state, despite provisions in Mozambique's General Peace Agreement guaranteeing the restitution of displaced persons' property, redress and reconciliation have been advanced through informal, customary approaches and the reform of national land laws to strengthen claimants' ability to resolve their concerns without recourse to formal institutions such as courts. My analysis suggests that these legal reforms and customary initiatives represent important, locally attuned contributions to the pursuit of justice and the resolution of displacement in Mozambique. The fact that the resolution of land claims and the redress of survivors' grievances took place largely outside the structure of formal state institutions does not mean that they are not significant contributions to creating conditions of just return. Indeed, given the government's extremely limited capacities and the

[5] For example, the 1994 Municipalities Law mandates a greater role for 'traditional authorities' in a wide range of state functions, including land management and dispute resolution (Alexander 1997: 1, 17–20).

popular demand for state recognition of the legitimacy of 'traditional authorities' in local governance, the *lack* of heavy-handed state intervention in locally mediated reparations processes (except to formally recognise the role of customary authorities, for example, in resolving land claims under the 1997 Land Law) is arguably one of the reasons the return process was relatively successful, both in terms of durability and the effective resolution of the grievances borne by returnees and their neighbours. Yet room remains for more formal responses to the violations experienced by returnees and other survivors of violence in Mozambique. Although the return operation technically ended more than 12 years ago, the work of redressing past injustices and (re)creating a robust relationship of rights and duties between citizens and the state is a much longer-term, unfinished endeavour.

Ending war in Mozambique

Mozambican President Joaquim Chissano and Renamo head Afonso Dhlakama did not so much lead their people to the negotiating table as accept that external pressures made a military victory unlikely for either side. The conflict was brought into stalemate by factors including the cessation of outside support for the warring parties, and the drought, which undermined the parties' ability to feed their troops.[6] At the same time, western backing for Frelimo rallied as the party formally abandoned its Marxist philosophy in 1987 and implemented extensive market-oriented reforms in an effort to revive the incapacitated Mozambican economy.[7]

The goal of the formal peace process was to end the war by transforming Renamo from a rebel group into a viable political party, a challenge pursued through 12 rounds of tortuous negotiations that culminated with the signing of the General Peace Agreement (GPA) in Rome on 4 October 1992.[8] The Rome negotiations were convened under the aegis

[6] Support for Renamo declined in the United States with the publication of a high-profile 1988 State Department report entitled *Summary of Mozambican Refugee Accounts of Principally Conflict-Related Experience in Mozambique*. Known as the Gersony Report, it focused attention on the indiscriminate killings, rapes and torture perpetrated by Renamo and, despite its methodological flaws, was instrumental to the withdrawal of support for Renamo among many conservative American politicians (Gersony 1988, Azevedo 2002: 8).

[7] The end of Frelimo's communist policies did not mean that Mozambicans forced into communal villages could return home, as the settlements were used as safe havens during the war. Although government protection from Renamo attacks on the safe havens was feeble, outside the safe havens protection was often non-existent (Unruh 2005: 151).

[8] The Rome negotiations were preceded by several rounds of talks between Frelimo and Renamo, and between Mozambique and South Africa, brokered by various African countries. See Armon, Hendrickson and Vines (1998: 82–87), Alden (2001) and Cabrita (2000).

of Santo Egidio, a Roman Catholic lay community, with the participation of the US, the European powers and the United Nations. The statement of principle Renamo released at the Nairobi talks preceding the Rome negotiations demonstrates only passing concern for the displaced, indicating that the party 'stands for the population of Mozambique and is against any massacre or violation of the population' (Armon, Hendrickson and Vines 1998: 39). The statement is more concerned with ensuring that Renamo's leaders would not be held accountable for the atrocities they sanctioned, arguing that 'we should emphasise the future and not the past', and asserting that 'Renamo wants a genuine negotiation conducive to national reconciliation without victors or vanquished and without recrimination' (Armon, Hendrickson and Vines 1998: 39). The government's 'Twelve Principles for Peace' released at the Nairobi talks offers a more detailed account of its concerns regarding the displaced, but both parties' practical disregard for the humanitarian cost of the war was evidenced by the fact that displacement rates actually escalated during the Rome negotiations, as neither side was wholly willing to forgo a violent resolution to the conflict and continued to carry out highly destructive attacks in order to strengthen their hands at the negotiating table (Armon, Hendrickson and Vines 1998: 38, RSG 1997).

The GPA provided for: the withdrawal of foreign troops; disarmament and demobilisation; multi-party democracy; presidential and parliamentary elections; humanitarian assistance and the return of refugees and IDPs. Although reconciliation was a key theme in the protagonists' statements of principle at the Nairobi talks, the issues of reconciliation and accountability are conspicuously absent from the GPA. Reconciliation is addressed only in the opening section of the agreement, which commits the 'President of the Republic of Mozambique and the President of Renamo to do everything within their power for the achievement of genuine national reconciliation' (GPA 1992). Renamo and the government refused to discuss victimisation, amnesties, prosecutions or civil claims during the Rome negotiations. Under the GPA, 'the Mozambican conflict had no victims who could be identified and be entitled to any kind of reparation or compensation and consequently there were no perpetrators who could be prosecuted or be eligible for amnesty' (Buford and van der Merwe 2004).

Protocol III of the GPA sets out comparatively detailed provisions (for the time) regarding the return of displaced persons. The GPA (1992: Protocol III, Section IV, Articles b and c) pledges that 'Mozambican refugees and displaced persons shall not forfeit any of the rights and freedoms of citizens for having left their original places of residence', and commits the signatories to 'organise the necessary assistance to refugees and displaced persons, preferably in their original places of residence'. The GPA was the first major peace treaty since World War II to recognise the explicit right of refugees and displaced persons to reclaim lost property. Article IV(e) of the treaty states,

> Mozambican refugees and displaced persons shall be guaranteed restitution of property owned by them which is still in existence and the right to take legal action to secure the return of such property from individuals in possession of it. (GPA 1992)[9]

Despite its relatively specific articles on restitution, the GPA's contribution to setting the stage for a just return of refugees to Mozambique was limited because in virtually all other areas the treaty reflects the signatories' complete disregard for issues of accountability and redress.

Some commentators have suggested that Article IV(e) does not in fact mandate land restitution, as all land in Mozambique was nationalised before the conflict and remained the possession of the state. Although it is unclear whether land use rights were to be considered ownership rights under the GPA, the 1993 tripartite agreement on voluntary repatriation between UNHCR, Mozambique and Zimbabwe provides greater detail on the Mozambican government's obligations regarding land access for returnees (Hanchinamani 2003, UNHCR 1995). Article 8 on the 'Treatment of the returnees' asserts that

> returnees shall have the right of return to their former places of residence or to any other places of their choice within Mozambique . . . The Mozambican Government shall ensure that returnees have access to land for settlement and use, in accordance with Mozambique laws . . . [and] shall, in accordance with the relevant provisions of Protocol III of the General Peace Accord, assist returnees who attempt to recover their lost property.

These provisions in fact expand the scope of the duties borne by the Mozambican state, as they oblige the government not only to facilitate the restitution of displaced persons' property, but also to ensure that all returnees, including the formerly landless, have access to land.

Although the correct interpretation of the GPA is a matter of legal debate, the restitution provisions are remarkably detailed for the standards of the time. However, it is unclear which parties around the table

[9] Annex 4 of the Agreement on a Comprehensive Political Settlement of the Cambodian Conflict, signed 1 year before the Mozambican GPA, emphasises that displaced Cambodians should be able to return to the place of their choice and underlines the need for 'full respect for the human rights and fundamental freedoms' of Cambodian returnees, including the 'right to property'. However, unlike the Mozambican GPA, the Cambodian treaty contains no specific provisions on the reclamation of lost assets.

championed the progressive step of entrenching returnees' right to restitution in the treaty. In advance of the Rome negotiations, neither the government nor Renamo exhibited particularly strong interest in the refugee issue or firm positions on resolving Mozambicans' displacement. Indeed, Chan and Venancio (1998: 58) suggest that Renamo was first and foremost concerned with securing money to sustain its operations as a political party and a more affluent lifestyle for its elites. Throughout the peace process, the Roman Catholic Church served as a crucial advocate for the rights and interests of the displaced; it is possible that their efforts prompted the inclusion of articles upholding refugees' rights to return and restitution in the GPA.

An unlikely success? Return and the consolidation of peace

The Mozambican peace and repatriation operations are regarded almost unanimously in humanitarian circles as unlikely but undoubted successes, if success is understood in the traditional terms of the creation of a relatively stable democracy and prompt, durable return.[10] The rapid return of millions of displaced persons was perhaps the most striking aspect of the fledgling peace process: tens of thousands spontaneously returned before the GPA was even signed, and within 30 months of the outbreak of peace, 1.7 million refugees and nearly 4 million IDPs headed 'home' in the largest return movement in African history (Unruh 1997: 28, Wilkinson 1998).[11] While the government initially assumed that refugees and IDPs would return to their 'areas of origin', in practice many were unable or unwilling to do so. Those subjected to repeated displacement during the colonial era, the independence struggle and the civil war did not necessarily have a clear 'area of origin' to which they were committed to return, and many attempted to enhance their security and economic prospects by relocating near markets and infrastructure. As I will discuss shortly, land conflicts involving returnees, 'stayees', elites and commercial interests also shaped returnees' destination options (Gengenbach 1998: 26, Meyers 1994: 603).

Refugees who returned in 1992 and early 1993 had to rely largely on their own resources and resourcefulness, while those who waited received

[10] For an ethnographic study that challenges the portrayal of repatriation as a straightforward success, see Englund (2002).

[11] UNHCR estimates that almost 80 per cent of returns to Mozambique were 'spontaneous'; that is, they were planned independently by refugees themselves and took place independently of direct support from the international community (Juergensen 2000: 18, Crisp et al. 1997: 31).

more assistance with transportation and reconstruction, and benefited from improved security conditions. However, as the return operation progressed, its voluntary nature was compromised by UNHCR's decision to accelerate repatriation from Malawi, where the vast majority of refugees were sheltered, by halting food distribution in the camps (Crisp 1996: 6). Refugees often returned to 'communities' that were completely deserted, and faced a truly staggering range of problems including poor or non-existent access to water, food, shelter, schools, roads, health care, seeds, employment opportunities, and reconciliation and rehabilitation programmes. However, according to UNHCR, the lack of popular desire for revenge meant that protection issues in Mozambique were not as complex as in other repatriation operations, such as the return to Bosnia (Crisp et al. 1997: 28).

The peace and repatriation processes were buoyed by good luck and good planning in the form of two particularly bountiful rainy seasons, and concentrated support from the international community. Humanitarian agencies' efforts were complemented by the work of the United Nations Operation in Mozambique (ONUMOZ), which was responsible for a complex mandate including: the demobilisation of some 110,000 combatants; the organisation of elections; and the return and reintegration of 5–6 million refugees and IDPs. The externally supported peace process culminated with elections in 1994, which were widely held to be free and fair. Almost 90 per cent of eligible voters cast their ballots, electing Chissano president with 53 per cent of the vote compared to Dhlakama's 34 per cent (Juergensen 2000: 14). As in Cambodia, the repatriation of refugees in time to participate in the election was seen as a critical plank of the peace process. Yet, unlike in Cambodia, the Mozambican peace process benefited from the pragmatic recognition by Frelimo, Renamo and UN leaders of the need to push the elections back a year, in order to allow sufficient time for demobilisation and reintegration.

The international community's efforts in Mozambique were not always so well crafted. UNHCR's efforts to support the repatriation of Mozambican refugees from South Africa were compromised by the agency's seeming inability to take into account how local-level motivations and practices, including individual, household and group concerns, shaped refugees' return strategies. UNHCR planned to support 2,500 returns from South Africa to Mozambique per week, totalling 240,000 returns over the course of a 2-year period. This goal was set after surveying refugees with the simple question 'Do you intend to return to Mozambique?', without probing the deeper issues of when, how, and in what circumstances the refugees envisioned their return (Dolan 1999: 88, 90). When it became clear that returns would not be forthcoming at the intended rate, UNHCR acted to suture a major programmatic failure and preserve the reputation of the Mozambican operation as a much-needed success story by simply cutting the goal to 120,000 returns over 12 months. Consequently, Mozambican refugees in South Africa had a 'very narrow window of opportunity' to repatriate with support from UNHCR; many chose not to return because they were not able to access reliable information about conditions in Mozambique in such a short timeframe (Dolan 1999: 92). By reducing its timeframe so severely, UNHCR 'automatically redefined those who remained as illegal immigrants' subject to deportation and heightened vulnerability in South Africa (Dolan 1999: 108).

Within Mozambique, the success of the operation was threatened by ill-advised policies such as the government and international actors' initial targeting of humanitarian assistance towards the displaced, which hampered reconciliation between returnees and stayees by exacerbating inequalities within and between communities (Crisp 1996: 12). UNHCR also found itself behind the curve in its reintegration efforts: by the time the agency finalised its reintegration strategy in 1994, the war had been over for more than 2 years, and 75 per cent of the refugees had already repatriated (Alden 2001: 58–9, Wilkinson 1998). Even more problematically, international support was overly focused on short-term needs and exacerbated Mozambique's already pronounced donor dependency. The international community 'effectively displaced the normal functions of government . . . [and] derailed the government's own efforts to reform' (Synge 1997: 149). By almost entirely neglecting the issues of redress and reconciliation, the international community also missed an opportunity to ensure that reforms resulted in greater state accountability for human rights violations, including the protracted displacement of millions of Mozambican civilians.

Unfinished business? Reparations, reconciliation and return

The neglect of reparation and reconciliation initiatives by the Mozambican government, Renamo and the international community was not simply a matter of limited budgets and competing priorities. As discussed above, Renamo and Frelimo leaders were careful to ensure that the GPA did not provide the grounds for them to be held responsible for the brutalities committed during the civil war. While western powers were adamant that accountability was integral to peace in regions such as the Balkans, they did not press this point in the southern African context. Indeed, various scholars and members of the international community espoused the view that Mozambicans were simply not interested in or culturally inclined to speak out about the crimes of the past. For example, Green and Honwana (1999) argue that in the Mozambican cultural context, 'To talk and recall the past is not necessarily seen as a prelude to healing or diminishing pain. Indeed, it is often believed to open the space for the malevolent forces to intervene.'[12] In a similar vein, a detailed UNHCR study on the Mozambican repatriation operation concluded that:

> Despite the intensity of the Mozambican conflict, the many atrocities which took place during the war and the enormous amount of social dislocation which it generated, there has been a remarkable absence of revenge and recrimination since the conflict came to an end. While War Crimes Tribunals and Truth Commissions may have an important role to play in other war-torn societies, the Mozambican experience demonstrates that some communities may be capable of reconciliation without such formal structures. (Crisp et al. 1997: 28)

Many Mozambicans would certainly concur with this assessment and the words of a local official who reflected, 'We were interested in planting seeds and not starting war tribunals to punish the guilty' (Wilkinson 1998). However, Azevedo (2002: 184) undoubtedly overstates the case when he argues that 'There are no indications whatsoever that, after more than fifteen years of war and massacres, the Mozambican people do not get along or are unwilling to forget and forgive the past.' The view that Mozambicans were (and are) uniformly uninterested in redress appears to be based largely on two assumptions. First, this view assumes that in the absence of formal state initiatives, Mozambicans have not been able to access any form of redress for the crimes they suffered. In fact, as I will discuss, many Mozambicans marshalled cultural practices and worked with traditional authorities to help themselves resolve their claims and grievances. As Mozambican laws and policies evolved to recognise and incorporate the contribution of customary authorities to local governance and dispute resolution, the activities of these actors occupied an increasingly nebulous space between informal cultural practice and official, state-sanctioned behaviour (Alexander 1997). Furthermore, through a 'Frelimo-specific politics of acknowledgement', the ruling party publicly recognised the foolhardiness of two of its most contested policies directly linked to displacement and the war: villagisation and the delegitimisation and persecution of traditional authorities (Dinerman 2006: 26). While Frelimo offered a 'full-throated' repudiation of its position on traditional authorities, it stopped short of offering a full apology for

[12] See also Englund (1998).

either policy, much less other forms of redress such as compensation for their effects (Dinerman 2006: 261, 287). 'Nonetheless,' Dinerman (2006: 287) argues,

> on a continent whose postcolonial rulers have evinced a marked predilection for blaming the detrimental effects of their own flawed policies on external factors, the ritualisation of public confession in the political arena is notable – even for a ruling party renowned for using strategically-timed critical self-appraisals as a powerful legitimating device.[13]

As the only party to have ruled Mozambique since independence, Frelimo is often conflated with the Mozambican state itself. Thus, when taken in combination with traditionally mediated approaches to redress, Frelimo's decrial of these policies represents a significant response to the grievances borne by returnees and other survivors against their state over the war.

The second assumption at work here is that because returnees and other survivors of political violence in Mozambique have not significantly disrupted the peace process or voiced loud calls for formal reparations, they are uninterested in the state attempting to address the injustices they suffered. In fact, during the first post-conflict election campaign, the 'conspicuous failure of the country's two grandees to address issues of substance, let alone own up to, and seek expiation for, past wrongdoing, prompted indignant cries that both sides were equally guilty of a fairly flagrant and thoroughly unwarranted arrogance' (Dinerman 2006: 265). Many if not most Mozambicans may have simply been too preoccupied with survival to channel this indignation into the organisation of formal reparations campaigns.[14] Indeed, Buford and van der Merwe (2004) argue that the 'sentiment persists among . . . Mozambicans that not nearly enough was done for ordinary victims after the 1992 ceasefire. Governmental focus in post-war Mozambique has been on the reintegration of soldiers and on the resettlement of the displaced, not on reparation to victims who suffered from the political violence.' Although displaced persons and victims of political violence are certainly not discrete categories, the technical difficulties associated with repatriation, resettlement and demobilisation have indeed detracted attention from issues of redress and accountability for past violations. Drawing on interviews with Mozambican civil society leaders, Buford and van der

[13] On Frelimo's 'selective cultivation of memory', see also Igreja (2008: 554).

[14] West and Myers (1996: 51) note the occurrence of 'collective demonstrations of discontent over land dispossession . . . [which] show that communities may tentatively emerge and assert themselves where their interests are held in common and space is open for expression.'

Merwe (2004) suggest that the Mozambican government should instigate an official reparation policy, in light of the need for the state to accept responsibility for its failure to protect its own citizens and relieve victims' suffering. Furthermore, engaging in a formal redress process may provide a valuable opportunity for the government to build closer relationships with its citizens.

In the following sections I examine how property restitution claims and broader questions of redress and reconciliation have been addressed in post-war Mozambique, despite the absence of formal government programmes and policies on these issues. While I highlight Mozambicans' remarkable resourcefulness in adapting and applying customary measures to resolve grievances and facilitate return and reintegration, customary approaches did not meet the needs of all claimants, and are not a panacea for formal efforts on the part of the state to uphold returnees' remedial rights (Unruh 2001). Although formal redress mechanisms were not identified as an urgent need in the early phases of the repatriation and reintegration process, interest in this issue may grow in the longer term (Armon, Hendrickson and Vines 1998: 7, Cobban 2007, Igreja, Dias-Lambrance and Richters 2008).

Restitution rights in post-war Mozambique: from customary approaches to legal reform

From the outset of the Mozambican peace and repatriation processes, observers typically described the question of land restitution as sensitive, volatile or explosive. Given these characterisations and the enshrinement of restitution guarantees in the GPA, the restoration of land access received surprisingly little attention from national and international actors in the early years of the peace process.[15] UNHCR's evaluation of the Mozambican repatriation operation is silent on the challenges of restitution and land access, while the agency's review of its reintegration programme devotes only passing reference to the issue (Crisp et al. 1997). The sidelining of the restitution issue was possible in part because of Mozambique's low population density: most returnees were able to access some land for building a shelter and planting crops, which relieved immediate pressure on the government and international actors to tackle the problem. However, after the 1994 elections, the national media began to direct attention to land conflicts, which had become increasingly common due to elite and corporate land-grabbing, and returnees' objection

[15] This analysis is based on the view that, properly interpreted, the GPA entitles returnees to regain land use rights, even if the land remains state property.

to being relegated to substandard land and denied the opportunity to reclaim their traditional territories (Gengenbach 1998: 8, Unruh 1997: 28, West and Myers 1996: 28, 37). Inconsistent colonial-era and post-independence land policies and repeated instances of forced displacement had created overlapping claims and serious confusion over entitlements. New political and business elites capitalised on this disorder in the early aftermath of the war by staking claims to huge swaths of territory occupied by the rural poor, with the assumption that the government would promptly denationalise land ownership, in accordance with its other neo-liberal economic reforms. At the same time, the government granted huge land use concessions to national and foreign companies in an effort to encourage investment in the crippled Mozambican economy (Unruh 1997, Waterhouse 1998, West and Myers 1996: 29–30). Unsurprisingly, conflicts between local farmers, displaced persons, elites and foreign investors were most frequent and intense where the land was most fertile (Unruh 1997: 31, 2001).

Although the GPA and the UNHCR-Zimbabwe-Mozambique tripartite agreement imply that the Mozambican state would help returnees to reclaim their property through formal legal channels, Mozambique's courts were (and are) largely under-resourced, overwhelmed with cases, and out of reach to poor, illiterate returnees who lacked formal documentation to prove their claims (Dinerman 2004: 152). Indeed, many returnees were most probably unaware that they had any formal restitution rights under the GPA.[16] Consequently, returnees and other claimants relied almost exclusively on customary authorities to resolve land disputes, or simply negotiated conflicts within family structures, 'at the lowest levels of "traditional authority"' (West and Kloeck-Jensen 1999: 484, 458).[17] Within the first one-and-a-half years of large-scale returns, customary authorities reportedly helped resolve more than 300,000 land conflicts, with UNHCR also playing a supportive role in mediating disputes (Crisp 1996: 12, RSG 1997). Although many Mozambicans have a longstanding preference for traditional methods of land dispute resolution, reliance on customary approaches resulted in uneven standards of justice across the country and was often detrimental to women, who have only limited rights under Mozambique's

[16] See Koser (1997: 10) for a discussion of refugee networks' limited access to information on the peace accords.

[17] As stated above, 'traditional authorities' do not represent a monolithic group in post-war Mozambique. These actors did not simply apply ancient, immutable conventions to resolve grievances associated with the war, but adapted and invented customs to serve survivors' needs, and their own interests, in varying measures. I am grateful to Dr. Graeme Rodgers for his insights on this issue.

various customary tenure systems (Dinerman 2004: 149, Geffray and Pedersen 1985: 37, Waterhouse 1998). Dinerman (2004: 123) suggests that in the early post-war years in Nampula province, the reinstatement of traditional authorities as local administration agents with responsibility for land management 'only served to widen the cascade of claims and counter-claims in many localities and, hence, to further undermine the legitimacy of official authority.' 'Retraditionalisation' inadvertently achieved this result in part by reigniting smouldering tensions between different local actors with competing claims to authority, 'title and turf' (Dinerman 2004: 139–140, 127).

In light of the shortcomings of customary systems and the persistence of land-related conflicts, resolving land claims gradually emerged as a priority concern for local, national, regional and international actors alike (Unruh 1997: 28). Mozambique's donors pressured the government to deal with the land rights question as a precondition to accessing further development aid, but were seemingly unwilling to provide the human and financial resources necessary for a discrete programme for resolving disputes, such as a streamlined claims adjudication mechanism (Hanchinamani 2003, Unruh 2005: 151). Instead, donors provided funds to enable the government to attempt to resolve some of the problems surrounding displacement, restitution and access to land through the creation of a new legal regime for land tenure and restitution. The legal reform effort took place against a backdrop of uneven and failed land policy; the need to attract and retain foreign and domestic investment; and the 'extreme lack of state capacity needed to manage a formal restitution programme' (Unruh 2005: 147, 148–149). The process struggled to weigh and respond to the strong and growing desire for restitution among diverse constituents with markedly different degrees of literacy, war-time allegiances, and access to state institutions, including millions of refugees and IDPs, as well as individuals and commercial interests keen to defend claims for land obtained under the colonial or independence regimes.[18]

The reform process resulted in the 1997 *Lei de Terras* (Land Law) which, contrary to expectations, did not denationalise land ownership in spite of pressure from Renamo MPs, Mozambican economic elites

[18] For example, Portuguese 'returnees' attempted to exploit the restitution process by establishing the Association of the Expropriated from Overseas Territories in the early 1990s and successfully pressuring the Portuguese government to create a department to advance their claims. Arguably, the Portuguese claimants are legally entitled to compensation, but the sums involved outstrip the Mozambican government's capacity to pay. Unruh (2005: 150) suggests that this is why the Mozambican government has been reluctant to address the Portuguese claims directly under national laws.

and several bilateral donors (Hanchinamani 2003). The 1997 Land Law revokes earlier land laws and focuses on rural territories where most of the Mozambican population lives, and where land conflicts have proven the most intractable. Unlike earlier laws, the *Lei de Terras* relies extensively on customary and informal approaches to tenure and conflict resolution, and requires that formal institutions such as national and regional courts consider verbal testimony on occupancy rights when formal ownership documents are unavailable.[19] The law strives to protect peasants while promoting partnership between local communities and commercial investors. By constructing a legal environment in which restitution claims can be 'self-managed' – that is, where claimants and other local actors can play a direct role in the negotiation and resolution of their own cases – the law attempts to sidestep the need for extensive assistance that the state lacks the capacity to provide (Unruh 2005: 153–154). Legitimising local governance systems in this manner also had the benefit of helping to redress Frelimo's longstanding rejection of Mozambican customary authorities, a major grievance for many disenfranchised citizens.

Under the Land Law, the state grants land use rights (known as DUAT, *direito de uso e aproveitamento da terra*) to individuals, communities or companies. In effect a type of lease, the DUAT stands for up to 100 years, and may be transferred, but not sold or mortgaged. Land use rights are conveyed either through a specific grant from the state or automatically, through occupancy 'according to customary norms and practices' for a period of at least 10 years (Hanchinamani 2003). This provision does not necessarily ensure that returnees may reoccupy their original lands but keeps that door open while granting a greater degree of tenure security for resettled populations.

The Land Law attempts to resolve restitution claims in various ways, including through compensation, the cancellation of lapsed claims and the imposition of the requirement that all actors granted land use rights by the state must have an approved development plan.[20] The goal of the latter approach is to rectify 'bad faith transactions' under which powerful landholders, elites or foreign interests obtained title at the

[19] These provisions are seen as a significant achievement and an appropriate response to challenges such as widespread illiteracy and the prevalence of informal tenure systems in Mozambique (Hanchinamani 2003). For a discussion of the perceived legitimacy of different forms of evidence and venues for deciding cases amongst claimants involved in land disputes, see Unruh (2001).

[20] Compensation is not addressed in detail in the 1997 Land Law but is in theory due for 'immovable property when rights are extinguished in the public interest' (1997 *Lei de Terras*, Article 18). See Unruh (2005: 257).

expense of peasants residing on the land without formal documentation. When investors signal their interest in pursuing claims for land on which peasants (including the displaced and resettled) have resided for at least 10 years, the Land Law mandates a formal consultation and negotiation process between the claimants. Under the law, local communities hold considerable power (at least in principle) in this encounter and in the approval of development plans. The investor's DUAT is to be revoked if implementation of the development plan has not commenced within 2 years of its provisional approval (Mozambican nationals are granted 5 years). According to Unruh (2005: 155), this is the 'primary way for the government to reclaim (for restitution purposes) land use rights from foreigners who may have for a number of years claimed rights under previous legal regimes, including the colonial regime'. The system creates two likely results. The first is the loss of largeholder rights, due to the strengthened rights of smallholders resident on the land. The second, more preferable option (from the point of view of the drafters of the 1997 Land Law), is the cooperative negotiation of a mutually beneficial agreement between local communities and investors with titles granted under previous regimes. Ideally, this system can 'provide concurrent restitution opportunities for both large and smallholders, even regarding the same land' (Unruh 2005: 157).

Albeit innovative, Mozambique's approach to restitution is contentious in several ways. First, the Land Law sets out a fairly comprehensive approach to resolving claims involving smallholders (including returnees) and investors, which formed the bulk of post-war disputes. However, it devotes insufficient attention to conflicts between returnees who wanted to reclaim to their original lands and IDPs who moved onto the land in their absence.[21] Indeed, the 1997 Land Law may in fact have been detrimental to the interests of returnees hoping to reclaim their original lands, as it backstops the rights of secondary occupants, provided they have been on the land for at least 10 years.[22] Second, when cooperative negotiations between claimants are unsuccessful, there is no specialised mechanism in place to adjudicate disputes.[23] As stated above, post-war Mozambican law encourages communities to resolve their own conflicts using traditional means, but when this fails, the only recourse is the formal court system, which for many years has been 'close to paralysis',

[21] For case studies of these conflicts, see Gengenbach (1998) and Myers (1994).

[22] This is not necessarily inappropriate, given that the rights, needs and interests of returnees must be negotiated alongside those of other stakeholders, such as secondary occupants.

[23] See, for example, the 1999 Law 11/99 on Extrajudicial Conflict Management (Unruh 2005: 160).

inundated by claims it lacks the resources to resolve (Unruh 2005: 159). This shortcoming has had particularly serious implications for poor Mozambicans who struggle to ensure the enforcement of their legal rights against uncooperative, powerful landholders and outside investors. However, it was also a major concern for displaced or migrant claimants engaged in disputes with other, non-migrant claimants. Unruh (2001) contends that in contrast to non-migrant disputants, customary approaches to land conflict resolution have often been perceived by migrant and displaced claimants as substantially less legitimate or 'just' than formal channels. As Unruh (2001) argues, for

> land dispute resolution to work in a context of recent armed conflict, the question of legitimacy becomes paramount . . . Dispute resolution rulings operating from a formal (state) tenure system which neglect to take into account post-war customary and migrant evidentiary constructs can result in outcomes which are considered inequitable and illegitimate, with aggregate adverse impacts on a peace process.

While the 1997 Land Law mandates the formal consideration of what is perceived as legitimate evidence by smallholder and migrant claimants (for example, verbal testimony), lack of access to the formal courts that are seen as the most just option by migrant claimants erodes the significance of these provisions. A third problem is that many rural Mozambicans may be unaware of their rights under the 1997 Land Law, in particular its prohibition of customary practices that discriminate against women claimants (Waterhouse 1998).[24]

In short, the 1997 *Lei de Terras* stands out as an innovative if inevitably imperfect attempt to uphold the right to land restitution in Mozambique. Certainly, Mozambique's land restitution efforts fall far short of the standard set in the Pinheiro Principles, which state in Principle 2.1 that 'All refugees and displaced persons have the right to have restored to them any housing, land and/or property of which they were arbitrarily or unlawfully deprived, or to be compensated for any housing, land and/or property that is factually impossible to restore as determined by an independent, impartial tribunal'. Yet one of the greatest strengths of Mozambique's approach to land restitution is that it is based on a pragmatic recognition of the state's severely constrained capacities, popular support for formally legitimising customary governance mechanisms, and a commitment to

[24] See Gengenbach (1998) for a discussion of women's land struggles in post-war Mozambique. Gengenbach argues that in Facazisse District, the most serious tensions involved women farmers struggling to ensure fair allocation of land, resolve boundary disputes, and deal with mounting resentment of displaced people who refused to return borrowed land.

making the most of limited state resources, rather than an ambitious standard impossible to realise in the country's present context. Property rights are particularly vulnerable to the 'lure of absolutes, which save us from the need to make context-governed judgements about claims of right' (Selznick 2002). By resisting this lure and adopting an approach suited to its capacities and context, Mozambique has created conditions in which it is more likely that returnees and their neighbours will benefit from the timely resolution of their land claims.

Looking beyond land

Just as there is no discrete, formal land restitution programme in Mozambique, there is no official policy on reconciliation or the provision of other forms of redress to the survivors of political violence in Mozambique, including returnees. As mentioned, the GPA failed to set the stage for the pursuit of redress, other than property restitution. At the same time, UNHCR's repatriation and reintegration programmes admittedly lacked the gender-sensitive and participatory components through which returnees' concerns about reconciliation and redress might have been expressed and carried to the government (Crisp 1996: 39–42). Given the dearth of concerted pressure from citizens, international agencies, regional powers and donor states, the post-conflict Mozambican government has made no serious efforts to commemorate or redress the atrocities of the war, beyond declaring 4 October national 'Peace Day' (Buford and van der Merwe 2004). Limited efforts were made by the government and among elected officials towards reconciliation, but this was primarily perceived as a process of *rapprochement* between Frelimo and Renamo as political parties, rather than as the broader creation or restoration of respectful, equitable relationships between citizens, communities and the state.

The pursuit of compensation, apologies and other forms of redress in Mozambique was complicated by the truly massive and yet personalised nature of suffering during the war. As one survivor expressed it, 'Each person suffered differently, but there is no doubt that all [of us] suffered' (Buford and van der Merwe 2004). An Africa Watch (1992: 5) study that attempted to assess the human suffering and damage caused by the civil war was forced to conclude that this was 'literally incalculable'. Yet, in the absence of state leadership, traditional spiritual healers and civil society institutions, including the Roman Catholic Church, made critical contributions to addressing the need for redress and reconciliation in return communities. Mozambican church leaders contributed to both the formal and informal peace processes by advocating a negotiated settlement to the conflict; serving as early intermediaries between Renamo and Frelimo; focusing attention on the needs of the displaced; and counselling divided communities on the meaning and value of peace, reconciliation and elections. The clergy were guided by the conviction that 'reconciliation was a basic vocation of the church', underlining that not only states and humanitarian agencies but also organisations such as churches may conceive of themselves as having a responsibility towards the displaced to create just conditions for return (Sengulane and Gonçalves 1998: 30).

Throughout much of Mozambique, Christianity blends with local cultures and belief systems, such that the churches' peacebuilding efforts were often paralleled by traditional spiritual practices intended to 'heal' violence and reintegrate combatants and returnees. Nordstrom (1997: 144) argues that at the local level, Mozambicans waged a remarkable 'war against violence' by using creative interpretations of spiritual traditions to treat, as a Mozambican *curandeiro* (traditional healer) expressed it, the 'rash on the soul' caused by conflict. Contrary to the premise that peace extends from elite-brokered treaties, Nordstrom (1997: 22) contends that the 'sophisticated institutions' crafted by rural Mozambicans 'set the stage for peace . . . [and] it was on this work that the peace accords were built'.

Yet as with customary approaches to land tenure and restitution, traditional healing practices are inevitably limited. The spiritual or religious rituals used to address past wrongs and enable reconciliation do not resonate across the board; many Mozambicans have found they cannot simply 'erase' memories of traumatic events, as some customary practices prescribe (Honwana 1998). In the longer term, a lack of formal approaches to redressing injustices may also foster denial and facilitate further social unrest, such as the violence that erupted in 2000 after Renamo narrowly lost the 1999 elections. These riots, in which 54 people were killed, reflected the incomplete nature of the national reconciliation process, with Dhlakama declaring that 'any victory [for Frelimo] is the fruit of theft' (Graybill 2004: 1127). The risks that could accompany a deterioration of relations between the country's most powerful parties are not to be underestimated, as the national constitution, which fails to impose adequate checks and balances on the exercise of political power, is 'tailor made to become a charter of revenge for sore winners lusting to punish their defeated rivals' (Weinstein 2002: 153).[25] 'Rather than being experienced as a mechanism of representation and a process heralding

[25] As Weinstein (2002: 142–146) explains, the Mozambican political system is based on an intense concentration of power in Maputo. This results in inadequate local-level

a break with the violent past', Mozambique's elections 'are an occasion when the wartime practices of geopolitical dominance are remembered and feared, and when politics turns dangerous' (Bertelsen 2004: 182–183). Importing foreign, formal approaches to justice and accountability may not necessarily rectify these problems. However, the Mozambican experience suggests that if a return is to be just, a balance may need to be sought between informal, traditionally-rooted approaches to reconciliation and redress, and state-level efforts to ensure peaceful reconciliation and accountability for the egregious crimes that forced citizens from their homes.

Just return and the responsibilities of a crippled state

Melding top-down and bottom-up approaches to creating peace and enabling return, the Mozambican case demonstrates that, in the short term at least, it is possible to have a rapid, durable return operation without formal reparations or acknowledgement of the state's role in perpetuating displacement. Does this vitiate the argument that state responsibility and redress are at the heart of a just return, and the suggestion that the justice of a repatriation operation can have important implications for its sustainability, and the strength of the broader peace process? What do responsibility and just return mean in the context of economically and administratively crippled states such as Mozambique?

Displaced Mozambicans' enthusiasm to return to their homes despite inordinately harsh conditions lends credence to the argument advanced in Chapter 2 that, from a refugee's perspective, voluntary repatriation may itself be seen as a form of redress and a powerful expression of justice.[26] As autonomous actors, refugees have the right to return to their homes even before minimum security conditions are in place; but the fact that some refugees are willing to return in chaotic, unsafe and ultimately unfair circumstances does not undermine the argument that states of origin and international actors have the duty to ensure that return can take place in conditions of safety and dignity. Mozambique's experience underlines that redress is only one of several various conditions that must be met in order for return to be fair and durable. Factors such as de-mining, the reconstruction of infrastructure, and the disarmament

power sharing, and the persistence of the deep regional cleavages that have troubled Mozambican politics since the colonial era.

26 The rapid return of refugees is also a testament to refugees' dissatisfaction with the conditions they faced in exile, such as a lack of access to land the refugees could farm for themselves. For more details on conditions in exile, see, for example, Andersson (1992) and McDermott Hughes (1999).

and demobilisation of combatants are also critical, and rightfully received concerted early attention from the Mozambican government and international actors during the repatriation process. However, it would be a mistake to conclude that redress did not play a significant role in the Mozambican return, even though it has been primarily provided through informal mechanisms outside the direct ambit of the state. Arguably, the repatriation process could have been more successful if the state and the international community had made more effort to strengthen the formal mechanisms necessary to backstop customary approaches to redress. For instance, accessible, specialised land claims courts could have helped circumvent violent conflict over restitution cases that customary authorities were unable to mediate effectively, while recognising and apologising for the crimes committed during the war may have engendered greater confidence among Mozambicans in their leaders and the state, or at least challenged the widespread perception of the state as simply 'a coercive mobiliser of unpaid labour' (Alexander 1997: 20). Yet return is not a tidy process with a neat cut-off date. Years after the formal resolution of the Mozambican civil war, returnees are still negotiating space for themselves at different levels in the national political community. Redress mechanisms such as apologies and truth commissions that were not applied in the early aftermath of the war may still have a role to play in facilitating this process.

How should we think about state responsibility and just return in cases such as Mozambique, where the state wanted to protect its citizens from displacement caused by non-state actors, but was unable to do so?[27] A state's inability to protect its citizens does not necessarily mean that it bears no moral responsibility for their plight: a state may be culpable for its citizens' displacement because it was negligent in developing the ability to protect and provide for them, duties that give the state its legitimacy. Yet this argument is not persuasive in the Mozambican case. While the government certainly exacerbated the alienation of large components of its citizenry through ill-conceived policies such as forced villagisation and its disdain for traditional authorities in their various manifestations, the state cannot be faulted for its inability to protect its citizens from Renamo attacks. Portuguese colonial rule in Mozambique was particularly brutal and exploitative, leaving Mozambican leaders little upon

[27] Two points of clarification are required here: First, as discussed, the Mozambican state was also complicit in actively causing forced migration and, thus, has a clear responsibility to redress those it arbitrarily or wrongfully displaced. Second, because the GPA legitimised Remano and paved the way for it to enter into the Mozambican political system, the state should arguably assume responsibility for promoting some form of redress for the atrocities Renamo committed during the war.

which to build when the country achieved its independence in 1975. Indeed, there were only 10 lawyers in the entire country at independence; 85 per cent of the population was illiterate; and democratic institutions, health care services and educational systems were essentially non-existent (UNHCR 1995). Mozambique had only 2 years of peace in which to build up its capacities before Renamo's destabilisation campaign began in 1977.[28] Although displaced Mozambicans were accustomed to expecting very little of their state, Chissano was well aware of the state's obligations towards its displaced citizens, commenting in 1988 that it would be wrong to ask the displaced to return when the conditions in Mozambique were untenable (Azevedo 2002: 149, Juergensen 2000: 27). In these circumstances, it was therefore highly appropriate for international actors, civil society and customary authorities to contribute to redressing past wrongs and enabling the refugees to return in safety and dignity. Following his mission to Mozambique in 1996, the former Representative of the UN Secretary-General on IDPs applauded the state for engaging outside actors in meeting the needs of the displaced, asserting, 'The flexible approach taken by the Government must be commended, in particular its willingness to transfer a major part of its coordinating responsibility to the United Nations during the peace implementation phase' (RSG 1997). This advanced the peace process by facilitating the more active involvement of Renamo in the repatriation movement and the provision of greater levels of support to civilians in Renamo-held areas. Similarly, by formally recognising the role of customary authorities in resolving land restitution claims, Mozambique both minimised the negative effect of its own limited capacity to adjudicate disputes and responded to the popular will of many rural Mozambicans who wanted to see a strong role for customary laws and officials in local and national governance. Indeed, 'peace was partly achieved on the promise of some kind of formal reinstatement for traditional leaders' (Lundin 1996, Waterhouse 1998). Yet the contributions made by international actors, civil society leaders and customary authorities to return and redress in Mozambique were not and are not a panacea for greater direct accountability from the state. (As discussed in Chapter 1, the state can still share remedial responsibility for displacement, even if it does not have direct causal or moral responsibility for uprooting its citizens.) Many Mozambicans frankly recognise that

[28] In this regard the struggle to redress the injustices associated with the Mozambican civil war segues with campaigns to achieve reparations for African countries from western countries for colonialism and slavery. The Mozambican case also raises the pressing question of what remedial responsibilities are borne by states such as South Africa, which were complicit in atrocities in other countries. However, these issues are outside the scope of this work.

remedies such as financial compensation for the violations committed during the war are unlikely to materialise, 'given the economic reality of [our] country', but object to the fact that other, inexpensive approaches to accountability and redress are also stymied because of insufficient political will among the former combatants who have now moved into mainstream party politics (Buford and van der Merwe 2004).

After the war, a survivor of the violence in Gurue was asked how he and his family were faring, and reflected, 'We are all right. Our child can now cry at night. Children were taught not to cry after dark during the armed conflict' (Azevedo 2002: 185). Not having to fear that a child's cries will attract a brutal attack is perhaps a sadly low bar for satisfaction with repatriation and reconstruction processes but reflects the relative nature of different communities' priorities, values and expectations regarding peace and justice. International standards such as the UN Reparations Principles may yet have an important role to play in prompting the Mozambican government to attend to its unresolved responsibilities. However, the country's experiences to date underline the importance of ensuring that emerging norms on redress for the displaced are flexible enough to be tailored to the challenging contexts in which many repatriation and redress processes play out, and to account for different conceptions and expectations of justice, some of which may best be served through informal or customary channels.

7 Analysis of case studies

Taken in total, the cases of Guatemala, Bosnia and Mozambique paint a rather bleak picture of the difficulties associated with efforts to redress returning refugees and uphold responsibility for their displacement. Far from being a 'silver bullet' to the safe, durable and ultimately just return of refugees, these cases demonstrate that, in some instances, concentrating on redress can detract attention from persistent obstacles to return and inadvertently generate new tensions that further complicate return and reintegration processes. This was illustrated in the Bosnian case, where international and domestic actors' concerted focus on property restitution effectively marginalised attempts to resolve other barriers to return, such as pervasive discrimination and unemployment, and sparked fresh grievances among evicted secondary occupants left without adequate humanitarian support. Indeed, each of these cases underlines the importance of critically examining and frankly recognising the limitations and unintended consequences of redress programmes involving returnees. Yet a critical approach should not obscure the advance these cases represent, when compared to repatriation operations in which returnees were denied any form of redress for the wrongs they suffered. While redress was not a panacea for the shortcomings of repatriation movements in Guatemala, Bosnia and Mozambique, the provision of reparations was nonetheless a significant response to returnees' concerns, and helped lay the foundation for continuing efforts to improve relations between returnees and their state, as well as quality of life in return communities.

Experiences in Guatemala, Bosnia and Mozambique both shaped and were shaped by the nascent international norms on redress for returnees examined in Chapter 3. The following section discusses the insights these cases offer in terms of how these norms may be effectively applied, thus contributing to the creation of conditions for a just return, understood in terms of the recasting of a new relationship of rights and duties between the state and its returning citizens. As discussed in Chapter 2, such a recasting of the state–citizen relationship should ensure that returnees and the non-displaced alike benefit from equal, effective protection for their security and basic human rights, including accountability for violations of these rights. The chapter then goes on to examine the implications of these cases for the conceptions of state responsibility and just return discussed in Part I. Given what these cases reveal about the difficulties associated with using reparations to enable just return, it may be argued that the 'minimum account' of just return discussed in Part I in fact sets a bar that is too high to reach in practice. I will respond to this potential criticism, and briefly address a number of the thorny questions the cases raise regarding the attribution and exercise of responsibility for displacement in practice; the culpability of actors beyond the state of origin, such as international organisations, foreign governments and insurgent groups; and whether reparations undertaken with a view to enabling just return should strive to restore the *status quo ante*.[1]

Crafting redress for returnees: insights from Guatemala, Bosnia and Mozambique

As Chapter 3 demonstrated, norms on redress for refugees are still in relatively early phases of development. International law does not yet offer firm guidance on the minimum requirements of reparations programmes for the victims of forced displacement, and while clear trends are emerging regarding the inclusion of provisions on redress for returnees in peace agreements and the institutionalisation of responsibility for post-conflict property restitution, practice remains scattered. Experiences in Guatemala, Bosnia and Mozambique make evident some of the main difficulties associated with devising and implementing reparations programmes that may benefit returnees and contribute to the resolution of displacement: reparations initiatives are often costly, legally and bureaucratically complex, and politically controversial, as they may run against the vested interests of local powerbrokers and state actors wedded to nationalistic or elitist ideologies. Yet through both their successes and shortcomings, the cases also provide insight into the development of effective redress programmes for returnees. As stated above, the goal of this analysis is not to generate a checklist or 'how-to' guide for the architects of reparations programmes. Rather, the aim is to highlight some of the broad characteristics of sensitively designed reparations initiatives, as evidenced by historical experience, and open up the theoretical questions they entail. Ill-fated attempts to provide redress to returnees to countries such as Afghanistan based on the Bosnian approach to property

[1] I will also examine some of these issues at greater length in Part III.

restitution underline the need for restraint in inferring universally applicable 'best practices' from a limited body of international experience.[2] Arguably, the clearest general 'lesson' from these cases is that the hallmark of effective reparations programmes for returnees is not a particular institutional configuration or resolute focus on an ideal principle, such as the restoration of the *status quo ante*, but the ability to respond to local needs, concerns, conditions and constraints.

As I have argued in the case studies above, specialised reparations initiatives for returnees cannot be pursued in isolation from broader transitional justice strategies. On the one hand, focusing on refugees' remedial rights to the exclusion of the non-displaced risks creating resentment among 'stayees', which may undermine return and reintegration processes. On the other, many returnees are survivors of the large-scale human rights violations investigated by institutions such as truth commissions and criminal tribunals, and should be able to access and participate in these bodies on an equitable basis. In order to draw out the insights these cases hold regarding the characteristics of reparations programmes that may contribute to the just return of refugees, I will build upon de Greiff's general account of the attributes of well-designed reparations programmes for the survivors of large-scale human rights violations (de Greiff 2006, 2007).[3] De Greiff's framework is particularly germane as his conception of the purpose of reparations processes segues closely with the arguments advanced in Part I on the role redress plays in just return processes by facilitating the restoration or creation of a legitimate relationship of rights and duties between the state and its repatriating citizens. According to de Greiff (2007: 154–167), the three primary goals of reparations programmes are to recognise past wrongs and victims' individual worth; build civic trust; and develop social solidarity, with a view to returning individuals to the status of citizens within trusting, trustworthy and empathetic political communities. To accomplish these goals, reparations programmes must be appropriately comprehensive, complete, complex and coherent. They must also adopt an apposite position on the issues of finality and munificence (de Greiff 2006: 6–13).

[2] Representatives of the international community and the Afghan government initially attempted to provide restitution to returnees through the creation of a Special Court for land claims, based on the Bosnian CRPC model. However, Afghanistan lacked the domestic capacity and robust international support that characterised the Bosnian operation, and the court collapsed without making a significant contribution to resolving returnees' claims (Foley 2008, Bradley 2009a).

[3] De Greiff focuses in particular on 'massive' reparations programmes that aim to provide different forms of compensation to survivors. However, his framework may inform a wider range of remedial activities.

While comprehensiveness refers to the specific types of crimes reparations programmes attempt to redress, completeness denotes an initiative's ability to 'cover, at the limit, the whole universe of potential beneficiaries' (de Greiff 2006: 6). Although property restitution programmes clearly conceive of forced migration as a crime in need of rectification, transitional justice initiatives, such as criminal tribunals, and compensation schemes do not always recognise territorial displacement as a violation perpetrating states are obliged to recognise and redress. When states have carried out a litany of abuses from murder and torture to forced sterilisation and rape, it may be difficult for reparations programmes to address each type of crime in a meaningful manner. However,

> All things considered, comprehensiveness is a desirable characteristic. It is better, both morally and practically, to repair as many categories of crime as feasible . . . Leaving important categories of victims unaddressed not only deprives a transitional administration of the gains in legitimacy that it might accrue by establishing a comprehensive reparations programme but it also virtually guarantees that the issue of reparations will continue to be on the political agenda. (de Greiff 2006: 9–10)

In the aftermath of violence causing large-scale displacement, returnees certainly must be considered an 'important category of victim'. The Guatemalan case illustrates the value for returnees of comprehensive reparations programmes that recognise displacement as a crime and attempt to redress it not only through specialised land claims systems, but also through truth commissions and court cases concerned with a broad range of interconnected human rights violations. Yet efforts to redress displacement in Guatemala were far from complete: only collective returnees from Mexico were able to benefit from property restitution and compensation programmes, excluding scores of 'potential beneficiaries' with similar claims. According to de Greiff (2006: 6), it 'goes without saying that completeness is a desirable characteristic in a reparations program', but the fact that reparations are mandated on paper does not mean they will reach all those who should be able to benefit from them. This was clearly evident in the Mozambican case, where provisions in the General Peace Agreement guaranteeing restitution for returnees did not translate into formal initiatives to ensure the implementation of this right. Setting appropriate evidentiary standards and eligibility guidelines, conducting outreach to raise awareness of remedial rights; and identifying or creating institutions capable of resolving large numbers of claims rapidly and even-handedly are essential steps towards ensuring that all those who deserve reparations, including displaced persons, are actually able to access them (de Greiff 2006: 6, Duthie 2012a). As experiences in Bosnia and Guatemala demonstrate, refugee-creating states may be highly resistant to taking the steps necessary to ensure that reparations programmes are appropriately comprehensive and complete. Concerted pressure and support from international actors and refugees themselves may play a critical role in ensuring that reparations initiatives tackle displacement as a crime, and that all those with similar claims can access redress on an equitable basis.

Beyond comprehensiveness and completeness, the architects of reparations programmes should also strive to achieve an appropriate level of complexity. 'Whereas comprehensiveness relates to the types of crimes reparations efforts seek to redress, complexity refers to the ways in which the efforts attempt to do so . . . A reparations programme is more complex if it distributes benefits of more distinct types, and in more distinct ways, than its alternatives' (de Greiff 2006: 10). A complex reparations programme might involve, for example, compensation in addition to official apologies and annual commemorations. Particularly if reparations are intended to open up a range of options regarding the resolution of displacement, it is desirable for reparations programmes to strike a balance between meaningful symbolic and material reparations. The implications of disproportionately focusing on material reparations were strikingly clear in the Bosnian case, where restitution was insufficient to make minority return a viable option for many displaced persons. Symbolic reparations that acknowledge past crimes and actively engage citizens in discussing their history and future are hardly a sure-fire route to peaceful reintegration in return communities, and it is debatable whether initiatives such as a truth commission would contribute to reintegration and the resolution of the final vestiges of displacement in the Balkans. Yet it is clear that in the absence of such symbolic reparations, minority return was rarely a practicable choice for the displaced.

Particularly in impoverished countries such as Guatemala, the question of whether community development initiatives such as building schools, wells or health centres should count as part of a complex reparations programme has attracted considerable debate among transitional justice advocates. Proponents of this approach argue that 'reparative' community development projects can 'provide recognition of the wrong done to a community as a whole and give members of divided communities a focus around which to begin rebuilding the fragile ties among neighbours stretched or broken during the conflict' (Roht-Arriaza 2004: 129). This approach may thus be particularly productive in return communities, conveniently sidestepping the dilemma of choosing between redress and other urgent needs such as healthcare. However, there are many problems associated with attempts to use redress as a proxy for basic social justice and public services (de Greiff and Duthie 2009). First, as transitional justice advocates in Guatemala point out, this approach conflates the state's separate duties to redress past wrongs and provide basic services to its citizens (Hayner 2011: 173–175, Roht-Arriaza 2004: 130). Second, it is often difficult to target the benefits of 'remedial' development projects to victims; even when this is accomplished, it risks generating resentment and social discontent. Third, focusing on community development as redress can overlook the special needs of the displaced, such as the resolution of land claims (Fitigu 2005, Roht-Arriaza 2004: 130–136). While experiences in Guatemala, Bosnia and Mozambique do not offer an incontestable answer to the question of the proper place of community development projects in reparations strategies, they highlight the importance of consulting with the intended beneficiaries of reparations programmes to ensure that whatever form redress takes, it responds to survivors' concerns and supports their ability to make choices about their futures. Furthermore, if 'reparative' community development projects are to advance a just return process through the creation or recreation of a legitimate relationship of rights and duties between the state and returnees, they must not conflate or confuse the state's responsibility to redress displacement and its broader duty to protect the basic human rights of all its citizens. If community development projects are to serve as a form of redress in the context of a just return process, they must be conscientiously framed as such, lest they be manipulated or perceived as a chance for governments to 'slap [on] a "reparations" label . . . and get off cheaply' (Roht-Arriaza 2004: 130).

Whether or not community development projects form part of 'complex' redress programmes, de Greiff argues that the different elements of these programmes must be internally and externally coherent. De Greiff (2006: 10–11) writes that 'internal coherence . . . refers to the relationship between the different types of benefits a reparations programme distributes . . . in order to reach the desired aims, it is important that benefits [both symbolic and material] internally support one another'. For example, restitution for returnees has typically been conceptualised and pursued separately from other transitional justice efforts. Administratively, this is often a strategic approach. However, the above cases demonstrate the importance of conceiving of restitution as an integral part of broader transitional justice processes in which displaced persons have an essential stake; in some cases, the degree to which restitution benefited Bosnian and Guatemalan returnees depended on the extent to which they were also able to benefit from other forms of redress, such as trials that removed the architects of displacement from return communities. In contrast to internal coherence, external coherence requires that reparations support broader national transitional processes (de Greiff 2006: 10–12). For example, as in the Bosnian case, efforts to resolve returnees' land claims can have a positive catalytic effect on post-conflict challenges, such as reforming legal systems and preparing the country to engage in trade and attract investment. By the same token, the Guatemalan experience demonstrates that if restitution efforts for returnees from highly tenure-insecure countries do not unfold alongside a broader process of land reform, the gains made for returnees may be fleeting at best.[4]

The last issues which, according to de Greiff (2006: 12–13), must be confronted in the construction of effective reparations programmes are finality and munificence. Finality refers to whether claimants who have received benefits through a particular reparations programme should still be able to pursue redress through other channels. For example, if a refugee receives compensation for her dispossession through a mass-claims system, should she still be able to file a case in court to obtain further redress? As de Greiff points out, it is difficult to come to firm conclusions about the desirability of finality in the abstract. While it is generally not desirable to foreclose citizens' access to justice institutions such as the courts, allowing the beneficiaries of large-scale reparations programmes to pursue further claims in court runs the risk of short circuiting the massive redress programme and generating dissatisfaction among its beneficiaries as court settlements are typically higher than those provided through mass claims systems. In terms of using reparations to facilitate the just return of refugees, the cases of Mozambique, Guatemala and Bosnia suggest that it may be legitimate to limit displaced persons' ability to make additional claims regarding the loss of their property if they have been able to access and benefit from restitution or compensation through a mass claims system. However, as I have argued, just return is a long-term process that may require numerous rapprochements between the state and its repatriated citizens regarding the acknowledgement and redress of the abuses inflicted on them. Generally speaking, as many avenues as possible should remain open to citizens in order to facilitate the renegotiation of their relationship with the state.

4 See Wily (2009) for a critique of the tendency of humanitarian actors to promote property restitution processes for displaced persons that are disjoined from local tenure norms and broader tenure reform processes.

Munificence refers to the magnitude of benefits available to individuals through specific material reparations efforts. The *worth* of the benefits of reparations programmes can rarely be reliably measured, as this depends on a range of factors such as the type of benefit distributed (for example, land or money), the context in which recipients live and how recipients perceive their own losses. De Greiff (2006: 12–13) argues that, by itself, munificence does not determine the success of a reparations programme, pointing out that although Argentina's provision of bonds for $224,000 to the families of those who 'disappeared' during the Dirty War is among the most munificent reparations settlements on record, the programme was not significantly more successful in terms of assuaging grievances than much less munificent agreements such as that reached between the US government and Japanese Americans interned during World War II. The experiences of Mozambique and Guatemala certainly bear out this conclusion: despite the shortcomings of customary approaches to redress for some claimants, studies of post-conflict Mozambican communities suggest that many returnees were reasonably satisfied by efforts to resolve their land claims with the assistance of customary authorities, which incurred virtually no financial cost to the Mozambican state or international donors (Unruh 2001). In contrast, although the Guatemalan government and its international backers channelled significant amounts of money into the purchase of land for returning refugees, this aspect of the reparations effort arguably did more to line the pockets of wealthy land-owners than it did to sustainably resolve returnees' grievances regarding systematic injustice in the national land tenure system. Indeed, the Guatemalan case underlines that while international support is often essential to returnees receiving any remedial benefits, it is also incumbent upon donors to ensure that their assistance translates into munificence for the victims, rather than the victimisers.

Critical analysis of efforts to redress refugees returning to Guatemala, Bosnia and Mozambique thus supports and adds nuance to de Greiff's contention that well-designed reparations programmes must offer fitting responses to the questions of comprehensiveness, completeness, complexity, coherence, finality and munificence. Yet these cases also point to some additional characteristics of reparations programmes that may contribute to the task of upholding state responsibility for displacement and enabling just return. First and perhaps most importantly, if reparations are to facilitate the just return of refugees, they must be based on suitable timeframes. This requires not only astute decisions concerning the finality of particular reparations schemes, but also timely and decisive action so that reparations programmes particularly those focused on property restitution, commence promptly, ideally in advance of large-scale returns. This is critical to building returnees' confidence in the viability of return, avoiding land conflicts and averting the internal displacement of returnees. The timely creation of restitution and compensation programmes for the displaced necessitates the inclusion of clear, detailed provisions on return and redress in peace agreements in order to leverage international support and set a clear standard to which the state can be held to account. Yet the timeliness of reparations programmes for returnees is not simply a question of being quick off the mark. It is also essential for the state of origin and its international backers to recognise that just return and the redress of displacement is a long-term endeavour. While experiences in countries such as Bosnia suggest that it is certainly reasonable and even advisable to 'front load' reparations efforts in the early years of peace and return processes in order to minimise complexities such as those posed by the protracted presence of secondary occupants on refugees' lands, governments and donors must temper their desire to quickly close the file on return and redress, and ensure that avenues to obtain redress remain open for refugees who are reluctant to embark on an early return.[5] At the same time, governments cannot expect that claims commissions and other remedial initiatives will quickly and neatly resolve all those grievances borne by returnees and other survivors of violence and atrocity. As Hamber and Wilson (2002: 5) argue, 'we should expect to have to live with the unsatisfied demands (for their own versions of truth, justice, compensation, and so on) of survivors for a long time'. Recasting the relationship between the state of origin and its returning citizens requires that space remains available within the political community for the expression of grievances without fear of recrimination.

Second, given the fierce opposition to the return of refugees and the restitution of their property that is often mounted by corporate elites, secondary occupants and politicians with deep-seated nationalistic or personal interests, these cases underline that effective redress programmes for returnees – particularly restitution schemes – require strong enforcement mechanisms at the local and national levels. Effective enforcement includes not only the availability of police forces trained and willing to evict secondary occupants from reclaimed properties but also concerted diplomatic pressure to ensure that institutions such as

[5] To argue that just return must be conceived as a long-term enterprise is not to imply that it is productive to encourage forced migrants to hold on to refugee or returnee labels long after repatriating. Rather, it means that domestic and international actors alike are well-advised to be attuned to the longer-term challenges of community reintegration and reconstruction, recognising that acknowledging and rectifying past injustices may take place in phases, over a long period as trust among neighbours and between citizens and the state is gradually rebuilt.

claims commissions get off the ground in the first place and run efficiently and effectively for the duration of their mandates. As the Bosnian case demonstrates, vesting a trusted domestic or international actor with the authority to dismiss recalcitrant officials and re-write obstructionist legislation may also be essential to ensuring the fair and timely adjudication and implementation of decisions.

Third, formal reparations programmes, even those supported with foreign funding, inevitably incur costs for the state and, by extension, its citizens as financial and human resources are diverted from normal government functions to support the provision of redress. Fairly distributing the costs of redress is a perennial challenge for reparations programmes. However, redressing returnees through restitution entails a particularly high price for secondary occupants, many of whom move onto refugees' properties not out of malicious intent, but stark necessity. Thus, a defining characteristic of reparations programmes conducive to just return is that they avoid the generation of new grievances by providing adequate support to secondary occupants evicted to make way for returnees. This may include assistance with transportation and securing alternative accommodation. Past experience demonstrates the importance of managing the positive and negative expectations of both returning claimants and secondary occupants facing the prospect of eviction by clearly communicating the purpose of reparations and the types of assistance and benefits that will be made available.

Last, experiences in Guatemala, Bosnia and Mozambique all illustrate, albeit in different ways, the costs and benefits associated with engaging displaced persons directly in the negotiation of reparations intended to enable their return. For example, as discussed above, Guatemalan refugees' determination to negotiate the conditions of their own return and redress with their government enabled them to develop sharp political skills; enhance their visibility and, by extension, their physical safety; and secure a comparatively munificent 'deal' in terms of access to land. Given the subjective nature of dignity and differing conceptions of justice, refugee involvement in articulating the nature and scope of reparations increases the likelihood that these measures will actually be perceived by the recipients as morally and politically significant, and relevant to their needs. This view is reflected in Long's argument that for the many Guatemalan refugees who saw return as a '*duty* to build a new Guatemala . . . dignity resided in their ability to shape the nature of this return' (Long 2008: 34). However, effective negotiations can be stymied by power struggles and lack of agreement within the refugee community. Furthermore, constant consultation and negotiation can become a proxy for government action, as it did in the Guatemalan case. The implication of this is that while refugees should ideally have the opportunity to participate directly in the negotiation of the terms of their own return and redress, vigilance is necessary on the part of refugee organisations and their international supporters to ensure that spoilers do not use negotiation as a cover for inaction or the detrimental pursuit of special interests.

Implications for theorising state responsibility and just return

The fact that this analysis of the characteristics of effective reparations programmes for returnees draws in equal measure from failures as it does from successes in Guatemala, Bosnia and Mozambique serves as a word of warning against underestimating the challenges associated with redressing displacement and enabling just return. Indeed, my critical appraisal of these cases and conclusion that none of them met the conditions of a just return begs some important questions: Does the 'minimum account' of just return set out in Part I represent an impossibly high bar? Is the standard for just return discussed in Chapter 2 legally and morally valid but simply unachievable in practice? In this section I will respond to these questions, and reflect on the implications of these cases for my account of state responsibility for displacement and just return, focusing on the challenge of conceptualising and upholding state responsibility for displacement in practice, the culpability and responsibility of actors beyond the state of origin and whether the restoration of the *status quo ante* should necessarily be the goal of reparations provided as part of a just return process.

While there is clearly a gap between the normative arguments I have developed and the historical record in these three cases, this does not vitiate my conception of the state of origin's remedial responsibility for displacement and just return, or render it irrelevant to 'real world' practice. This is true for a number of reasons. First, although my argument presents marked challenges for refugee-creating states who have traditionally never been called to account for the injustice of uprooting their citizens, it is ultimately austere: when exiled citizens return to their countries of origin, they should be able to do so in safety and dignity, with the expectation that their state of origin will protect and provide for their basic human rights. This obliges the state to recognise returnees' legitimate grievances and attempt to remedy the injustices that forced refugees from their homes, but it need not necessarily involve adherence to a specific transitional justice 'blueprint', the creation of costly and complex institutions such as criminal tribunals, or the attainment of distributive justice and the resolution of debates on the nature of a just society.[6] Rather, I have offered a *minimum account* of just return, stressing the importance of adopting a flexible approach to reparations and post-conflict justice that takes into account local histories, values and limitations. It is therefore difficult to see how the bar for just return could be lowered and still maintain that it speaks to the issue of justice. Achieving even a modicum of justice in countries decimated by violence will always be a Herculean task, but it is counter-productive (and potentially also nonsensical) to lower the bar simply in order to make it easier to meet.

Second, many of the obstacles to just return experienced in these cases, particularly in Guatemala and Bosnia, are traceable to state actors' opposition to the return and redress of refugees. The problem is not that the conditions for just return are too high to meet, but that state actors have to *want* to reach this bar and receive the necessary support from the international community to do so. When actors within the state of origin are divided in their support for return, the challenge is for domestic and international proponents of repatriation and redress to make a convincing case and apply incentives and pressure to secure the unified cooperation of all those actors with important roles to play in the just return process. In this connection, it would be instructive to examine cases where returnees were warmly welcomed by the vast majority of actors in new or transformed states, such as when exiled activists returned to South Africa after the collapse of apartheid, and to East Timor after the withdrawal of Indonesia. The minimum conditions of just return are perhaps more easily achieved in cases such as these, which involve relatively small numbers of refugees from elite backgrounds who return to help lead new or radically reformed states.

Third, it is clear that in all three cases the efforts made to redress returnees represented, on the whole, a positive contribution to national peace processes. This suggests that even in cases in which there are major barriers impeding the achievement of conditions of just return, the concept of providing reparations with a view to recasting returnees' relationships with the state may provide a relevant and productive framework to guide and improve practice. This is not to excuse

[6] Granted, the principles of comprehensiveness and complexity, discussed above, may backstop calls for the creation of institutions such as criminal tribunals. However, comprehensiveness and complexity are values that need to be weighed against other considerations and constraints faced by the architects of reparations programmes, who ultimately have to decide which approaches to redress are most appropriate in the circumstances. At any rate, costliness is clearly not a prerequisite for the successfulness of a transitional justice initiative. In many cases supporting local or national reparations initiatives may be more economically efficient and politically effective than establishing ad hoc, high budget international institutions.

attempts to push refugees to return in sub-standard conditions, but to recognise that even morally and legally problematic repatriation operations can benefit from normative analysis through this lens, and may be improved by the instigation or revision of reparations programmes, with a view to addressing returnees' justice claims. As I have argued, just return must be seen as a long-term endeavour that unfolds alongside broader reintegration, reconciliation and peacebuilding processes. Some of the difficulties encountered in the early years of repatriation movements may eventually be negotiated and resolved, underlining that the need is not for lax criteria that may be easily and promptly satisfied but for apposite standards calibrated to facilitate the transition to durable peace.

While these cases therefore do not undermine the relevance and cogency of my conception of just return, they do raise important questions regarding the allocation and implications of responsibility for forced migration. I have already discussed some of the these issues in the case studies above, such as how state responsibility for displacement may be understood and acted upon in the context of state collapse. However, some concluding reflections are warranted on the challenges these cases present for conceptualising and operationalising responsibility for the creation of refugees. As the cases make clear, a state's ability to effectively exercise remedial responsibility for displacement depends on the complexity of the justice claims at stake, as well as the availability of financial and human resources, cooperation among different state actors and the strength of the state's bureaucracy. The actions and policies of international organisations and donors definitively shape the latter variables. In this respect, my conception of state responsibility and just return intersects with an inherent tension in contemporary peacebuilding: both my theory of state responsibility and just return and the international community's broader engagement in post-war nation-building are 'premised on the certitude of the need for the reconstruction of the state (or, indeed, the nation-state) in the aftermath of conflict. However . . . this imperative is [often] actively undercut by the thrust of the international financial institutions and donor programmes which seek, in effect, to dismantle the state' (Alden 2001: 123–124). In cases such as Guatemala and Mozambique, the state's ability to exercise responsibility for its most vulnerable citizens, including returnees, is limited not only by its commitment to privileging the interests of elites, but also by the ill-conceived policies of donors and international organisations, which often foster aid dependency and cut back critical social programmes in the name of economic reform. Maximising the potential of 'nation-building' initiatives and the capacity of post-conflict states to exercise remedial responsibility for displacement and enable just return therefore requires greater coherence in the policies of international actors.

Paradoxically, many returnees may be wary of a stronger state, even if it is ostensibly reformed. Such hesitancy was exemplified by Mozambicans who sought a stronger role for customary rather than formal state authorities in local governance, and the behaviour of Guatemalan returnees who created social and economic networks to increase their own autonomy and reduce the presence of the state in their lives (Long 2008: 32). Must a responsible state be directly and extensively involved in returnees' lives? The experience of countries such as Mozambique suggests that while it is clearly desirable that state institutions be available to protect citizens' rights and help resolve their claims, formal institutions need not necessarily be the first 'port of call' in a just return process. Creating room for customary mechanisms to work alongside formal institutions such as courts in the resolution of returnees' claims may indeed, in some cases, be the mark of a responsible state cognisant of its own limitations, and responsive to the needs and values of its citizens.

In the conventional refugee paradigm, the state of origin is assumed to be the actor that is causally and morally responsible for causing its citizens' exile. The Guatemalan, Bosnian and Mozambican cases alike demonstrate that, in practice, the attribution of these aspects of responsibility for displacement is rarely so clean cut. In these three cases, actors such as hostile foreign governments and insurgent groups played a direct role in creating refugee crises. Morally and legally, there are strong grounds for arguing that these actors should have to exercise responsibility for their actions by redressing the wronged state and its citizens.[7] Yet due to factors such as the lack of compelling political pressure and the dearth of accessible legal mechanisms with the power to prosecute violations of international human right laws, these actors are rarely held to account. While an in-depth discussion of the responsibility of agents other than the state of origin for causing and rectifying displacement is outside the ambit of this project, it may be argued that greater accountability on the part of actors such as the US, which orchestrated the Guatemalan coup and backstopped the country's genocidal government, would bolster efforts to hold refugees' states of origin responsible for their own parts in creating refugee flows. Yet progress on this front could not, in any event, substitute for efforts to ensure that the state of origin exercises *remedial responsibility* for displacement. The enduring and most important political relationship at stake in repatriation processes is that linking returnees and their state of origin. Therefore, the state of origin's remedial responsibility for displacement (which may or may not be linked

[7] For discussion of legal arguments to this effect, see, for example, Shelton (2006).

to causal and moral responsibility for displacement) and the rectification of the relationship between returnees and their state generally remain the most salient issues for those concerned with accountability for forced migration and the use of repatriation as an ethically defensible solution to displacement. To return to the discussion in Chapter 1 of Miller's theory of responsibility, while other actors may share causal and moral responsibility for displacement, the state of origin bears the lion's share of *remedial responsibility* for displacement. That is, the state of origin has a 'special obligation to put the bad situation right'; it has been 'picked out, either individually or along with others, as having a responsibility towards the deprived or suffering party that is not shared equally among all agents' (Miller 2001: 454). That 'special obligation' is the bond of citizenship, albeit strained, between the state and its displaced citizens.

Yet, as discussed in Chapter 1, the allocation of remedial responsibility depends on variables such as the capabilities of the actors involved and the effectiveness of the aid they are able to provide (Miller 2001: 461). This points to the final set of issues these case studies raise concerning remedial responsibility for displacement and just return: the role of the international community, including international organisations, foreign governments and donors. The experiences of Guatemala, Bosnia and Mozambique suggest that states will rarely step up and embrace responsibility for redressing displacement on their own accord; even if the state of origin is in principle willing to acknowledge its role in the creation of refugees and its obligation to redress their displacement, it may lack the capacity to act on this duty without external support. From the outset, international pressure is needed to prompt states to acknowledge and shoulder their responsibilities in the initial phases of the repatriations process, as well as in the long term. These cases suggest that supporting reparations programmes for returnees is a prudent course of action not only for states of origin but also for donors and international organisations, as these initiatives are often conducive to the durable resolution of displacement, the avoidance of land conflicts and the reform of post-conflict state structures. International actors committed to promoting responsibility for displacement and just return are well advised, first and foremost, to engage in the early phases of the peace and return processes, in order to ensure that detailed, enforceable provisions outlining refugees' right to return and redress are included in peace agreements. While international actors may be well placed to push for the timely and equitable resolution of returnees' claims, these cases suggest that it is also prudent to recognise that attempts to rush return and repatriations processes are likely to be counter-productive. Instead, the cooperative involvement of international actors may be productively used to build returnees' trust in the repatriation and redress processes and, eventually, in their state of origin. In addition, international actors can facilitate the effective exercise of remedial responsibility for displacement by bringing the insights gained from previous return and redress processes to bear on new operations, keeping in mind that the transfer of 'lessons' must take into account factors such as different political, historical, socio-economic and cultural contexts. Last, international actors may improve their contribution to upholding remedial responsibility for displacement by investing more consistently in reparations programmes for returnees and supporting the development of a cadre of experts who can help international organisations such as the United Nations move beyond an ad hoc approach to this ubiquitous post-conflict challenge (Leckie 2008).

Beyond these observations on the effective engagement of international actors in helping states of origin to shoulder remedial responsibility for displacement, the case studies evoke further questions regarding the responsibilities of international actors themselves. What can be expected, minimally, of the international community regarding support for return and redress? What are the responsibilities of donors who support redress programmes? If donors push for and bankroll reparations programmes, to what extent can they still be seen as an expression of responsibility and accountability on the part of the state of origin? What are the moral and political implications of donors and host states supporting reparations programmes for returnees with the self-interested goal of facilitating or justifying the revocation of asylum and the 'mandated' repatriation of refugees? Although it is not possible to respond to these questions in detail here, they highlight the diverse and not necessarily altruistic motivations for international involvement in redressing displacement, which must be taken into consideration in the design and implementation of reparations programmes intended to support the just return of refugees.

The last and perhaps most contentious insight that emerges from these cases pertains to the proper goal of redress itself: that is, must reparations aim to restore the *status quo ante* if they are to enable just return? As I discussed in earlier chapters, restitution has traditionally been seen as the 'first form of reparations', required unless it is 'materially impossible' or 'involves a burden out of all proportion to the benefit deriving from restitution instead of compensation' (Shelton 2002: 849). Many refugee advocates, particularly those concerned with the plight of the Palestinian refugees, have ardently argued that the just resolution of refugee crises must involve *restitutio in integrum* ('full restitution') at least in terms of the restoration of lost property and the return of refugees to their original homes and lands. In Bosnia, particularly strenuous efforts were made to meet this demand, which is reflected in documents such as the UN Principles on Housing and Property Restitution for Refugees and

Displaced Persons (Pinheiro Principles 2005).[8] However, experiences in Bosnia as well as in Guatemala and Mozambique underline that the restoration of the *status quo ante* is often impossible: many of the crimes associated with displacement, such as torture, rape and murder simply cannot be undone. Restoration of the *status quo ante* in terms of the distribution of properties and populations may also be extremely difficult if not impossible to achieve, and is not necessarily of foremost relevance to enabling just return, defined in terms of the restoration or creation of a viable relationship of rights and duties between the state and its returning citizens.

As Torpey (2006: 7) argues, 'the ethic of responsibility enjoins finding the seam where the normatively desirable meets the historically possible'. These cases demonstrate that this equation does not necessarily result in the restoration of the *status quo ante*. In Mozambique, for example, state officials assumed that it was both desirable and plausible for refugees to return to their 'areas of origin' after the war, but in fact this was not always an historically clear-cut or desirable proposition from the returnees' point of view. The term 'areas of origin' itself 'defies definition in the context of Mozambique. This area may be one of numerous locations, including the land held by one's parents, land given as part of a colonial villagisation scheme, land given as part of a government villagisation or other agricultural scheme, or land held before the most recent displacement . . . smallholders themselves often selectively determine[d] these areas based upon economic and other opportunities' (Myers 1994: 615). 'Areas of origin' and the '*status quo ante*' were also slippery, volatile concepts in Guatemala, where indigenous refugee communities traced their displacement to the invasion of Spanish colonisers. In Guatemala as in many other repatriation operations, returnees were not necessarily interested in the restoration of the *status quo ante*, which saw their communities marginalised on unproductive scraps of land, while powerful elites controlled vast swaths of the country's most fertile territory. Rather, the refugees strived to use the return process to challenge the legitimacy of the *status quo ante* and, if possible, improve their families' lot in life, both literally and figuratively. For many returnees, the desire to reclaim land with deep historical or spiritual significance was tempered by the aspiration to improve their socio-economic conditions and preserve communities formed in exile, as well as by recognition of the need to compromise with secondary occupants who had also formed

[8] For example, Principle 2.2 of the Pinheiro Principles calls on states to 'demonstrably prioritise the right to restitution as the preferred remedy for displacement and as a key element of restorative justice'.

attachments to the land in the refugees' absence, in order to achieve a reasonably just outcome for all.

Yet for other returnees in Guatemala and elsewhere, *attempting* to restore the *status quo ante*, at least in some respects, is seen as essential to bringing at least a sliver of justice to the return process, and confirming that in the future, the relationship between citizens and state will be based on principles of equity and respect for human rights. For example, in the aftermath of the ethnic cleansing of Bosnia, failing to restore property to its displaced owners would have been tantamount to condoning genocide and accepting outright that the notions of freedom of movement and equality before the law were an unmitigated sham in the newly constituted state of Bosnia and Herzegovina. The theoretical upshot of these cases is that there is no hard-and-fast rule on the role of the restoration of the *status quo ante* in the pursuit of just return. In other words, restoring the *status quo ante* cannot be considered a minimum condition of just return. In some cases, particularly those involving recent ethnic cleansings, achieving just return and the reconstitution of the relationship between returnees and the state of origin will require reparations that *attempt* to restore aspects of the *status quo ante*, or at least make this an option for returnees who desire it. In other cases the restoration of the *status quo ante* is neither an historically lucid proposition nor an approach that adequately balances the rights and interests of returnees and secondary occupants. In all cases, the scope and aims of reparations processes have to be negotiated, recognising that even with intense international support, as was made available in Bosnia, successfully restoring the *status quo ante* is rarely practicable, even in terms of property and population distribution. Part III will further develop this argument, exploring how the passage of time affects claims for the restoration of the *status quo ante*, and the implications of my arguments on state responsibility and just return for cases such as that of the Palestinian refugees, where there is no bond of citizenship between the exiled and the state that arguably bears a significant measure of causal, moral and potentially also remedial responsibility for their displacement. In the context of efforts to resolve and redress displacement in Guatemala, Bosnia and Mozambique, at least, it is clear that ultimately redress is 'less about how to restore the *status quo ante* and more about how to repair broken relationships between people', and, equally, between citizens and the state (Miller and Kumar 2007: vi).

Part III

Beyond repair? Grappling with hard cases

Introduction to Part III

A just return, as argued in Part I, must recast the fragmented relationship between the state of origin and its exiled citizens. Ultimately, a just return should put refugees back on equal footing with their non-displaced co-nationals by restoring (or, indeed, creating for the first time) a respectful relationship of rights and duties between the state and returnees. Part I contended that reparations play an important role in this reconstitution of the state–citizen relationship, and in ensuring that refugees enjoy the minimum conditions of a just return, namely equal, effective protection for their security and basic human rights, including accountability for any violations of these rights. Part II of this book explored past efforts to redress refugees returning to Guatemala, Bosnia and Mozambique, and examined the insights these cases offer for the theory of just return developed in Part I and the challenge of holding states accountable for displacing their citizens.

The conception of just return mapped out in Part I speaks primarily to those paradigmatic cases in which returnees are citizens of the state that is remedially responsible for their displacement. However, contemporary refugee crises often do not fit neatly into this model. While factors such as state collapse and the involvement of non-state actors complicated the attribution and exercise of the state's causal and moral responsibility for forced migration in Guatemala, Bosnia and Mozambique, my analysis of these cases demonstrated that these issues did not fundamentally challenge the cogency of the theoretical framework on the state's remedial responsibility for displacement and enabling just return that was laid out in Part I. For the purposes of my theory of just return, the truly hard cases are those in which there is no bond of citizenship linking refugees and the state to which they would return, and protracted exile has heightened the complexity of the claims at stake in the return process. These hard cases raise significant questions about the meaning and scope of the right of return itself, and the broad relevance of my conception of just return.

In order to tease out the implications of my theory of just return in these hard cases, this section will examine statelessness and protracted displacement as the characteristics of cases that are 'hard' *vis-à-vis* my theory of just return, and will provide brief snapshots of two hard cases, the Biharis in Bangladesh and the Lhotshampa refugees from Bhutan. (Following Article 1.1 of the 1954 Convention Relating to the Status of Stateless Persons, this discussion focuses on stateless persons as those who are 'not considered as a national by any State under the operation of its law'.) It will then discuss the importance of grappling with hard cases and the implications of the notion of just return for these particularly perplexing situations. Briefly, I will argue that the just resolution of paradigmatic and hard cases alike demands that a premium be placed on equity and maximising the range of choices available to returnees, with a view to upholding conditions of safety and dignity throughout the repatriation process. In hard cases in which there is no state–citizen relationship, a just return must result in refugees returning to land under the control of a state through which they acquire 'effective' or functional citizenship.[1] That is, if their return is to be just, stateless refugees must return to states in which they are recognised as equal citizens in the political community and benefit from effective protection of their security and basic human rights.[2] Securing citizenship for stateless returnees is a critical component of a just return because 'under international law there is no replacement for citizenship' (Batchelor 1998: 160). Citizenship is essential in ensuring that formerly stateless returnees can effectively make claims for equal rights, including the right to redress. Indeed, reparations from those actors responsible for protracted displacement can play a key role in enabling the resolution of statelessness and exile. This discussion will set the stage for Chapter 8, in which I will use the situation of the Palestinian refugees as an entry point to explore in greater detail the challenges raised by hard cases, and demonstrate how my conception of just return may be used as a starting point to elucidate states' responsibilities

1 As Gibney (2006: 2) points out, citizenship carries a variety of meanings. Legally, it implies the formal right of membership in a particular state. Citizenship may also be interpreted as 'standing'; that is, it conveys the notion that a person has a legitimate claim to equal respect and treatment within the state. In the republican tradition, citizenship is conceived normatively as the acts of participating in governance and public life. This discussion focuses on citizenship as a legal status and in terms of standing.

2 This is not to say that return is necessarily the 'preferred' solution in these (or any) cases. Particularly in hard cases, it may be especially important for displaced persons to have access to alternative solutions such as resettlement or local integration.

towards stateless refugees seeking to resolve their displacement through various forms of return.

Characteristics of hard cases

The intersection of statelessness and protracted displacement renders cases particularly hard, from the perspective of the conception of just return laid out in Chapter 2. Cases such as the displacement of the Palestinians, Lhotshampas and Biharis raise complex questions about political membership and challenge the logic of my conception of just return because, while many refugees involved in these cases demand the right to return, they cannot make this claim straightforwardly, as citizens of the states responsible for their displacement. Indeed, while refugees are in many instances pushed to repatriate against their will, in hard cases the tables are often turned, with refugees themselves pushing to return, only to be rebuffed by states unwilling to consider the claims of non-citizens and unmoved by arguments regarding their responsibility for events that unfolded decades ago.

Statelessness

The 1954 Convention Relating to the Status of Stateless Persons defines a 'stateless person' as an individual 'who is not considered as a national by any State under the operation of its law' (Article 1). This definition focuses on the *de jure* or technically stateless.[3] In contrast, *de facto* stateless persons are those who have not necessarily been formally stripped of their citizenship but, nonetheless, cannot prove their nationality and are unable to exercise their rights as citizens (Batchelor 1998: 171, Goris, Harrington and Köhn 2009: 4). While it is sometimes assumed that *de facto* statelessness is synonymous with refugeehood, 'neither *de jure* nor *de facto* statelessness necessarily signifies the existence of a well-founded fear of persecution under the terms of the 1951 [Refugee] Convention', and

[3] I use the terms citizenship and nationality as synonyms. It is important to note that the 1954 Convention does not in fact use the phrase '*de jure* stateless', but the term has emerged as a way to clarify that an individual falls under the Convention's definition of a stateless person. Passing reference is made to '*de facto*' stateless persons in the Final Act of the 1961 Convention on the Reduction of Statelessness. However, 'the term *de facto* statelessness is not defined in any international instrument and there is no treaty regime specific to this category of persons' (UNHCR 2012b: 3). UNHCR (2012b: 3) stresses that 'Care must be taken that those who qualify as "stateless persons" under Article 1(1) of the 1954 Convention are recognised as such and not mistakenly referred to as *de facto* stateless persons as otherwise they may fail to receive the protection guaranteed under the 1954 Convention.'

it is now widely accepted in legal circles that a distinction can and should be made between the conditions of refugeehood and statelessness (Batchelor 1998: 172).[4] As argued in the introduction to this book, it is also important from a theoretical perspective to make this distinction. While many scholars accept at face value Arendt's broad-brush characterisation of refugees as stateless, I suggested that if it is to maintain its analytic incisiveness statelessness cannot simply mean marginalisation and a lack of robust state protection, as this is a predicament that unfortunately befalls not only refugees but also most non-displaced citizens of dysfunctional states such as Haiti and Somalia (Bradley in press). That said, the individuals implicated in the hard cases under consideration are *both* refugees and stateless persons: a just return in these instances must resolve both their physical displacement and their lack of moorings in the state system.

Statelessness arises for a variety of reasons including the deliberate and arbitrary deprivation of citizenship; territorial transfers; and, more commonly, administrative glitches and conflicts in nationality laws (Batchelor 1998: 175, UNHCR 2006c: 8–9). UNHCR (2011: 4) estimates that 12 million people around the world are either *de jure* stateless or unable to conclusively prove their nationality. These individuals are slipping through a 'genuine normative gap in international law' (Goris, Harrington and Köhn 2009: 6). The essence of the gap is this: international law prohibits arbitrarily rendering individuals stateless, and further indicates that every person has a right to citizenship, which is the 'gateway' to the enjoyment of rights in the state system (Gibney 2009: 50).[5] Although a positive right to citizenship must entail a corresponding duty for states to provide it, international law is largely silent on the issue of how to resolve the predicament of those who are currently stateless, leaving the attribution of citizenship to the domestic jurisdiction of states (Batchelor 1998: 156, Gibney 2009: 50, Goris, Harrington and Köhn 2009: 6). Batchelor (1998: 168) succinctly captures the problem: 'While human rights law states clearly in several international instruments that everyone has the right to a nationality, little direction is given in these instruments as to *which* nationality.'

The upshot of this legal lacuna is that there is no clear avenue for resolving the limbo endured by stateless refugees.[6] Many stateless refugees

[4] See Weis (1979), UNHCR (2005), Batchelor (1995, 2006), Sawyer and Blitz (2011) and van Waas (2008) for detailed discussions of statelessness and international law.

[5] For example, Article 15 of the Universal Declaration of Human Rights states that 'Everyone has the right to a nationality' and prohibits the arbitrary deprivation of citizenship.

[6] The situation is further complicated by the fact that many of the states implicated in 'hard cases' involving the protracted displacement of stateless refugees have not signed those

would prefer to resolve their displacement by gaining citizenship and locally integrating in their country of asylum. Those who favour repatriation face the difficult task of convincing the state governing the territory to which they would return to recognise their right to do so and, ultimately, to grant them citizenship. Stateless refugees' repatriation claims are underpinned by the argument that properly interpreted, the provisions in agreements such as the Universal Declaration of Human Rights (Article 13.2) and the International Covenant on Civil and Political Rights (Article 12.4) on the individual's right to enter or return to 'his own country' extend to stateless persons seeking to return to their families' original places of residence. As Hurst (1987: 56–59, Lee 1998: 148–149) maintains, the ordinary meaning of the phrase 'his own country' is not commensurable with 'the country of which he is a national'. The argument can also be made that it is the responsibility of the state that instituted the policies resulting in statelessness to resolve the problem, presumably by extending citizenship to those in limbo. Although this may at first appear to be a reasonable and straightforward proposition, it becomes much more complicated in practice, owing to differing presumptions regarding the rights, obligations and procedures surrounding the conferment of nationality (Batchelor 1998: 169). The challenges associated with the attribution of responsibility for resolving the displacement of stateless persons are further compounded when one considers that there are presumably differences between the moral obligations of a state that purposefully stripped individuals of their citizenship before they fled, and the obligations of a state that was implicated in the displacement of individuals who were never its citizens. It is unsurprising that, in the absence of clear legal provisions and regular state practice to inform the resolution of statelessness and compel states to grant citizenship to stateless refugees, the prospect of a just return (or other solutions) becomes elusive, and many statelessness situations become protracted.

Protracted displacement

A practical problem with complex implications for theory, the protraction of refugee situations is increasingly common due to lacklustre international support for resettlement and local integration, and the difficulty of implementing durable solutions such as voluntary repatriation in regions characterised by instability and state fragility. Whereas the average

pieces of international law that provide some guidance, albeit limited, on the resolution of statelessness, such as the 1954 Convention Relating to the Status of Stateless Persons and the 1961 Convention on the Reduction of Statelessness.

duration of a refugee situation in 1993 was 9 years, by 2004 refugees typically had to wait some 17 years for a solution to their displacement (Loescher et al. 2007: 1). Some hard cases, such as that of the Palestinian refugees, have stretched out in excess of 6 decades.

When coupled with statelessness, protracted displacement renders cases 'hard' *vis-à-vis* just return for a number of intertwined practical and theoretical reasons.[7] First, in protracted refugee situations, secondary occupants typically move onto refugees' land and often into their actual homes. Longstanding secondary occupants arguably develop a right to remain on the land and evicting them to make way for returning refugees risks creating a second wave of displacement and instability. Particularly if the right of return and refugees' remedial rights are interpreted as requiring the restitution of original properties, this situation can result in seemingly intractable conflicts over land claims and major obstacles to the physical return of refugees.

Second, with the passage of time the restoration of the *status quo ante* typically becomes less and less of a viable proposition, not only in terms of the distribution of land but also in terms of social relations and occupations. 'Turning back the clock' to reconstruct lost ways of life is rarely possible, nor is it necessarily even desirable. Yet as displacement becomes protracted, the refugee community's conception of the *status quo ante* may become progressively more idealised, such that no feasible solution or form of redress can begin to speak to the magnitude of the perceived loss.[8] In this way, narratives of grievance and dreams of a utopian return may inadvertently hinder the resolution of displacement by limiting the scope available for negotiating a just return (or other solutions) in practice.

Third, protracted displacement makes it difficult for would-be returnees to mount convincing claims for membership in political communities that may have always regarded them as 'outsiders', and within which they have no formal status. The fact that these political communities may have radically transformed in the refugees' absence further complicates the refugees' claim to belong. When the violations that led to displacement and statelessness took place under the watch of previous generations, it is often difficult to impress upon current leaders and citizens that they have an obligation to redress and resolve the present suffering stemming from these past wrongs, especially when the wrongs

[7] While these issues are common to many different hard cases, they are not necessarily relevant to every hard case.

[8] Unfortunately, a more detailed discussion of the mythologising of return is beyond the scope of this work. For in-depth examinations of this issue, see Zetter (1994, 1999).

were inflicted on non-citizens. Although the legal principle of state continuity indicates that the institution of the state bears responsibility for the acts of past regimes, terse legal principles rarely evoke a strong popular sense of shared responsibility for historical injustices or generate readiness among citizens to welcome returning stateless refugees into their polity. Without such popular support, it may be extremely difficult for states to effectively exercise responsibility towards stateless refugees, particularly by granting them the opportunity to return as citizens.

Snapshots of hard cases

The experiences of ethnic Nepalese exiled from Bhutan and the Bihari refugees 'stranded' in Bangladesh illustrate the difficulties of understanding and acting upon the requirements of a just return process in cases involving the intersection of statelessness and protracted displacement. These cases raise some key challenges that are also encountered in the situation of the Palestinian refugees, which will be explored in greater detail in Chapter 8.

The exile of Lhotshampas from Bhutan

In the late 1980s and early 1990s, the Kingdom of Bhutan expelled some 102,000 Lhotshampas, who were promptly channelled through India and eventually ensconced in seven UNHCR-run camps in Nepal. One of Bhutan's four main ethnic groups, the Lhotshampas are the descendants of Nepalese farmers who migrated to southern Bhutan between 1865 and the 1930s. Although the Bhutanese political elite hailed from the Ngalong and Central Bhutanese ethnic groups, many Lhotshampas served in the government and the community was an important economic engine in this isolated state of only 680,000 people. However, in the mid-1980s, the integration of southerners slowed due to elite opposition to Lhotshampa involvement in democratic activism (Bose 2003: 73, Hutt 2005: 44).[9]

In the late 1980s, the government instigated an annual census in the south of Bhutan, the stated purpose of which was to identify and crack down on the purported problem of illegal immigration from Nepal. The Lhotshampas perceived the census as a calculated step towards pushing them out of Bhutan, despite the fact that they had long been considered Bhutanese citizens and held national identity cards. To register as citizens, individuals were required to produce tax receipts dated 1958, the year Bhutan's first Nationality Law came into effect. The census was

[9] For detailed discussions of this case, see Hutt (1996, 2003).

criticised for being arbitrarily implemented and unfairly resulting in the denationalisation of some of those unable to produce 1958 tax receipts. In the autumn of 1990, Lhotshampa activists organised large demonstrations for equal civil and political rights. The arrest and abuse of many protestors triggered the beginning of the refugee outflow, which by 1991 became a 'flood' as the Lhotshampas were subjected to evictions, torture, rape and beatings by the policy and army (Hutt 2005: 46–47, Lee 1998: 124–125). Refugee leaders contend that half of the Lhotshampas of southern Bhutan were forced to flee their homes; today 35 per cent of Bhutan's population remains ethnic Nepalese (Lee 1998: 121, CIA 2012).

The exodus resulted in mass denationalisation, leaving the Lhotshampa refugees *de jure* stateless. Denationalisation was achieved through the confiscation of citizenship cards and the application of restrictive Bhutanese nationality laws, which provide for the revocation of the citizenship of those who choose to move abroad. In addition, before leaving Bhutan, approximately 50 per cent of refugee families were coerced into signing forms indicating that they were migrating voluntarily. Ironically, the forms confirm that the signatories used to hold Bhutanese nationality and, thus, were not simply illegal migrants (Bose 2003: 75, Hutt 2005: 50, Lee 1998: 128–131, 145).

While Nepal has regularly called for the refugees to be allowed to return to Bhutan 'with honour and dignity', it has in practice consistently bowed to Bhutanese pressure on the refugee issue (Hutt 2005: 44, 48). For its part, the National Assembly of Bhutan has each year called for a ban on return, and the government has attempted to undercut return by instituting a policy of resettling Bhutanese from elsewhere in the country onto the refugees' land. Bhutan's avers that only 'genuine Bhutanese nationals' are eligible to return; those who left 'voluntarily', as well as 'anti-nationals' and 'non-nationals' must be barred (Bose 2003: 78, Hutt 2005: 48–49, Lee 1998: 118–119).

In 2003, Nepal and Bhutan released the results of a drawn-out and sharply criticised 'verification process' designed to confirm the status of the residents of Khudunabari camp. The verification process determined that only 2.5 per cent of the camp residents were Bhutanese citizens with valid refugee claims. 70.5 per cent were found to have voluntarily emigrated and, thus, lost their Bhutanese citizenship; 24.2 per cent were determined simply to be 'non-Bhutanese'; and 2.8 per cent were labelled Bhutanese criminals. Of those surveyed, 94 per cent appealed their classification, to no avail (Hutt 2005: 48–50). Bhutan's declaration that it would take 'full responsibility' for the return of the 2.5 per cent determined to be 'real' refugees was presented as a major concession, as the government faced serious internal opposition to any return whatsoever. While the 2.5 per cent categorised as 'real refugees' were to benefit from limited assistance and remedies, those refugees labelled as 'emigrants' faced much greater uncertainty. 'Emigrants' who wished to repatriate permanently would be allowed to reapply for citizenship, but they would have to do so from within Bhutan and then wait in the country for 2 years while their claims were processed. No guarantees were made regarding where the refugees would live during this period, or whether they would benefit from restitution, family reunification, and access to education and health care. Bhutan also refused any international monitoring of the process. Unsurprisingly, most were unwilling to return under such circumstances. Those who declined to return were to have had the opportunity to apply for citizenship in Nepal, but after gaining power Maoist leaders reneged on this commitment and reiterated demands for the refugees to return to Bhutan (Hutt 2005: 49–52).

Faced with stagnation in the camps and steadfast opposition from Bhutan to return movements, in 2008 UNHCR launched a rare large-scale resettlement process for the Lhotshampas. The US set a target of resettling 60,000 Lhotshampa refugees, and has expressed willingness to accept more if needed. As of 2011, some 43,500 refugees had been resettled, but the process has been complicated by the Maoists' opposition to the operation, on the grounds that the refugees should first return to Bhutan. Furthermore, refugee activists determined to return mounted concerted opposition to this strategy. Indeed, the resettlement issue polarised refugees in the camps, leading to violent clashes between 'pro' and 'anti' resettlement groups, causing deaths. Approximately 17,000 refugees have not pursued resettlement opportunities; many of those in this group prefer to return to Bhutan. While UNHCR has pledged to continue to advocate for voluntary repatriation for all those interested, critics contend that the resettlement operation implies that Bhutan can evade responsibility for ethnic cleansing and will be able to carry out further expulsions with impunity (Bose 2003: 81–82, Frelick 2011, Sarkar 2008, UN News Service 2009).

Somewhat counter-intuitively, alongside these debates Bhutan has embarked on a democratisation process resulting in a new constitution, and the country's first democratic elections in July 2008. No provisions were made to enable the participation of refugee voters in this election, and the longer term implications of the democratisation process for the stateless Lhotshampas remain unclear (Hutt 2005: 53–55, Sengupta 2008). Under an optimistic reading of the situation, the democratisation process may result in a more equitable, pluralistic conception of

Bhutanese citizenship that creates new opportunities to negotiate the just return of refugees who were deprived of their citizenship more than 18 years ago. Prime Minister Jigme Y Thinley's July 2010 public characterisation of the refugees as illegal immigrants underlines that such changes are likely not to be realised soon, but if they do eventually come to pass, the restoration of the Lhotshampas' citizenship will undoubtedly be one of the most salient forms of redress extended in the context of the return process (Frelick 2011).

Bihari refugees in Bangladesh

Known also as 'stranded Pakistanis', the Bihari refugees in Bangladesh represent another 'hard case' for the purposes of the theory of just return discussed in Part I. The Biharis are Urdu-speaking Muslims who migrated to East Pakistan, mostly from the Indian state of Bihar, when the subcontinent was partitioned in 1947. Following an initially warm welcome, rifts emerged between the Biharis and the predominantly Bengali population of East Pakistan, due to linguistic, cultural and socioeconomic differences. Under the patronage of the West Pakistan elite, the Biharis enjoyed a privileged position in East Pakistan, but relations with the Bengali majority deteriorated sharply in the 1950s and 1960s. During the 1970–1971 civil war that led to the independence of Bangladesh, many Biharis joined the Pakistani army in inflicting violence on Bengalis, while Bengali attacks led to the death of 10,000–15,000 Biharis (Ahmad 2003: 173–174, Paulsen 2006, Sen 1999: 628).

After the war, 60–95 per cent of Biharis expressed their wish to 'repatriate' to Pakistan (Paulsen 2006: 55, Sen 1999: 640). Although the Biharis had never physically lived in West Pakistan, the Pakistani government initially accepted their claimed right to 'return' to the state with which they identified. However, in practice Pakistan limited repatriation rights to former residents of West Pakistan, government employees and their families. In addition, a modest number were to be admitted on humanitarian grounds. Under the 1974 New Delhi Tripartite Agreement, some 170,000 Biharis repatriated to Pakistan in the early aftermath of the war. However, the majority were denied repatriation rights, denationalised by Pakistan, and left 'stranded' in Bangladesh in a situation of *de facto*, if not also *de jure*, statelessness. Crowded into camps after their properties were seized by members of the new Bangladeshi elite, by 2000, some 240,000–500,000 Biharis lived in squalid camps across the country (Paulsen 2006, Sen 1999: 625, 637–638, UNHCR 2000: 74).

While Bangladesh, Pakistan, UNHCR and various scholars contend that the Biharis are not refugees in the strict sense of the 1951 Convention, researchers such as Sen (1999: 645) argue that Pakistan's unilateral denationalisation of the Bihari minority and its refusal to allow a broad right of return may be interpreted as acts of persecution sufficient to establish refugee status for the group. Certainly the Biharis are dislocated within Bangladesh, and have faced institutionalised discrimination linked to their tenuous citizenship status. Virtually all Biharis would have citizenship under Bangladesh's nationality laws if they were interpreted straightforwardly, as these laws extend citizenship to all those born in Bangladesh, as well as to all those whose fathers or grandfathers were permanent residents in the country as of 25 March 1971 (Paulsen 2006: 58). Two main reasons explain the Biharis' struggle to conclusively establish their citizenship and resolve their displacement. First, under Bangladeshi nationality law, a person does not quality to be a citizen if he or she 'owes, affirms or acknowledges, expressly or by conduct, allegiance to a foreign state' (Ahmad 2003: 176). This provision has historically been used to deny Biharis equal access to rights as Bangladeshi citizens, although several court rulings have determined that this provision cannot be applied *en masse* to disqualify the Biharis from Bangladeshi citizenship, and a May 2008 High Court ruling definitively concluded that all Biharis who were minors when Bangladesh became independent, or who were born afterwards, have the right to be citizens and to vote. However, entrenched, institutionalised discrimination has undercut efforts to uphold these rulings and ensure that all Biharis can enjoy full rights as Bangladeshi citizens (BBC News 2008a, Hussain 2009: 30, Lynch 2008, Paulsen 2006: 61–62, 67). For example, the government has taken steps to prevent the return of the Biharis to their former homes and properties in Bangladesh, passing a 1972 Presidential Order that granted the state custodial rights over the Biharis' 'abandoned' properties (Ahmad 2003: 176–177).

The second reason underlying the Biharis' longstanding dislocation is that although integration as citizens in Bangladesh appears to be an increasingly viable option preferred by the younger generations, a significant proportion of Biharis, including the community's traditional leaders, continue to press for repatriation to Pakistan (Ahmad 2003: 177, Paulsen 2006: 55). It is this subsection of the Bihari population that is truly perplexing when considering the question of just return. For these individuals, Bangladeshi citizenship is not functional or effective, due to systemic discrimination and the fact that they simply consider themselves to be members of a different political community. In 1984, Pakistani General Zia-ul-Haq promised to secure the Biharis' return, 'even if I have to carry them on my back', and a trust was established with $278 million from Saudi Arabia to facilitate the repatriation (Ahmad 2003: 178). However, the would-be returnees have continued to languish in Bangladeshi camps, largely because of Pakistan's concerns that such a population movement would increase tensions in the already fragile country, particularly within the Sindhi community. Indeed, the return of a mere 53 Bihari families to Pakistan in 1993 sparked protests that put a halt to further repatriation plans. Pakistan has also indicated that the burden of hosting a large Afghan refugee population renders it unable to open up to an additional population of impoverished returnees (Ahmad 2003: 178, BBC News 2002c, Sen 2000: 59–60, UNHCR 2000: 74).

Negotiating a just and permanent resolution to the Biharis' dislocation has been hampered by Pakistan's perception that the Biharis' predicament is a humanitarian issue, rather than a question of remedial responsibility for nationals displaced in a conflict for which Pakistan is partially culpable (Refugees International 2006). While UNHCR has promoted a strong focus on local integration in Bangladesh over repatriation to Pakistan, scholars such as Ahmad and Sen argue that as far as possible, the Biharis should be allowed to choose between durable solutions. In any case, scholars and advocates contend, the Biharis' citizenship status must be clearly resolved, and both Pakistan and Bangladesh must acknowledge their shared responsibility for the past suffering and future wellbeing of this long marginalised population (Ahmad 2003: 178, Paulsen 2006: 68, Sen 2000: 45).

Just return in hard cases

Although they raise intriguing issues from the scope of the right of return to what it means for a particular state to be a refugee's 'country of origin', the cases of the Biharis and Lhotshampas are admittedly quite esoteric. Why not dismiss hard cases such as these as insignificant anomalies and focus exclusively on more 'paradigmatic' cases of refugeehood? Or, why not argue that return is simply not viable as a durable solution in these hard cases? One could conceivably argue that in the absence of a bond of citizenship between a refugee-creating state and the displaced, states may effectively exercise responsibility for the crime of forced migration without promoting or enabling return, but by helping to create local integration opportunities in host states, and financing resettlement processes. In some cases, this may be true. However, whether through the insistence of reluctant host states or refugees themselves, demands for some form of return figure centrally in many refugee scenarios, including 'hard cases'. Even if return is not the predominant solution in these cases, it is important to consider what a just return might look like in cases where displacement is protracted and there is no state-citizen relationship to structure the repatriation process.

Thinking about hard cases is also important because while cases such as the Biharis and the Lhotshampas are hardly in the international political limelight, they involve a significant number of people whose concerns deserve attention. Furthermore, certain hard cases such as that of the Palestinian refugees involve millions of refugees, attract major international political attention, and have critical implications in terms of peacebuilding and regional security. As the largest and most longstanding refugee situation in the world, the Palestinian case is often the 'elephant in the room' for scholars of forced migration. It is often overlooked because of its unique facets, yet the Palestinian case in fact embodies many of the same issues and complexities that characterise other cases. An exploration of the Palestinian case may thus serve as a window into other hard cases; if a theory of just return cannot speak to at least some of the critical challenges raised in this case, its practical and theoretical value is questionable. Before proceeding to a detailed examination of the Palestinian case in Chapter 8, I will briefly discuss the principal implications of my theory of just return in these hard cases.

In recent years, there has been a strong focus among refugee advocates and scholars on repatriation as the return of refugees to their 'original' homes and land. In the preceding chapters, I have argued that while the restoration of refugees' property *may* play an important role in enabling safe and dignified repatriation, just return is more fundamentally concerned with repositioning the refugee as an equal member in the political community of the state of origin. As acknowledged above, this is a particularly difficult prospect when refugees have languished in a protracted situation of statelessness. What might a just return look like in these hard cases?

Simply put, in cases of the protracted displacement of stateless refugees, a just return would mean that refugees return to territory governed by a state willing to grant them effective or functional citizenship. For such a migration to be considered 'return', refugees would need to have a significant link to the land itself, or a bond of nationality or common identity with the political community they (re)enter. For such a return to be considered just, returnees must be recognised as equal citizens, and be able to access effective state protection in terms of security and basic human rights. Depending on the circumstances, a just return in hard cases may or may not entail the return of stateless refugees to the country that is primarily causally or morally responsible for their displacement. In any event, reparations from those agents bearing the lion's share of remedial responsibility for displacement play a prominent role in enabling just return in hard cases by providing refugees with valuable resources to support the pursuit of durable solutions, and creating the good will and space for compromise needed to resolve complex cases of conflict, displacement and statelessness.

What hinders the just resolution of hard cases along these lines? Arguably, the thorniest issue is establishing which state should open up to and extend citizenship rights to returnees. In some cases, such as that of the Lhotshampas, there is only one state to which the refugees could logically 'return'; a just return in this case would involve those refugees who wish to repatriate having the opportunity to regain their Bhutanese citizenship and return to Bhutan in conditions of safety and dignity, with the support of remedies that recognise and contribute to repairing the violations that forced the refugees from their homes decades ago.[10] Other solutions such as resettlement or local integration in Nepal could resolve their limbo, but would not constitute return. In other cases, such as the displacement of the Biharis, there are a number of states within which the Biharis could conceivably acquire citizenship and exercise the right to return: they could repatriate as citizens to Pakistan; negotiate a return to prepartition communities in India; or return as citizens to their prewar homes in Bangladesh. Although there is no simple recipe for determining which country stateless refugees should be able to return to, the closely related legal principles of 'effective nationality', 'genuine and effective link' and 'appropriate connection' offer valuable insight into this conundrum.[11]

The notion of effective nationality refers to the fact that in the context of the state system, citizenship is an essential precursor for exercising many fundamental rights (Batchelor 1998: 156). Thus, the 'right to a nationality is a positive right. It is more than the unilateral obligation on a State to avoid the creation of statelessness under its own legislation . . . The right to a nationality is, or should be, based on a recognition of the link, or bond, established between an individual and a State' (Batchelor 1998: 181). The principle of the genuine and effective link informs the determination of the country in which a stateless individual should have the

[10] As Frelick (2011) points out, and as discussed in Chapter 2, for this population having the opportunity to return to their country of origin could function as a form of redress in its own right.

[11] See Gibney (2006) for a more theoretical discussion of the dilemmas associated with the fair distribution of citizenship to the stateless. Gibney identifies three principles that may help determine who should be granted formal status in the demos: the lack of alternative membership principle; the informal membership principle; and the principle of democratic inclusion.

right to acquire effective nationality. The principle was articulated by the International Court of Justice (ICJ) in the 1955 Nottebohm Case, in which the ICJ ruled that nationality is a bond 'having as its basis a social fact of attachment, a genuine connection of existence, interest and sentiments, together with the existence of reciprocal rights and duties' (ICJ 1955: 23). According to the ICJ, place of birth, descent and residence are evidence of a link to the state, which may serve as the foundation for determining and extending citizenship. While place of birth, descent and residence remain the primary reference points for determining such a connection, genuine and effective link is a 'subtle and fluid concept', which can be reflected in a wide variety of other factors such as participation in public life, extended family ties and demonstrated social attachment to the country, which is passed on to children (Batchelor 1998: 157, Sen 2000).[12] While some Bihari refugees, for example, may demonstrate genuine and effective links with Bangladesh, others may conceivably have a stronger link to Pakistan.

Interestingly, the view is now widespread (but by no means universal) that particularly when statelessness has arisen as a result of state succession, individuals should be given a 'right of option' regarding their nationality. That is, when there is more than one state with which the individual might have a genuine and effective link, the stateless person's will should be taken into account in the attribution of citizenship (Batchelor 1998: 163). This incorporation of individual preferences may be particularly conducive to enabling just return in hard cases since, as argued in Chapter 2, backstopping the refugee's capacity to make free choices is an important demonstration of respect for the dignity of the returnee, and may be an important form of redress insofar as it restores a valuable measure of control to the refugee over the refugee's life direction.

The principle of the genuine and effective link therefore offers valuable insight into the difficult question of which country should extend citizenship to stateless refugees in the context of just return processes in hard cases. The critical point is that just return in hard cases must address both physical and political displacement: returnees must acquire not merely homes and passports but also effective citizenship within political communities where they may stand as equals, with the ability to access essential services and protections. Resolving their statelessness may be

12 The International Law Commission (ILC) has suggested that an 'appropriate connection' between an individual and a state should inform the attribution of citizenship and contends that this 'appropriate connection' should be interpreted more broadly than the concept of a 'genuine link'. However, the genuine link doctrine has been broadly interpreted by states in practice, and the terms arguably carry the same meaning and should be harmonised (Batchelor 1998: 162–164).

the most salient form of redress for refugees who have long lacked firm footing in the state system. Yet refugees in hard cases may also bear a host of other complex claims for lost land, undermined livelihoods and grievous suffering due to human rights violations. The insights gleaned from return and redress processes in Guatemala, Bosnia and Mozambique, and discussed in Chapter 7, may also inform efforts to redress returnees in hard cases. In hard and more 'paradigmatic' cases alike, the hallmark of effective redress programmes for returnees is not a particular institutional configuration or resolute focus on an ideal principle such as the restoration of the *status quo ante*. Rather, successful reparations programmes in hard cases respond to local needs, concerns, conditions and constraints and are integrated into broader transitional justice strategies. Effective reparations programmes in hard cases must be appropriately comprehensive, complete, complex and coherent, and respond effectively to the issues of finality and munificence, bearing in mind the need for suitable time frames, strong enforcement mechanisms, fair cost distribution systems, protections for secondary occupants, and the engagement of international actors and displaced persons themselves.[13] In spite of the insights offered by concepts such as the 'genuine and effective link', outstanding challenges remain, as the following chapter illustrates, in terms of understanding and distributing responsibility for the resolution of displacement and statelessness and implementing reparations programmes that speak to refugees' grievances, thereby opening up opportunities to resolve the broader conflicts that generate and perpetuate displacement. While the concept of just return offers no tidy answers to these dilemmas, the following case demonstrates how it may help elucidate the various ways in which states may exercise responsibility for creating refugees and apply different forms of redress to enable safe and dignified resolutions to displacement.

[13] See Chapter 7 and de Greiff (2006, 2007) for more detailed discussion of these concepts.

8 Just return and the Palestinian refugees

'We travel like other people', wrote revered Palestinian poet Mahmoud Darwish (1984: 31) from the rubble of besieged Beirut in 1982, 'but we return to nowhere . . . We have a country of words. Speak, speak so we may know the end of this travel.' The struggle of the Palestinian refugees to return from 'nowhere' to their homeland is at the core of the Israeli–Palestinian conflict. The largest and most longstanding refugee situation in the world, the Palestinian exodus is an indisputably hard case: displaced for more than six decades, over half of the refugees are *de jure* stateless. Owing to its unique and complex facets, the Palestinian situation has often been treated as a *sui generis* case in which neither the norms that structure the mainstream refugee regime nor insights gained from other refugee crises pertain. The aim of this chapter is to explore the implications for the Palestinian refugee situation of the conception of just return mapped out in Part I and revisited in the introduction to Part III. Building on the previous discussion, this chapter will use the Palestinian refugee situation as an entry point to examine some of the challenges raised by hard cases, particularly the claims of secondary occupants and the allocation of citizenship rights. This chapter will thereby add to a growing body of scholarship that recognises the unique aspects of the Palestinian situation but challenges its unqualified designation as *sui generis*.[1] Infighting between Hamas and Fatah, multiple sieges on Gaza and the stagnation of the peace process leave no room for optimism on the imminent resolution of the refugees' displacement. Nonetheless, considering what a just return would entail for the Palestinian refugees and absorbing the insights gained through return processes in countries such as Bosnia, Guatemala and Mozambique are important steps towards the eventual resolution of this dispiriting case.

Part I argued that in 'paradigmatic' cases in which refugees are citizens of the state that bears primary remedial responsibility for their displacement, a just return process entails the recasting of a new relationship of

[1] For examples of this scholarship, see Dumper (2006b).

rights and duties between the state of origin and its returnees, such that returnees and the non-displaced alike benefit from equal, effective protection for their security and human rights, which must include accountability for past abrogation of these rights. In the introduction to Part III, I suggested that in 'hard cases' involving the intersection of statelessness and protracted displacement, a just return must result in refugees returning to locations that have some significance to them due to prior inhabitance, ancestral connections, or because it is part of their national or traditional homeland. Furthermore, a just return process must result in the (re)acquisition of effective citizenship for the displaced. That is, returnees must be formally recognised as equal members of a state that will protect their security and basic human rights. In the Palestinian case, this could be achieved in three main ways.[2] First, in the event of a one-state solution, the refugees would return to a binational state where they would live as citizens alongside other Palestinians and Jewish Israelis.[3] Second, in the event of a two-state solution in which a viable, independent Palestinian state is created largely on the West Bank and Gaza Strip, the 1948 refugees would nonetheless return to their original homes behind the Green Line, where they would acquire Israeli citizenship and live peacefully as equal citizens. Third, in the event of a two-state solution, the 1948 refugees would return as citizens not to their original properties, but to a portion of their historic national homeland, newly constituted as the independent state of Palestine.

Whatever its moral merits might be, the first scenario is extremely improbable. Despite growing interest among scholars and activists in a one-state solution, Israel's vociferous opposition to it is highly unlikely to change in the foreseeable future.[4] Furthermore, despite abysmal progress in peace negotiations, the vast majority of Israelis and Palestinians still support a negotiated two-state solution (Geneva Initiative 2009).[5] In this

[2] This discussion focuses on the role of different forms of return in resolving the Palestinians' displacement. However, local integration and resettlement outside the region may also play significant roles in resolving the Palestinians' displacement. For a discussion of the obstacles and opportunities associated with these solutions, see Dumper (2007).

[3] It is important to note that a one-state solution does not necessarily mean that all refugees would be able to reoccupy their original lands without complex negotiations and compromises, as many of these properties have now been occupied by others for decades. Furthermore, many families have grown so much that even if they all wanted to return to their ancestral lands, they could not all be easily accommodated (R. Khalidi 1998: 244).

[4] For work reflecting this renewed interest in the one-state solution, see, for example, Bisharat (2008), Said (2000: 312–321) and Hilal (2007).

[5] For example, an April 2009 study concluded that a two-state solution is considered 'essential' or 'desirable' by 78 per cent of Israelis and 74 per cent of Palestinians. Such

discussion, I will therefore focus on the question of a just return in the context of a two-state solution, as envisioned in scenarios two and three. These scenarios are not mutually exclusive: a two-state solution could involve a mixture of return to the Palestinian state and to the refugees' original homes in Israel. Indeed, I will contend that a just return should ideally open up this option to as many refugees as possible, given the centrality of choice to dignified and ultimately just returns. However, it must be recognised that large-scale return to Israel undermines the rationale of the two-state solution from the Israeli perspective, as it could leave Jews in the minority in Israel, thus changing the 'Jewish nature' of the state, and its role as a vehicle for Jewish national self-determination. While debates on the legitimacy of exclusivist interpretations of the right to self-determination are outside the scope of this chapter, the commitment of the Israeli government, and many of its citizens and international backers, to this view cannot be doubted.[6] Equally, Israel's readiness to block any proposal that features the large-scale return of 1948 refugees to their original homes is beyond contestation. Moral argument need not and arguably should not necessarily be limited by such pragmatic calculations of political possibility. Yet as Rashid Khalidi (1998: 252) underscores, solutions 'must be grounded in the difficult process of accepting the truth. This includes both the truth about what happened in 1948 and the truth about what is attainable [more than 60] years later.' Without underestimating the difficulty of determining what is in fact attainable in this troubled region, in this chapter I will argue that *under some circumstances*, a just return may be achieved within the context of scenario three.[7] Albeit unlikely, scenario two could also represent a just return, but will not be the focus of this discussion.[8]

surveys do not typically poll refugees outside the occupied territories, which could significantly alter the results. On the exclusion of Palestinians outside the occupied territories not only from polls but also from debates and decision-making processes on these issues, see Nabulsi (2007).

6 On alternatives to singularist conceptions of self-determination, see Iris Marion Young's (2007) 'Self-Determination as Nondomination: Ideals Applied to Palestine/Israel' and Levy (2008).

7 See Adelman and Barkan (2011) for a related argument on the possibility of finding solutions to displacement through return to an independent Palestinian state.

8 This discussion of just return in the context of a negotiated two-state solution presumes that the Palestinian state emerging from such an agreement would be independent and viable. On 29 November 2012, the UN General Assembly passed Resolution 67/19 granting Palestine Non-Member Observer State status. Of 193 Member States, 138 voted in favour of the resolution, however, debate persists over whether Palestine meets the Montevideo criteria governing the establishment of statehood. Two pivotal states in the conflict, Israel and the US, voted against the resolution while 20 per cent of states abstained. Meanwhile, 'several of the states that voted in favour of the resolution underscored that statehood could only be achieved through dialogue between the parties,

Enabling just return within the parameters of scenario three will require that all the actors involved make maximising equitable treatment and access to choice for the Palestinian refugees a high priority. It will also require the thoughtful and strategic use of reparations at both the individual and collective levels to strengthen the Palestinian state; ensure accountability for human rights violations; nurture a willingness to compromise; and broaden the range of options available to refugees regarding the resolution of their displacement. While many different actors bear shared responsibility for the refugees' displacement and protracted exile, I will argue that owing to its involvement in ousting the refugees and preventing their return, Israel needs to take a leading role in developing and implementing a reparations strategy that draws on many different types of redress, including restitution, compensation, truth-telling and apologies and explicitly recognises its shared moral responsibility for the refugees' plight. Beyond redressing the loss of land, these initiatives must also speak to the atrocities that have scarred the refugee community, such as the massacres at Deir Yasin and Sabra and Shatilla camps, and must segue effectively with efforts to resolve core concerns such as control over Jerusalem and access to water.[9] As reparations will undoubtedly play a critical role in resolving the refugee situation and, by extension, the conflict, this is a duty Israel owes not only to the Palestinians but also to its own citizens.

The 'person who seeks absolute justice', according to prominent Israeli author and peace advocate David Grossman (2002: 41), 'is evading practical decisions . . . I do not seek pure justice, nor the settling of historical accounts, but rather possible life, no more than imperfect and tolerable, causing as little injustice as possible.' While I share Grossman's reservations about pursuing an ever-elusive standard of absolute justice,

implying that Palestine had not yet achieved statehood' (Cerone 2012: 3). Even if Palestine is currently recognised as a state, it is certainly not independent. The vast majority of the Palestinian refugees remains stateless, and the present viability of Palestine may be questioned. While a detailed discussion of what viability entails in this case is not possible here, it is important to note that at a minimum viability must require that the Palestinian state is politically independent, and founded on territory that is sufficiently contiguous to allow for reasonable freedom of movement and economic development. My focus on the possibility of enabling just return to such a viable and independent Palestinian state should not be confused with support for the 'transfer solution' in any form. This putative solution to Israel's demographic 'problem' envisions transferring territory occupied largely by Palestinian citizens of Israel to the Palestinian state. It is contrary to international law and the wishes of the vast majority of Israel's Palestinian citizens (Blecher 2005).

9 As Edward Said (2001: 446) argues, 'What is needed, at the very least, is an acknowledgment of the destruction of Palestinian society, of the dispossession of the Palestinian people and the confiscation of their land. And also of the deprivation and the suffering over the last 52 years, including such actions as the killing at Sabra and Chatila refugee camps. I believe that the conflict can only end when Israel assumes the burden of all that. I think an attempt should be made to say "this is what happened". This is the narrative.'

my arguments rest on the conviction that confronting major historical injustices and ensuring minimum conditions of just return for the Palestinian refugees is central to the practical pursuit of peace in the Middle East. To explore and support these views, the first section of this chapter will examine the contested terms at stake, the origins of the refugee situation and the attribution of responsibility for the Palestinians' longstanding displacement. The second section of the chapter will review the key international frameworks on the Palestinian refugees that may inform a just return process, and the history of stillborn efforts to negotiate the closure of the refugee file. The final section will reflect on what a just return would entail in the Palestinian case, focusing on how different interpretations of the rights of return, redress and self-determination may affect the resolution of the refugees' statelessness and physical displacement.

Before moving in this direction, some provisos are in order. First, this is merely a *preliminary* discussion of what a just return might look like in the Palestinian case that cannot engage in detail with the case's manifold intricacies. Second, many groups have unfortunately been displaced over the course of the conflict, including Mizrahi Jews from Arab countries; Palestinians uprooted by the 1967 war; internally displaced citizens of Israel, and those made homeless through the construction of the security barrier; widespread house demolitions and other human rights violations associated with the occupation.[10] Although this chapter will focus on the 1948 refugees, the claims of all these groups will need to be addressed in a comprehensive solution to the Middle East conflict. Third, this chapter assumes that Jews and Palestinians represent distinct political communities with legitimate claims to nationhood. The evolution of Palestinian nationalism and identity has been ably addressed elsewhere, and will not be discussed in detail.[11]

Contested lands and terms

The conditions endured by displaced Palestinians are not unlike those faced by refugees in other longstanding, urban or semi-urban situations: tent cities have given way to camps cast in concrete, densely populated and impoverished. Yet the Palestinian case is unique in terms of its longevity; legal complexity; the nature of the conflict that spawned the

10 On the Mizrahi claims, see Shenhav (1999, 2002, 2003, 2005), Fischbach (2005, 2008a, 2008b), Shulewitz (1999), Levin (2001), Cotler, Matas and Urman (2007) and Abu Shakrah (2001). It is important to note that many Israeli Mizrahi Jews do not conceive of themselves as refugees but as Zionists who chose to build new lives in Israel. However, even those who voluntarily migrated to Israel may still have legitimate claims for reparations for lost property. On the 1967 refugees, see Segev (2007). On the claims of Palestinian IDPs, see Wakim (2001), Schechla (2001) and Bradley (in press).

11 See Schulz (2003), R. Khalidi (1997), Bisharat (1997) and Swedenburg (1995).

displacement situation; and its lack of territoriality, in that there is currently no Palestinian state or uncontested place to which the refugees might return. The situation is also unique in terms of the number of refugees involved, both in absolute terms and as a percentage of the Palestinian population (Dumper 2006c: 5–8). Some 750,000 refugees were forced from their homes in 1948. This population has grown to include 4.82 million registered with the United Nations Relief and Works Agency (UNRWA), comprising more than 30 per cent of the 15.4 million refugees worldwide (UNHCR 2011: 2). In addition, approximately 1.54 million Palestinian refugees are not registered with UNRWA. More than 70 per cent of the global Palestinian population of 10 million are refugees or displaced persons; one-third of the refugees live in the West Bank and Gaza Strip, while the majority are sheltered in Jordan, Syria and Lebanon (Shiblak 2009: 2).[12]

The remarkable size of the population is partially attributable to another unique aspect of this case: the definition used to identify the refugees. There is no formal definition of a Palestinian refugee under international law (Takkenberg 1998: 68). Under UNRWA's operational definition, which I will use in this chapter, Palestinian refugees are those persons 'whose normal place of residence was Palestine between June 1946 and May 1948, who lost both their homes and means of livelihood as a result of the 1948 Arab-Israeli conflict' (UNRWA 2009). UNRWA's operational definition includes the descendents of Palestinians exiled in 1948 and those who have secured citizenship in another state such as Jordan. In contrast, under the 1951 Refugee Convention, refugees are generally no longer counted as such when they have obtained citizenship in another state.[13] Although UNRWA's definitional approach has attracted pointed criticism from observers who contend that it artificially prolongs the refugee problem, it helpfully recognises that those who have managed to obtain citizenship elsewhere may nonetheless hold strong claims for return and redress.

The terminology surrounding durable solutions in this case is also contested. In mainstream Palestinian Arabic discourse, 'return' generally means the act of refugees going back to their original lands; the Arabic term '*tawtin*' (resettlement) is more often used to denote

[12] UNRWA statistics are contested but offer a helpful general indication of the size of the population. In addition to the 1948 refugees, approximately 400,000 Palestinians were exiled by the 1967 war; 240,000 are internally displaced within Israel; and 150,000 are internally displaced in the occupied territories (Shiblak 2009: 2).

[13] See Article 1C(3) of the 1951 Convention relating to the Status of Refugees. For a comprehensive discussion of the status of Palestinian refugees in international law, see Takkenberg (1998).

migration to an independent Palestinian state (Dumper 2007: 20). While conscious of this tradition, I will follow the lead of Palestinian scholars such as Rashid Khalidi (1992, 1998) and use the terms 'return' and 'repatriation' interchangeably to refer to the movement of refugees to territory within the borders of historic Palestine, including return to the refugees' original homes, and to an independent Palestinian state. Many refugees live within a short commute or even eye sight of their original lands, and may prefer to move freely between their host communities and return destinations. Thus, 'return' may not be a 'durable solution' in the sense of a permanent end to migration, but rather the cessation of imposed exile (Hanafi 2007: 283, Shehadi 2009).

Last, the struggle to control historic Palestine is reflected in wrangling over words for the land itself. I use 'Israel' to refer to the Jewish state within its 1948 borders, and the 'Palestinian territories' to refer to the West Bank and Gaza Strip.

The 1948 exodus: origins and attribution of responsibility

Hailed as 'miraculous' by Israeli President Chaim Weizman, the Palestinian exodus is known among the displaced as the great catastrophe (*al Nakba*) (Gabbay 1959: 110, Segev 2007: 7). Such diametrically opposed perceptions render the refugees' displacement particularly difficult to resolve: the refugee issue cuts to the core of each group's collective identity, placing their competing historical narratives and constituting myths in sharp relief (Gal 2008: 2).

Before the birth of Israel in 1948, Jews owned 7 per cent of the land in Mandate Palestine and represented 35 per cent of the population. Under the original UN partition plan, Israel would have governed 56 per cent of Mandate Palestine, with a sizable Arab minority of 45 per cent (Pappé 1994: 98–99, R. Khalidi 1998: 233–235). However, by the conclusion of the 1948 war, Israel controlled 76 per cent of Mandate Palestine, which was emptied of all but 156,000 of its Arab residents (Ben-Ze'ev and Aburaiya 2004, R. Khalidi 1998: 233). Israel quickly moved to entrench the refugees' dispossession, authorising large-scale demolitions in approximately 400 villages (Fischbach 2003: 3–5, 14–15, 2006: 15, W. Khalidi 1991). In 1950, the adoption of the Basic Law on Absentee Property 'retrospectively and prospectively' enabled Israel to confiscate land from 'absentees' (Cohen 2003: 8). Under this law, the Custodian of Absentee Property is considered the owner of absentees' lands and is prohibited from transferring ownership of the land to any party other than the Jewish development authority. The government transfers payment for the land to the Custodian so that it can be argued, albeit with Kafkaesque logic, that the property was acquired legally (Holzman-Gazit 2007: 108–109).

Traditional Israeli narratives of the 1948 war present a blameless Israel attacked without provocation by Arab states unwilling to accept the terms of the UN Partition Plan for Palestine.[14] Prime Minister David Ben Gurion's explanation for the Palestinians' convenient departure has generally been taken at face value by many in the Israeli populace: speaking to the Knesset in 1961, Ben Gurion stated that 'we have explicit documents testifying that they left Palestine following instructions by the Arab leaders . . . under the assumption that the invasion of the Arab armies . . . will destroy the Jewish state and push all the Jews into the sea' (Pappé 1994: 88–89). This account has been compellingly refuted through archival research by Israeli 'new historians'.[15] 'Without exception', these Israeli historians and their Palestinian counterparts have concluded that 'the flight of the vast majority was the result not of orders from their leaders (many of whom urged them to stay as soon as the scope of the exodus was revealed), but rather of forcible eviction by Israeli forces, fear and terror, and disorganisation and lack of leadership among the Palestinians' (R. Khalidi 1998: 239).[16]

Certainly, these scholars are hardly a unanimous group. Dissent abounds on numerous issues, particularly the extent to which the expulsion was a concerted Zionist strategy and whether the Palestinian exodus constitutes ethnic cleansing (Morris 2004b, Pappé 2004). Without wading far into these debates, it may be clearly established that Israel bears significant causal and moral responsibility for the refugees' ongoing plight. This is because, beyond the active involvement of Jewish forces in displacing Palestinians, resolutely refusing the return of refugees to their homes has been a cornerstone of Israeli policy since 1948 (Morris 1988, 2004a).[17] With a handful of minor exceptions, the refugees' aspiration to return has continually been frustrated, while Jewish people from around the world enjoy the right to 'return' to Israel under the national Law of Return. This frustration has been compounded by Israel's

[14] For unreconstructed presentations of this narrative, see Teveth (1985) and Karsh (1997). Lustick (1997) offers a comprehensive response to Karsh.

[15] Key pieces of Israeli revisionist scholarship addressing the 1948 war and the refugees' expulsion include Segev (1986), Shlaim (1988), Flapan (1987), Shafir (1989), Pappé (1994), and, in particular, the work of Benny Morris (1988, 1990, 2004a).

[16] Seminal Palestinian texts include W. Khalidi (1991), (2005), Masalha (1992, 2000, 2003) and Khalaf (1991). Research by scholars including Rafi Nets-Zehngut (2011, 2012) suggests that Israelis are increasingly accepting of 'critical' narratives of 1948.

[17] My assumption is that the state of Israel bears moral responsibility for the actions of the *yishuv*, since the *yishuv* functioned as a proto-state and its leaders promptly assumed positions of formal authority upon Israel's independence.

longstanding denial of any moral responsibility for the refugees' predicament (R. Khalidi 1998: 249).

Responsibility for the refugees

Just return hinges on accountability for displacement. To interpret and allocate responsibility for the Palestinians' displacement as a first step towards understanding what a just return might entail in this case, one must consider who is accountable for *creating* the problem in the first place; *sustaining* it over the past six decades; and, ultimately, *resolving* it. Understanding responsibility for the Palestinian refugee situation is complicated by tensions between what is owed to individual victims and to the collective Palestinian community. As Feldman (2008: 500) recognises, 'there is sometimes conflict between individual and collective claims to Palestine': for Palestinians in exile (and many in the West Bank and Gaza Strip), the possibility that their individual claims for restitution and return might be traded to secure the collective right to self-determination in an independent state is deeply dissatisfying – as evidenced by the furore over the Palestine Papers, a massive collection of leaked documents detailing concessions on key peace process issues, including the refugee file, floated by Palestinian negotiators.[18] Interpreting responsibility in this case is further complicated by the possibility that the experience of the Holocaust and the need to provide security for Jewish survivors might mitigate the responsibility of Israel and the international community for putting an unfair burden on the Palestinians.

Given these complexities, it is unsurprising that while establishing a minimum amount of common ground regarding responsibility for past crimes has been a first step in many successful negotiation processes, in the Palestinian-Israeli case, debates on responsibility for the injustices of the conflict have typically been sidelined or shelved (Lustick 2005: 112–115). However, the Palestine Papers 'provide evidence of a growing awareness of the importance of narratives and the potential of moral acknowledgement especially on the Palestinian side . . . analysts from the Palestinian Negotiations Support Unit (NSU; who produced many of the leaked documents on the refugee file) showed growing sophistication and a surprising sensitivity to Israeli concerns regarding their narrative'

[18] Leaked to Al-Jazeera in January 2011, the Palestine Papers are available at www.aljazeera.com/palestinepapers/ and www.guardian.co.uk/world/palestine-papers. See Molloy et al. (2011) for a discussion of the implications of the thinking revealed in the Palestine Papers for the resolution of the refugee situation.

(Molloy et al. 2011). For example, one of the documents in the Palestine Papers is a July 2008 memo on 'Recognition of Israel's Responsibility' from the NSU to (former) chief Palestinian negotiator Saeb Erekat in which the negotiating team insisted that 'Israel acknowledges its moral and legal responsibility for the longstanding displacement and dispossession of the Palestinian civilian population as a result of Israeli action during and following the conflict of 1948'. Yet in the same document, this straight-forward call for accountability is accompanied by highly nuanced draft positions such as the following, laid out under the heading 'Adapting to Israel's concern as to its national narrative':

> Israel has expressed its reluctance to acknowledge its responsibility out of fear that it would contradict its national narrative of triumph and homecoming. In fact, the acknowledgement Palestinians are seeking takes into account these concerns and does not lay responsibility for the creation of the refugee problem per se at the feet of the Israelis [alone]. Nor does it necessarily contradict the Israeli national self-perception as it is undeniable to all Israelis that the state has taken measures to oppose Palestinian return despite their efforts to come back... States frequently make mistakes or take actions which harm others. Acknowledging these mistakes and the harms that have resulted does not undermine the legitimacy of the state. Rather it shows its strengthen (sic) of character and determination to move forward.[19]

Widespread anger among Palestinians over the contents of the Palestine Papers forced the resignation of chief Palestinian negotiator Saeb Erekat and may have left his successors with greater hesitancy to attempt to address the complex narratives of the conflict. However, delaying confrontation with the historical record, as suggested by scholars such as Arzt (1997), may ultimately prove unwise. As prominent Palestinian critic Edward Said (2000: 158, 186) contended, acknowledgement of Palestinians' past sacrifices and losses is 'more important than peace for us'. Israeli recognition of its moral responsibility for the Palestinians' dispossession constitutes an essential component of a just return process for the Palestinian refugees. If Israel hopes to facilitate the resolution of the refugee situation without recourse to restitution and large-scale return behind the Green Line, recognising its moral responsibility for the Palestinians' displacement may prove critical to creating willingness among

[19] The memo goes on to state, under the heading 'Recognition of suffering is inadequate', that 'Simply recognizing the suffering of the Palestinians is inadequate for reaching an agreement. Palestinians need acknowledgement from Israel as to its actions which left them stateless, homeless and exiled. This is the history and underlying cause of the conflict. Acknowledgement is necessary to reverse the elements of conflict which has been built upon denial of the Palestinian humanity and dignity. It is through acknowledgement that the Palestinians can reclaim their dignity and put to rest their victimization.' See Molloy et al. (2011).

the refugees to consider alternative forms of return. In this connection, Rashid Khalid, Palestinian delegate to the 1992 Multilateral Working Group on Refugees, argued that it was 'essential' that 'the existential hurt that was done to the majority of the Palestinian people be acknowledged by those who caused that hurt, or their successors in power', precisely because 'there can probably be no fundamental redress of that grievance' (Lustick 2005: 124, R. Khalidi 1995: 74).

Israel bears only partial responsibility for the creation and resolution of the Palestinian refugee crisis. This weight is shared with the international community, including the Arab states involved in the 1948 war, and with the Palestinian leadership. The potential legitimacy of Arab grievances over partition aside, traditional Israeli accounts of 1948 correctly point out the role Egypt, Jordan, Lebanon, Syria, Iraq, Yemen and Saudi Arabia played as aggressors alongside the Palestinian forces. Through collusion with Israel, Jordan secured control of the West Bank and imposed a harsh occupation regime, which exacerbated the lamentable repercussions of the war for Palestinian refugees pushed onto the West Bank (Shlaim 1988). The Arab parties' decision to violently oppose partition must translate into a degree of shared responsibility for the attendant refugee crisis. However, the troubling role of great powers and international organisations in Palestine long predates the 1948 war. For example, the extension of the League of Nations Mandate for Palestine to Britain in 1922 almost perfectly mimicked the Balfour Declaration, calling for the creation of a Jewish homeland in Palestine, despite its 90 per cent Arab majority, and declining to explain how this could be accomplished without violence (R. Khalidi 1998: 245–246). In the lead up to 1948, the western powers were guided by the conviction that creating a Jewish state would compensate at least in part for the appalling legacy of anti-Semitic persecution (Said 2000: 184). Soon after the war, however, the international community was compelled to recognise that through its support for the partition of Palestine it had created special responsibilities for itself towards the Palestinian refugees (Nabulsi 2003: 482). Effective action on these responsibilities was another matter: the UN spawned two bodies with special mandates for the Palestinian refugees, UNRWA and the United Nations Conciliation Commission for Palestine (UNCCP). UNRWA was tasked with providing relief to the Palestinian refugees in the region, while the UNCCP was charged with the legal dimensions of refugee protection and operationalising solutions (Fischbach 2006: 17–18). Neither body represented an adequate expression of international responsibility towards the Palestinian refugees. Lacking a robust protection mandate, UNRWA is limited to a caretaker role; after compiling extensive data on the Palestinians' land claims, the UNCCP gradually became inert and now exists only on paper (Fischbach 2002, Forsythe 1972). Since the instigation of the Oslo peace process, the Palestinians have received international aid at one of the highest per capita rates in the world, yet portraying this assistance as an expression of international responsibility is also questionable: critics contend that it simply subsidises the occupation (Alpher 2005: 155–156).

Beyond palliative aid, effective international accountability towards the Palestinian refugees requires that the United Nations and its leading powers publicly recognise their own role in the Palestinians' dispossession, and support a 'permanent, just, and comprehensive resolution of the question of Palestine' (R. Khalidi 1998: 245–246). The western powers and potentially the Arab states are likely to contribute to compensation for the Palestinian refugees as part of this elusive solution and may also open their doors to some refugee resettlement or local integration. However, international donors are unwilling to foot the entire compensation bill or resettle large numbers of refugees, and are more likely to portray their contributions as strategic investments in the stability of the region and downplay any recognition of their role in the Palestinians' dispossession (Brynen 2008: 8).

Under the presidency of George W. Bush, a transformation was effected such that in the eyes of many western observers the 'Palestinians are no longer a people suffering military occupation or deserving rights and protections, but instead are entirely responsible for their predicament' (Nabulsi 2004: 228). Reasoning from entirely different vantage points, various Palestinian commentators have also concluded that their leadership must shoulder some of the responsibility for the refugees' plight. The Palestinians' own 'massive political failures in the decades preceding and following 1948' and their penchant for the 'portrayal of failure as triumph' have come under scrutiny from various Palestinian historians and commentators (R. Khalidi 1998: 245).[20] Beyond such scholarly recognition, the Palestinian leadership has also gradually prepared itself to exercise a significant degree of remedial responsibility for the refugees. As the sole representative of the Palestinian people, the Palestine Liberation Organisation (PLO) and the Palestinian National Authority (PA) recognise that they have, as Miller (2001: 454) says, a 'special obligation to put [this] bad situation right'. In other words, as the potential government of a future Palestinian state in which the refugees would have the right of citizenship, the PLO/PA has a particular 'responsibility towards the deprived or suffering party that is not shared equally among all agents,' irrespective of their causal or moral responsibilities for

[20] See also Khalaf (1991), R. Khalidi (1997) and Mattar (1988).

the *Nakba* (Miller 2001: 454). This duty was grounded in the Palestine National Council's 1988 Palestinian Declaration of Independence, which proclaimed that the 'State of Palestine is the state of Palestinians wherever they may be', thereby establishing a collective right of return to a Palestinian state existing peacefully alongside Israel (R. Khalidi 1998: 250, Nabulsi 2003: 486, PNC 1988). Since the instigation of the Oslo peace process, the Palestinian Authority's Ministry of Planning and Department of Refugee Affairs have conducted important policy research on the integration of returnees, in preparation for exercising its remedial responsibility through enabling large-scale return to an independent Palestinian state.[21]

Historically, Palestinians have been loath to discuss their own responsibility and that of the international community for the refugees, out of fear that this might detract from the push for Israeli accountability (R. Khalidi 1998: 245). As I have argued, Israeli revisionist historiography and Israel's longstanding policy of barring return provide strong grounds for attributing a significant degree of causal, moral and remedial responsibility for the refugees to Israel. Revisionist histories 'have greatly increased Israeli appreciation of the suffering of Palestinians in 1948 and the injustice of acts of expulsion and of enforced exile that produced and have maintained that suffering. Still, these findings have not achieved the emotionally reassuring status (for Palestinians) of official truth in Israel' (Lustick 2005: 119).[22] Rather, through policies such as unilateral disengagement, Israel has unsuccessfully attempted to divest itself of responsibility for the Palestinians' fate, without confronting its own moral culpability (Alpher 2005).

Israeli acceptance of even shared moral responsibility is hindered by the popular 'lack of conceptual and emotional distinction made between the events of the war itself and the creation of the state of Israel'; consequently, the suggestion that Israel should accept some moral responsibility for the Palestinians' displacement is often conflated with challenges to the legitimacy of the Jewish presence in the Middle East (Gal 2008: 3). Accountability for displacement is further hindered by the government's conviction that its fundamental responsibility is to preserve Israel's Jewish nature. Recognising even a modicum of moral responsibility for the refugees is seen as an abrogation of this duty, as it purportedly risks opening the floodgates to return. Yet Israeli imperviousness to accountability towards the refugees may ultimately undermine its ability to uphold its responsibility to guarantee the security and wellbeing of its

[21] See, for example, Nijem (2007). [22] See also Hirsch (2007).

citizens by perpetuating the conflict. From the Palestinian perspective, culpability for their uprooting matters enormously; taking steps to defuse hostilities by recognising Israel's part in the refugee crisis may in fact be seen as a responsibility Israel owes to its own citizens, because it is an essential condition for improving their security (Oz 2007).

Amos Elon's 1967 reflections on this issue were quite extraordinary at the time: 'We have a moral obligation', Elon wrote in *Ha'aretz*, 'because the road to Israel's independence was paved on the backs of these people, and they paid, with their bodies, their property, and their future, for the pogroms in the Ukraine and the Nazi gas chambers' (Segev 2007: 7). In the early years of the Oslo process, this type of public recognition was still rare (Gal 2008: 3–4). However, the need to accept shared moral responsibility for the refugee crisis is now more widely recognised; indeed, Nets-Zehngut (2011) suggests that in the Israeli 'collective memory', critical narratives of 1948 were already well established and quite widely accepted long before the Oslo process. For example, although he forthrightly rejects the return of Palestinian refugees to their original homes, Oz (2007) reflects that if Israel is to enjoy security and 'rest',

> The time has come to openly admit that we are partly responsible for the plight of the Palestinian refugees; not exclusive responsibility or exclusive guilt, but our hands are not entirely clean. The State of Israel is mature and strong enough to accept its partial guilt.

In 1999, former Israeli Prime Minister Ehud Barak took a small step in this direction by expressing 'regret for the suffering caused [by Israel's establishment] for the Palestinian people'; however, recognition of legal or moral responsibility for the refugees was one of Barak's four 'red lines' at the 2000 Camp David negotiations (Lustick 2005: 121–122). Lustick (2005: 107, 125–126) opines that Barak's reasons for this refusal were predominantly economic and legal, suggesting implicit recognition of the fairness of the demand and scope for acting upon it if practical concerns regarding the scope of Israel's liability were resolved. Importantly, the Palestinian negotiating position on moral responsibility, tabled at Taba in 2001, did not insist on Israeli acceptance of the right of return, or wording such as 'sole', 'central', or even 'primary' responsibility for the refugees' plight (Lustick 2005: 107, 125–126). This suggests room for compromise, as do documents released in the Palestine Papers, and survey data from 2000 indicating that more Israelis than previously assumed would be willing to go beyond Barak's 'red line': some 35 per cent of Israelis accept shared responsibility with the Arab countries for the problem; 22 per cent accept more limited Israeli responsibility (Yuchtman-Yaar and Hermann 2001: 309). To be sure, Israeli public opinion on refugee issues has hardened considerably since the outbreak of the second *intifada* and the effective collapse of the peace process (Brynen 2008: 1). Former Prime Minister Olmert's outright refusal – on moral grounds – to accept 'any kind of responsibility for the creation of this problem' also serves as a warning against premature optimism that opportunities to negotiate a just return will be opened up by the sides coming to an early agreement on the foundational issue of causal or moral responsibility for the refugees' displacement (Keinon and Horovitz 2007).

Resolving and redressing Palestinian displacement: frameworks and past efforts

One of the accomplishments of the Palestinian struggle has been to assert the rights of the displaced, so that it is now widely recognised that peace must involve redress for the refugees. Various international frameworks have consistently connected reparations to the resolution of the Palestinians' displacement, thus contributing to the emergence of international norms on redress for refugees (Lynk 2003). However, many frameworks and negotiations to date have fixated on compensation. The analysis offered in Chapter 7 suggests that in order to serve as springboards towards a just return, such frameworks and negotiations would need to incorporate equitable access to different forms of redress that clearly reflect shared moral and remedial responsibility for displacement.

International frameworks relevant to just return

In 1948, the UN Mediator on Palestine identified the 'twin rights of repatriation and compensation' as essential to the settlement of the Palestinian question (Lee 1986: 534). UN Member States echoed this view in General Assembly Resolution 194 (III) of 1948, which resolved that

> refugees wishing to return to their homes and live at peace with their neighbours should be permitted to do so at the earliest practicable date, and that compensation should be paid for the property of those choosing not to return and for loss of or damage to property which, under principles of international law or in equity, should be made good by the Governments or authorities responsible. (UNGA 1948)

Resolution 194 is reaffirmed annually by the General Assembly, prompting some to argue that it now represents customary international law (Boling 2001). Until the 1960s, the Arab states rejected Resolution 194 as not going far enough in support of the refugees' claims but now contend that Resolution 194 is the bedrock of the rights to return, restitution and compensation. Israel rejects this argument as wishful legal thinking, underscoring that Resolution 194 does not recognise any rights but merely resolves that the refugees '*should* be permitted' to return (Israel MFA 2007, italics added, Israel MFA 2009). Although it was only in the 1980s that Resolution 194 became a focal point for Palestinian advocacy, Khalidi (1992, 1998: 243) argues that the resolution is integral to a peaceful conclusion to the conflict, because it 'embodies a modicum of justice, which must be the basis for any settlement'. However, Khalidi also recognises several pragmatic barriers to its implementation, including the destruction of the vast majority of refugees' homes; the growth of refugee families; and lack of clarity on whether Resolution 194 covers refugees' descendents. Furthermore, two-thirds of refugees were legally landless upon their exile in 1948 (Fischbach 2006: 20). Focusing predominantly on reparations for lost property, as per Resolution 194, is unlikely to ensure a just return for those from the bottom rungs of the socio-economic ladder.

Alongside General Assembly Resolution 194, United Nations Security Council Resolution 242 of 1967 may also serve as a touchstone in enabling a just return process. Resolution 242 simply 'affirms' the 'necessity . . . [of] achieving a just settlement of the refugee problem', without proposing a specific solution. Both sides have expressed support for Resolution 242 as a basis for the resolution of the conflict, although the Palestinians also stress the continued importance of General Assembly Resolution 194.

In addition to the negotiation of these resolutions, various actors have developed detailed frameworks to assess the Palestinians' land claims and other grievances. For example, the IOM has carried out extensive research on lessons learned through different reparations processes for forced migrants that may inform the Palestinian case (Brynen 2008: 4). Independent researchers have reached a wide variety of figures on the scope of Palestinian losses. For example, Kubursi (1996, 2001) has estimated that it would cost Israel $132 billion to compensate the Palestinian refugees for lost land; adding damages for injury and psychological suffering would double this figure (Badil 1999). However, other estimates indicate that only $5.7–27.3 billion in compensation would be economically feasible for Israel, while a mere $1–5 billion would be acceptable to the Israeli electorate (Rempel 1999: 45). Indeed, most of the restitution and compensation frameworks developed to date sidestep these sticky questions of financing and convincing dubious constituents on both sides to support the plans.[23]

[23] On the under-examined issue of financing redress, see Segovia (2006) and Brynen (1999).

One of the most significant conceptual frameworks to emerge from international debates is the 'adequate compensation' model. This framework was discussed by the General Assembly in 1981 and elaborated upon by Benvenisti (1999) and the UN Group of Governmental Experts on International Cooperation to Avert New Flows of Refugees. Although the ideas at the heart of this model have been reflected in various stages of the Israeli-Palestinian negotiations, many of its elements are incongruous with a just return process. A principal aim of the adequate compensation framework is to take into account both parties' interests and constraints. Calculations of adequate compensation factor in Israel's financial limitations; the time elapsed since 1948; refugees' ability to prove property ownership; and the massive and growing number of claimants (Rempel 1999: 42). The adequate compensation framework rejects the ICJ's ruling that restitution must eliminate the consequences of a harmful act on the grounds that it is not pragmatic when dealing with large refugee communities. Proponents argue that paying full compensation could drain state resources, creating instability during delicate transition periods. Because adequate compensation attempts to balance the parties' interests and constraints, it could result in compensation levels below full market value. However, this model strives to ensure that compensation not only responds to individual grievances, but also advances the broader development of refugee communities: if rehabilitation will require more money than refugees' properties are worth, adequate compensation rates may in principle exceed the market value of their property. As Benvenisti (1999) writes, 'These principles are not just backward looking; they are also, and not less importantly, forward looking'.

As discussed in Chapter 1, efforts to uphold responsibility for displacement must be both backward and forward looking; indeed, these aspects of responsibility are deeply intertwined. Yet the adequate compensation framework, albeit practical and adaptable, fails to model the type of reparations process that could enable just conditions of return. Efforts to redress injustices are weakened by unrealistic or impracticable demands; however, if redress is to promote justice for refugees, it must involve not only compensation for lost property, but also some degree of property restitution and accountability for the violations that led to and prolonged the refugees' displacement (Du Plessis 2003: 659). While 'compensation may in certain circumstances be a favourable alternative to restitution it is by no means a panacea' (Bagshaw 2000: 214). Among restitution advocates, there is concern that relying entirely on compensation may be seen as a means of legitimising human rights violations, especially ethnic cleansing (Goodwin-Gill 1996: 269). Particularly troubling is the fact that, under this model, compensation would release

Israel from any further obligations towards refugees, without necessarily admitting responsibility for any wrong-doing. This undermines what the former UN Special Rapporteur on the Right to Reparations identified as the purpose of remedies for human rights abuses: 'relieving the suffering of and affording justice to victims by removing or redressing to the extent possible the consequences of the wrongful acts and by preventing and deterring violations' (Redress 2002: 5).

Return and redress: persistent hurdles for the peace process

Despite the existence of these frameworks, and the centrality of the Palestinian exodus to the conflict itself, the refugee question has struggled to find space on negotiation agendas preoccupied with '1967 issues'. However, it is now widely recognised in both camps that resolving the Palestinians' displacement cannot simply be sidelined or postponed, and the refugee issue has 'taken centre stage' as a critical challenge for negotiation (Gal 2008: 1).

The Oslo process was to have facilitated the immediate return of the 1967 refugees, leaving the 1948 refugee file to final status negotiations.[24] However, the process failed on both fronts: the 1967 refugees were denied return, while the collapse of the 2000 Camp David Summit is widely attributed to deadlock over the 1948 refugee issue (Brynen 2008: 3). At Camp David, Barak made what was perceived among Israelis to be the most generous offer possible of a Palestinian state on the entire Gaza Strip and over 90 per cent of the West Bank, only to be rebuffed by the Palestinians, for whom the issue is not generosity but a solution that at least approaches their conceptions of justice: from the Palestinian perspective, Israel's refusal to recognise even in principle the refugees' right to return was insupportable. At last-ditch talks convened in Taba in the final days of the Clinton presidency, the two sides arguably came closer to agreement on the refugee file than ever before, reaching consensus on definitions; mechanisms to finance compensation and development; and the broad structure of an international compensation commission. The negotiators' suggestion that their failure was due more to lack of time than fundamental impediments has, however, been met by scepticism from observers who point out that the negotiators went well beyond their instructions, and had no agreement on compensation figures or the number of refugees who would be able to return to Israel (Brynen 2008:

[24] On bilateral refugee negotiations since the early 1990s, see Sher (2006), Klein (2007), Zureik (1994, 1996), Tamari (1999) and Brynen (2008). On the multilateral process, see Rempel (1999) and Brynen (1997b).

8). In response to the Palestinian demand that Israel recognise its moral responsibility for the refugee crisis, Israel prepared a private response that obliquely broached the question of moral responsibility, stating that

> For all those parties directly or indirectly responsible for the creation of the status of Palestinian refugeeism [*sic*], as well as those for whom a just and stable peace in the region is an imperative, it is incumbent to take upon themselves responsibility to assist in resolving the Palestinian refugee problem of 1948. (Brynen 2008: 17)

While these steps represented significant advances, the Oslo process was far from yielding a comprehensive agreement that would be acceptable to the two sides and that could be seen as conducive to a just return.

The failure at Taba and the outbreak of the second *intifada* left the Oslo process on life support. Multilateral and track-two initiatives launched with a view to reviving serious bilateral talks did not, for the most part, address the refugee issue in detail.[25] The Quartet's 'performance-based road map' to peace simply calls for an 'agreed, just, fair and realistic solution to the refugee issue' (Quartet 2003). In contrast, the 2002 Arab Peace Initiative calls for the 'achievement of a just solution to the Palestinian refugee problem to be agreed upon in accordance with UN General Assembly Resolution 194' (Council of the League of Arab States 2002). Prominent track-two initiatives tended to be more explicit in their focus on the resolution of displacement through repatriation to a future Palestinian state. For example, the controversial 2002 Ayalon-Nusseibeh Plan bluntly stated that the 'Palestinian refugees will return only to the State of Palestine; Jews will return only to the State of Israel' (Ayalon and Nusseibeh 2002). The 2003 Geneva Accord attempted a more careful finesse of the issue, indicating that the refugees were entitled to compensation for property losses and 'refugeehood' itself and that General Assembly Resolution 194, Security Council Resolution 242, and the Arab Peace Initiative would underpin a just end to the refugee situation. This would be achieved by giving the refugees a choice between five options. Mirroring the Clinton Parameters, the options included permanent residence in the state of Palestine, areas in Israel transferred to the Palestinians through land swaps, third countries, the state of Israel

[25] Major post-Oslo multilateral initiatives include the 'road map' proposed by the 'Quartet' of the United States, Russia, the European Union and the United Nations and the Arab Peace Initiative proposed by the League of Arab States. Significant track-two initiatives include the 2002 Ayalon-Nusseibeh Plan ('People's Voice') and the 2003 Geneva Accord. The Ayalon-Nusseibeh Plan was drafted by Amihai Ayalon, a former Knesset Member for the Labour Party and head of Shin Bet, and Sari Nusseibeh, a professor and former representative of the Palestinian Authority in Jerusalem. The Geneva Accord was negotiated and signed by more than two dozen prominent Palestinian and Israeli leaders and peace advocates, acting in their individual capacities.

and current host countries. While the first and second options would be rights for all Palestinians, access to the latter options would be at the sovereign discretion of the states involved. Hailed by some as a pragmatic balancing act, this compromise has been decried by others as a perversion of international norms. Nabulsi (2004: 224), for example, charges that while the Geneva Accord purports to embody the implementation of Resolution 194, by leaving restitution to Israel's discretion 'the Accord's "implementation" of Resolution 194 is, in very real terms, it repudiation'.

In short, like the frameworks discussed above, attempts to negotiate the refugee issue have had at best a mixed record in terms of broaching the sensitive issues essential to enabling just return: equity, choice, the expression of responsibility through different forms of redress and ultimately the acquisition of effective citizenship for the Palestinian refugees. It is now widely accepted that in the event of a comprehensive two-state solution, all refugees outside the territories would have the right to return as citizens to the Palestinian state. This represents a major advance over the early years of negotiations, when Israel attempted to assert a right on security grounds to control even this form of return (Gal 2008: 5). Guaranteeing equal citizenship for all returning refugees in the Palestinian state would address some of the core components of a just return process. However, efforts to ensure equity in the resolution of the refugee situation are arguably compromised by the concerted focus in negotiations on reparations for property losses. Dealing fairly with land claims is central to the resolution of the conflict; however, this preoccupation risks marginalising the needs of the substantial proportion of the refugee population who have no land to claim. In addition, as landholding patterns in Palestine were heavily patriarchal, simply restoring property to male owners could exacerbate gender inequalities (Farha 2000). Given this wide range of shortcomings, refugees' dissatisfaction with the peace talks and the eventual implosion of the Oslo process is unsurprising. Indeed, the collapse of the talks shows 'just how fragile is a framework erected on a weak foundation. If it is not grounded in history, if it has no reference to international legitimacy and to the principle of justice, such a framework is inherently unstable' (R. Khalidi 1998: 252).

The best we can do? Imagining just return in the Palestinian case

At the end of his attempt to mediate compromise on the refugee issue in late 2000, President Clinton simply stated: 'This is the best I can do' (Clinton 2000). Although sharply criticised in many quarters, the Clinton parameters frankly grappled with some of the compromises that may well be the price of peace. Are the types of compromise Clinton proposed on issues including the rights of return, redress and self-determination and the resolution of statelessness conducive to a just return and a just peace, or do they inadvertently undermine their own endgame?

Looking beyond the right of return as restitution?

Understanding what a just return would entail in the Palestinian case requires coming to terms with perhaps the most hotly contested issue in the conflict: the right of return. The right of return has been portrayed in innumerable ways, from a steadfast practical demand to a negotiable principle and from the national aspiration of a downtrodden people to the demise of another. Palestinian reflections and negotiating positions on the right of return are broadly united by their conception of the right of return as the restitution of and repatriation to refugees' lost lands. International law arguably reinforces this position, insofar as it suggests that restitution should usually be the 'first form of redress' (Shelton 2002: 849). Are there satisfactory reasons for diverging from this norm in this case? Is it acceptable – and even cogent – to recognise the right of return in principle but limit the ways in which it can be implemented in practice? What would this mean for the prospect of a just return for the Palestinian refugees? I have argued that models such as the adequate compensation framework are incompatible with a just return because they fail to address moral responsibility for the refugees' exile and unilaterally foreclose restitution and return to original lands as options for even a small number of refugees. However, two factors caution against approaches at the opposite end of the spectrum, which assert virtually unfettered rights of restitution and return. First, interpreting the right of return as restitution may impose large and even catastrophic burdens on secondary occupants. Second, if Palestinian refugees returning to their original lands are to benefit from the resolution of not only their dispossession but also their statelessness, they would presumably need to acquire Israeli citizenship, or at least residency rights. This would challenge and arguably undermine the rights of both peoples to self-determination.

Taken in conjunction with practical insights gained through efforts to redress returnees in Bosnia, Guatemala and Mozambique, Jeremy Waldron's work on superseding historical injustice provides valuable insight into the first issue of balancing the claims of returnees and secondary occupants. It is widely accepted that some rights 'fade' in their moral importance and practical effect as time passes; this idea underlies the use of statutes of limitations for the prosecution of certain crimes.

Yet is there a statute of limitations on a state's obligation to redress the wrongfully uprooted? It certainly seems harsh to use the fact of refugees' longstanding dispossession as a way of weakening their claim to restitution (Waldron 1992: 15).[26] Waldron's principal contribution to navigating this conundrum is his argument that entitlements may be sensitive to circumstances; in other words, 'certain things that were unjust when they occurred may be overtaken by events in a way that means their injustice has been superseded' (Waldron 2004: 240). For example, a returnee may have a clear entitlement to property restitution, but this entitlement may be weakened if upholding the returnee's rights will have a disproportionately negative impact on the secondary occupants who will be evicted. Waldron's argument effectively demonstrates that refugees' rights to restitution and return to their original lands must be balanced against and may potentially be superseded by the claims of others, as 'the only thing that can trump the enterprise [of repairing historical injustice] is an honest and committed resolve to do justice for the future, a resolve to address present circumstances in a way that respects the claims and needs of everyone' (Waldron 1992: 27).

Putting aside for a moment the obvious rebuttals that it is by no means clear that the parties are motivated by such an egalitarian resolve and that it may be unjust to deny the refugees' claims in order to enable an exclusive form of self-determination for another group, Waldron's argument is compelling. Arbitrary dispossession and the fact of having 'been there first' are only two of the many variables that must be considered when determining the justice of a particular approach to resolving past wrongs. The notion of having 'been there first' is particularly troublesome in historic Palestine, where both peoples have deep roots in addition to particular religious claims to the land that may arguably trump entitlements generated by residency or legal ownership.[27] Although the supersession thesis may limit the refugees' restitution rights, Waldron (2004: 261) importantly stresses that 'no amount of discussion about

[26] See Waldron (2004) for a more detailed discussion of the implications of the supersession thesis for the Middle East conflict. Waldron (2004: 248) acknowledges that certain readings of the supersession thesis might seem to legitimise Israeli settlements in the occupied territories and create a 'set of perverse incentives' to undertake and then sustain unjust acts. However, he underscores that the application of the supersession thesis fundamentally depends not 'on the passage of *time*, but on *changes in circumstances* that a theory of justice makes relevant' (Waldron 2004: 237, italics added). See Thornton (2012) for further discussion of the philosophical challenges associated with property restitution after longstanding displacement.

[27] See Waldron (2007) on the limitations of first residency as a guiding principle for resolving land claims.

supersession can make the character of that injustice evaporate, nor remove the right of those who suffered it to some sort of remedy'.

Coupled with Waldron's theoretical arguments, the experiences of countries such as Guatemala and Mozambique further reinforce the argument that an unqualified right to reclaim original homes cannot be considered a minimum condition of just return.[28] The Bosnian case, in which the vast majority of displaced persons benefitted from restitution, is often used to backstop Palestinians' claims. However, comparisons between this case and the Palestinian situation are often misleading. Restitution was possible in Bosnia in large part because displacement was relatively short-lived, the different groups had recent experience of sharing a political community (however volatile) and there was a clear desire among the Bosniaks (not to mention the international community), who represent a significant proportion of the population, to maintain a multi-ethnic state. As discussed in Chapter 5, property restitution did not translate into widespread, long-term minority returns. In Guatemala and Mozambique, where displacement spanned decades, the reclamation of refugees' original properties was a negotiated affair that took into account factors such as the long-term presence of secondary occupants. To the limited extent that these repatriations processes approached the conditions of a just return discussed in Chapter 2, this was in part because the claims of different stakeholders were weighed, and compromises were made on all sides to ensure that upholding refugees' rights did not come at the expense of the rights of others. This experience runs counter to the stance of many Palestinian refugee advocates. However, if activists and academics wish to seriously defend the claim that the Palestinian case is not *sui generis*, they must refrain from 'cherry picking' only those insights that support their perspective, and undertake dispassionate analysis of what these cases reveal about the nature of just return and the right of return in theory and practice.

While Waldron's work and experiences in Guatemala and Mozambique caution against displacing longstanding secondary occupants to make way for returnees, the Palestinian refugees may nonetheless have strong grounds to reclaim those expropriated lands that are standing vacant. Indeed, Abu-Sitta (2001) estimates that 68 per cent of the Jewish Israeli population is concentrated on 8 per cent of Israeli territory, and suggests that much of the refugees' land is unoccupied or is used for agriculture. Is it not unacceptable to deny the refugees the chance to return to these lands? Opponents of restitution and return cite Israel's need for

[28] See Samy (2010) and Dumper (2006a, 2007) for detailed comparative perspectives on the provision of redress to the Palestinian refugees.

the land in order to maintain its economic prosperity and accommodate new immigrants. However, these needs pale in comparison to the refugees' need for new lives beyond the camps and could probably be met without Israel retaining all of the refugees' unoccupied land. Rather, the main barrier to returning this land is the implications this would have for Israel's demographic composition and both peoples' right to self-determination.

Allocating citizenship, interpreting self-determination and ending statelessness

As Waldron (2004: 262) points out, 'Not everyone has the right – even the moral right – to settle in any country to which they claim a connection, and the effect of the supersession thesis might be that the particular connection of the Palestinian refugees to this country rooted in the fact that they used to live there may have less and less force, as a matter of justice, as the character of their attachment changes.' The possibility that the Palestinian refugees may have a claim to acquire Israeli citizenship appears increasingly tenuous when one further considers that 'states are not simply legal membership organisations: they are communities, or, at least federations of communities, and membership in these communities should correspond to membership in the state' (Gibney 2006: 10).[29] While Israeli conceptions of citizenship might be best described as communitarian, the refugees' claim to Israeli citizenship is more instrumental, a status required for them to return to their lands. Clarifying different conceptions of citizenship and the principles that should inform the allocation of citizenship to stateless refugees is a significant element of enabling just return in hard cases because how citizenship is distributed can significantly affect future inequalities between groups within the state (Gibney 2006).

An obvious way to enable at least some restitution for the Palestinian refugees without changing Israel's demographic composition is to transfer control of this land to a future Palestinian state, or, more controversially, to 'swap' the land for settlements in the West Bank. Depending on the

[29] Of course there is a sizable group of Palestinians who live within the 1948 borders of Israel and hold Israeli citizenship. Refugees who returned as citizens to live behind the Green Line would presumably share some affinity and develop links with this community. However, it is important to recognise the marginalised status of the Palestinian minority within Israel and the fact that many if not most Palestinians who hold Israeli passports do not identify themselves as Israelis, given that the predominant conceptions of citizenship in Israel are directly linked to membership in the Jewish community. See Shafir and Peled 2002.

location of the land, however, this approach may not be viable. In these cases, it may be possible to restore the refugees' titles and allow them to return as citizens of the Palestinian state with residency rights in Israel. Such creative accommodations should not be ruled out, although it is admittedly difficult to imagine conditions in which Israel would agree to them. To the extremely limited extent that Israel has been willing to discuss the return of refugees to their original properties, it has generally been on the condition that these returnees would become Israeli citizens, entitled to the protections of the state but also formally bound to abide by its norms. Are restrictions on the number of refugees able to benefit from the restitution of unoccupied properties and the conferral of Israeli citizenship compatible with a just return? Various legal and moral principles come into play here. The two most immediately relevant are the right of national self-determination and the international legal principle of genuine and effective link, discussed in the introduction to Part III. Neither conclusively establishes nor refutes the claim that Palestinian refugees should have the opportunity to return to live on their lands behind the Green Line and become Israeli citizens.

The principle of the genuine and effective link suggests that factors including place of birth, descent, residence and social attachment may underpin a claim to citizenship (Batchelor 1998: 157, 163). Under this principle, the Palestinian refugees may have grounds to claim citizenship in a Palestinian state or in Israel. Significantly, the 1988 Palestinian Declaration of Independence established that all Palestinians would have the right to citizenship in Palestine, confirming in advance a genuine link between the refugees, the Palestinian leadership and the independent state they hope to create.[30] Israel does not consider this principle to legitimise the refugees' claim to return as citizens to their lands, and no legal rulings provide definitive precedents to inform this case. The utility of this principle in this case is further limited because it is intended to inform situations in which the claimants are stateless. The Palestinian case involves a large number of stateless refugees, in addition to many with citizenship status, such as the 1.9 million Palestinian refugees who

30 This raises an interesting point *vis-à-vis* my earlier argument that refugeehood is not simply about being ousted from a particular piece of land; rather, it is the intersection of physical displacement and the denial of citizens' right to claim membership in the political community of the state. The Palestinian refugees' claim to membership in the Palestinian political community is clearly not in doubt. Indeed, in many senses the modern Palestinian political community was forged in the refugee camps and now spans the globe (Nabulsi 2006). However, the refugees' membership claims cannot be truly effective in the absence of an independent state; thus, the Palestinians and other refugees find themselves in similar circumstances, insofar as their membership claims do not translate into effective state protection of their rights.

are citizens of Jordan (Shiblak 2009: 3). Does the possession of alternate citizenship weaken refugees' claim to return to their lands and access Israeli citizenship, particularly when their claims are compared to those refugees who are stateless? Although significant changes are required to render Jordanian citizenship equitable and effective for Palestinians, it is reasonable and compatible with the conditions of a just return process to focus first and foremost on providing solutions to those who are in the greatest need: the stateless refugees in Lebanon (Brynen 1997a, Clinton 2000). Yet enabling only the refugees in Lebanon to access restitution and citizenship rights in Israel would still have major impacts on the principle of self-determination.

Defences and critiques of the right to self-determination are abundant in philosophical, political and legal quarters.[31] Backers of both the two-state solution and the refugees' right to return to their original homes contend that while each group has a legitimate collective claim to self-determination in historic Palestine, on an individual basis the refugees still have the right to return to live on their properties, which would presumably involve becoming Israeli citizens. Many of these commentators question the legitimacy and justice of defining citizenship rights in terms of membership in a particular ethnic or national group. I have no definitive answers to this debate. Without wishing to undercut individual rights, it is however, important to reiterate that my concern is with the question of just return in the context of a negotiated two-state solution; such a solution presumably takes as its point of departure the idea that Israel represents the Jewish homeland, while a Palestinian state would be the Palestinian homeland. For many if not most Israelis, 'the right of the State of Israel to exist is inseparable from its claim to exist *as a Jewish state* and its status as the embodiment of the right to self-determination of the Jewish people' (Waldron 2004: 258). Collective and individual rights are not exercised in isolation from one another: enabling a sizable number of *individual* refugees to reclaim their unoccupied lands and return to them as citizens of Israel would alter if not undermine the Jewish people's collective right of self-determination in the state of Israel, at least in its current form. Thus, extending citizenship rights in Israel to a large number of Palestinian refugees is incompatible with the political rationale for the two-state solution. Some argue that Israel's ethnically-based approach to allocating citizenship and its insistence on self-determination separate from the Palestinians is simply incompatible with justice and respect for human rights. If these arguments are accepted, the only recourse for those

[31] See, for example, Kymlicka (1989), Tamir (1993), Margalit and Raz (1990) and Butenschon (2006).

concerned with justice is to reject the two-state solution and refocus on completely transforming the debate. However, if the two-state solution is accepted as a starting point for discussion, extending citizenship to at least some of those refugees who wish to return to their unoccupied lands appears to be something that could be morally *good* for Israel to do (and potentially politically expedient, at least in terms of facilitating a resolution to the conflict), rather than an *obligation* that represents a minimum condition of just return.

This discussion may seem to imply that the Palestinian refugees are scrambling for the chance to become Israeli citizens. In fact, Palestinians' experience of Israeli citizenship has been highly problematic: although Palestinian citizens of Israel are clearly cognisant of the protections afforded by this status, they have struggled with Israel's unwillingness 'in principle as well as in practice, to consider non-Jews, and particularly Arabs, as capable of becoming full-fledged members of the Israeli-Jewish national community' (Lustick 1980, 1993: 577, Peled 1992, Shafir and Peled 2002). The attitudes of current Palestinian refugees towards becoming Israeli citizens are often ambivalent or simply unknown. Conducting empirical research on the refugees' actual preferences has been fraught with challenges. A survey conducted in 2003 by the well-reputed Palestinian Centre for Policy and Survey Research (PSR) among refugees in the occupied territories and neighbouring host states concluded that if Israel recognised the Palestinian right of return under a comprehensive settlement to the conflict, only 10 per cent would seek to take up this right if it meant living under Israeli sovereignty (ICG 2004b: 8, PCPSR 2003). These results were denounced by refugee activists who allegedly ransacked the PSR offices and assaulted the Centre's director (ICG 2004b: 8). A 2006 survey among the broader Palestinian population found that 41 per cent support and 54 per cent oppose a settlement agreed to be based on Resolutions 194 and 242, in which refugees choose between five permanent residency options including unrestricted return to the Palestinian state and swapped territories and return to original homes subject to Israeli approval (PCPSR 2006).

Some refugees have objected to the very premise of these questions: Palestinian refugee Amna Ghanayam told the UK Joint Parliamentary Commission of Enquiry on the Palestinian Refugees that

> Holding a referendum about this right [of return] is an insult to the Palestinian people because it questions their loyalty to their homeland. Every Palestinian dreams of return. I have been asked 'Return or Jerusalem?' This question, as far as I am concerned, is the same as 'which one of your eyes do you want to knock out, the left or the right?'. (Joint Parliamentary Middle East Councils 2001: 83)

However, Hart's (2005) qualitative research with young Palestinian refugees in Jordan also problematises the claim that all refugees wish to return to their original homes, demonstrating that while young Palestinians may support the right to return in principle, many dream not of returning to a bucolic rural life, but of exciting urban lifestyles. Hanafi (2005) underscores that decision-making regarding return is shaped by social factors such as capital and transnational networks, more so than by nostalgia and political convictions. Such nuanced accounts of refugees' aspirations are extremely useful from both theoretical and practical points of view, as they begin to indicate how the actual preferences of each party may be simultaneously accommodated. Broaching the notion that many Palestinians may prefer not to exercise their right to return in practice, despite their commitment to the principle, has been incredibly difficult because of the Palestinians' weak negotiating position: neither the refugees nor their negotiators have much incentive to divulge any willingness to imagine forms of return beyond reclaiming and resuming life on their original lands. Thus, the Palestinians' fear of weakening their hand, coupled with Israel's unwillingness to recognise its moral responsibility and the right of return, even in principle, short circuit opportunities to craft a just return that speaks to real needs and aspirations on both sides.

Enabling return through redress

Compromise is a central theme cross-cutting the Israeli-Palestinian conflict. As Margalit (2005) argues, there may be circumstances in which the weaker party in a conflict, such as the Palestinians, are morally called upon to accept compromises that fall short of idealised conceptions of justice. The types of compromise that may bring peace after a protracted conflict in which both sides are arguably 'in the right' will always be difficult, but must never be humiliating. For a people who have built a national identity on the foundations of the dream of returning to their original homes, compromising on this principle may be a form of humiliation. The challenge for those committed to enabling a just return for the Palestinian refugees in the context of a two-state solution will be to strategically craft and apply different forms of redress that make it possible for the refugees to accept compromise, without compromising their dignity.

Whether they return as citizens of a Palestinian state or as Israeli citizens to their original, unoccupied homes, reparations therefore promise to play a central role in realising a just return for the Palestinian refugees. For those who may return to Israel, reparations will be essential to building goodwill and laying the foundation for a viable state-citizen relationship between Israel and Palestinian returnees. For the greater number likely to return to an independent Palestinian state, securing a decent redress 'package' will be critical to creating confidence among returnees in their new state. The material benefits obtained through redress may prove vital to improving returnees' living conditions, while Israel's expression of shared moral responsibility for the refugees through mechanisms such as apologies and truth commissions will likely be essential to ensuring stable, peaceful relations between Israel and Palestine. Thus, in this case, reparations play a dual role, strengthening both state-citizen relations and relations between states.

Given the centrality of reparations to the resolution of this high-profile conflict, the marginalisation of the Palestinian case from modern reparations politics is striking (Said 2000: 187). When transitional justice advocates and scholars have turned their attention to the Palestinian case, the results, such as the adequate compensation model and, at the other end of the spectrum, calls for restitution across the board of refugees' lost properties, have often failed to account for key facets of the case, such as the longstanding presence of secondary occupants and the need for remedies to involve explicit acknowledgement of shared moral responsibility for the Palestinian exodus. For reparations to advance a just return, a diversified approach is required that puts a premium on the even-handed treatment of all claimants, who must have the chance to choose to engage in a variety of remedies that tackle material and moral wrongs. The architects of a reparations strategy for the Palestinian refugees would be well advised to heed the insights gained through other return and redress processes, such as those that played out in Bosnia, Guatemala and Mozambique. As Chapter 7 argued, these experiences underline the need for redress programmes that are sufficiently comprehensive, complete, complex and coherent, and that respond appropriately to the issues of finality and munificence. In addition, reparations programmes must be based on suitable time frames that recognise that the application of redress to support the construction of respectful relationships of rights and duties between returnees and their states is a long-term endeavour. Successful reparations programmes for the Palestinian refugees will require strong monitoring and enforcement mechanisms; the targeted engagement of the international community; and well-calibrated strategies to facilitate the participation of displaced populations themselves, as well as the Israeli public. However, such engagement strategies must be informed by the pragmatic recognition that while reparations programmes can be vastly improved through the active involvement of refugees and returnees, in such tense and complex situations, it is impossible to craft solutions that will meet each individual's conceptions and expectations of justice.

An approach to reparations for the Palestinian refugees that takes these insights into account would entail broadening from a potentially myopic focus on restitution and compensation to engage with other remedies, such as truth commissions, apologies, public commemorations of massacres and former villages and the reform of educational curricula to ensure appropriate treatment of the narratives of each group.[32] Although it runs the risk of appearing tokenistic, at least a small number of refugees should be enabled to reclaim and return to their original, unoccupied lands, in order to be sure the process is not seen to tacitly condone the expulsion of an ethnic group from a particular region (Arzt 2001). Whether this is achieved through land transfers, swaps, repatriation to Israel, or other innovative means such as short-term returns to visit families' former homes would be subject to negotiation. (Such innovative approaches to conceptualising and enabling return would be particularly important for those Palestinian refugees who currently live on the West Bank or in the Gaza Strip and, thus, would not physically return to a newly independent Palestinian state.) David Grossman's discussions with Palestinians from Waki Alfuqin, one of the few groups of refugees who were granted restitution and the chance to return, illustrate the pitfalls of assuming that restitution is the 'silver bullet' to resolving the refugees' concerns. Grossman (2002: 75) reflects that despite the refugees' joy in reclaiming their land, 'Returning home did not turn the heart of any one of them into one which loves us, the Israelis. Maybe it was foolish to even hope for that.' While love and even basic reconciliation do indeed appear to be far too lofty goals for all but the most idealistic of commentators, the experiences of the Waki Alfuqin returnees underscore the fact that a remedy for land losses alone is insufficient to transform such deeply antagonistic relationships.

Irrespective of whether they access real property restitution, all refugees will need to be financially compensated for their material and moral injuries. An extensive body of literature has evolved to help inform policymakers crafting reparations programmes as part of a comprehensive solution to the conflict.[33] Much of this research advances figures

[32] On commemorative activities, see Khalili (2004, 2005) and Bronstein (2005). On representing diverse narratives in school textbooks, see Podeh (2005). For discussions of the link between reparations, the resolution of the refugee situation and reconciliation, see R. Khalidi (1999) and Rouhana (2004, 2005).

[33] For a major compilation of this research, see Brynen and El-Rifai (in press). See also Samy (2010). Key pieces of research on compensation for the Palestinian refugees are also available on the Palestinian Refugee Research Net at http://prrn.mcgill.ca/prrn/

for compensation that at first appear to be well beyond the bounds of practicality, given Israel's relatively modest GDP of $31,500 per capita and the limited willingness of international actors to foot the bill. In considering such figures, it is important to bear in mind that these amounts pale in comparison to the cost of continued conflict. Presenting compensation not as a 'good deed' but as an *investment*, grounded in respect for justice and a commitment to peace, may increase the palatability of these figures. At the same time, providing compensation alongside other forms of redress such as truth commissions, apologies and commemorations may make somewhat lower levels of compensation more acceptable. The potential of remedies such as apologies is underexplored by both scholars and negotiators; more concertedly examining such approaches may hasten the advent of a just return for the Palestinian refugees (Samy 2007).

When Argentina moved to redress the families of those who 'disappeared' during Argentina's Dirty War, a subset of the famous *Madres de Plaza de Mayo* refused to receive any redress from the government, as this would mean accepting their children's death and giving up on the dream of their return (Hamber and Wilson 2002: 10). A similar dynamic animates the Palestinian case: psychological and political barriers on both sides obstruct open discussions on reparations for the refugees, which are easily portrayed as a governmental strategy to buy survivors' silence and 'close the books' on their suffering. Premature attempts to link reparations and reconciliation can also undermine refugees' willingness to discuss different forms of redress that may plausibly contribute to the resolution of their displacement. A 2005 survey strikingly illustrates the gulf between Israelis and Palestinians on the reconciliation question: while 67.3 per cent of Israeli Jews indicated that reconciliation between Israeli Jews and Palestinians is 'very desirable', only 5.6 per cent of Palestinians felt the same; 23.3 per cent of Israeli Jews stated that reconciliation was 'desirable', compared to 48.5 per cent of Palestinians (Gal 2008: 10, Yuchtman-Yaar and Hermann 2001). These drastically differing perceptions underline that a distinction must be made between a minimally just political settlement and reconciliation; indeed, reconciliation may simply not be a realistic aim at this point (Rouhana 2005: 262–264). It may well be that it is only after the Palestinian refugees have had the chance to return to their homeland, in conditions of safety, dignity and with a

prcomp3.html#papers. Much of this literature addresses technical issues such as the composition of claims mechanisms and the merits of different approaches to assessing and delivering compensation, which are outside the scope of this chapter.

minimum measure of justice that the challenge of reconciliation between neighbours may finally be broached.

At the present juncture, talk of just return and eventual reconciliation in Palestine and Israel risks appearing hopelessly disconnected from the reality of increasingly hawkish politics in the Knesset, sectarian violence in the Palestinian territories and unabated suffering in the camps in Gaza. Yet, looking back on the history of failed negotiations characterised by 'red lines' or neglect of the refugee issue, the need for a fresh approach is abundantly clear. Reflecting on the meaning of just return in this quintessentially hard case, and not only the costs but also the opportunities presented by the compromises necessary to achieve it, may prove an essential first step in this direction.

Conclusion

Exile and return are themes that thread throughout the lives of individuals and nations, constantly reflected in literature, mythology, history and politics. Although few refugees ever know a return as triumphant as Homer's Odysseus, many could recognise themselves in his constant 'straining for no more than a glimpse of hearth-smoke drifting up from his own land', and his fear that outside powers, whether gods or states, had 'wiped from sight the day of their return' (Homer 1996: 77, 79). While various researchers have probed this mythologising of return and the personal significance of repatriation for refugees from different countries and cultures, the academic literature has lacked an integrated moral, legal and political analysis of the justice claims raised by repatriation. The preceding chapters have tackled this challenge, articulating a minimum conception of a just return process, and exploring how states responsible for creating refugees may be held accountable for this crime in the context of efforts to resolve displacement. These chapters have also underscored the practical value, as well as the challenges, of using different forms of redress such as restitution, compensation and trials to acknowledge and attempt to remedy the violations associated with displacement.

The point of departure for this book was the observation that debates on responsibility for forced migration have often fixated on the duties of host states and international organisations, leaving the responsibilities of states of origin in the margins. This sidelining of the duties of refugee-creating states is especially troubling because factors such as the end of the Cold War, compounded by more recent events including the terrorist attacks of 11 September 2001, have shifted the parameters for the pursuit of durable solutions for refugees in the context of the international refugee regime, leading to the consolidation of repatriation as the 'preferred' and predominant solution to displacement, at least from many states' perspectives. In light of this shift, there is a pressing need for deeper scholarly understanding of the responsibilities of refugee-creating states, especially in the context of return.

Accordingly, this book applied the tools of moral theory, international law and political and historical analysis to elucidate the remedial responsibility states of origin bear towards their repatriating citizens. The book's principal aim was to develop a normative account of the minimum conditions of a just return process. The account I have offered suggests that while international law requires that refugee repatriation takes place voluntarily, in conditions of safety and dignity, a *just* return builds on these standards with a view to (re)establishing returnees as equal members of the political community of the state by recasting a new, legitimate relationship of rights and duties between the state and its returning citizens. I maintained that a just return must ensure that returnees can access effective, equal protection for their security and basic human rights, including accountability for abuses of these rights. Drawing on international law and political theory, I argued that different forms of redress such as property restitution, compensation, apologies and truth commissions play a critical role in enabling just return, as it is through reparations that the state of origin may affirm or re-establish its legitimacy by acknowledging and attempting to make good on the duties it abrogated by forcing its citizens into exile.

This work's second main aim was to connect this theoretical argument to the practice of states and other key actors in the refugee regime, first by tracing the emergence and evolution of international norms on reparations for refugees and then by exploring the challenges associated with redressing refugees returning to Guatemala, Bosnia and Mozambique. These cases underlined the messiness of moving from theory to practice: legally and morally, returnees' right to redress is well-founded, but in practice efforts to 'do justice' by returnees are complicated by a host of practical challenges. These include recalcitrant authorities, lacklustre international support, competing priorities, chaotic post-conflict circumstances and the simple impossibility of offering reparations that even approach the magnitude of many refugees' losses. Whether refugees are repatriating to states emerging from genocide, war, occupation or other systemic human rights abuses, return and redress will inevitably be flawed processes. However, these cases underlined the valuable role reparations may play in upholding at least a degree of state responsibility for forced migration, and enabling returnees to rebuild their lives and their place in the political community. They also served as rich sources of insight into the characteristics of reparations programmes through which states of origin may make good on their obligation to enable just return for their exiled citizens. These insights were explored in Chapter 7, and informed my discussion in Part III of 'hard cases' involving the protracted displacement of stateless refugees who cannot mount claims as citizens against the states to which they would return. Chapter 8 examined the implications of the notion of just return for the Palestinian refugee situation, a quintessentially hard case. In this section I suggested that my account of just return is indeed relevant in these hard cases and that in such cases a just return must involve the return of refugees to land with which they have some prior ties, whether through former residence, ancestral links or community membership, and to which they may return as citizens benefitting from redress from those actors responsible for their displacement.

Several of the ideas, observations and arguments that emerged through this combined theoretical and empirical analysis require a final word of emphasis or clarification. First, I have underscored the duty of states of origin to shoulder remedial responsibility for their citizens' displacement by creating just conditions of return, but many refugee-creating states clearly lack the capacity, material resources and even the will to take seriously returnees' rights and claims. Indeed, many refugee-generating states are clearly colonial creations that cobble together members of different social groups while carving up other groups that happen to span the boundaries drawn by the colonial powers; in such circumstances, a lack of affinity between state and citizen is often widespread. This effort to understand state responsibility for forced migration and the minimum conditions of a just return process should not be seen as an apologia for the state system, with its troubled origins and in its equally troubling present manifestation, but rather as an attempt to grapple with how these flawed institutions may nonetheless bolster some measure of present legitimacy by protecting and upholding the rights of their citizens. Where states lack the capacity or will to execute this responsibility, international actors play a critical role in strengthening the ability and resolve of states of origin to enable the just return and reintegration of their citizens. In short, while just return is primarily a duty of states of origin, supporting its achievement may be both a moral requirement and a prudential policy decision for other actors in the refugee regime.

Second, both my normative arguments and empirical analyses of attempts to redress displacement in Bosnia, Guatemala and Mozambique underscore that recasting the relationship between states and their returning citizens requires confronting and attempting to redress not only refugees' loss of land but also other human rights violations at the root of displacement, such as discrimination, rape and torture. The 'norm entrepreneurs' responsible for instigating and advancing the development of international standards on reparations for refugees have focused squarely on real property restitution as the form of redress most intimately connected to the crime of forced migration and the implementation of return as the 'preferred' solution to displacement. The negotiation of hundreds of provisions on refugees' right to reclaim their lost lands and the creation of more than a dozen institutions to operationalise these standards represents an important advance for the refugee regime. However, the effective implementation of these norms with a view to enabling just return requires that refugees' non-material claims are also integrated into broader reparations programmes and transitional justice strategies. This is a challenge that has only recently begun to be appreciated (Duthie 2012a).

Third, it bears emphasising that the creation of conditions of just return is a long-term process for which there is no definitive blueprint. While I have sketched minimum conditions of a just return that may serve as a guide for states and international organisations seeking to understand their basic obligations in different circumstances, the unique characteristics of each case must be taken into account in order to ensure that to the extent possible, remedial interventions respond to different communities' and individuals' priorities and conceptions of justice. The direct participation of refugees in negotiating the terms of their return, as exemplified by the Guatemalan case, may be extremely valuable in this regard. Indeed, as the Mozambican experience demonstrated, in some cases the most appropriate way forward may be for the state to reinforce citizens' efforts to apply their own tools and traditions to resolve land conflicts and other challenges surrounding return and reintegration.[1] Of course participation is not a sure-fire route to a successful and just return process. While refugees have the right to expect that minimum conditions of safety and dignity are in place before they cross the border, renegotiating the relationship between returnees, their former neighbours and the state is a long-term process necessitating the sustained engagement of national and international actors, and a commitment to ensuring that efforts to redress returnees are embedded in longer-term peacebuilding processes. Efforts to enable a just return for refugees must be strategically rooted in broader post-conflict policies; otherwise, refugees may be left out of critical political, development and justice processes. Equally, if returnees are perceived to be receiving special treatment, this may generate grievances that undermine reconciliation and the transition from conflict. In a related vein, this study has demonstrated that while reparations and transitional justice more broadly have often been perceived

[1] The Afghanistan case also illustrates the utility of approaches that draw on traditional dispute resolution mechanisms to address grievances associated with return. See Foley (2008) and Bradley (2009a).

and portrayed as 'soft' challenges in post-conflict environments, compared to overtly securitised issues such as disarmament, demobilisation and security-sector reform, the emergence of international norms on redress for refugees represents a significant 'realpolitik' streak in reparations politics. An examination of refugees' role in reparations politics shows that the provision of redress to displaced persons (particularly restitution) is often a question of post-conflict stability and political and economic interests on the part of both states of origin and asylum.

Fourth, I have argued that repatriation and efforts to redress the suffering of returnees and other survivors are inescapably flawed processes: there is simply no way to turn back the clock on the violence of war and the crimes that foment refugeehood. The reclamation of homes, the prosecution of offenders and the acknowledgement of their experiences and suffering in the reports of national truth commissions may be powerful experiences for some returnees. Yet for others such remedies may be largely irrelevant to resolving their most pressing concerns or woefully incommensurate with the depth of their wounds. It may well be that for some refugees a just return through the reconstitution of their relationship with their state of origin is simply an impossibility. It is therefore essential not to confuse efforts to articulate and realise conditions of just return with support for the foreclosure of other solutions to displacement. (In some cases, return may be undertaken alongside other solutions to displacement. For example, many resettled refugees eventually return to their original states, to visit if not to live, and would thus benefit from serious efforts to resolve their claims and create a functional relationship between the state and its citizens, including those who left as refugees and now also hold other passports.) The shortcomings of return and redress processes are exacerbated by the fact that refugees often have pitifully little recourse if the problems they encounter upon their return turn out to be intolerable. Hathaway (2007: 5, 2005) points out that under the 1951 Refugee Convention, those who voluntarily return to their home countries still retain refugee status until they 're-establish' themselves, a process that entails 'durable, ongoing presence in the home country'. This should make it possible for refugees interested in long-term return to 'test the water' and re-avail themselves of protection in their country of asylum if they conclude that the conditions are not tenable. However, UNHCR and host states eager to clear up refugee situations sometimes behave as if the decision to return automatically precludes any further enjoyment of asylum rights, thus short-circuiting returnees' options in the event that minimum conditions of safety, dignity and justice are absent in their states of origin. Taken in combination, these limitations may prompt those concerned with justice for forced migrants to question whether there is any point in discussing the possibility of a just return. However, as Shklar (1964: 122–123) reflects, 'To show that justice has its practical and ideological limitations is not to slight it . . . The entire aim is rather to account for the difficulties which the morality of justice faces in a morally pluralistic world and to help it recognise its real place in it – not above the political world but in its very midst.'

All this attests to the need for a profound reconceptualisation of return as a political process. Just return is not a matter of restoring a lost way of life, an elusive *status quo ante* or the natural *qua* national 'order of things' (Malkki 1995). Scholars concerned with political membership and the shortcomings of the state system have debunked the notion that individuals necessarily 'belong' in a particular geographic place or within a particular political community (Benhabib 2004, Malkki 1992, 1995, Turton 2005). Rather than relying on essentialised assumptions about membership and belonging, my account of just return builds on the widely accepted view that if a state is to retain a legitimate claim to sovereignty, it must protect the rights of its citizens, irrespective of factors such as their ethnicity, religion or political views. This does not preclude refugees joining new political communities; certainly, refugees should be able to exercise and enjoy their human rights wherever they find themselves. However, the bleak history of the refugee regime testifies to the difficulty refugees face in securing respect for these rights when seeking shelter in states where they do not hold citizenship. I have contended that it is neither productive nor analytically accurate to indiscriminately portray refugees as stateless victims exclusively reliant on the mercy of foreign governments and humanitarian agencies. Instead, it is important to begin to consider how refugees' citizenship in their state of origin may be leveraged to enable them to make claims against their state, particularly in the context of the repatriation process, for the protection of their rights, including redress for past violations. Of course in many recent and current repatriation operations, citizenship has not functioned as such an empowering tool but as a label to legitimise coercive return and the premature withdrawal of protection and assistance. This bleak reality cannot be denied, but one of the assumptions underpinning this book is that despite the changes globalisation has engendered for the exercise of sovereignty, the state system is far from collapse; there is value in scholarship that confronts this reality, recognising that in a world of states unwilling to extend sufficient resettlement and local integration opportunities to millions of refugees, increasing the efficacy of refugees' citizenship claims *vis-à-vis* their states of origin is critical to ensuring that more refugees may enjoy a durable and just solution to their displacement. Ultimately, the challenge is to ensure that the process of redressing past wrongs, which is at the heart of a just return process, serves as an entry point for a more profound renegotiation of the relationship between the state and its citizens, including those in exile and returnees. As Kymlicka and Norman (1994: 368) point out,

> In most post-war political theory, the fundamental normative concepts were democracy (for evaluating procedures) and justice (for evaluating outcomes). Citizenship, if it was discussed at all, was usually seen as a derivative of democracy and justice – that is, a citizen is someone who has democratic rights and claims of justice. There is increasing support, however, from all points of the political spectrum, for the view that citizenship must play an independent normative role in any plausible political theory and that the promotion of responsible citizenship is an urgent aim of public policy.

This discussion of state responsibility for displacement and just return has drawn on a relatively austere conception of citizenship as the ability to enjoy basic rights and exercise fundamental justice claims. However, in the long term, it is in the interest of states recovering from war and large-scale forced migrations to develop more vibrant, active conceptions of responsible citizenship because 'what the state needs from the citizenry cannot be secured by coercion, but only cooperation and self-restraint in the exercise of private power' (Cairns and Williams 1985: 43). Reparations provided in the context of a just return process may play a critical part in first making good on a minimal conception of citizenship as equal rights and legal status and eventually supporting the articulation and enactment of more dynamic conceptions of citizenship as the exercise of responsibility and civic virtues.

This examination of state responsibility for displacement, just return and the provision of redress to refugees raises a range of questions for future research. Further empirical study is required to understand variation in the implementation of norms on redress for the displaced, and to appreciate the relative efficacy of different approaches to reparations involving displaced persons, such as restitution in comparison to compensation, and high-level interventions in contrast with locally based processes.[2] Redress may contribute to the achievement of justice in the abstract, but further research could advance comprehension of the significance of reparations on a practical level, in the daily lives of returnees and other survivors of large-scale human rights violations. In this connection, productive links could be built between the emerging body of research on reparations for refugees uprooted by war and human rights

[2] See Duthie (2012a) for an important contribution to this discussion.

violations, and the more well-established literature on compensation for those ousted by development projects.[3] As displacement linked to the effects of climate change emerges as a major issue on the forced migration research agenda, it would also be beneficial to explore the role of different forms of redress in responding to the justice claims of those whose homes and even states are destroyed by disasters associated with climate change. How should those concerned with accountability for forced migration interpret responsibility for so-called environmental displacement? I have focused on different forms of redress as tools that may be used to help enable a just return for refugees, but what is the moral and practical significance of reparations in cases of environmental displacement where return may be physically impossible?

It is abundantly clear that return happens in inappropriate and often heinous circumstances, with no pretence of voluntariness or respect for refugees' dignity. While such cases could not qualify as just returns, there is still value in trying to ensure that even when repatriation falls short of international standards, the conditions returnees encounter are as just as possible. It is, however, important to consider whether there are cases in which, from a moral point of view, return should not even be contemplated. Even the most comprehensive processes of redress and reform may in some cases be unable to restore any bonds of 'trust, loyalty, protection, and assistance between the citizen and the state' (Shacknove 1985: 275). In such instances, should return simply be beyond the pale? Interestingly, Article 1 C(5) of the 1951 Refugee Convention provides support for the notion that some refugees should never have to countenance return. It states that an individual no longer qualifies for refugee status if the circumstances that led to flight have been resolved, unless the refugee has 'compelling reasons arising out of his previous persecution for refusing to avail himself of the protection of the country of nationality'. Understanding how this may be determined would release states and agencies such as UNHCR to focus on those cases in which just return is a practically, legally and morally valid option.

Ultimately, the concept of just return has a two-fold aim: most immediately, a just return process strives to ensure that refugee-creating states effectively shoulder remedial responsibility for the expulsion of their own citizens, thus opening up opportunities to resolve displacement by recasting the relationship between the state and returnees. In the longer term, the deterrence of future abuses is an ever-present, overarching goal of reparations politics and of redress provided to refugees in the context of

[3] See, for example, Cernea and Mathur (2008), Cernea and McDowell (2000), Penz (2003) and Penz, Drydyk and Bose (2011).

a just return process. The continuous uprooting of refugees from Syria to the Democratic Republic of Congo leaves little room for optimism that the gradually growing push for accountability for human rights abuses currently serves to dissuade institutions and individuals from committing atrocities. Yet this will be a challenge for researchers and practitioners to monitor in the future, in the hope that norms on redress and responsibility for displacement will grow constantly sharper, to the point where they not only provide remedy after injustice but also deter the crimes that create refugees in the first place.

Bibliography

TREATIES, AGREEMENTS, CONVENTIONS AND DECLARATIONS

(1944) Annotations of the Text of the Treaty of Versailles.
(1948) Universal Declaration of Human Rights.
(1951) Convention Relating to the Status of Refugees.
(1954) Convention Relating to the Status of Stateless Persons.
(1961) Convention on the Reduction of Statelessness.
(1969) Convention Governing the Specific Aspects of Refugee Problems in Africa.
(1989) CIREFCA Declaration and Concerted Plan of Action in Favour of Central American Refugees, Returnees and Displaced Persons.
(1991) Agreement on a Comprehensive Political Settlement of the Cambodian Conflict.
(1992) General Peace Agreement for Mozambique.
(1992) Sochi Agreement on Resolving the Georgian-Ossetian Conflict.
(1993) Tripartite Agreement between the Government of the Republic of Mozambique, the Government of Zimbabwe and UNHCR for the Voluntary Repatriation of Mozambican Refugees from Zimbabwe.
(1994) Accord on the Resettlement of Populations Uprooted by the Armed Conflict in Guatemala.
(1995) General Framework Agreement for Peace in Bosnia and Herzegovina.

OTHER SOURCES

Abu Shakrah, J. (2001) 'Deconstructing the Link: Palestinian Refugees and Jewish Immigrants from Arab Countries'. In Aruri, N. (ed.) *Palestinian Refugees: The Right of Return*. London: Pluto Press (pp. 208–216).

Abu-Sitta, S. (2001) 'The Right of Return: Sacred, Legal and Possible'. In Aruri, N. (ed.) *Palestinian Refugees: The Right of Return*. London: Pluto Press (pp. 195–207).

ACCORD (1997) *Negotiating Rights: The Guatemalan Peace Process*. London: Conciliation Resources.

Adejumobi, S. (2001) 'Citizenship, Rights and the Problem of Conflict and Civil Wars in Africa'. *Human Rights Quarterly* 23(1), 148–170.

Adelman, H. (2002) 'Refugee Repatriation'. In Stedman, S. J., Rothchild, D. and Cousens, E. (eds.) *Ending Civil Wars: The Implementation of Peace Agreements*. Boulder: Lynne Rienner (pp. 273–302).

Adelman, H. and Barken, E. (2011) *No Return, No Refuge: Rights and Rites in Minority Repatriation*. New York: Columbia University Press.

AFP (2011) 'Humanitarian Aid: "The Biggest Mistake UNHCR Ever Made"'. *The Express Tribune/International Herald Tribune*, 28 December 2011.

Africa Watch (1992) *Conspicuous Destruction: War, Famine and the Reform Process in Mozambique*. London: Human Rights Watch.

Agamben, G. (1994) 'We Refugees' (trans. M. Rocke). Available at: www.egs.edu/faculty/Agamben/agamben-we-refugees.html.

Ahmad, Z. (2003) 'The Bihari Muslims of Bangladesh: In a State of Statelessness'. In Chari, P. R., Joseph, M. and Chandran, S. (eds.) *Missing Boundaries: Refugees, Migrants, Stateless and Internally Displaced Persons in South Asia*. New Delhi: Manohar Publishers (pp. 173–180).

Alden, C. (2001) *Mozambique and the Construction of the New African State*. New York: Palgrave.

Alexander, J. (1997) 'The Local State in Post-War Mozambique: Political Practice and Ideas about Authority'. *Africa* 67(1), 41–69.

Allen, T. and Turton, D. (1996) 'Introduction: In Search of Cool Ground'. In Allen, T. (ed.) *In Search of Cool Ground: War, Flight and Homecoming in Northeast Africa*. Oxford: James Currey Publishers (pp. 1–22).

Alpher, J. (2005) 'Israel's Aid Responsibilities towards the Palestinian Population'. In Keating, M., Le More, A. and Lowe, R. (eds.) *Aid, Diplomacy and Facts on the Ground: The Case of Palestine*. London: Royal Institute of International Affairs.

Amnesty International (2007) 'Human Rights in Bosnia and Herzegovina'. In *Amnesty International Report 2007*. London: Amnesty International. Available at: www.amnesty.org/en/region/bosnia-herzegovina/report-2007.

(2008) 'Human Rights in Bosnia and Herzegovina'. In *Amnesty International Report 2008*. London: Amnesty International. Available at: www.amnesty.org/en/region/bosnia-herzegovina/report-2008.

Andersson, H. (1992) *Mozambique: A War against the People*. New York: St Martin's Press.

Andreu-Guzmán, F. (2012) 'Criminal Justice and Forced Displacement'. In Duthie, R. (ed.) *Transitional Justice and Displacement*. New York: SSRC (pp. 233–276).

Annan, K. (2005) 'United Nations Secretary-General's Address'. Statement Delivered to the UNHCR Executive Committee'. Geneva, 6 October 2005.

Arendt, H. (2004) *The Origins of Totalitarianism*. New York: Schocken Books.

(2006) *Eichmann in Jerusalem: A Report on the Banality of Evil*. London: Penguin.

Armon, J., Hendrickson, D. and Vines, A. (eds.) (1998) *The Mozambican Peace Process in Perspective*. London: Conciliation Resources.

Arzt, D. (1997) *Refugees into Citizens: Palestinians and the End of the Arab-Israeli Conflict*. Syracuse: Syracuse University Press.

(1999) 'The Right to Compensation: Basic Principles Under International Law'. Paper delivered at the Workshop on Compensation for Palestinian Refugees, International Development Research Centre, Ottawa, 14–15 July 1999.

(2001) 'Actual Repatriation: A Minimal Israeli Gesture'. In Ginat, J. and Perkins, B. (eds.) *The Palestinian Refugees: Old Problems, New Solutions*. Brighton: Sussex Academy Press (pp. 122–136).

Atran, S. and Alexrod, R. (2008) 'Reframing Sacred Values'. *Negotiation Journal* 24(3), 221–246.

Auden, W. H. (1940) *Another Time*. New York: Random House.

Ayalon, A. and Nusseibeh, S. (2002) Ayalon-Nusseibeh Plan ('People's Voice'). Available at: www.jewishvirtuallibrary.org/jsource/Peace/peoplesvoiceplan.html.

Azevedo, M. J. (2002) *Tragedy and Triumph: Mozambique Refugees in Southern Africa, 1977–2001*. Portsmouth: Heinemann.

B92 (2005) 'Zatvorski dani B. Plavšić', 15 March 2005. Available at: www.b92.net/info/vesti/index.php?yyyy=2005amp;mm=03amp;dd=12amp;nav_category=64amp;nav_id=164146.

Babbitt, E. et al. (2002) *Imagine Coexistence: Assessing Refugee Reintegration Efforts in Divided Communities*. Geneva: Tufts University Center for Human Rights and Conflict Resolution.

Badil (1999) 'The Impact of Return on Compensation for Palestinian Refugees'. Background paper delivered at the Workshop on Compensation for Palestinian Refugees, International Development Research Centre, Ottawa, 14–15 July 1999.

(2002) 'Palestinian Refugees Visit Bosnia-Herzegovina to Learn About Return and Real Property Restitution'. Available at: www.badil.org/Press/2002/press262-02.htm.

Bagshaw, S. (1997) 'Benchmarks or Deutschmarks? Determining the Criteria for the Repatriation of Refugees to Bosnia and Herzegovina'. *International Journal of Refugee Law* 9(4), 566–592.

(2000) 'Property Restitution and the Development of a Normative Framework for the Internally Displaced'. *Refugee Survey Quarterly* 19(3), 209–223.

Bailliet, C. (2000a) 'Preventing Internal Displacement: Conciliating Land Conflicts in Guatemala'. *Refugee Survey Quarterly* 19(3), 187–200.

(2000b) 'Unfinished Business: The IDP Land Question'. *Forced Migration Review* 7, 7–19.

(2003) 'Property Restitution in Guatemala: A Transnational Dilemma'. In Leckie, S. (ed.) *Returning Home: Housing and Property Restitution Rights of Refugees and Displaced Persons*. New York: Transnational Publishers (pp. 1–14).

Ballard, M. (2010) 'Post-Conflict Property Restitution: Flawed Legal and Theoretical Foundations'. *Berkeley Journal of International Law* 28(2), 462–496.

Barnett, M. and Finnemore, M. (2004) *Rules for the World: International Organizations in Global Politics*. Ithaca: Cornell University Press.

Barkan, E. (2001) *The Guilt of Nations: Restitution and Negotiating Historical Injustices*. Baltimore, MD: Johns Hopkins University Press.

(2005) 'Considerations Toward Accepting Historical Responsibility'. In Lustick, I. and Lesch, A. (eds.) *Exile and Return: Predicaments of Palestinians and Jews*. Philadelphia: University of Pennsylvania Press (pp. 85–160).

(2007) 'Reparation: A Moral and Political Dilemma'. In Miller, J. and Kumar, R. (eds.) *Reparations: Interdisciplinary Inquiries*. Oxford: Oxford University Press (pp. 1–20).

Batchelor, C. A. (1995) 'Stateless Persons: Some Gaps in International Protection'. *International Journal of Refugee Law* 7(2), 232–256.

(1998) 'Statelessness and the Problem of Resolving Nationality Status'. *International Journal of Refugee Law* 10(1/2), 156–183.

(2006) 'Transforming International Legal Principles into National Law: The Right to a Nationality and the Avoidance of Statelessness'. *Refugee Survey Quarterly* 25(3), 8–25.

Bazyler, M. (2002) 'The Holocaust Restitution Movement in Comparative Perspective'. *Berkeley Journal of International Law* 20 (1), 11–44.

BBC News (2002a) 'Dutch Government Quits over Srebrenica', 16 April 2002. Available at: http://news.bbc.co.uk/2/hi/europe/1933144.stm.

(2002b) 'Dutch General Joins Srebrenica Exodus', 17 April 2002. Available at: http://news.bbc.co.uk/2/hi/europe/1935484.stm.

(2002c) 'Musharraf Wraps up Bangladesh Visit', 31 July 2002. Available at: http://news.bbc.co.uk/2/hi/south_asia/2163374.stm.

(2003a) 'Belgrade Apology for Bosnia War', 13 November 2003. Available at: http://news.bbc.co.uk/2/hi/europe/3267683.stm.

(2003b) 'Bosnia's "Iron Lady" Jailed', 27 February 2003. Available at: http://news.bbc.co.uk/2/hi/europe/2803303.stm.

(2008a) 'Citizenship for Bihari Refugees', 19 May 2008. Available at: http://news.bbc.co.uk/2/hi/south_asia/7407757.stm.

(2008b) 'Srebrenica Reburies 300 Victims', 11 July 2008. Available at: http://news.bbc.co.uk/2/hi/europe/7501523.stm.

Beigbeder, Y. (2002) *Judging Criminal Leaders: The Slow Erosion of Impunity*. The Hague: Kluwer Law International.

Belloni, R. (2001) 'Civil Society and Peacebuilding in Bosnia and Herzegovina'. *Journal of Peace Research* 38(2), 163–180.

(2005) 'Peacebuilding at the Local Level: Refugee Return to Prijedor'. *International Peacekeeping* 12(3), 434–447.

Benhabib, S. (2004) *The Rights of Others: Aliens, Residents and Citizens*. Cambridge: Cambridge University Press.

Benvenisti, E. (1999) 'Principles and Procedures for Compensating Palestinian Refugees: International Legal Perspectives'. Paper delivered at the Workshop on Compensation for Palestinian Refugees, International Development Research Centre, Ottawa, 14–15 July 1999.

Ben-ze'ev, E. and Aburaiya, I. (2004) '"Middle-Ground" Politics and the Re-Palestinization of Places in Israel'. *International Journal of Middle East Studies* 36(4), 639–655.

Bertelsen, B. (2004) '"It will rain until we are in power!" Floods, Elections and Memory in Mozambique. In Englund, H. and Nyamnjoh, F. (eds.) *Rights and the Politics of Recognition in Africa*. London: Zed Books, pp. 169–191.

Bhargava, R. (2000) 'Restoring Decency to Barbaric Societies'. In Rotberg, R. and Thompson, D. (eds.) *Truth v. Justice: The Morality of Truth Commissions*. Princeton: Princeton University Press (pp. 45–67).

Biro, M. et al. (2004) 'Attitudes toward Justice and Social Reconstruction in Bosnia and Herzegovina and Croatia'. In Stover, E. and Weinstein, H. (eds.) *My Neighbor, My Enemy: Justice and Community in the Aftermath of Mass Atrocity*. Cambridge: Cambridge University Press (pp. 183–205).

Bisharat, G. (1997) 'Exile to Compatriot: Transformations in the Social Identity of Palestinian Refugees in the West Bank'. In Gupta, A. and Ferguson, J. (eds.) *Culture, Power, Place: Explorations in Critical Anthropology*. Durham: Duke University Press (pp. 203–233).

(2008) 'Maximizing Rights: The One State Solution to the Palestinian-Israeli Conflict'. *Global Jurist* 8(2), 1–38.

Black, R. (2002) 'Conceptions of 'Home' and the Political Geography of Refugee Repatriation: Between Assumption and Contested Reality in Bosnia-Herzegovina'. *Applied Geography* 22(2), 123–138.

Black, R., Eastmond, M. and Gent, S. (2006) 'Introduction – Sustainable Return in the Balkans: Beyond Property Restitution and Policy'. *International Migration* 44(3), 5–13.

Black, R. and Koser, K. (eds.) (1999) *The End of the Refugee Cycle? Refugee Repatriation and Reconstruction*. Oxford: Berghahn Books.

Blecher, R. (2005) 'Citizens without Sovereignty: Transfer and Ethnic Cleansing in Israel'. *Comparative Studies in Society and History* 47(4), 725–754.

Boemeke, M., Feldman, G. and Glaser, E. (eds.) (1998) *The Treaty of Versailles: A Reassessment after 75 Years*. Cambridge: Cambridge University Press.

Boling, G. (2001) 'Palestinian Refugees and the Right of Return: An International Law Analysis'. *BADIL Information and Discussion Briefs*, Working Paper 8.

Borneman, J. (2004) 'Returning German Jews and Questions of Identity'. In Long, L.D. and Oxfeld, E. (eds.) *Coming Home? Refugees, Migrants and Those Who Stayed Behind*. Philadelphia: University of Pennsylvania Press (pp. 127–149).

Bose, T. K. (2003) 'Bhutan: Creating Statelessness – A Recipe for Regional Instability'. In Chari, P. R., Joseph, M. and Chandran, S. (eds.) *Missing Boundaries: Refugees, Migrants, Stateless and Internally Displaced Persons in South Asia*. New Delhi: Manohar Publishers (pp. 61–87).

Bosnia and Herzegovina Ministry for Human Rights and Refugees (2003) *Strategy of Bosnia and Herzegovina for the Implementation of Annex VII*. Available at: www.internal-displacement.org.

Bowen, M. (2000) *The State Against the Peasantry: Rural Struggles in Colonial and Postcolonial Mozambique*. Charlottesville, VA: University Press of Virginia.

Bradley, M. (2008) 'Back to Basics: The Conditions of Just Refugee Returns'. *Journal of Refugee Studies* 21(3), 285–304.

(2009a) 'Obstacles to Realising Guiding Principle 29 in Afghanistan'. *Forced Migration Review* (Special Edition), 24–25.

(2009b) 'Return in Dignity: A Neglected Refugee Protection Challenge'. *Canadian Journal of Development Studies* 28(3), 371–382.
(2011) 'Unlocking Protracted Displacement: Central America's "Success Story" Reconsidered'. *Refugee Survey Quarterly* 30(4), 84–121.
(2012a) 'Displacement, Transitional Justice and Reconciliation: Assumptions, Challenges and Lessons'. *Refugee Studies Centre Policy Brief* 9. Available at: www.rsc.ox.ac.uk/publications/policy-briefings/rscpb9-displacement-transitional-justice-reconciliation-250412-en.pdf/view.
(2012b) '"Migrants in a Feverland": State Obligations towards "Environmental Refugees"'. *International Journal of Political Theory* 8 (1–2), 147–158.
(2012c) 'Truth-Telling and Displacement: Patterns and Prospects'. In Duthie, R. (ed.) *Transitional Justice and Displacement*. New York: Social Science Research Council (pp. 189–231).
(in press) 'Redressing Internally Displaced Persons in Israel'. In Brynen, R. and El-Rifai, R. (eds.) *Palestinian Refugee Compensation and the Peace Process*. London: Pluto.
(in press) 'Rethinking Refugeehood: Statelessness, Repatriation and Refugee Agency'. *Review of International Studies*.
Brkic, C. A. (2007) 'Justice Denied in Bosnia'. *Dissent* 54(3), 19–22.
Bronstein, E. (2005) 'The *Nakba* in Hebrew: Israeli-Jewish Awareness of the Palestinian Catastrophe and Internal Refugees'. In Masalha, N. (ed.) *Catastrophe Remembered: Palestine, Israel and the Internal Refugees*. London: Zed Books (pp. 178–196).
Brynen, R. (1997a) 'Imagining a Solution: Final Status Arrangements and Palestinian Refugees in Lebanon'. *Journal of Palestine Studies* 26(2), 42–58.
(1997b) 'Much Ado about Nothing? The Refugee Working Group and the Perils of Multilateral Quasi-negotiation'. *International Negotiations* 2(2), 279–302.
(1999) 'Financing Palestinian Refugee Compensation'. Paper presented at Workshop on Compensation for Palestinian Refugees, IDRC, Ottawa, 14–15 July 1999.
(2008) *The Past as Prelude? Negotiating the Palestinian Refugee Issue*. London: Chatham House.
Brynen, R. and El-Rifai, R. (eds.) (in press) *Palestinian Refugee Compensation and the Peace Process*. London: Pluto.
Buchanan, A. (2004) *Justice, Legitimacy, and Self-Determination: Moral Foundations for International Law*. Oxford: Oxford University Press.
Buchanan, J. (1975) *The Limits of Liberty: Between Anarchy and Leviathan*. Chicago: University of Chicago Press.
Buford, W. and van der Merwe, H. (2004) 'Reparations in Southern Africa'. *Cahiers d'études africaines* 44(1–2). Available at: http://etudesafricaines.revues.org/4617.
Butenschon, N. (2006) 'Accommodating Conflicting Claims to National Self- Determination: The Intractable Case of Israel/Palestine'. *International Journal on Minority and Group Rights* 13(2), 285–306.
Buur, L. and Kyed, H. M. (2005) *State Recognition of Traditional Authority in Mozambique: The Nexus of Community Representation and State Assistance*. Uppsala: Nordiska Afrikainstitutet.

Buyse, A. C. (2009) 'Home Sweet Home? Restitution in Post-Conflict Bosnia and Herzegovina'. *Netherlands Quarterly of Human Rights* 27(1), 9–26.

Cabrita, J. (2000) *Mozambique: The Tortuous Road to Democracy*. New York: Palgrave.

Cairns, A. and Williams, C. (1985) *Constitutionalism, Citizenship and Society in Canada*. Toronto: University of Toronto Press.

Cann, J. (1997) *Counterinsurgency in Africa: The Portuguese Way of War, 1961–1974*. Westport, CT: Greenwood Press.

Cantor, D. (2011) *Restitution, Compensation, Satisfaction: Transnational Reparations and Colombia's Victims' Law*. Geneva: UNHCR, Policy Development and Evaluation Service.

Caparini, M. (2012) 'Justice-Sensitive Security Sector Reform and Displacement'. In Duthie, R. (ed.) *Transitional Justice and Displacement*. New York: Social Science Research Council (pp. 279–326).

Caplan, R. (2000) 'Assessing the Dayton Accord: The Structural Weaknesses of the General Framework Agreement for Peace in Bosnia and Herzegovina'. *Diplomacy & Statecraft* 11(2), 213–232.

(2005a) *Europe and the Recognition of New States in Yugoslavia*. Cambridge: Cambridge University Press.

(2005b) 'Who Guards the Guardians? International Accountability in Bosnia'. *International Peacekeeping* 12(3), 463–476.

Carey, D. (2004) 'Maya Perspectives on the 1999 Referendum in Guatemala: Ethnic Equality Rejected?'. *Latin American Perspectives* 31(6), 69–95.

Castles, S. (2003) 'Towards a Sociology of Forced Migration and Social Transformation'. *Sociology* 37(13), 13–34.

Centre on Housing Rights and Evictions (COHRE) (2001) *Housing and Property Restitution for Refugees and Internally Displaced Persons: International, Regional and National Legal Resources*. Geneva: COHRE.

(2005) 'UN to Adopt Pathbreaking New Global Standard which Demands Return of Confiscated Refugee Land and Housing'. Media Release, 11 August 2005.

Cernea, M. and Mathur, H. (eds.) (2008) *Can Compensation Prevent Impoverishment? Reforming Resettlement through Investments and Benefit-Sharing*. Oxford: Oxford University Press.

Cernea, M. and McDowell, C. (eds.) (2000) *Risks and Reconstruction: Experiences of Resettlers and Refugees*. Washington, DC: World Bank.

Cerone, J. (2012) 'Legal Implications of the UN General Assembly Vote to Accord Palestine the Status of Observer State'. *ASIL Insights* 16(37), 1–7.

Chan, S. and Venancio, M. (1998) *War and Peace in Mozambique*. Basingstoke: Palgrave.

Chandler, D. (2000) *Bosnia: Faking Democracy after Dayton*. London: Pluto Press.

Chayes, A. and Minow, M. (eds.) (2003) *Imagine Coexistence: Restoring Humanity After Violent Ethnic Conflict*. San Francisco: Jossey-Bass.

Cheng, C. and Chudoba, J. (2003) *Moving Beyond Long-Term Refugee Situations: The Case of Guatemala*. Geneva: UNHCR.

Chimni, B. S. (1993) 'The Meaning of Words and the Role of UNHCR in Voluntary Repatriation'. *International Journal of Refugee Law* 5(3), 442–460.

Chingono, M. (1996) *The State, Violence and Development: The Political Economy of War in Mozambique, 1975–1992*. Aldershot: Avebury.

CIA (2012) 'Bhutan'. Available at: www.cia.gov/library/publications/the-world-factbook/geos/bt.html.

Clinton, W. J. (2000) 'Clinton Parameters Regarding Israel and Palestine'. Available at: www.cfr.org/publication/13838/clinton_parameters_regarding_israel_and_ palestine.html.

Cobban, H. (2007) *Amnesty after Atrocity? Healing Nations after Genocide and War Crimes*. Boulder: Paradigm Publishers.

Coelho, J. (1998) 'State Resettlement Policies in Post-Colonial Rural Mozambique: The Impact of the Communal Village Programme on Tete Province, 1977–1982'. *Journal of Southern African Studies* 24(1), 61–91.

Cohen, H. (2003) 'Land, Memory and Identity: The Palestinian Internal Refugees in Israel'. *Refuge* 21(2), 6–13.

Commission for Historical Clarification (CEH) (1999) *Guatemala: Memory of Silence: Report of the Commission for Historical Clarification*. Guatemala City: CEH. English translation of conclusions and recommendations available at: http://shr.aaas.org/guatemala/ceh/report/english/toc.html.

Corkalo, D. et al. (2004) 'Neighbors again? Intercommunity Relations after Ethnic Cleansing'. In Stover, S. and Weinstein, H. M. (eds.) *My Neighbor, My Enemy: Justice and Community in the Aftermath of Mass Atrocity*. Cambridge: Cambridge University Press (pp. 143–161).

Costello, P. (1995) *Guatemala: Displacement, Return and the Peace Process – WRITENET Report*. Geneva: UNHCR.

Cotler, I., Matas, D. and Urman, S. (2007) *Jewish Refugees from Arab Countries: The Case for Rights and Redress*. New York: Justice for Jews from Arab Countries.

Council of the League of Arab States (2002) *Arab Peace Initiative*. Available at: www.reliefweb.int/rw/rwb.nsf/AllDocsByUNID/5a7229b652beb9c5c1256b8a005-4b62e.

Cousens, E. and Harland, D. (2006) 'Post-Dayton Bosnia and Herzegovina'. In Durch, W. (ed.) *Twenty-First-Century Peace Operations*. Washington, DC: USIP (pp. 49–140).

Cox, M. (1998) 'The Right to Return Home: International Intervention and Ethnic Cleansing in Bosnia and Herzegovina'. *International and Comparative Law Quarterly* 47(3), 599–631.

Cox, M. and Garlick, M. (2003) 'Musical Chairs: Property Repossession and Return Strategies in Bosnia and Herzegovina'. In Leckie, S. (ed.) *Returning Home: Housing and Property Restitution Rights of Refugees and Displaced Persons*. New York: Transnational Publishers (pp. 65–81).

Crawford, J. (2002) *The International Law Commission Articles on State Responsibility: Introduction, Text and Commentaries*. Cambridge: Cambridge University Press.

Crisp, J. (1996) 'From Social Disarticulation to Social Reconstruction: A Critical Review of the UNHCR Reintegration Programme for Returning Refugees and Displaced People in Mozambique'. Paper delivered at the Second International Conference on Displacement and Resettlement, Queen Elizabeth House, Oxford, 9–13 September 1996.

Crisp, J. et al. (1997) 'Rebuilding a War-Torn Society: A Review of the UNHCR Reintegration Program for Mozambique'. *Refugee Survey Quarterly* 16(2), 24–71.

Crook, J. (1993) 'The United Nations Compensation Commission: A New Structure to Enforce State Responsibility'. *American Journal of International Law* 87(1), 144–157.

Darwish, M. (1984) 'We Travel Like Other People'. In *Victims of a Map* (trans. Adballah Udhari). London: El Saqi (p. 31).

Davies, A. (2004) 'Restitution of Land and Property Rights'. *Forced Migration Review* 21, 12–13.

de Greiff, P. (2006) 'Repairing the Past: Compensation for Victims of Human Rights Violations'. In de Greiff, P. (ed.) *The Handbook of Reparations*. Oxford: Oxford University Press (pp. 1–18).

(2007) 'Justice and Reparations'. In Miller, J. and Kumar, R. (eds.) *Reparations: Interdisciplinary Inquiries*. Oxford: Oxford University Press (pp. 153–175).

de Greiff, P. and Duthie, R. (2009) *Transitional Justice and Development: Making Connections*. New York: SSRC.

de Rivero, J. (2001) 'Reinventing Communities: The Resettlement of Guatemalan Refugees'. *Forced Migration Review* 11, 8–11.

Deng, F. (1995) *Sovereignty, Responsibility and Accountability*. Washington, DC: Brookings Institution Press.

Dinerman, A. (2004) 'Processes of State Delegitimization in Post-Independence Rural Mozambique: The Case of Namapa District, Nampula Province'. *Journal of Historical Sociology* 17(2–3), 123–184.

(2006) *Revolution, Counter-Revolution and Revisionism in Postcolonial Africa: The Case of Mozambique, 1975–1994*. London: Routledge.

Dolan, C. (1999) 'Repatriation from South Africa to Mozambique – Undermining Durable Solutions?'. In Black, R. and Koser, K. (eds.) *The End of the Refugee Cycle? Refugee Repatriation and Reconstruction*. Oxford: Berghahn Books (pp. 85–109).

Dowty, A. (1994) 'Return or Compensation: The Legal and Political Context of the Palestinian Refugee Issue'. In U.S. Committee for Refugees (ed.) *World Refugee Survey 1994*. Washington, DC: U.S. Committee for Refugees (p. 29).

Druke, L. (2000) 'Housing and Property Restitution for Returnees in Tajikistan in the 1990s'. *Refugee Survey Quarterly* 19(3), 113–129.

Drumbl, M. (2007) *Atrocity, Punishment and International Law*. Cambridge: Cambridge University Press.

du Plessis, M. (2003) 'Historical Injustice and International Law: An Exploratory Discussion of Reparations for Slavery'. *Human Rights Quarterly* 25(3), 624–659.

Dumper, M. (2006a) 'Palestinian Refugees in Comparative Perspective: The cases of Guatemala, Bosnia and Afghanistan'. In Benvenisti, E. and Hanafi, S. (eds.) *The Palestinian Refugee Issue and the Arab-Israeli Conflict*. Heidelberg: Max Planck Institute (pp. 387–407).

(ed.) (2006b) *Palestinian Refugee Repatriation in Global Perspective*. London: Routledge.

(2006c) 'Introduction: The Comparative Study of Refugee Repatriation Programmes and the Palestinian Case'. In Dumper, M. (ed.) *Palestinian Refugee Repatriation: Global Perspectives*. London: Routledge (pp. 1–20).

(2007) *The Future for Palestinian Refugees: Toward Equity and Peace*. Boulder: Lynne Rienner.

Duthie, R. (2011) 'Transitional Justice and Displacement'. *International Journal of Transitional Justice* 5, 241–261.

(ed.) (2012a) *Transitional Justice and Displacement*. New York: Social Science Research Council.

(2012b) 'Transitional Justice and the Reintegration of Displaced Persons'. In Duthie, R. (ed.) *Transitional Justice and Displacement*. New York: Social Science Research Council (pp. 37–63).

Echeverria, G. (2002) 'The Draft Basic Principles and Guidelines on the Right to Remedy and Reparation: An Effort to Develop a Coherent Theory and Consistent Practice of Reparations for Victims'. *Article 2* 1(6), 6–19.

Egan, B. (1999) '"Somos de la Tierra": Land and the Guatemalan Refugee Return'. In North, L. and Simmons, A. (eds.) *Journeys of Fear: Refugee Return and National Transformation in Guatemala*. Montreal: McGill-Queen's University Press (pp. 95–111).

Eldar, A. (2012) 'A Softer Touch on the Nakba', *Haaretz*, 24 January 2012.

Ellis, M. and Hutton, E. (2002) 'Policy Implications of World War II Reparations and Restitution as Applied to the Former Yugoslavia'. *Berkeley Journal of International Law* 20, 342.

Englbrecht, W. (2001) 'Bosnia and Herzegovina: No Future without Reconciliation'. *Forced Migration Review* 11, 18–20.

(2003) 'Property Rights in Bosnia and Herzegovina: The Contributions of the Human Rights Ombudsperson and the Human Rights Chamber towards their Protection'. In Leckie, S. (ed.) *Returning Home: Housing and Property Restitution Rights for Refugees and Displaced Persons*. New York: Transnational Publishers (pp. 83–142).

(2004) 'Bosnia and Herzegovina, Croatia and Kosovo: Voluntary Return in Safety and Dignity?'. *Refugee Survey Quarterly* 23(3), 100–148.

Englund, H. (1998) 'Death, Trauma and Ritual: Mozambican Refugees in Malawi'. *Social Science and Medicine* 46(9), 1165–1174.

(2002) *From War to Peace on the Mozambique-Malawi Borderland*. Edinburgh: University of Edinburgh Press.

Erskine, T. (2001) 'Assigning Responsibilities to Institutional Moral Agents: The Case of States and Quasi-States'. *Ethics and International Affairs* 15(2), 67–86.

(ed.) (2003) *Can Institutions Have Responsibilities? Collective Moral Agency and International Relations*. New York: Palgrave Macmillan.

Falk, R. (2006) 'Reparations, International Law, and Global Justice: A New Frontier'. In de Greiff, P. (ed.) *The Handbook of Reparations*. Oxford: Oxford University Press (pp. 478–503).

FAO et al. (2007) *Handbook on Housing and Property Restitution for Refugees and Displaced Persons: Implementing the 'Pinheiro Principles'*. Turin: International Training Centre of the ILO.

Farha, L. (2000) 'Women's Rights to Land, Property and Housing'. *Forced Migration Review* 7, 23–26.

Fauvet, P. (1984) 'Roots of Counter-Revolution: The Mozambique National Resistance'. *Review of African Political Economy* 29, 108–121.

Feinberg, J. (1970) 'The Nature and Value of Rights'. *Journal of Value Inquiry* 4(4), 243–260.

Feldman, I. (2008) 'Refusing Invisibility: Documentation and Memorialization in Palestinian Refugee Claims'. *Journal of Refugee Studies* 21 (4): 498–516.

Feller, E. (2009) 'Giving Peace a Chance: Displacement and Rule of Law During Peacebuilding'. *Refugee Survey Quarterly* 28(1), 78–94.

Ferris, E. (2002) 'NGO Statement on Voluntary Repatriation'. Statement delivered at the UNHCR Global Consultations on International Protection, Geneva, 22–24 May 2002.

Finnegan, W. (1992) *A Complicated War*. Berkeley: University of California Press.

Finnemore, M. (2000) 'Are Legal Norms Distinctive?'. *Journal of International Law and Politics* 32(3), 699–705.

Finnemore, M. and Sikkink, K. (1998) 'International Norm Dynamics and Political Change'. *International Organization* 52(4), 887–917.

Fischbach, M. (2002) 'The United Nations and Palestinian Refugee Property Compensation'. *Journal of Palestine Studies* 31(2), 34–50.

(2003) *Records of Dispossession: Palestinian Refugee Property and the Arab-Israeli Conflict*. New York: Columbia University Press.

(2005) 'Palestinian and Mizrahi Jewish Property Claims in Discourse and Diplomacy'. In Lustick, I. and Lesch, A. (eds.) *Exile and Return: Predicaments of Palestinians and Jews*. Philadelphia: University of Pennsylvania Press (pp. 207–224).

(2006) *The Peace Process and Palestinian Refugee Claims: Addressing Claims for Property Compensation and Restitution*. Washington, DC: United States Institute of Peace.

(2008a) *Jewish Property Claims Against Arab Countries*. New York: Columbia University Press.

(2008b) 'Palestinian Refugee Compensation and Israeli Counterclaims for Jewish Property in Arab Countries'. *Journal of Palestine Studies* 31(1), 6–24.

Fitigu, Y. (2005) 'Forgotten People: Internally Displaced Persons in Guatemala'. Available at: http://www.internal-displacement.org/8025708F004CE90B/%28httpDocuments%29/9B3742CBE13D7097802570B7005943EA/$file/6341_file_Guatemala_Forgotten_People.pdf.

Flapan, S. (1987) *The Birth of Israel: Myth and Reality*. New York: Pantheon.

Fletcher, L. and Weinstein, H. (2002) 'Violence and Social Repair: Rethinking the Contribution of Justice to Reconciliation'. *Human Rights Quarterly* 24(3), 573–639.

(2004) A World unto Itself? The Application of International Justice in the Former Yugoslavia'. In Stover, E. and Weinstein, H. (eds.) *My Neighbor, My Enemy: Justice and Community in the Aftermath of Mass Atrocity*. Cambridge: Cambridge University Press (pp. 29–48).

Foley, C. (2008) 'Housing, Land and Property Restitution Rights in Afghanistan'. In Leckie, S. (ed.) *Housing, Land and Property Rights in*

Post-Conflict United Nations and Other Peace Operations: A Comparative Survey and Proposal for Reform. Cambridge: Cambridge University Press (pp. 136–178).

Forsythe, D. (1972) *United Nations Peacemaking: The Conciliation Commission for Palestine*. Baltimore, MD: Johns Hopkins University Press.

(2001) *UNHCR's Mandate: The Politics of Being Non-political*. Geneva: UNHCR.

Frelick, B. (2011) 'For Bhutan's Refugees, there's No Place Like Home'. Available at: www.hrw.org/news/2011/03/30/bhutan-s-refugees-there-s-no-place-home.

Gabbay, R. (1959) *A Political Study of the Arab-Jewish Conflict: The Arab Refugee Problem*. Geneva: Droz.

Gal, O. (2008) *Israeli Perspectives on the Palestinian Refugee Issue: A Chatham House Briefing Paper*. London: Chatham House.

Garlick, M. (2000) 'Protection for Property Rights: A Partial Solution? The Commission for Real Property Claims of Displaced Persons and Refugees (CRPC) in Bosnia and Herzegovina'. *Refugee Survey Quarterly* 19(3), 64–85.

Garry, H. (1998) 'The Right to Compensation and Refugee Flows: A "Preventative Mechanism" in International Law?'. *International Journal of Refugee Law* 10(1/2), 97–117.

Geffray, C. (1990) *La Cause des armes au Mozambique: anthropologie d'une guerre civile*. Paris: Karthala.

Geffray, C. and Pedersen, M. (1985) *Transformação da organização social e do sistema agrário do campesinato do Distrito do Erati: processo de socialização do campo e diferenciação social*. Maputo: Departamento de Arquelogia e Antropologia, Universidade Eduardo Mondlane e o Departamento Rural, Ministério da Agricultura.

Geneva Initiative (2003) *Geneva Accord*. Available at: www.geneva-accord.org.

(2009) 'New Poll Finds Two-State Solution is the Preferred Option for Majority of Israelis and Palestinians'. Available at: www.geneva-accord.org/mainmenu/new-poll-finds-two-state-solution-is-the-preferred-option-for-majority-of-israelis-and-palestinians.

Gengenbach, H. (1998) '"I'll Bury You in the Border!": Women's Land Struggles in Post-War Facazisse (Magude District), Mozambique'. *Journal of Southern African Studies* 24(1), 7–36.

Gersony, R. (1988) *Summary of Mozambican Refugee Accounts of Principally Conflict-Related Experience in Mozambique*. Washington, DC: United States Department of State.

Gibney, M. (ed.) (1988) *Open Borders? Closed Societies?: The Ethical and Political Issues*. Westport: Greenwood Press.

Gibney, M. J. (1999) 'Liberal Democratic States and Responsibilities to Refugees'. *American Political Science Review* 93(1), 169–181.

(2004) *The Ethics and Politics of Asylum: Liberal Democracy and the Response to Refugees*. Cambridge: Cambridge University Press.

(2006) *Who Should be Included? Non-Citizens, Conflict and the Constitution of the Citizenry*. Oxford: Centre for Research on Inequality, Human Security and Ethnicity.

(2009) 'Statelessness and the Right to Citizenship'. *Forced Migration Review* 32, 50–51.

Gibson, J. (2009) *Overcoming Historical Injustices: Land Reconciliation in South Africa*. Cambridge: Cambridge University Press.

Gillard, E. (2003) 'Reparation for Violations of International Humanitarian Law'. *International Review of the Red Cross* 85(851), 529–553.

Goodwin-Gill, G. (1989) 'The Language of Protection'. *International Journal of Refugee Law* 1(1), 6–9.

(1995) 'The Principles of International Refugee Law'. In Council of Europe (ed.) *Asylum (Debates)*. Brussels: Council of Europe (pp. 11–42).

(1996) *The Refugee in International Law* (2nd edn). Oxford: Clarendon Press.

Goris, I., Harrington, J. and Köhn, S. (2009) 'Statelessness: What it is and Why it Matters'. *Forced Migration Review* 32, 4–6.

Graham, M. and Khosravi, S. (1997) 'Home is Where You Make It: Repatriation and Diaspora Culture among Iranians in Sweden'. *Journal of Refugee Studies* 10(2), 115–133.

Graybill, L. (2004) 'Pardon, Punishment, and Amnesia: Three African Post-Conflict Methods'. *Third World Quarterly* 25(6), 1117–1130.

Green, E. and Honwana, A. (1999) 'Indigenous Healing of War-Affected Children in Africa'. *IK Notes*, No. 10, July 1999, World Bank. Available at: www.worldbank.org/afr/ik/iknt10.pdf.

Green, M. (2002) 'Institutional Responsibility for Global Problems'. *Philosophical Topics* 30(2), 79–95.

Grossman, D. (2002) *The Yellow Wind* (trans. Watzman, H.). New York: Picador.

Groult, S. (2007) 'Lebanon Refugees Yearn to Return Home Once Fighting Ends'. *Agence France-Presse*, 1 September 2007.

Guterres, A. (2010) 'Statement to the Third Committee of the General Assembly, 65th Session'. Speech delivered to the United Nations General Assembly (Third Committee), New York, 2 November 2010.

Haider, H. (2009) '(Re)Imagining Coexistence: Striving for Sustainable Return, Reintegration and Reconciliation in Bosnia and Herzegovina'. *International Journal of Transitional Justice* 3(1), 91–113.

Hall, M. (1990) 'The Mozambican National Resistance Movement (Renamo): A Study in the Destruction of an African Country'. *Africa* 60(1), 39–68.

Hamber, B. and Wilson, R. (2002) 'Symbolic Closure through Memory, Reparation and Revenge in Post-Conflict Societies'. *Journal of Human Rights* 1(1), 35–53.

Hammerstad, A. (2000) 'Whose Security?: UNHCR, Refugee Protection and State Security After the Cold War'. *Security Dialogue* 31(4), 391–403.

Hammond, L. (1999) 'Examining the Discourse of Repatriation: Towards a More Proactive Theory of Return Migration'. In Black, R. and Koser, K. (eds.) *The End of the Refugee Cycle? Refugee Repatriation and Reconstruction*. Oxford: Berghahn Books (pp. 227–244).

Hanafi, S. (2005) 'Social Capital and Refugee Repatriation: A Study of Economic and Social Translations Kinship Networks in Palestine/Israel'. In Lustick, I. and Lesch, A. (eds.) *Exile and Return: Predicaments of Palestinians and Jews*. Philadelphia: University of Pennsylvania Press (pp. 57–82).

(2007) 'Palestinian Return Migration: Lessons from the International Refugee Regime'. In Dumper, M. (ed.) *Palestinian Refugee Repatriation: Global Perspectives*. London: Routledge (pp. 273–286).

Hanchinamani, B. (2003) 'The Impact of Mozambique's Land Tenure Policy on Refugees and Internally Displaced Persons'. *Law Human Rights Brief* 7(2), 10–12.

Hanlon, J. (1991) *Mozambique: Who Calls the Shots?* Bloomington: Indiana University Press.

Hansen, G. (1999) 'Displacement and Return'. In Cohen, J. (ed.) *A Question of Sovereignty: The Georgia-Abkhazia Peace Process*. London: Conciliation Resources (pp. 58–63).

Harrell-Bond, B. (1989) 'Repatriation: Under What Conditions is it the Most Desirable Solution for Refugees? An Agenda for Research'. *African Studies Review* 32(1), 41–69.

Harris-Rimmer, S. (2010) 'Women Cut in Half: Refugee Women and the Commission for Reception, Truth-Seeking and Reconciliation in Timor-Leste'. *Refugee Survey Quarterly* 29, 85–103.

Hart, H. L. A. and Honoré, T. (1985) *Causation in the Law* (2nd edn). Oxford: Clarendon Press.

Hart, J. (2005) 'Beyond Struggle and Aid: Children's Identities in a Palestinian Refugee Camp in Jordan'. In Boyden, J. and de Berry, J. (eds.) *Children and Youth on the Front Lines: Ethnography, Armed Conflict and Displacement*. Oxford: Berghahn Books (pp. 167–188).

Harvey, J. (2006) 'Return Dynamics in Bosnia and Croatia: A Comparative Analysis'. *International Migration* 44(3), 89–114.

Hass, A. (2012) 'The Real Palestinian Concession'. *Haaretz*, 26 January 2011.

Hastings, L. (2001) 'Implementation of the Property Legislation in Bosnia Herzegovina'. *Stanford Journal of International Law* 37(2), 221–254.

Hathaway, J. (1994) 'Introduction to the Law of Refugee Status'. Presentation delivered at the Centre for Refugee Studies, York University, Toronto, 23 June 1994.

(1997) 'The Meaning of Repatriation'. *International Journal of Refugee Law* 9(4), 551–558.

(2005) *The Rights of Refugees Under International Law*. Cambridge: Cambridge University Press.

(2007) 'Refugee Solutions, or Solutions to Refugeehood?'. *Refuge* 24(2), 3–10.

Hayner, P. (2011) *Unspeakable Truths: Transitional Justice and the Challenge of Truth Commissions* (2nd edn). London: Routledge.

Heimerl, D. (2005) 'The Return of Refugees and Internally Displaced Persons: From Coercion to Sustainability?'. *International Peacekeeping* 12(3), 377–390.

Hilal, J. (ed.) (2007) *Where Now for Palestine? The Demise of the Two State Solution*. London: Zed Press.

Hirsch, M. B. (2007) 'From Taboo to the Negotiable: The Israeli New Historians and the Changing Representation of the Palestinian Refugee Problem'. *Perspectives on Politics* 5(2), 241–258.

Hodzic, R. (2012) 'Twenty Years On, Bosnia Struggles to Reckon with the Past'. ICTJ Pod- Cast available at: http://ictj.org/news/twenty-years-bosnia-struggles-reckon-past.

Hoffman, E. (2002) 'The Balm of Recognition: Rectifying Wrongs Through the Generations'. In Owen, N. (ed.) *Human Rights, Human Wrongs*. Oxford: Oxford University Press (pp. 274–303).

Holborn, L.W. (1975) *Refugees: A Problem of our Time*. Metuchen, NJ: Scarecrow Press.

Holbrooke, R. (1999) *To End a War*. New York: The Modern Library.

Holzman-Gazit, Y. (2007) *Land Expropriation in Israel*. London: Ashgate.

Homer (1996) *The Odyssey* (trans. R. Fagles). London: Penguin.

Honoré, T. (1999) *Responsibility and Fault*. Oxford: Hart Publishing.

Honwana, A. (1998) 'Sealing the Past, Facing the Future: Trauma and Healing in Rural Mozambique'. In Armon, J., Hendrickson, D. and Vines, A. (eds.) *The Mozambican Peace Process in Perspective*. London: Conciliation Resources (pp. 75–81).

(1999) 'The Collective Body: Challenging Western Concepts of Trauma and Healing'. *Track Two* 8(1), online.

Hovey, G. (2000) 'The Rehabilitation of Homes and Return of Minorities to Republika Srpska, Bosnia and Herzegovina'. *Forced Migration Review* 7, 8–11.

Hovil, L. (2012) 'The Nexus Between Displacement and Transitional Justice: A Gender-Justice Dimension'. In Duthie, R. (ed.) *Transitional Justice and Displacement*. New York: Social Science Research Council (pp. 329–359).

Human Rights Watch (2004) *Claims in Conflict: Reversing Ethnic Cleansing in Northern Iraq*. New York: Human Rights Watch.

(2006) *A Chance for Justice: War Crime Prosecution in Bosnia's Serb Republic*. New York: Human Rights Watch.

(2007) *Narrowing the Impunity Gap: Trials before Bosnia's War Crimes Chamber*. New York: Human Rights Watch.

Hume, C. (1994) *Ending Mozambique's War*. Washington, DC: United States Institute of Peace.

Humphrey, M. (2003) 'International Intervention, Justice and National Reconciliation: The Role of the ICTY and ICTY in Bosnia and Rwanda'. *Journal of Human Rights* 2(4), 495–505.

Hurst, H. (1987) *The Right to Leave and Return in International Law and Practice*. Dordrecht: Martinus Nijhoff Publishers.

Hussain, K. (2009) 'The End of Bihari Statelessness'. *Forced Migration Review* 32, 30–31.

Hutt, M. (1996) 'Ethnic Nationalism, Refugees and Bhutan'. *Journal of Refugee Studies* 9(4), 397–420.

(2003) *Unbecoming Citizens: Culture, Nationhood and the Flight of Refugees from Bhutan*. Oxford: Oxford University Press.

(2005) 'The Bhutanese Refugees: Between Verification, Repatriation and Royal Realpolitik'. *Journal of Peace and Democracy in South Asia* 1(1), 44–55.

Iasiello, L. V. (2004) '*Just Post Bellum*: The Moral Responsibilities of Victors in War'. *Naval War College Review* 57, 33–52.

ICISS (2001) *The Responsibility to Protect: Report of the International Commission on Intervention and State Sovereignty* (ICISS). Ottawa: International Development Research Centre.

Igreja, V. (2008) 'Memories as Weapons: The Politics of Peace and Silence in Post-Conflict Mozambique'. *Journal of Southern African Studies* 34(3), 539–556.

Igreja, V., Dias-Lambranca, B. and Richters, A. (2008) 'Gamba Spirits, Gender Relations, and Healing in Post-Civil War Gorongosa, Mozambique'. *Journal of the Royal Anthropological Institute* 14(2), 353–371.

Inter-Agency Standing Committee (2010) *IASC Framework on Durable Solutions for Internally Displaced Persons*. Washington, DC: Brookings-Bern Project on Internal Displacement.

Inter-American Commission on Human Rights (IACHR) (1994) *Special Report on the Human Rights Situation in the so-called 'Communities of Peoples in Resistance' in Guatemala*. Washington, DC: Inter-American Commission on Human Rights.

Inter-American Court of Human Rights (IACHR) (2004) *Case of the Plan de Sánchez Massacre v. Guatemala: Reparations and Costs: Judgment of 19 November 2004*. Washington, DC: Inter-American Court on Human Rights.

Internal Displacement Monitoring Centre (IDMC) (2006) 'Guatemala: Ten Years After Peace Accords, Key Provisions Benefiting the Displaced Remain Unimplemented', 9 June 2006. Available at: www.internal-displacement.org/8025708F004BE3B1/%28httpInfoFiles%29/097D0D136EE4FD7BC12571860046E2A6/$file/Guatemala%20-June%202006.pdf.

(2007) *Internal Displacement: Global Overview of Trends and Developments in 2006*. Geneva: IDMC.

(2012) *Global Overview 2011: People Internally Displaced by Conflict and Violence*. Geneva: IDMC.

International Center for Transitional Justice (ICTJ) (2008) 'The Former Yugoslavia: ICTJ Activity', March 2007. Available at: http://ictj.org/our-work/regions-and-countries/former-yugoslavia?gclid=CPST3NLOhbMCFUfNOgod7j0ANw.

International Court of Justice (ICJ) (1955) *Reports – Nottebohm Case*. The Hague: International Court of Justice.

(2007) *Application of the Convention on the Prevention and Punishment of the Crime of Genocide (Bosnia and Herzegovina v. Republic of Serbia and Montenegro): Judgment of 26 February 2007*. The Hague: International Court of Justice.

International Crisis Group (ICG) (1998) *The Konjic Conundrum: Why Minorities have Failed to Return to Model Open City*. Brussels: ICG.

(1999) *Preventing Minority Return in Bosnia and Herzegovina: The Anatomy of Hate and Fear*. Brussels: ICG.

(2000) *Bosnia's Refugee Logjam Breaks: Is the International Community Ready?*. Sarajevo: ICG.

(2002) *The Continuing Challenge of Refugee Returns in Bosnia and Herzegovina*. Brussels: ICG.

(2004a) *Blood and Soil: Land, Politics and Conflict Prevention in Zimbabwe and South Africa*. New York: ICG.

(2004b) *Palestinian Refugees and the Politics of Peacemaking*. Amman, Brussels: International Crisis Group

International Herald Tribune (2007) 'Survivors of Srebrenica Massacre Sue United Nations and Dutch Government'. *International Herald Tribune*, 3 June 2007.

International Law Association (ILA) International Committee on the Legal Status of Refugees (1992) *Cairo Declaration of Principles of International Law on Compensation to Refugees*. Cairo: International Law Association.

International Organization for Migration (IOM) (2009) *Property Restitution and Compensation: Practices and Experiences of Claims Programs*. Geneva: IOM.

IRIN (2012) 'Afghanistan: Towards More Sustainable Solutions for Returnees'. Available at: www.irinnews.org/report.aspx?reportID=94965.

Isaac, J. C. (2002) 'Hannah Arendt on Human Rights and the Limits of Exposure, or Why Noam Chomsky is Wrong about the Meaning of Kosovo'. *Social Research* 69(2), 505–537.

Isaacman, A. and Isaacman, B. (1983) *Mozambique: From Colonialism to Revolution, 1900–1982*. Boulder: Westview Press.

Israel Ministry of Foreign Affairs (2007) 'Israel, the Conflict and Peace'. Available at: www.mfa.gov.il/MFA/MFAArchive/2000_2009/2003/11/Israel-%20the%20Conflict%20and%20Peace-%20Answers%20to%20Frequen.

(2009) 'Israel, the Conflict and Peace' (updated). Available at: www.mfa.gov.il/MFA/FAQ/FAQ_Peace_process_with_Palestinians_Dec_2009.

ITO, A. (2000) 'Politicisation of Minority Return in Bosnia and Herzegovina: The First Five Years Examined'. *International Journal of Refugee Law* 13(1/2), 98–122.

Jamal, A. (2000) *Refugee Repatriation and Reintegration in Guatemala: Lessons from UNHCR's Experience*. Geneva: UNHCR Evaluation and Policy Analysis Unit.

Jansen, S. (2007) 'Troubled Locations: Return, the Life Course, and Transformations of "Home" in Bosnia-Herzegovina'. *Focaal – European Journal of Anthropology* 49, 15–30.

Johns, F. (2004) 'The Madness of Migration: Disquiet in the International Law Relating to Refugees'. *International Journal of Law and Psychiatry* 27(6), 587–607.

Joint Parliamentary Middle East Councils (2001) *Right of Return: Report of the Joint Parliamentary Middle East Councils Commission of Enquiry on the Palestinian Refugees*. London: Labour Middle East Council, Conservative Middle East Council, and Liberal Democrat Middle East Council.

Jonas, S. (2000) *Of Centaurs and Doves: Guatemala's Peace Process*. Boulder: Westview Press.

Jorda, C. (2001) 'The ICTY and the Truth and Reconciliation Commission in Bosnia and Herzegovina'. Speech delivered by ICTY President Claude Jorda, The Hague, 17 May 2001.

Juergensen, O. T. (2000) 'Repatriation as Peacebuilding and Reconstruction: The Case of Northern Mozambique, 1992–1995'. *New Issues in*

Refugee Research Working Papers 31, available at: www.unhcr.org/refworld/topic,45a5199f2,4ba0ac9e2,4ff580ee2,0,UNHCR,,.html.

Kabeer, N. (2002) 'Citizenship, Affiliation and Exclusion: Perspectives from the South'. *IDS Bulletin* 33(2), 12–23.

Kahler, M. (2000) 'Conclusion: The Causes and Consequences of Legalization'. *International Organization* 54(3), 661–683.

Kälin, W. (2008) *The Guiding Principles on Internal Displacement* (rev.edn). Washington, DC: ASIL Brookings Institution.

Kant, I. (1991) 'Toward Perpetual Peace: A Philosophical Sketch'. In Reiss, H. (ed.) *Kant's Political Writings*. Cambridge: Cambridge University Press (pp. 54–60).

Karsh, E. (1997) *Fabricating Israel's History: The 'New Historians'*. London: Cass.

Keinon, H. and Horovitz, D. (2007) 'Diplomacy: It has not been the Easiest Year (Interview with Ehud Olmert)'. *Jerusalem Post*, 29 March 2007.

Kennan, G. F. (1996) *At a Century's Ending: Reflections 1982–1995*. New York: W.W. Norton.

Khalaf, I. (1991) *Politics in Palestine: Arab Factionalism and Social Disintegration, 1939–1948*. Albany: State University of New York.

Khalidi, R. (1992) 'Observations on the Right of Return'. *Journal of Palestine Studies* 21(2), 29–40.

(1995) 'The Palestinian Refugee Problem: A Possible Solution'. *Palestine-Israel Journal* 2(4), 72–87.

(1997) *Palestinian Identity: The Construction of Modern National Consciousness*. New York: Columbia University Press.

(1998) 'Attainable Justice: Elements of a Solution to the Palestinian Refugee Issue'. *International Journal* 53(2), 233–252.

(1999) 'Truth, Justice and Reconciliation'. In Karmi, G. and Cotran, E. (eds.) *The Palestinian Exodus*. London: Ithaca (pp. 221–242).

Khalidi, W. (ed.) (1991) *All that Remains: The Palestinian Villages Occupied and Destroyed by Israel in 1948*. Washington, DC: Institute for Palestine Studies.

Khalili, L. (2004) 'Grass-roots Commemorations: Remembering the Land in the Camps of Lebanon'. *Journal of Palestine Studies* 34(1), 6–22.

(2005) 'Commemorating Contested Lands'. In Lustick, I. and Lesch, A. (eds.) *Exile and Return: Predicaments of Palestinians and Jews*. Philadelphia: University of Pennsylvania Press (pp. 19–40).

Kibreab, G. (2003) 'Citizenship Rights and Repatriation of Refugees'. *International Migration Review* 37(1), 24–73.

Klein, M. (2007) 'The Palestinian Refugees of 1948: Models of Allowed and Denied Return'. In Dumper, M. (ed.) *Palestinian Refugee Repatriation: Global Perspectives*. London: Routledge (pp. 88–106).

Konefal, B. O. (2003) 'Defending the Pueblo: Indigenous Identity and Struggles for Social Justice in Guatemala, 1970 to 1980'. *Social Justice* 30(3), 32–47.

Koning AbuZayd, K. (2006) 'UNRWA Commissioner-General's Address'. Public lecture at the Middle East Institute 60th Annual Conference, Washington, DC, 13 November 2006.

Koser, K. (1997) 'Information and Repatriation: The Case of Mozambican Refugees in Malawi'. *Journal of Refugee Studies* 10(1), 1–18.

Krasner, S. D. (1983) 'Structural Causes and Regime Consequences: Regimes as Intervening Variables'. In Krasner, S. D. (ed.) *International Regimes*. Ithaca: Cornell University Press (pp. 1–21).

Kritz, N. and Finci, J. (2001) 'A Truth and Reconciliation Commission in Bosnia and Herzegovina: An Idea Whose Time has Come'. *International Law FORUM du droit international* 3(1), 50–58.

Krznaric, R. (1997) 'Guatemalan Returnees and the Dilemma of Political Mobilization'. *Journal of Refugee Studies* 10(1), 61–78.

Kubursi, A. (1996) *Palestinian Losses in 1948: The Quest for Precision*. Washington, DC: Center for Policy Analysis on Palestine.

(2001) 'Valuing Palestinian Losses in Today's Dollars'. In Aruri, N. (ed.) *Palestinian Refugees: The Right of Return*. London: Pluto Press.

Kundera, M. (2002) *Ignorance* (trans. Asher, L.) London: Faber and Faber.

Kymlicka, W. (1989) *Liberalism, Community and Culture*. Oxford: Oxford University Press.

(1991) 'The Social Contract Tradition'. In Singer, P. (ed.) *A Companion to Ethics*. Oxford: Blackwell Publishers (pp. 186–196).

(2007) 'Keynote Address'. Presentation delivered at the Conference on Immigration, Multiculturalism, Minorities and Democracy, Montreal, 26 October 2007.

Kymlicka, W. and Norman, W. (1994) 'Return of the Citizen: A Survey of Recent Work on Citizenship Theory'. *Ethics* 104(2), 352–381.

Leckie, S. (2003a) 'Peace in the Middle East: Getting Real on the Issue of Palestinian Refugee Property'. *Forced Migration Review* 16, 41–44.

(ed.) (2003b) *Returning Home: Housing and Property Restitution Rights of Refugees and Displaced Persons*. New York: Transnational Publishers.

(2003c) 'Introduction'. In Leckie, S. (ed.) *Returning Home: Housing and Property Restitution Rights of Refugees and Displaced Persons*. New York: Transnational Publishers (pp. 3–61).

(2005) 'An Introduction to the "Pinheiro Principles"'. In *The Pinheiro Principles: United Nations Principles on Housing and Property Restitution for Refugees and Displaced Persons*. Geneva: Centre on Housing Rights and Evictions (pp. 3–6).

(ed.) (2007) *Housing, Land and Property Restitution Rights of Refugees and Displaced Persons: Laws, Cases, and Materials*. Cambridge: Cambridge University Press.

(ed.) (2008) *Housing, Land, and Property Rights in Post-Conflict United Nations and Other Peace Operations: A Comparative Survey and Proposal for Reform*. Cambridge: Cambridge University Press.

Lee, L. (1986) 'The Right to Compensation: Refugees and Countries of Asylum'. *American Journal of International Law* 80, 532–567.

(1993) 'The Cairo Declaration of Principles of International Law on Compensation to Refugees'. *American Journal of International Law* 87(1), 157–159.

(1998) 'Refugees from Bhutan: Nationality, Statelessness and the Right to Return'. *International Journal of Refugee Law* 10 (1/2), 118–155.

Leffert, M. (2001) 'Women's Organizations in Guatemalan Refugee and Returnee Populations'. In Smillie, I. (ed.) *Patronage or Partnership: Local Capacity Building in Humanitarian Crises*. Bloomfield: Kumarian Press (pp. 131–155).

Levin, I. (2001) *Locked Doors: The Seizure of Jewish Property in Arab Countries*. Westport: Praeger.

Levitt, B. (1999) 'Theorizing Accompaniment'. In North, L. and Simmons, A. (eds.) *Journeys of Fear: Refugee Return and National Transformation in Guatemala*. Montreal: McGill-Queen's University Press (pp. 237–254).

Levy, J. (2008) 'Self-Determination, Non-Domination, and Federalism'. *Hypatia* 23(3), 60–78.

Loescher, G. (2001a) *The UNHCR and World Politics: A Perilous Path*. Oxford: Oxford University Press.

(2001b) 'The UNHCR and World Politics: State Interests versus Institutional Autonomy'. *International Migration Review* 35(1), 33–56.

Loescher, G., Betts, A. and Milner, J. (2008) *The United Nations High Commissioner for Refugees: The Politics and Practice of Refugee Protection into the 21st Century*. New York: Routledge.

Loescher, G., Milner, J., Newman, E. and Troeller, G. (2007) 'Protracted Refugee Situations and Peacebuilding'. *UNU Policy Briefs* 1, available at: http://unu.edu/publications/policy-briefs/protracted-refugee-situations-and-peacebuilding.html.

Long, K. (2008) *State, Nation, Citizen: Rethinking Repatriation*. Oxford: Refugee Studies Centre.

(2009) 'Early Repatriation Policy: Russian Refugee Return 1922–1924'. *Journal of Refugee Studies* 22(2), 133–154.

Lowe, V. (2001) 'The Politics of Law-Making: Are the Method and Character of Norm Creation Changing?'. In Byers, M. (ed.) *The Role of Law in International Politics: Essays in International Relations and International Law*. Oxford: Oxford University Press (pp. 207–226).

Lu, C. (2002) 'Justice and Moral Regeneration: Lessons from the Treaty of Versailles'. *International Studies Review* 4(3), 3–25.

Luban, D., Strudler, A. and Wasserman, D. (1992) 'Moral Responsibility in the Age of Bureaucracy'. *Michigan Law Review* 90(8), 2348–2392.

Lubkemann, S. (2008) *Culture in Chaos: An Anthropology of the Social Condition in War*. Chicago: University of Chicago Press.

Lundin, I. (1996) 'Political Parties: A Reading of the Ethnic and Regional Factor in the Democratisation Process'. In Mazula, B. (ed.) *Mozambique: Elections, Democracy and Development*. Maputo: Inter-Africa Group (pp. 407–454).

(2004) 'Reflections on Conflict Resolution and "Prevention": The State and Citizens in Mozambique'. In Batchelor, P. and Kingma, K. (eds.) *Demilitarisation and Peace-Building in Southern Africa: Volume II – National and Regional Experiences*. Aldershot: Ashgate (pp. 1–18).

Lustick, I. (1980) *Arabs in the Jewish State: Israel's Control of a National Minority*. Austin: University of Texas Press.

Lustick, I. (1993) 'Writing the Intifada: Collective Action in the Occupied Territories'. *World Politics* 45, 560–594.

(1997) 'Israeli History: Who is Fabricating What?'. *Survival* 39, 156–166.
(2005) 'Negotiating Truth: The Holocaust, Lehavdil, and al-Nakba'. In Lustick, I. and Lesch, A. (eds.) *Exile and Return: Predicaments of Palestinians and Jews*. Philadelphia: University of Pennsylvania Press (pp. 106–130).
Lynch, M. (2008) 'Bihari: From Statelessness to Citizenship'. Available at: www.refugeesinternational.org/blog/bihari-statelessness-citizenship.
Lynk, M. (2003) 'The Right to Restitution and Compensation in International Law and the Displaced Palestinians'. *Refuge* 21(2), 96–113.
Madsen, L. (2001) 'Homes of Origin: Return and Property Rights in Post-Dayton Bosnia and Herzegovina'. *Refuge* 19(3), 157–174.
Mahony, L. (1999) *Risking Return: NGOs in the Guatemalan Refugee Repatriation*. Uppsala: Life and Peace Institute.
Malcolm, N. (2002) *Bosnia: A Short History*. London: Macmillan.
Malkki, L. (1992) 'National Geographic: The Rooting of Peoples and the Territorialisation of National Identity among Scholars and Refugees'. *Cultural Anthropology* 7(1), 24–44.
(1995) 'Refugees and Exile: From "Refugee Studies" to the National Order of Things'. *Annual Review of Anthropology* 24, 295–523.
Mallison, W. and Mallison, S. (1980) 'The Right of Return'. *Journal of Palestine Studies* 9(3), 125–136.
Mandela, N. (1995) *Long Walk to Freedom*. London: Abacus.
Manly, M. (2007) 'The Spirit of Geneva – Traditional and New Actors in the Field of Statelessness'. *Refugee Survey Quarterly* 26(4), 255–261.
Manning, C. (2002) *The Politics of Peace in Mozambique: Post-conflict Democratization, 1992–2000*. Westport, CT: Greenwood Publishing Group.
Margalit, A. (1995) *The Decent Society* (trans. Goldblum, N.). Cambridge, MA: Harvard University Press.
(2005) 'I. Indecent Compromise; II. Decent Peace'. *Tanner Lectures on Human Values*, Stanford University, Stanford, 4–5 May 2005. Available at: http://tannerlectures.utah.edu/lectures/documents/Margalit_2006.pdf.
(2010) *On Compromise and Rotten Compromises*. Princeton: Princeton University Press.
Margalit, A. and Raz, J. (1990) 'National Self-Determination'. *Journal of Philosophy* 87(9), 439–461.
Martin, S. et al. (2005) *The Uprooted: Improving Humanitarian Responses to Forced Migration*. Lanham, MD: Lexington Books.
Martín Beristain, C. (1998) 'Guatemala: Never Again'. *Forced Migration Review* 3, 23–26.
(2007) 'The Legacy of Genocide in Guatemala: Memory and Psychosocial Recovery in Affected Communities'. In Sisson, J. (ed.) *Dealing with the Past in Post-Conflict Societies: Ten Years after the Peace Accords in Guatemala and Bosnia-Herzegovina*. Bern: Swisspeace (pp. 34–44).
Masalha, N. (1992) *Expulsion of the Palestinians: The Concept of 'Transfer' in Zionist Political Thought, 1882–1948*. Washington, DC: Institute for Palestine Studies.
(2000) *Imperial Israel and the Palestinians: The Politics of Expansion*. London: Pluto.

(2003) *The Politics of Denial: Israel and the Palestinian Refugee Problem*. London: Pluto Press.

Massad, J. (2001) 'Return or Permanent Exile?'. In Aruri, N. (ed.) *Palestinian Refugees: The Right of Return*. London: Pluto Press (pp. 71–76).

Massagee, A. (in press) 'Beyond Compensation: Reparations, Transitional Justice and the Palestinian Refugee Question'. In Brynen, R. and El-Rifai, R. (eds.) *Palestinian Refugee Compensation and the Peace Process*. London: Pluto.

Mattar, P. (1988) *The Mufti of Jerusalem: Al-Hajj Amin al-Husayni and the Palestinian National Movement*. New York: Columbia University Press.

McDermott Hughes, D. (1999) 'Refugees and Squatters: Immigration and the Politics of Territory on the Zimbabwe-Mozambique Border'. *Journal of Southern African Studies* 25(4), 533–552.

McGregor, J. (1998) 'Violence and Social Change in a Border Economy: War in the Maputo Hinterland 1984–1992'. *Journal of Southern African Studies* 24(1), 37–60.

Meernik, J. (2005) 'Justice and Peace How the International Criminal Tribunal Affects Societal Peace in Bosnia'. *Journal of Peace Research* 42(3), 271–289.

Mendez, J. E. (1997) 'Accountability for Past Abuses'. *Human Rights Quarterly* 19(2), 255–282.

Meyer, L. (2004) 'Historical Injustice and the Right of Return'. *Theoretical Inquiries in Law* 5(2), 295–306.

Meyer, M. (1989) 'Dignity, Rights and Self-Control'. *Ethics* 99(3), 520–534.

Miller, D. (2001) 'Distributing Responsibilities'. *The Journal of Political Philosophy* 9(4), 453–471.

(2004) 'Holding Nations Responsible'. *Ethics* 114(2), 240–268.

(2005) 'Inheriting Responsibilities'. Available at: www.trinitinture.com/documents/miller.pdf.

(2007) *National Responsibility and Global Justice*. Oxford: Oxford University Press.

Miller, J. and Kumar, R. (2007) 'Preface'. In Miller, J. and Kumar, R. (eds.) *Reparations: Interdisciplinary Inquiries*. Oxford: Oxford University Press (pp. v–vii).

Milner, J. (2009) 'Refugees and the Regional Dynamics of Peacebuilding'. *Refugee Studies Quarterly* 28(1), 13–30.

Minow, M. (1998) *Between Vengeance and Forgiveness: Facing History After Genocide and Mass Violence*. Boston: Beacon Press.

Minter, W. (1994) *Apartheid's Contras: An Inquiry into the Roots of War in Angola and Mozambique*. Johannesburg: Witwatersrand University Press.

MINUGUA (2004) *Report of the Secretary-General*. New York: United Nations Department of Peacekeeping Operations.

Molloy, M., Bell, J., Waintraub, N. and Anderson, I. (2011) 'The Palestinian Refugee Issue: Intangible Needs and Moral Acknowledgement'. Paper presented at Conference on Displacement and Reconciliation, Saint Paul University, Ottawa, 9–10 June 2011.

Mooney, E. (2006) 'Protecting and Reintegrating Displaced Women and Children Post-Conflict'. In Ndulo, M. (ed.) *Security, Reconciliation and*

Reconstruction in Africa: When the Wars End. Ithaca: Cornell University Press (pp. 111–124).

Morris, B. (1988) *The Birth of the Palestinian Refugee Problem, 1947–1949*. Cambridge: Cambridge University Press.

(1990) *1948 and After: Israel and the Palestinians*. Oxford: Clarendon Press.

(2004a) *The Birth of the Palestinian Refugee Problem Revisited*. Cambridge: Cambridge University Press.

(2004b) 'Politics by Other Means'. *The New Republic*, 22 March.

Myers, G. (1994) 'Competitive Rights, Competitive Claims: Land Access in Post-War Mozambique'. *Journal of Southern African Studies* 20(4), 603–632.

Nabulsi, K. (2003) 'Being Palestinian'. *Government and Opposition* 38(4), 479–496.

(2004) 'The Peace Process and the Palestinians: A Road Map to Mars'. *International Affairs* 80(2), 221–231.

(2006) *Palestinians Register: Laying Foundations and Setting Directions – Report of the Civitas Project*. Oxford: Nuffield College.

(2007) 'Justice as the Way Forward'. In Hilal, J. (ed.) *Where Now for Palestine? The Demise of the Two-State Solution*. London: Zed Books (pp. 253–254).

Nadelman, E. (1990) 'Global Prohibition Regimes: The Evolution of Norms in International Society'. *International Organization* 44(4), 479–526.

Nalepa, M. (2012) 'Reconciliation, Refugee Returns, and the Impact of International Criminal Justice: The Case of Bosnia and Herzegovina'. In Williams, M., Nagy, R. and Elster, J. (eds.) *Nomos L: Transitional Justice*. New York: New York University Press.

Naqvi, Y. (2004) 'Between a Rock and a Hard Place? A Legal Analysis of the Voluntary Repatriation of Guatemalan Refugees'. *Refugee Survey Quarterly* 23(3), 74–99.

Netherlands Institute for War Documentation (NIWD) (2002) *Srebrenica: A 'Safe' Area*. Amsterdam: Netherlands Institute for War Documentation.

Nets-Zehngut, R. (2011) 'Origins of the Palestinian Refugee Problem: Changes in the Historical Memory of Israelis/Jews, 1949–2004'. *Journal of Peace Research* 48(2), 235–248.

(2012) 'The Passing of Time and Collective Memory of Conflicts: Israel and the 1948 Palestinian Exodus'. *Peace and Change* 37(2): 253–285.

Nettelfield, L. (2010) *Courting Democracy in Bosnia and Herzegovina: The Hague Tribunal's Impact in a Postwar State*. Cambridge: Cambridge University Press.

Newitt, M. (1995) *A History of Mozambique*. Bloomington: Indiana University Press.

Ni Aolain (2001) 'The Fractured Soul of the Dayton Peace Agreement: A Legal Analysis'. In Sokolović, D. and Bieber, F. (eds.) *Reconstructing Multiethnic Societies: The Case of Bosnia- Herzegovina*. Burlington: Ashgate (pp. 63–94).

Nijem, K. (2007) 'Planning in Support of Negotiations: The Refugee Issue'. In Brynen, R. and El-Rifai, R. (eds.) *Palestinian Refugees: Challenges of Repatriation and Development*. London: I.B. Tauris (pp. 121–131).

Nine, C. (2008) 'Superseding Historic Injustice and Territorial Rights'. *Critical Review of International Social and Political Philosophy* 11(1), 79–87.

Nolin, C. (1997) *Guatemalan Refugees and Returnees: Local Geography and Maya Identity*. Toronto: Centre for Research on Latin America and the Caribbean (CERLAC)

Nordstrom, C. (1997) *A Different Kind of War Story*. Philadelphia: University of Pennsylvania Press.

North, L. and Simmons, A. (eds.) *Journeys of Fear: Refugee Return and National Transformation in Guatemala*. Montreal: McGill-Queen's University Press.

Office of the UN High Commissioner for Human Rights (OHCHR) (2008) *Rule-of-Law Tools for Post-Conflict States: Reparations Programmes*. Geneva: OHCHR.

Office of the High Representative in Bosnia and Herzegovina (OHR) (1999) *Comprehensive Strategy for a Just and Efficient Return Process in Bosnia- Herzegovina*. Sarajevo: OHR.

(2000a) 'PLIP Inter-Agency Framework Document', 15 October 2000. Available at: www.ohr.int/plip/key-doc/default.asp?content_id=5510.

(2000b) 'PLIP: Non Negotiable Principles in the Context of the Property Law Implementation', 1 March 2000. Available at: www.ohr.int/plip/key-doc/default.asp?content_id=5511.

(2002) Decision on Constitutional Amendments in Republika Srpska, amend. LXXXV, 19 April 2002. Available at: www.ohr.int/print/?content_id=7474.

(2003) 'BiH Institutions Assume Responsibility for Return Process'. Press Release, 30 December 2003.

(2004) 'Return in the Hands of the Domestic Authorities'. Accessed 3 April 2008 at: www.ohr.int/ohr-dept/presso/pic/rrtf-resp-w-bih-authorities/images/Return%20in%20the%20Hands%20of%20the%20Domestic%20Authorities%20-%20press%20ad.doc.

Ogata, S. (1992) 'Statement of the United Nations High Commissioner for Refugees'. Statement delivered at the International Meeting on Humanitarian Aid for Victims of the Conflict in the Former Yugoslavia, Geneva, 29 July 1992.

(2003) 'Foreword: Imaging Coexistence in Conflict Communities'. In Chayes, A. and Minow, M. (eds.) *Imagine Coexistence: Restoring Humanity After Violent Ethnic Conflict*. San Francisco: Jossey-Bass (pp. xi–xvi).

(2005) *The Turbulent Decade: Confronting the Refugee Crises of the 1990s*. New York: W. W. Norton & Company.

Oz, A. (2007) 'Israel Partly at Fault: We Must Assume Partial Blame for Refugee Problem in Order to Resolve it'. Available at: www.ynetnews.com/articles/0,7340,L-3393299,00.html.

Painter, R. A. (1996) 'Property Rights of Returning Displaced Persons: The Guatemalan Experience'. *Harvard Human Rights Journal* 9, 145–183.

Palestine National Council (PNC) (1988) *Palestinian Declaration of Independence*, Algiers, 15 November 1988.

Palestinian Centre for Policy and Survey Research (PCPSR) (2003) 'Press Release on Refugee Views on the Settlement of the Refugee Issue'. Ramallah, 18 July 2003. Printed in *Journal of Palestine Studies* 33(1), 160–161.

(2006) 'Strong Preference among Palestinians and Israelis for a Comprehensive Settlement Over an Interim Political Track'. Available at: www.pcpsr.org/survey/polls/2006/p22ejoint.html#b2refugees.

Palmer, B. (2005) 'Can Peace Trump Justice?'. *Stanford Report*, 11 May 2005. Available at: http://news-service.stanford.edu/news/2005/may11/tanner-051105.html.

Pantuliano, S. (ed.) (2009) *Uncharted Territory: Land, Conflict and Humanitarian Action*. Bourton-on-Dunsmore, UK: Practical Action Publishing Ltd.

Pantuliano, S. and Elhawary, S. (2009) 'Uncharted Territory: Land, Conflict and Humanitarian Action'. *HPG Policy Brief* 39, 193–212.

Pappé, I. (1994) *The Making of the Arab-Israeli Conflict: 1947–1951*. London: I.B. Tauris.

(2004) *A History of Modern Palestine: One Land, Two Peoples*. Cambridge: Cambridge University Press.

Partos, G. (2006) 'Analysis: Serbia in the Dock', 27 February 2006. http://news.bbc.co.uk/go/pr/fr/-/2/hi/europe/4748960.stm.

Paulsen, E. (2006) 'The Citizenship Status of the Urdu-speakers/Biharis in Bangladesh'. *Refugee Survey Quarterly* 25, 54–69.

Peled, Y. (1992) 'Ethnic Democratic and the Legal Construction of Citizenship: Arab Citizens of the Jewish State'. *American Political Science Review* 86(2), 432–443.

Penz, P. (2003) 'Development, Displacement and International Ethics'. In Van Ufford, P. and Giri, A. (eds.) *A Moral Critique of Development: In Search of Global Responsibilities*. London: Routledge (pp. 135–192).

Penz, P., Drydyk, J. and Bose, P. (2011) *Displacement by Development: Ethics, Rights and Responsibilities*. Cambridge: Cambridge University Press.

Percy, S. (2007) 'Mercenaries: Strong Norm, Weak Law'. *International Organization* 61(2), 367–397.

Permanent Court of International Justice (PCIJ) (1928) *Case Concerning the Factory at Chorzów: Judgement No. 13, 47*. The Hague: Permanent Court of International Justice.

Petrin, S. (2002) *Refugee Return and State Reconstruction*. Geneva: UNHCR.

Pfeiffer, J. (2004) 'Civil Society, NGOs and the Holy Spirit in Mozambique'. *Human Organization* 63(3), 359.

Philpott, C. (2005) 'Though the Dog is Dead, the Pig Must be Killed: Finishing with Property Restitution to Bosnia-Herzegovina's IDPs and Refugees'. *Journal of Refugee Studies* 18(1), 1–24

Phuong, C. (2000a) 'At the Heart of the Return Process: Solving Property Issues in Bosnia and Herzegovina'. *Forced Migration Review* 7, 5–7.

(2000b) '"Freely to Return": Reversing Ethnic Cleansing in Bosnia-Herzegovina'. *Journal of Refugee Studies* 13(2), 165–183.

(2005) *Forcible Displacement in Peace Agreements*. Geneva: International Council on Human Rights Policy. Available at: www.ichrp.org/files/papers/52/128_-_Forcible_Displacement_in_Peace_Agreements_Phuong__Catherine__2005.pdf.

Podeh, E. (2005) 'The Right of Return versus the Law of Return: Contrasting Historical Narratives in Israeli and Palestinian School

Textbooks'. In Lustick, I. and Lesch, A. (eds.) *Exile and Return: Predicaments of Palestinians and Jews*. Philadelphia: University of Pennsylvania Press (pp. 41–56).

Pollack, C. (2003) 'Returning to a Safe Area? The Importance of Burial for Return to Srebrenica'. *Journal of Refugee Studies* 16(2), 186–201.

Prettitore, P. (2006) 'Refugee Return in Bosnia and Herzegovina'. In Dumper, M. (ed.) *Palestinian Refugee Repatriation: Global Perspectives*. New York: Routledge (pp. 180–208).

Price, R. (ed.) (2008) *Moral Limit and Possibility in World Politics*. Cambridge: Cambridge University Press.

Pritchard, M. (1972) 'Human Dignity and Justice'. *Ethics* 82(4), 299–313.

Public International Law and Policy Group (2005) *Peace Agreement Drafters' Handbook*. Washington, DC: Public International Law and Policy Group.

Quartet (2003) 'Performance-Based Roadmap to a Permanent Two-State Solution to the Israeli-Palestinian Conflict'. Available at: http://news.bbc.co.uk/2/hi/middle_east/2989783.stm.

Quinn, J. R. and Freeman, M. (2003) 'Lessons Learned: Practical Lessons Gleaned from Inside the Truth Commissions of Guatemala and South Africa'. *Human Rights Quarterly* 25(4), 1117–1149.

Radio Free Europe (2007) 'Bosnian Serbs Apologize to War Victims in Bosnia', 28 February 2007. Available at: www.rferl.org/featuresarticle/2007/02/1C5B0C6F-9F0C- 4E46–829F-C569E15B85F9.html.

Ranger, T. (1994) 'Studying Repatriation as Part of African Social History'. In Allen, T. and Morsink, H. (eds.) *When Refugees Go Home*. Trenton, NJ: Africa World Press (pp. 279–294).

Redress (2002) *The Reparation Sourcebook*. London: Redress.

Refugees International (2006) 'Bangladesh: Stateless Biharis Grasp for a Resolution and their Rights'. Available at: www.refugeesinternational.org/policy/field- report/bangladesh-stateless-biharis-grasp-resolution-and-their-rights.

(2007) 'Guatemalan Refugees Return to a Hard Life'. http://refugeesinternational.org/content/article/detail/1220/?output=printer.

Rempel, T. (1999) 'The Ottawa Process: Workshop on Compensation and Palestinian Refugees'. *Journal of Palestine Studies* 29(1), 36–49.

Representative of the United Nations Secretary-General on Internally Displaced Persons (RSG) (1997) *Profiles in Displacement: Mozambique*, E/CN.4/1997/43/Add.1.

(2005) *Report of the Representative of the Secretary-General on the Human Rights of Internally Displaced Persons: Addendum – Mission to Bosnia and Herzegovina*, E/CN.4/2006/71/Add.4.

Representative of the United Nations Secretary-General on the Human Rights of Internally Displaced Persons (2009) *Report to the UN Human Rights Council of the Representative of the Secretary-General on the Human Rights of Internally Displaced Persons, Addendum: Framework on Durable Solutions for Internally Displaced Persons*, A/HRC/13/21/Add.4, 29 December 2009.

Republic of Mozambique (1997) *Lei de Terras*. Institutio da Estatística-Maputo.

(1999) *Law 11/99 on Extrajudicial Conflict Management*. Institutio da Estatística-Maputo.

Republic of South Africa (1994) *Restitution of Land Rights Act of 1994*. www.info.gov.za/acts/1994/a22-94.pdf.

Reus-Smit, C. (2004) 'Introduction'. In Reus-Smit, C. (ed.) *The Politics of International Law*. Oxford: Oxford University Press (pp. 1–13).

Reus-Smit, C. and Snidal, D. (2008) 'Reuniting Ethics and Social Science'. *Ethics and International Affairs* 22(2), 261–271.

Reuters (2007) 'Bosnians Raise Monument to Canned Beef', 6 April 2007. Available at: http://uk.reuters.com/article/oddlyEnoughNews/idUKL0657786020070406.

Richardson, H. (1999) 'Institutionally Divided Moral Responsibility'. *Social Philosophy and Policy* 16(2): 218–249.

Riess, S. (2000) '"Return is Struggle, not Resignation": Lessons from the Repatriation of Guatemalan Refugees from Mexico'. Geneva: UNHCR.

Roberts, L. (1996) 'Long Path Home for Guatemalan Refugees'. *Peace Magazine* 12(5), 12–14.

Rodicio, A. (2001) 'Restoration of Life: A New Theoretical Approach to Voluntary Repatriation Based on a Cambodian Experience of Return'. *International Journal of Refugee Law* 13(1/2), 123–141.

(2006) 'Re-approaching Voluntary Repatriation within a Reconciliation Framework: A Proposal Drawn from the Cambodian Return Process'. In Dumper, M. (ed.) *Palestinian Refugee Repatriation: Global Perspectives*. New York: Routledge (pp. 209–231).

Roesch, O. (1992) 'Renamo and the Peasantry in Southern Africa: A View from Gaza Province'. *Canadian Journal of African Studies* 26(3), 462–484.

Roht-Arriaza, N. (2004) 'Reparations in the Aftermath of Repression and Mass Violence'. In Stover, E. and Weinstein, H. (eds.) *My Neighbor, My Enemy: Justice and Community in the Aftermath of Mass Atrocity*. Cambridge: Cambridge University Press (pp. 121–140).

Roucek, J. (1929) *The Working of the Minorities System under the League of Nations*. Prague: Orbis Publishing Company.

Rouhana, N. (2004) 'Group Identity and Power Asymmetry in Reconciliation Processes: The Israeli-Palestinian Case'. *Peace and Conflict* 10(1), 33–52.

(2005) 'Truth and Reconciliation: The Right of Return in the Context of Past Injustice'. In Lustick, I. and Lesch, A. (eds.) *Exile and Return: Predicaments of Palestinians and Jews*. Philadelphia: University of Pennsylvania Press (pp. 261–278).

Rubin, S. and Schwartz, A. (1951) 'Refugees and Reparations'. *Law and Contemporary Problems* 16(3), 377–394.

Said, E. (2000) *The End of the Peace Process: Oslo and After*. New York: Pantheon Books.

(2001) *Power, Politics, and Culture*. New York: Vintage.

Samy, S. (2007) 'Would "Sorry" Repair my Loss? Why Palestinian Refugees Should Seek an Apology for their Displacement'. Paper delivered at From Exodus to Exile: Palestinian Lives in the Levant, Christian Michelsen Institute, Bergen, 7–8 September 2007.

(2010) *Reparations to Palestinian Refugees: A Comparative Perspective*. London: Routledge.

Sarkar, S. (2008) 'Maoist Victory Casts Shadow Over Bhutan Refugee Resettlement'. Available at: www.thaindian.com/newsportal/world-news/maoist-victory-casts-shadow-over-bhutan-refugee-resettlement_10042445.html.

Sawyer, S. and Blitz, B. (eds.) (2011) *Statelessness in the European Union: Displaced, Undocumented, Unwanted*. Cambridge: Cambridge University Press.

Schechla, J. (2001) 'The Invisible People Come to Light: Israel's "Internally Displaced" and "Unrecognized Villages"'. *Journal of Palestine Studies* 31(1), 20–31.

Schirmer, J. (1991) 'The Guatemalan Military Project: An Interview with Gen. Héctor Gramajo'. *Harvard International Review* 13(1), 10–13.

(1999) *The Guatemalan Military Project: A Violence Called Democracy*. Philadelphia: University of Pennsylvania Press.

Schlesinger, S. and Kinzer, S. (2005) *Bitter Fruit: The Untold Story of the American Coup in Guatemala* (rev. edn). Cambridge, MA: David Rockefeller Center for Latin American Studies.

Schulz, H. L. (2003) *The Palestinian Diaspora: Formation of Identities and Politics of Homeland*. London: Routledge.

Segev, T. (1986) *The First Israelis*. New York: Free Press.

(2007) 'The June 1967 War and the Palestinian Refugee Problem'. *Journal of Palestine Studies* 36(3), 6–22.

Segovia, A. (2006) 'Financing Reparations Programs: Reflections from International Experience'. In de Greiff, P. (ed.) *The Handbook of Reparations*. Oxford: Oxford University Press (pp. 154–175).

Seils, P. (2002) 'Reconciliation in Guatemala: The Role of Intelligent Justice'. *Race and Class* 44(1), 33–60.

(2012) 'Guatemala Genocide Ruling a Triumph for Survivors'. http://ictj.org/news/guatemala-genocide-ruling-triumph-survivors.

Selznick, P. (2002) *Law in Context, Fidelity to Context*. Berkeley: Center for the Study of Law and Society, Jurisprudence and Social Policy Program.

Sen, S. (1999) 'Stateless Refugees and the Right to Return: The Bihari Refugees of South Asia, Part 1'. *International Journal of Refugee Law* 11(4), 625–645.

(2000) 'Stateless Refugees and the Right to Return: The Bihari Refugees of South Asia, Part 2'. *International Journal of Refugee Law* 12(1), 41–70.

Sengulane, D. S. and Gonçalves, J. P. (1998) 'A Calling for Peace: Christian Leaders and the Quest for Reconciliation in Mozambique'. In Armon, J., Hendrickson. D. and Vines, A. (eds.) *The Mozambican Peace Process in Perspective*. London: Conciliation Resources.

Sengupta, S. (2008) 'Heavy Turnout in First Bhutan Election'. *New York Times*, 25 March 2008.

Shacknove, A. (1985) 'Who Is a Refugee?'. *Ethics* 95(2), 274–284.

Shafir, G. (1989) *Land, Labour and the Origins of the Israeli-Palestinian Conflict 1882–1914*. Cambridge: Cambridge University Press.

Shafir, G. and Peled, Y. (2002) *Being Israeli: The Dynamics of Multiple Citizenship*. Cambridge: Cambridge University Press.

Shawcross, W. (2000) *Deliver Us From Evil: Warlords and Peacekeepers in a World of Endless Conflict*. London: Bloomsbury.

Shehadi, N. (2009) *Palestinian Refugees: The Regional Perspective*. London: Chatham House.

Shelton, D. (2000) *Remedies in International Human Rights Law*. Oxford: Oxford University Press.

(2002) 'Righting Wrongs: Reparations in the Articles on State Responsibility'. *American Journal of International Law* 96(4), 833–856.

Shelton, D. (2006) *Remedies in International Human Rights Law* (2nd edn). Oxford: Oxford University Press.

Shenhav, Y. (1999) 'The Jews of Iraq, Zionist Ideology, and the Property of the Palestinian Refugees of 1948: An Anomaly of National Accounting'. *International Journal of Middle East Studies* 31(4), 605–630.

(2002) 'Ethnicity and National Memory: The World Organization of Jews from Arab Countries (WOJAC) in the Context of the Palestinian National Struggle'. *British Journal of Middle Eastern Studies* 29(1), 27–56.

(2003) 'Hitching a Ride on the Magic Carpet: Any Analogy Between Palestinian Refugees and Jewish Immigrants from Arab Lands is Folly in Historical and Political Terms'. *Haaretz*, 8 August 2003.

(2005) 'Arab Jews, Population Exchange, and the Palestinian Right of Return'. In Lustick, I. and Lesch, A. (eds.) *Exile and Return: Predicaments of Palestinians and Jews*. Philadelphia: University of Pennsylvania Press (pp. 225–245).

Sher, G. (2006) *The Israeli-Palestinian Peace Negotiations, 1999–2001: Within Reach*. New York: Routledge.

Shiblak, A. (2009) *The Palestinian Refugee Issue: A Palestinian Perspective*. London: Chatham House.

Shklar, J. (1964) *Legalism*. Cambridge: Harvard University Press.

(1993) 'Obligation, Loyalty, Exile'. *Political Theory* 21(2), 181–197.

Shlaim, A. (1988) *Collusion across the Jordan: King Abdullah, the Zionist Movement and the Partition of Palestine*. New York: Columbia University Press.

Shue, H. (1996) *Basic Rights: Subsistence, Affluence and US Foreign Policy* (2nd edn). Princeton: Princeton University Press.

Shulewitz, M. H. (ed.) (1999) *The Forgotten Millions: The Modern Jewish Exodus from Arab Lands*. London: Cassell.

Simpson, G. (1997) 'Reconstruction and Reconciliation: Emerging from Transition'. *Development in Practice* 7(4), 475–478.

Smit, A. R. (2004) 'International Approaches to Post-Conflict Housing and Property Restitution and Refugee/IDP Returns: Case Studies of Georgia and Kosovo'. Presentation delivered at the Refugee Studies Centre Informal Seminar Series, Queen Elizabeth House, University of Oxford, Oxford, 17 February 2004.

(2012) *The Property Rights of Refugees and Internally Displaced Persons: Beyond Restitution*. London: Routledge.

Souter, J. (in press) 'Towards a Theory of Asylum as Reparation for Past Injustice'. *Political Studies*.

Soyinka, W. (1999) *The Burden of Memory, the Muse of Forgiveness*. New York: Oxford University Press.

Special Rapporteur on Housing and Property Restitution for Refugees and Internally Displaced Persons (2002) *The Return of Refugees' or*

Displaced Persons' Property: Working Paper Submitted Pursuant to Sub- Commission on the Promotion and Protection of Human Rights decision 2001/122, E/CN.4/Sub.2/2002/17.

Special Rapporteur on the Right to Reparation to Victims of Gross Violations of Human Rights (1993) *Study Concerning the Right to Restitution, Compensation and Rehabilitation for Victims of Gross Violations of Human Rights and Fundamental Freedoms*, E/CN.4/Sub.2/1993/8.

Spiegelberg, H. (1971) 'Human Dignity: A Challenge to Contemporary Philosophy'. *World Futures* 9(1), 39–64.

Spiro, P. (2011) 'A New International Law of Citizenship'. *American Journal of International Law* 105, 694–746.

Stefansson, A. (2006) 'Homes in the Making: Property Restitution, Refugee Return, and Senses of Belonging in a Post-War Bosnian Town'. *International Migration* 44(3), 115–139.

Stepputat, F. (1994) 'Repatriation and the Politics of Space: The Case of the Mayan Diaspora and Return Movement'. *Journal of Refugee Studies* 7(2/3), 175–185.

(1999) 'Repatriation and Everyday Forms of State Formation in Guatemala'. In Black, R. and Koser, K. (eds.) *The End of the Refugee Cycle? Refugee Repatriation and Reconstruction*. Oxford: Berghahn Books (pp. 223–224).

(2001) 'Review of *Journeys of Fear: Refugee Return and National Transformation in Guatemala*'. *Journal of Refugee Studies* 14(1), 90–91.

(2006) '"Sustainable Returns"?: State, Politics and Mobile Livelihoods – The Guatemalan Case'. In Dumper, M. (ed.) *Palestinian Refugee Repatriation: Global Perspectives*. New York: Routledge (pp. 109–131).

Stover, E. (2004) 'Witnesses and the Promise of Justice in The Hague'. In Stover, E. and Weinstein, H. (eds.) *My Neighbor, My Enemy: Justice and Community in the Aftermath of Mass Atrocity*. Cambridge: Cambridge University Press (pp. 104–120).

Stover, E. and Weinstein, H. (2004) 'Introduction: Conflict, Justice and Reclamation'. In Stover, E. and Weinstein, H. (eds.) *My Neighbor, My Enemy: Justice and Community in the Aftermath of Mass Atrocity*. Cambridge: Cambridge University Press (pp. 1–24).

Sudetic, C. (1998) *Blood and Vengeance: One Family's Story of the War in Bosnia*. New York: W.W. Norton & Company.

Swedenburg, T. (1995) *Memories of Revolt: The 1936–1939 Rebellion and the Palestinian Past*. Minneapolis: University of Minnesota Press.

Synge, R. (1997) *Mozambique: UN Peacekeeping in Action, 1992–1994*. Washington, DC: United States Institute of Peace Press.

Takahashi, S. (1997) 'The UNHCR Handbook on Voluntary Repatriation: The Emphasis of Return over Protection'. *International Journal of Refugee Law* 9(4), 593–612.

Takkenberg, L. (1998) *The Status of Palestinian Refugees in International Law*. Oxford: Oxford University Press.

Tamari, S. (1999) 'Palestinian Refugees and the Palestinian-Israeli Negotiations (interview)'. *Journal of Palestine Studies* 29(1), 81–89.

Tamir, Y. (1993) *Liberal Nationalism*. Princeton, NJ: Princeton University Press.

Taylor, C. (1998) *Return of Guatemala's Refugees: Reweaving the Torn*. Philadelphia, PA: Temple University Press.

Teveth, S. (1985) *Ben Gurion and the Palestinian Arabs: From Peace to War*. Oxford: Oxford University Press.

Thiele, B. (2001) 'Recent Development in United Nations Policy on Housing and Property Restitution for Refugee Return'. *Refuge* 19(3), 3–7.

Thoresen, B. (1995) 'The Return of Guatemalan Refugees: Two Years After'. *Migration World* 23(5), 22–27.

Thornton, C. (2012) 'Pinheiro and the Political Philosophers: Achieving Justice Through Post-Conflict Property Restitution'. Available at: http://terra0nullius.wordpress.com/2012/03/06/pinheiro-and-the-political-philosophers-achieving-justice-through-post-conflict-property-restitution/#more-2603.

Toal, G. and Dahlman, C. (2011) *Bosnia Remade: Ethnic Cleansing and its Reversal*. Oxford: Oxford University Press.

Torpey, J. (2006) *Making Whole What Has Been Smashed: On Reparations Politics*. Cambridge: Harvard University Press.

Tuathail, G. (2010) 'Localizing Geopolitics: Disaggregating Violence and Return in Conflict Regions'. *Political Geography* 29(5), 256–265.

Tuathail, G. and O'Loughlin, J. (2009) 'After Ethnic Cleansing: Return Outcomes in Bosnia-Herzegovina a Decade beyond War'. *Annals of the Association of American Geographers* 99(5), 1045–1053.

Turton, D. (2005) 'The Meaning of Place in a World of Movement'. *Journal of Refugee Studies* 18(3), 258–280.

UNIFEM (2000) *Proceedings of the All-Party Burundi Women's Peace Conference*. New York: UNIFEM.

United Nations Commission on Human Rights (1998) *Report of the Representative of the Secretary-General, Mr. Francis M. Deng, Submitted Pursuant to Commission Resolution 1997/39 – Addendum: Guiding Principles on Internal Displacement*, E/CN.4/1998/53/Add.2.

(2003) *Resolution on Human Rights and Mass Exoduses*, 2003/52, E/CN.4/RES/2003/52.

United Nations Commission on Human Rights Sub-Commission On The Prevention of Discrimination and Protection of Minorities (1998) *Resolution on Housing and Property Restitution in the Context of Return of Refugees and Internally Displaced Persons*, 1998/26.

United Nations General Assembly (UNGA) (1948) *Resolution 194 (III)*.

(1950) *Resolution 428(v)*. Statute of the Office of the United Nations High Commissioner for Refugees.

(2005a) *Basic Principles and Guidelines on the Right to a Remedy and Reparation for Victims of Gross Violations of International Human Rights Law and Serious Violations of International Humanitarian Law (UN Reparations Principles)*. UN Doc. A/RES/60/147.

(2005b) *World Summit Outcome*, A/60/L.1.

United Nations Group of Governmental Experts (1986) *Report of the UN Group of Governmental Experts on International Cooperation to Avert New Flows of Refugees*, UN Doc. A/41/324.

United Nations High Commissioner for Refugees (UNHCR) (1978–2006) 'Speeches of the UN High Commissioners for Refugees'. Speeches delivered by the UN High Commissioners for Refugees, various locations, 1978–2006.

(1995) *The Future for Mozambique*. Geneva: UNHCR.

(1996) *UNHCR Handbook on Voluntary Repatriation: International Protection*. Geneva: UNHCR.

(2000) *State of the World's Refugees: Fifty Years of Humanitarian Action*. Oxford: Oxford University Press.

(2001) 'Checklist on the Restitution of Housing and Property'. 28 November 2001. Available at: www.unhcr.org/cgi-bin/texis/vtx/refworld/rwmain?docid=3c0e327d4.

(2002) *Global Consultations on International Protection – Background Paper on Voluntary Repatriation*, EC/GC/02/5.

UNHCR (2003) *Resolution on Human Rights and Mass Exoduses*, 2003/52. E/CN.4/RES/2003/52.

(2004) *Handbook for Repatriation and Reintegration Activities*. Geneva: UNHCR.

(2005) *Nationality and Statelessness: A Handbook for Parliamentarians*. Geneva: UNHCR/Inter-Parliamentary Union.

(2006a) *Refugees By Number 2005*. Geneva: UNHCR. Available at: www.unhcr.orgcgi-bintexisvtxbasicsopendoc.htm?tbl=BASICSamp;id=3b028097c#Returnees.

(2006b) *State of the World's Refugees: Human Displacement in the New Millennium*. Oxford: Oxford University Press.

(2006c) *The World's Stateless People: Questions and Answers*. Geneva: UNHCR.

(2007) *Statistical Yearbook 2006: Trends in Displacement, Protection and Solutions*. Geneva: UNHCR.

(2008) *2007 Global Trends: Refugees, Asylum-seekers, Returnees, Internally Displaced and Stateless Persons*. Geneva: UNHCR. Available at: www.unhcr.org/statistics/STATISTICS/4852366f2.pdf.

(2010) *2010 UNHCR Country Operations Profile: Bosnia and Herzegovina*. Available at: www.unhcr.org/cgi-bin/texis/vtx/page?page=49e48d766.

(2011) *60 Years and Still Counting: UNHCR Global Trends 2010*. Geneva: UNHCR.

(2012a) *2012 UNHCR Country Operations Profile: Bosnia and Herzegovina*. Geneva: UNHCR. Available at: www.unhcr.org/cgi-bin/texis/vtx/page?page=49e48d766.

(2012b) *Guidelines on Statelessness No. 1: The Definition of "Stateless Person" in Article 1(1) of the 1954 Convention Relating to the Status of Stateless Persons*, HCR/GS/12/01.

United Nations High Commissioner for Refugees Executive Committee (EXCOM) (1985) *Conclusion No. 40 (XXXVI)-1985 Voluntary Repatriation*, A/AC.96/673.

(2006) *Statelessness: Prevention and Reduction of Statelessness and Protection of Stateless Persons*, EC/57/SC/CRP.6.

United Nations High Commissioner for Refugees, UNDP and World Bank (2010) *Concept Note: Transitional Solutions Initiative*. Available at: www.unhcr.org/4e27e2f06.html.

United Nations Mediator on Palestine (1948) *Supplement to Part 3 of Progress Report of the United Nations Mediator on Palestine*, 3 UN GAOR Supp. (No. 11), UN Doc. A/648.

United Nations News Service (2009) 'Number of Bhutanese Refugees Resettled from Nepal Last Year Tops 8,000 – UN'. UN News Service, 7 January 2009. Available at: www.unhcr.org/refworld/countryBTN,4562d8cf2,4982d0bb20,0.html.

United Nations Relief and Works Agency for Palestine Refugees in the Near East (UNRWA) (2009) 'Who is a Palestine Refugee?'. Available at: www.un.org/unrwa/refugees/whois.html.

United Nations Secretary-General (UNSG) (1992) *An Agenda for Peace: Preventive Diplomacy, Peacemaking and Peace-keeping*. A/47/277-S/24111.

(2004) *The Rule of Law and Transitional Justice in Conflict and Post-Conflict Societies: Report of the Secretary-General*. S/2004/616.

(2009) *Report of the Secretary-General on Peacebuilding in the Immediate Aftermath of Conflict*. A/63/881-S/2009/304.

(2011a) 'Durable Solutions: Follow up to the Secretary-General's 2009 Report on Peacebuilding'. Secretary-General's Policy Committee Decision 2011/20.

(2011b) *The Rule of Law and Transitional Justice in Conflict and Post-Conflict Societies: Report of the Secretary-General*. S/2011/634.

United Nations Security Council (1967) *Resolution 242: The Situation in the Middle East*. S/RES/242.

(1973) *Resolution 338: Cease-fire in the Middle East*. S/RES/338.

(1967) *Resolution 237: The Situation in the Middle East*. S/RES/237.

(1992) *Resolution 787: The Situation in Bosnia and Herzegovina*. S/RES/787.

(1993a) *Resolution 820: Bosnia and Herzegovina, 17 April 1993*. S/RES/820.

(1993b) *Resolution 874: The Situation in Armenia-Azerbaijan*. S/RES/874.

(1995) *Resolution 999: The Situation in Tajikistan*. S/RES/999.

(1996) *Resolution 1036: The Situation in Georgia*. S/RES/1036.

(1999a) *Resolution 1244: The Situation in Kosovo*. S/RES/1244.

(1999b) *Resolution 1258: The Situation in the Democratic Republic of Congo*. S/RES/1258.

(2004a) *Resolution 1545: The Situation in Burundi*. S/RES/1545.

(2004b) *Report of the Secretary-General on Sudan*. S/RES/1564.

United Nations Sub-Commission on the Promotion and Protection of Human Rights (2005) *Final Report of Mr. Pinheiro, Special Rapporteur on Housing and Property Restitution in the Context of the Return of Refugees and Internally Displaced Persons: Principles on Housing and Property Restitution for Refugees and Displaced Persons*. E/CN.4/Sub.2/2005/17.

United States House of Representatives (2007) *House of Representatives Resolution 185: Expressing the Sense of the House of Representatives Regarding the Creation of Refugee Populations in the Middle East, North Africa, and the Persian Gulf Region as a Result of Human Rights Violations*, 110th Congress, 1st Session.

United States Senate (2007) *Senate Resolution 85: Expressing the Sense of the Senate Regarding the Creation of Refugee Populations in the Middle East, North Africa, and the Persian Gulf Region as a Result of Human Rights Violations*, 110th Congress, 1st Session.

Unruh, J. (1997) 'The Role of Land Conflict and Land Conflict Resolution in a Peace Process: Mozambique's Return to Agriculture'. *Refuge* 16, 28–33.

(2001) 'Postwar Land Dispute Resolution: Land Tenure and the Peace Process in Mozambique'. *International Journal of World Peace* 18, 3–30.

(2005) 'Property Restitution Laws in a Post-War Context: The Case of Mozambique'. *African Journal of Legal Studies* 3, 147–165.

Utting, P. (ed.) (1994) *Between Hope and Insecurity: The Cambodia Peace Process*. Geneva: UNRISD.

van Boven, T. (1993) *Study Concerning the Right to Restitution, Compensation and Rehabilitation for Victims of Gross Violations of Human Rights and Fundamental Freedoms*. E/CN.4/Sub.2/1993/8.

van der Auweraert, P. (2012) 'Reparations and Large-Scale Forced Displacement'. In Duthie, R. (ed.) *Transitional Justice and Displacement*. New York: Social Science Research Council (pp. 139–186).

van Hear, N. (1998) *New Diasporas: The Mass Exodus, Dispersal and Regrouping of Migrant Communities*. Seattle: University of Washington Press.

van Heuven Goedhart, G. J. (1955) 'Refugee Problems and Their Solutions'. Nobel Lecture at the Nobel Institute, Oslo, Norway, 12 December 1955.

van Houtte, H. (1999) 'Mass Property Claim Resolution in a Post-War Society: The Commission for Real Property Claims in Bosnia and Herzegovina'. *International Comparative Law Quarterly* 48(3), 625–638.

van Metre, L. and Akan, B. (1997) *Dayton Implementation: The Return of Refugees*. Washington, DC: USIP.

van Waas, L. (2008) *Nationality Matters: Statelessness under International Law*. Oxford: Intersentia.

Vieira, L. (2012) *The CAVR and the 2006 Displacement Crisis in East Timor: Reflections on Truth-Telling, Dialogue and Durable Solutions*. New York/Washington, DC: International Centre for Transitional Justice/Brookings Institution.

Vines, A. (1991) *Renamo: Terrorism in Mozambique*. London: James Currey.

Vogel, T. K. (2007) 'Bosnia-Herzegovina: Hague Ruling Won't Bring Closure', 27 February 2007. Available at: www.rferl.org/featuresarticle/2007/02/af969725-ffe5-432a-a29c-b676f47027f6.html.

von Carlowitz, L. (2005) 'Resolution of Property Disputes in Bosnia and Kosovo: The Contribution to Peacebuilding'. *International Peacekeeping* 12(4), 547–561.

Wakim, W. (2001) 'The "Internally Displaced": Seeking Return within One's Own Land (interview)'. *Journal of Palestine Studies* 31(1), 32–38.

Waldron, J. (1992) 'Superseding Historic Injustice'. *Ethics* 103(1), 4–28.

(2004) 'Settlement, Return and the Supersession Thesis'. *Theoretical Inquiries in Law* 5(2), 237–268.

(2007) 'Why is Indigeneity Important?'. In Miller, J. and Kumar, R. (eds.) *Reparations: Interdisciplinary Inquiries*. Oxford: Oxford University Press (pp. 23–42).

Walzer, M. (1983) *Spheres of Justice*. New York: Basic Books.

(1994) *Thick and Thin: Moral Argument at Home and Abroad.* Notre Dame: University of Notre Dame Press.

Warner, D. (1996) 'Voluntary Repatriation and the Meaning of Return to Home: A Critique of Liberal Mathematics'. *Journal of Refugee Studies* 7(2/3), 160–174.

Washington Office on Latin America (WOLA) (1989) *Uncertain Return: Refugees and Reconciliation in Guatemala.* Washington: WOLA.

Waterhouse, R. (1998) 'Women's Land Rights in Post-War Mozambique'. In UNIFEM (ed.) *Women's Land and Property Rights in Situations of Conflict and Reconstruction.* New York: UNIFEM.

Weinstein, J. (2002) 'Mozambique: A Fading UN Success Story'. *Journal of Democracy* 13(1), 141–156.

Weis, P. (1979) *Nationality and Statelessness in International Law* (2nd rev. edn). Alphen aan den Rijn: Sijthoff and Noordhoff International Publishers.

Weiss Fagen, P. (2003) 'Post-Conflict Reintegration and Reconstruction: Doing it Right Takes a While'. In Steiner, N., Loescher, G. and Gibney, M. (eds.) *Refugee Protection: Ethical, Legal and Political Problems and the Role of UNHCR.* New York: Routledge (pp.197–223).

(2005) 'Repatriation'. In Gibney, M. J. and Hansen, R. (eds.) *Immigration and Asylum: From 1900 to the Present.* Santa Barbara: ABC Clio (pp. 513–519).

(2006) 'UNHCR and repatriation'. In Dumper, M. (ed.) *Palestinian Refugee Repatriation in Global Perspective.* London: Routledge (pp. 42–63).

West, H. (1998a) '"This Neighbour Is Not My Uncle!": Changing Relations of Power and Authority on the Mueda Plateau'. *Journal of Southern African Studies* 24(1), 141–160.

(1998b) 'Traditional Authorities and the Mozambican Transition to Democratic Governance'. In Graybill, L. and Thompson, K. (eds.) *Africa's Second Wave of Freedom: Development, Democracy and Rights.* Lanham, MD: University Press of America (pp. 65–80).

(2005) *Kupilikula: Governance and the Invisible Realm in Mozambique.* Chicago: University of Chicago Press.

West, H. and Kloeck-Jenson, S. (1999) 'Betwixt and Between: "Traditional Authority" and Democratic Decentralisation in Post-War Mozambique'. *African Affairs* 98(393), 455–484.

West, H. and Myers, G. (1996) 'A Piece of Land in a Land of Peace? State Farm Divestiture in Mozambique'. *Journal of Modern African Studies* 34(1), 27–51.

Wilkinson, R. (1998) 'Mozambique Revisited'. *Refugees* 112, 4–10.

Williams, R. (2004) 'Post-Conflict Property Restitution in Croatia and Bosnia and Herzegovina'. *Forced Migration Review* 21, 15–16

(2006a) 'Post-Conflict Property Restitution and Refugee Return in Bosnia and Herzegovina: Implications for International Standard-Setting and Practice'. *New York University Journal of International Law and Politics* 37(3), 441–554.

(2006b) 'The Significance of Property Restitution to Sustainable Return in Bosnia and Herzegovina'. *International Migration* 44(3), 39–61.

(2007) *The Contemporary Right to Property Restitution in the Context of Transitional Justice.* New York: International Center for Transitional Justice.

(2010a) 'Introductory Note – European Court of Human Rights: Demopoulos v. Turkey'. *International Legal Materials* 49(3), 816.

(2010b) 'The Pinheiro Principles Take a Licking (and Keep on Ticking?)', *Terra Nullis*. Available at: http://terra0nullius.wordpress.com/?s=The+Pinheiro+Principles+Take+a+Licking+%28and+Keep+on+Ticking%3F.

(2012) 'Protection in the Past Tense: Restitution at the Juncture of Humanitarian Response to Displacement and Transitional Justice'. In Duthie, R. (ed.) *Transitional Justice and Displacement*. New York: Social Science Research Council (pp. 85–136).

Williams, R. and Gurel, A. (2011) 'The European Court of Human Rights and the Cyprus Property Issue: Charting a Way Forward'. *PRIO Cyprus Centre Paper* 1. Available at: www.prio.no/upload/Report%20European%20Court%20WEB.PDF.

Wily, L. A. (2009) 'Tackling Land Tenure in the Emergency to Development Transition in Post-Conflict States: From Restitution to Reform'. In Pantuliano, S. (ed.) *Uncharted Territory: Land, Conflict and Humanitarian Action*. Warwickshire: Practical Action Publishing (pp. 27–50).

Wood, N. (2004) 'Bosnian Serbs Apologize for Srebrenica Massacre'. *New York Times* 11 November 2004.

Wooldridge, F. and Elias, O. (2003) 'Humanitarian Considerations in the Work of the United Nations Compensation Commission'. *International Review of the Red Cross* 85(851), 555–581.

Worby, P. (1999) *Lessons Learned from UNHCR's Involvement in the Guatemalan Refugee Repatriation and Reintegration Programme (1987–1999)*. Geneva: UNHCR.

(2001) 'Security and Dignity: Land Access and Guatemala's Returned Refugees'. *Refuge* 19(3), 17–24.

World Bank (2004) 'Colombia: Protection of Patrimonial Assets of Internally Displaced Populations'. Accessed 19 September 2007 at: available at: http:wbln0018.worldbank.orglaclacinfoclient.nsf DateBy+Author_Country600F35A7B210920F85256F3A0078A5D5?OpenDocument.

World Organisation of Jews from Arab Countries (WOJAC) (2007) 'Israeli Cabinet Resolutions'. *Leadership Report* 4(1), online.

Young, I. M. (2006) 'Responsibility and Global Justice: A Social Connection Model'. *Social Philosophy and Policy* 23(1), 102–130.

(2007) *Global Challenges: War, Self-Determination and Responsibility for Justice*. Cambridge: Policy Press.

Young, L. and Park, R. (2009) 'Engaging Diasporas in Truth Commissions: Lessons from the Liberia Truth and Reconciliation Commission Diaspora Project'. *International Journal of Transitional Justice* 3(3), 341–361.

Yuchtman-Yaar, E. and Hermann, T. (2001) 'How the Palestinian and Israeli-Jewish Publics Perceive the Issues'. In Ginat, J. and Perkins, E. (eds.) *The Palestinian Refugees: Old Problems – New Solutions*. Sussex: Sussex University Press and University of Oklahoma Press (pp. 303–316).

Zegveld, L. (2003) 'Remedies for Victims of Violations of International Humanitarian Law'. *International Review of the Red Cross* 85(851), 499–528.

Zetter, R. (1994) 'The Greek-Cypriot Refugees: Perceptions of Return under Conditions of Protracted Exile'. *International Migration Review* 28(2), 307–322.

(1999) 'Reconceptualizing the Myth of Return: Continuity and Transformation amongst the Greek-Cypriot Refugees of 1974'. *Journal of Refugee Studies* 12(1), 1–22.

(2004) '"Returning to Yerussalem": Exile, Return and Oral History'. *History Workshop Journal* 58, 296–306.

(2005) 'Land, Housing and the Reconstruction of the Built Environment'. In Barakat, S. and Wardell, G. (eds.) *After the Conflict: Reconstruction and Development in the Aftermath of War*. New York: Palgrave (pp. 155–172).

Zieck, M. (2004) 'Voluntary Repatriation: Paradigm, Pitfalls, Progress'. *Refugee Survey Quarterly* 23(3), 33–54.

Zondervan Corp. (1998) *The NIV Study Bible*. London: Hodder & Stoughton.

Zureik, E. (1994) 'Palestinian Refugees and Peace'. *Journal of Palestine Studies* 24(1), 5–17.

(1996) *Palestinian Refugees and the Peace Process*. Washington, DC: Institute for Palestine Studies.

Index